Ultimate LLMOps for LLM Engineering

Engineering Reliable, Observable, and Scalable LLM Systems

Kinjal Dand

www.orangeava.com

First Published: February 2026

Published By: Orange Education Pvt Ltd, AVA®

Address: 9, Daryaganj, Delhi, 110002, India

275 New North Road Islington Suite 1314 London,
N1 7AA, United Kingdom

ISBN (PBK): 978-93-49887-53-4

ISBN (E-BOOK): 978-93-49887-62-6

Scan the QR code to explore our entire catalogue

www.orangeava.com

Dedicated to

My Family, for Their Endless Support, Love, and Patience that Provided the Time and Peace Needed for this Intellectual Journey.

And

To the Many Colleagues, Leaders, and Mentors, Who Opened Doors, Provided Opportunities, and Fostered the Environment for Continuous Learning, Allowing Me to Contribute to the Exciting Future of Large Language Model Engineering.

About the Author

Kinjal Dand is a distinguished Data Science Architect with over 12 years of profound experience in the fields of Data Science, Cloud Engineering, and robust Machine Learning Operations (MLOps). Her career is defined by a relentless drive to translate complex artificial intelligence and machine learning models into scalable, production-ready systems that deliver tangible business value.

Kinjal is a recognized expert in the highly specialized and rapidly evolving domain of Large Language Model Operations (LLMOps). Her expertise covers the entire lifecycle of LLMs, from initial experimentation and secure deployment to continuous monitoring, fine-tuning, and performance optimization. She has a proven track record of architecting multi-cloud solutions, enabling enterprises to leverage the full power of Generative AI across AWS, Google Cloud Platform, and Microsoft Azure.

Holding a B.E. in Computer Science and a Post-Graduate Program (PGP) in Big Data and Data Science, Kinjal backs her deep theoretical knowledge with an exceptional array of high-level certifications. She is certified as a Chartered Data Scientist, an AWS Certified Solutions Architect Professional, an AWS Certified Data Analytics Specialty, a Google Cloud Platform Professional Data Engineer, and a Microsoft Certified: Azure Developer Associate, among others.

In her professional capacity, Kinjal focuses on building resilient data pipelines, developing sophisticated Deep Learning and NLP solutions, and integrating rigorous DevSecOps principles to ensure that models are not just accurate, but secure, compliant, and highly performant in production environments.

Through this book, ***Ultimate LLMOps for LLM Engineering***, Kinjal shares the comprehensive architectural patterns and practical strategies necessary to navigate the complexities of the LLM landscape. Her goal is to empower the next generation of GenAI Developers, Machine Learning Engineers, and Data Scientists to transform ground-breaking research into world-changing applications!

About the Technical Reviewers

Jay Mangi is a results-driven machine learning and data science professional with 11 years of IT experience, including seven years dedicated to applied ML, MLOps, and LLMOps across enterprise environments at firms such as EY and Infosys. He specializes in building end-to-end solutions—spanning data ingestion, feature engineering, model development, and production deployment—with a particular focus on Generative AI, Large Language Models (LLMs), and Computer Vision. Jay's work emphasizes measurable impact, translating complex ML initiatives into tangible outcomes while maintaining robust engineering practices and operational reliability at scale.

He holds multiple cloud certifications, most notably the Google Cloud Professional Machine Learning Engineer credential, alongside additional multi-cloud certifications on GCP and Azure. These highlight his fluency in cloud-native ML tooling and production patterns, including orchestration, CI/CD for models, and platform-aligned best practices that reduce time-to-value. Jay is also recognized for his commitment to knowledge sharing and community engagement, helping teams effectively adopt ML solutions across predictive analytics, NLP, and vision domains.

Gaurav Jain is a technology leader with 15 years of experience in AI, MLOps, LLMOps, systems design, and enterprise-grade solution architecture. He specializes in helping organizations build, scale, and operationalize AI and LLM applications across cloud platforms, including AWS, Azure, and GCP. Gaurav has been honored with the '40 Under 40 Data Scientists' award by Analytics India Magazine. Throughout his career, he has worked across industries with leading organizations such as Deloitte, S&P Global, and Adani, bringing deep domain knowledge and technical leadership to each engagement.

Currently, Gaurav serves as a Senior Manager, assisting Fortune 500 companies in defining strategic AI roadmaps, leading AI platform development, and designing scalable architectures. He is also instrumental in driving client partnerships and mentoring junior team members. Gaurav is passionate about enabling organizations to unlock the full potential of AI through robust operational frameworks, scalable architectures, and continuous innovation.

Acknowledgments

Writing a technical book in a field that moves as quickly as LLMOps is a challenging yet rewarding endeavor. This work would not have been possible without the support and opportunities provided by many people along the way.

First and foremost, my deepest gratitude goes to my family. Their enduring love, patience, and understanding during the many nights and weekends dedicated to this project were the foundation that allowed me to complete this book. I thank them for their unwavering belief in my commitment.

Professionally, I want to express my appreciation to the mentors and leaders who invested in my growth, trusted my vision, and gave me significant opportunities throughout my career. The experience and exposure gained from these chances were crucial in developing the expertise shared within these pages. Similarly, I am thankful to the numerous colleagues and teams I have collaborated with. Their technical insights, challenging discussions, and collaborative spirit directly contributed to the quality and real-world applicability of this material.

I am also grateful to the reviewers whose technical scrutiny and feedback ensured that the concepts are accurate and relevant to the current industry standards. Finally, I thank my friends, for the encouragement, timely distractions, and the constant reminders to maintain balance. Their support kept my spirits high throughout the writing process.

This book is a product of these collective contributions and opportunities. Thank you all.

A Note to Our Readers on Code Examples

Throughout this book, you will encounter numerous **code examples**—often presented in Python—designed to illustrate key LLMOps concepts, from setting up a RAG pipeline to instrumenting an application with an observability platform. Please treat all the codes in this book as **executable pseudocode**.

These snippets are intentionally kept short and simplified for the sake of clarity and brevity. Their primary purpose is to explain a concept's logic and structure, not to serve as production-ready, drop-in solutions. Consequently, there is no guarantee that these examples are bug-free, fully up-to-date with the latest library versions, or immediately runnable without modifications.

We strongly encourage you to use these snippets as a starting point for understanding the mechanics of a solution. You should always adapt, test, and integrate any code into your specific production environment, following your team's established engineering practices.

Preface

The world of **Large Language Models (LLMs)** has moved at a breakneck pace, shifting from academic curiosity to a foundational technology transforming nearly every industry. As an LLM enthusiast, you have likely felt the dual pull of this revolution: the sheer excitement of what is possible, and the daunting complexity of actually making it work reliably in the real world.

That complexity—the process of taking a brilliant model from a notebook prototype to a robust, scalable, and secure production system—is what **LLMOps** is all about. It is a comprehensive roadmap that connects the dots between foundational concepts like **prompt management** and the advanced architecture of **AI agents** and **Retrieval Augmented Generation (RAG)**.

Hence, whether you are a seasoned MLOps professional, a software engineer, or a data scientist, you will find a structured path here to master the specialized challenges of this domain: from securing your model against prompt injection to ensuring that its performance does not **drift** over time. The speed of change is dizzying; this constant, rapid evolution is why a solid operational framework is no longer optional—it is essential.

Hope that this book serves its purpose well, and does not just teach you the how of LLMOps, but empowers you to build the next generation of intelligent applications with confidence, clarity, and control. So, let us get started on this journey of turning ground-breaking models into world-changing products!

Get a Free eBook

We hope you are enjoying your recently purchased book! Your feedback is incredibly valuable to us, and to all other readers looking for great books.

If you found this book helpful or enjoyable, we would truly appreciate it, if you could take a moment to leave a short review with a 5 star rating on Amazon. It helps us grow, and lets other readers discover our books.

As a thank you, we would love to send you a free digital copy of this book, and a **30%** discount code on your next cart value on our official websites:

www.orangeava.com

www.orangeava.in (For Indian Subcontinent)

☑ **Here's how:**

Leave a review for the book on Amazon.

Take a screenshot of your review, and send an email to **info@orangeava.com** (it can be just the confirmation screen).

Once, we receive your screenshot, we will send you the digital file, within 24 hours.

Thank you so much for your support — it means a lot to us!

Downloading the code bundles and colored images

Please follow the links or scan the QR codes to download the ***Code Bundles and Images*** of the book:

https://github.com/ava-orange-education/Ultimate-LLMOps-for-LLM-Engineering

The code bundles and images of the book are also hosted on ***https://rebrand.ly/d3d8aa***

In case there's an update to the code, it will be updated on the existing GitHub repository.

Errata

We take immense pride in our work at **Orange Education Pvt Ltd,** and follow best practices to ensure the accuracy of our content to provide an indulging reading experience to our subscribers. Our readers are our mirrors, and we use their inputs to reflect and improve upon human errors, if any, that may have occurred during the publishing processes involved. To let us maintain the quality and help us reach out to any readers who might be having difficulties due to any unforeseen errors, please write to us at :

errata@orangeava.com

Your support, suggestions, and feedback are highly appreciated.

DID YOU KNOW

Did you know that Orange Education Pvt Ltd offers eBook versions of every book published, with PDF and ePub files available? You can upgrade to the eBook version at **www.orangeava.com** and as a print book customer, you are entitled to a discount on the eBook copy. Get in touch with us at: **info@orangeava.com** for more details.

At **www.orangeava.com**, you can also read a collection of free technical articles, sign up for a range of free newsletters, and receive exclusive discounts and offers on Print Books and eBooks.

PIRACY

If you come across any illegal copies of our works in any form on the internet, we would be grateful if you would provide us with the location address or website name. Please contact us at **info@orangeava.com** with a link to the material.

ARE YOU INTERESTED IN AUTHORING WITH US?

If there is a topic that you have expertise in, and you are interested in either writing or contributing to a book, please write to us at **business@orangeava.com**. We are on a journey to help developers and tech professionals to gain insights on the present technological advancements and innovations happening across the globe and build a community that believes Knowledge is best acquired by sharing and learning with others. Please reach out to us to learn what our audience demands and how you can be part of this educational reform. We also welcome ideas from tech experts and help them build learning and development content for their domains.

REVIEWS

Please leave a review. Once you have read and used this book, why not leave a review on the site that you purchased it from? Potential readers can then see and use your unbiased opinion to make purchase decisions. We at Orange Education would love to know what you think about our products, and our authors can learn from your feedback. Thank you!

For more information about Orange Education, please visit
www.orangeava.com.

Table of Contents

CHAPTER 1
Unveiling the World of Large Language Models

Introduction

Welcome to an exciting exploration into the world of Large Language Models (LLMs), Artificial Intelligence's (AI's) game-changers that are reshaping how we interact with technology and process information. This book, ***Ultimate LLMOps for LLM Engineering***, will guide you through the practical journey of deploying, managing, and scaling these sophisticated models in real-world environments.

Our first chapter sets the stage by tracing the remarkable ascent of Large Language Models. We will journey from the foundational concepts of Natural Language Processing (NLP) to the revolutionary Transformer architecture, introducing you to prominent models such as **BERT, GPT, and DALL-E**. You will also gain an understanding of their diverse architectures and the wide array of applications they enable, from enhancing customer service and generating creative content to supporting critical tasks in legal and software development. However, bringing these powerful models into production comes with its own set of challenges. We will also discuss the significant hurdles involved, including managing computational resources and costs, how to ensure data privacy and security, address biases and fairness, navigate interpretability, and tackle integration and regulatory compliance. These foundational challenges and their operational defenses are the subject of the deep dive in Chapter 10.

Consider this chapter your essential introduction to the LLM landscape, providing the context necessary for our deeper dive into the operational excellence central to LLMOps. So, let us begin this insightful journey together.

Structure

In this chapter, we will discuss the following topics:

- Rise of Large Language Models
- Types of Large Language Models
- Applications of Large Language Models
- Challenges in Deployment of Large Language Models

Rise of Large Language Models

The digital age has witnessed a profound transformation in how machines understand and generate human language. Suddenly, advanced artificial intelligence has ***crossed a major threshold***, shifting **from theoretical** promise to **practical reality** across industries. This section delves into the foundational developments and key innovations that propelled sophisticated conversational agents and generative systems into the mainstream, inaugurating an era where machines seamlessly communicate, create, and reason alongside us.

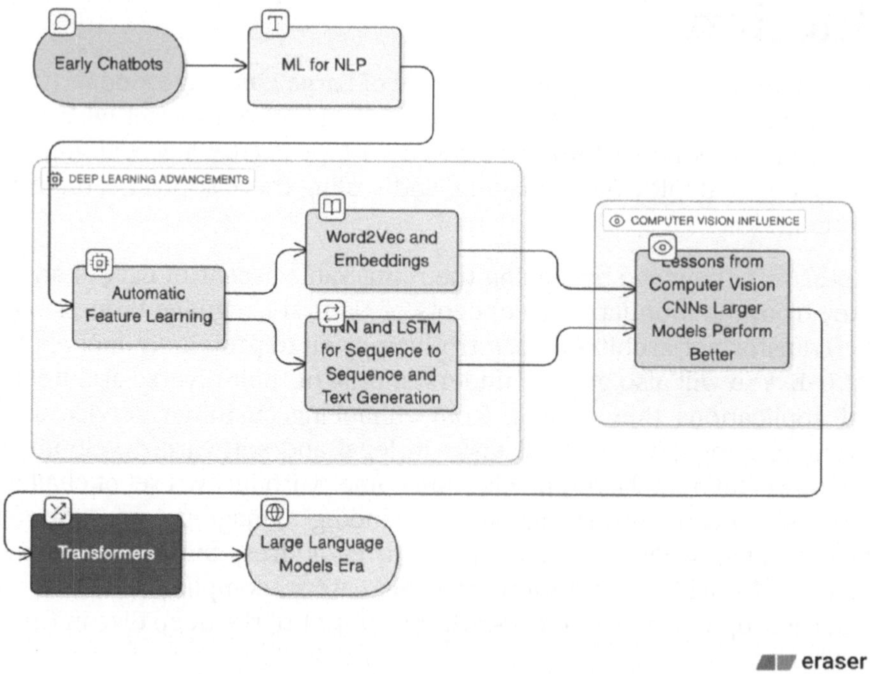

Figure 1.1: *Evolution of AI Chatbot Technology*

Early Chatbots

The ability of computers to interact with humans using natural language processing has a long history. Some of the earliest examples include **ELIZA** developed at MIT in the 1960's. Widely considered as the first chatbot, it was a "*rules*"-based program consisting of if-else and substitution methods. These rules were mostly derived from understanding and breakdown of the grammar of natural language (specifically English in this case). For example, first-person, "*I*" (user) is converted to "*you*" (by chatbot) while referring to the user and so on. Interested readers can refer to this link[1] for more details and associated challenges.

In terms of **size**, the program was small enough to run on personal computers of the time. This contrasts with modern GPT-4 which needs to run on **multiple GPUs**, even during the **inference stage**. Although pioneering at the time, it had limited functionality, best described as "*psychotherapist*" by experts. Nevertheless, the initial fascination and hype paved the way for more advancements in the field of NLP.

Use of Machine Learning for Natural Language Processing

The problem with the preceding **rule-based systems** is that these rules need to be coded by humans in very fine granularity, and the system can only do what the rules tell it to do. It **does not learn** from experience or change its rules on its own. If it encounters a situation that does not fit in any of the rules, it will not know what to do. In contrast, a machine learning system learns from examples, rather than following strict rules. A machine learning system is given a lot of data (like texts, images, or anything else depending on the task), and it looks for **patterns** as well as learns from them. As it processes more data, it gets better at making predictions or decisions. It can also adapt to new situations because it is not limited to a fixed set of rules.

Given the complexities of human language, the preceding rule-based methods were very **difficult to scale out**, and scientists quickly started looking for techniques to automate the process of this rule creation. This led to the building of some early machine learning models which were based on the bag of words concept.[2] (**for example, "Sentence 1: '`The cat is happy.`'** Sentence 2: '**`The dog is happy`**.' **Bag of words** for Sentence 1: **`{the:1, cat:1, is:1, happy:1}`**") The idea was simple, a sentence which has a negative word like "no" will most likely carry a negative sentiment and so on. The problem with this model was that it was not oblivious to sentence structure and word order. Moreover, the larger the corpus aka vocabulary, the higher the number of predictors which led to the classical problem of "***curse of dimensionality***" [Appendix 1] and in turn **overfitting**. Also from a usability perspective, this model could only classify the input but **could not generate** any new input of any kind.

Advancements in Deep Learning

Some of the preceding problems were solved when deep learning picked up its pace after its big AI winter. In the early 2000s, deep learning was not widely used due to the limitations in computational power and the lack of large datasets needed to train deep neural networks. Traditional Machine Learning (ML) techniques, which relied on handcrafted features extracted from images, were the norm. However, machine learning, although powerful, still relies on the programmer to generate and select the features of the data that are important for the system to learn from. The system is then trained on a dataset to recognize patterns based on these features. Deep learning, on the other hand, can identify these patterns in data, without much guidance only by "*looking*" at the data. In deep learning, the system is designed with layers of artificial "neurons" that mimic the human brain. These layers can process data in a more complex and abstract way, learning from the data itself, without needing specific feature selection by a programmer. The system can identify intricate patterns that might not be immediately obvious to humans.

For example, traditional machine learning for face detection relied on *human-engineered* features like Geometric features or Edge Detectors, where experts manually design algorithms to identify specific visual patterns (for example, edges, textures, and so on) indicative of a face. In contrast, deep learning, particularly with CNNs, automates this process: the network learns to extract relevant features directly from raw image pixels through multiple layers, progressively building a hierarchy from simple edges in early layers to complex, abstract facial representations in deeper layers, ultimately optimizing these features automatically for the task of face detection during end-to-end training.

In the context of Natural Language Processing (NLP), traditional machine learning algorithms need to train themselves on explicit features like the frequency of certain words, the presence of named entities, parts of speech, or n-grams (sequences of n words). The process requires significant human intervention to identify which features are relevant and how they should be encoded. Deep learning, on the other hand, takes a more holistic approach to NLP. It utilizes neural networks with multiple layers that automatically discover the representations needed for feature detection from raw data. As the data progresses through each layer of the network, the model learns increasingly complex features. In the lower layers, it might learn about individual words and their meanings, while in the higher layers, it could learn about sentence structure, context, and the subtleties of language, such as idioms, sarcasm, and ambiguity.

There is one problem though. Text cannot be directly fed to neural networks. It must be transformed into numbers. But the English language alone contains over 1 million words with varying frequency, and this list keeps changing every day. As such an earlier approach of mapping this individual word aka tokens to number, and feeding it to DL brought many challenges with it.

The concept of **embedding generation** from the **`word2vec`**[3] model changed this landscape. Unlike the **bag of words model** which represented the sentence means of once and zeros for the presence and absence of every word, the **word2vec model** created a more concise representation. Every word would generate a fixed size embedding (N-dimensional) and words with similar meaning tended to be "**nearby**" to each other in this N-dimensional space. (that is mathematically, you can roughly do this: `king - man + woman = queen`) This concept of embedding when combined with advanced neural network architecture such as RNN and LSTM made it possible to not only classify the input but also generate new text. For example, sequence-to-sequence models showed promising results in new use cases like generating summaries or answering questions.

Lessons from Computer Vision

While deep learning models were showing huge advances in text analytics space, their impact on the computer vision field was even more forthcoming. Especially the concept of Convolutional Neural Networks (CNNs) helped to learn the patterns in the image, and thereby find its applications in a huge number of areas. For example, face recognition, autonomous vehicles, medical image analysis, object detection, OCR and so on. A landmark event in the field was the **ImageNet Large Scale Visual Recognition Challenge (ILSVRC)**. A deep neural network called AlexNet, designed by Alex Krizhevsky, Ilya Sutskever, and Geoffrey Hinton, significantly outperformed traditional methods by using a deep convolutional neural network. This model was able to automatically learn features directly from the raw image pixels, and its success demonstrated the potential of deep learning for computer vision tasks.

Following the success of AlexNet, the use of deep learning in computer vision exploded. Researchers developed **more sophisticated and deeper CNN architectures**, such as VGG, Google Net, and ResNet, each improving upon the previous model's performance and efficiency. These networks were trained on **ever-larger datasets** and benefited from advances in GPU technology, which made it feasible to train deep networks in a reasonable amount of time. One common pattern across various deep learning models was that the larger the model size, the better the predictive power. The **large number of neurons** or **nodes** in deep learning corresponds to the model **better capturing** the intricacies of patterns in various images.

While deep learning models, particularly CNNs, revolutionized computer vision by enabling parallel processing of images, one major hurdle in using large models for text processing was that of **sequential nature**. While convolution neural networks allowed processing of various parts of the image in parallel, the same could not be applied effectively in text space. This limitation in text processing, especially for larger models, was ultimately addressed by a **groundbreaking architecture**: The **Transformer** using the **attention mechanism.**

Transformers - Sequence to Parallel Processing

The attention mechanism can "*look*" at the entire sentence in one go, unlike RNN or LSTM which inspect the sentence, one word at a time. Moreover, the Transformer Model includes multiple such attention modules. This means that it can "look" at the sentence from multiple "***angles***". For example: One module could concentrate on "*sentiment*" and another on the "*subject-object*" relationship. In essence, it could capture the information in the given text from various perspectives, and at the same time (in parallel). One can imagine a candidate being observed by multiple panels at the same time, and each panel evaluating on a certain specific aspect, they are interested in. This led to the model capturing the finer contextual information from the input and hence, generating better-quality output.

One finer detail to add is that "*attention*" in Transformers is often quoted as "***self-attention***" which stretches on the fact that the model is looking for a relationship between the words in the sentence. To elaborate more, the model is not just trying to build a relationship with input and output, or every token in input with output token. Instead, it specifically focuses on ***detecting the relationship*** between various words within the input sentence. This way, it can capture dependencies between words over a longer range, and produce contextual aware outputs.

Finally, apart from the attention module, the Transformer model has also included the *Positional Encoding* of every word in the input sentence, along with their corresponding word embedding. This helped it to **retain the order of words** in sentences during training, and hence, maintain the context in its entirety. This powerful combination is one of the key aspects behind the success of Transformer architecture. It not only allows models to capture richer contextual information from text but also made it feasible to train '*large*' models with unprecedented numbers of parameters on vast text corpuses, ushering in the era of LLMs. Interested readers can refer to more details in the original paper[4] "Attention is all you need".

The Era of Large Language Models

When we say large, to be specific, OpenAI released GPT 1 with 117 million parameters, followed by GPT2 with 1.5 billion and GPT 3 with 175 billion parameters. OpenAI has not officially released the architecture and number of parameters of GPT-4 but speculation suggests the parameter count is expected to be trillions.! Similarly, other organizations have trained their own large language models such as Google Gemini and LLAMA from Meta.

One key characteristic and effect of large models is their ability to handle larger context windows (such as longer input sequences) and generate superior-quality output, especially in terms of grammar and vocabulary. Additionally, GPT-4 and Gemini are classified as ***multimodal*** meaning they are capable of handling images, along with text. This has increased the scope of use cases in which these models could be used.

Types of Large Language Models

In this section, we will briefly look at various large language models, their architecture, datasets, size and so on which will help readers choose suitable models for their use case.

Baseline Transformer

We will begin with briefly describing the baseline transformer model introduced in the paper[4] "*Attention is all you need*". This model was primarily trained as a translator; hence, its architecture consists of encoder and decoder modules. Both the encoder and decoder use a self-attention mechanism to capture the context of input. One big difference is that whereas the **encoder** has **multi-head attention**, the **decoder** has **masked multi-head attention**. This is done to prevent the decoder from using future information during the prediction task. Depending upon the scenario and the end usage, variants of transformer either use both encoder-decoder, only encoder or only decoder. We will discuss examples with specific models shortly.

It was trained on two datasets, English-German and English-French, and achieved **BLEU**[5] scores of 28.4 and 41.8 respectively on the test dataset: the highest at the time in comparison to others. Given that the second **dataset**, English French was significantly **larger** than the former, we see its **impact** of a **higher bleu** score. Its code is publicly available on GitHub, and took 12 hours to train on 8 NVIDIA P100 GPUs. To test its applicability on other tasks, the authors of the paper also tested it on other tasks such as "*English Constituency Parsing*". Their results showed that it surpassed most other models, even without task-specific tuning. This significant achievement led to many advancements and models described as follows.

Also, the general scenario here is that the "*base*" model: Transformer and its variants are largely trained with a huge language corpus and its main aim is to understand language structure in general. This base model is then fine-tuned to achieve accuracy on the actual task at hand. This is like image models wherein pre-trained large models could be *repurposed(fine-tuned)* to perform image classification and other tasks. Usually, lower layers would be "*freezed*" as they generally capture common image patterns like lines and angles, whereas higher layers are fine-tuned to classify images as required, and so on.

BERT

The full form of BERT is **Bidirectional Encoder Representation** from Transformer. Let us now break down this to fully understand what BERT is. Firstly, BERT only consists of the "**encoder**" part from the transformer architecture described in the preceding paragraphs. An encoder as named performs the job of "encoding" the input into a suitable "representation". Moreover, BERT reads the entire text sequence in one go due to the attention mechanism. (Please note this is slightly different from other Bidirectional RNNs or Bidirectional LSTM. Usually, they consist of two RNNs or LSTMs, one processing the input from left to right, and the other from right to left. The outputs of both are combined at each step to produce the final representation.) Because of this, **BERT can capture context** from **both directions** at the same time. Hence, the term used is "*Bidirectional Encoder Representation from Transformer*".

The BERT model is trained on two tasks which help it to capture language representation effectively. First is the Masked Language Model. In this technique, tokens are chosen at random, and replaced with mask tokens like "**[MASK]**". The model is trained to accurately predict this masked word. The second task is the Next Sentence Prediction. Here pairs of sentences are chosen, and the model is supposed to predict if the second sentence logically follows the first one or not. Thus, BERT is trained to capture context within a sentence as well as in between two sentences. On its release, it surpassed many other models in a variety of NLP tasks such as a high bleu score on the SQUAD dataset.

Over the years, many variants from the base architecture of BERT have been released. Among them, the popular ones include RoBERTa, DistilBERT, ALBERT, and so on.

GPT

GPT stands for **Generative Pretrained Transformer**. It largely consists of training a base model consisting of decoder architecture from Transformer. This base model is then trained for specific tasks such as ChatGPT which is trained to "*chat*" with the user by following instructions. Encoders are generally used to draw outputs like yes/no or predefined categories, based on representations they learn from data. The **decoder** on the other hand, is expected to **generate** sequential output, commonly being the next word that follows the given sequence of input. The idea of the decoder is to "*generate*" output. Hence, the term "*Generative Pretrained Transformer*".

GPT 3 and 4 were not only increased in size but also in capability commonly called "*in-context learning*". This capability is generally attributed to a huge number of parameters, a longer context window, and a diverse set of data which enables it to generalize on a vast set of topics. What this means for the end-user is that the model can generate the required output without fine-tuning, and simply based on instructions as well as one or more examples. This is the basis of "*prompt engineering*" which we will later cover in this book. Refer to *Figure 1.2, BERT vs GPT* for quick contrast between BERT and GPT.

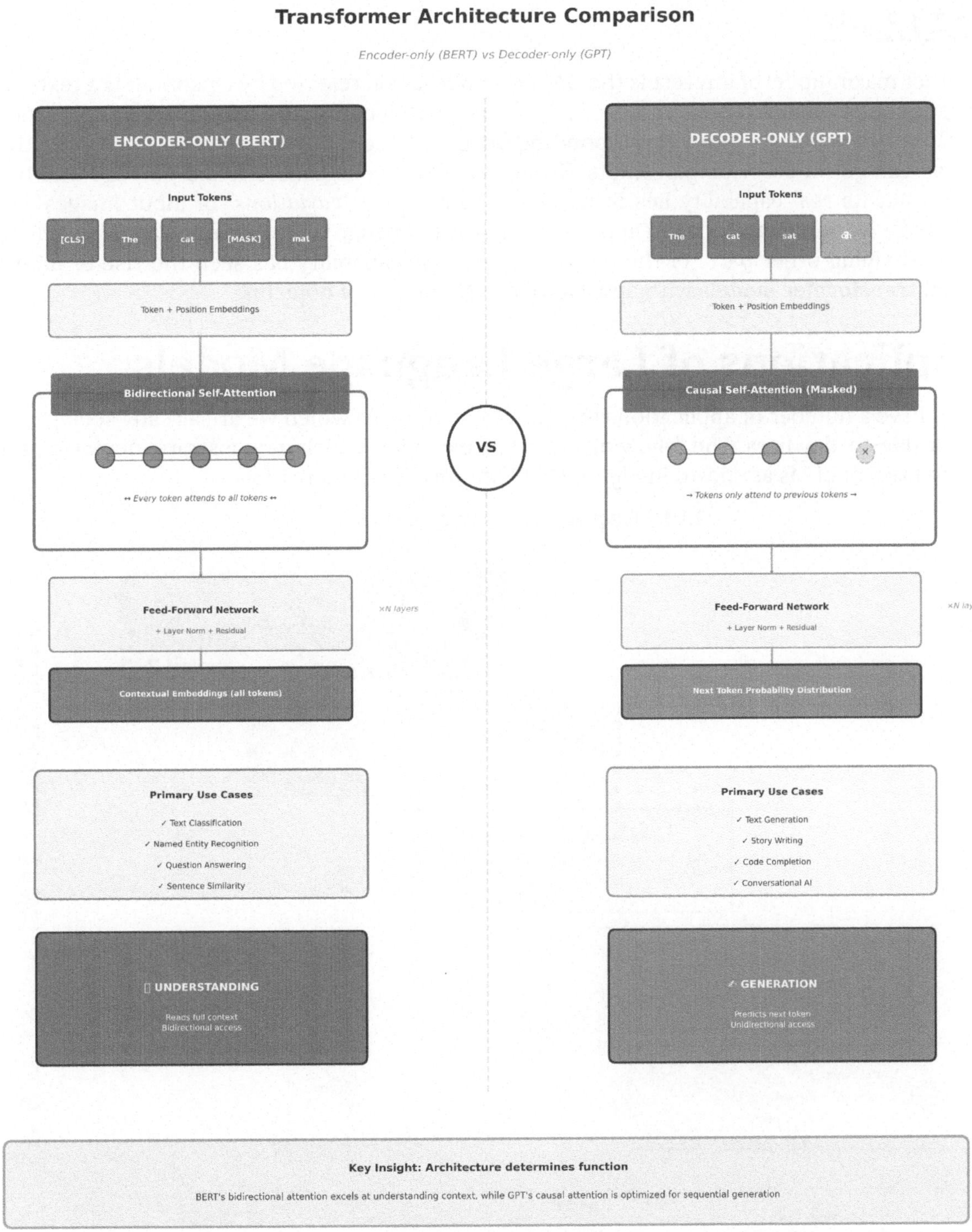

Figure 1.2: BERT *vs* GPT

DALL-E

Another major model of interest is the DALL-E model again released by OpenAI. It is a text-to-image generation model built on top of GPT. At its heart, it **converts** a **text prompt** (description or caption of an image) into a **corresponding image**. The generated image could be as creative as one can get in describing prompts. Examples of the same can be found on Page 2 of this paper. But its real capability lies in its ability to produce "*variations*" of input images. For example, given an image of a red apple, you can ask to change the color of the apple to yellow, while retaining other parts of the image as it is. This capability has seen the rise of **multi-modal transformer models** with applications in N number of domains.

Applications of Large Language Models

LLMs have a number of applications in a variety of domains which we are already seeing now in our day-to-day lives. The following are a few examples which demonstrate increasing the capabilities of LLMs as shown in *Figure 1.3, LLM Capability Progression.*

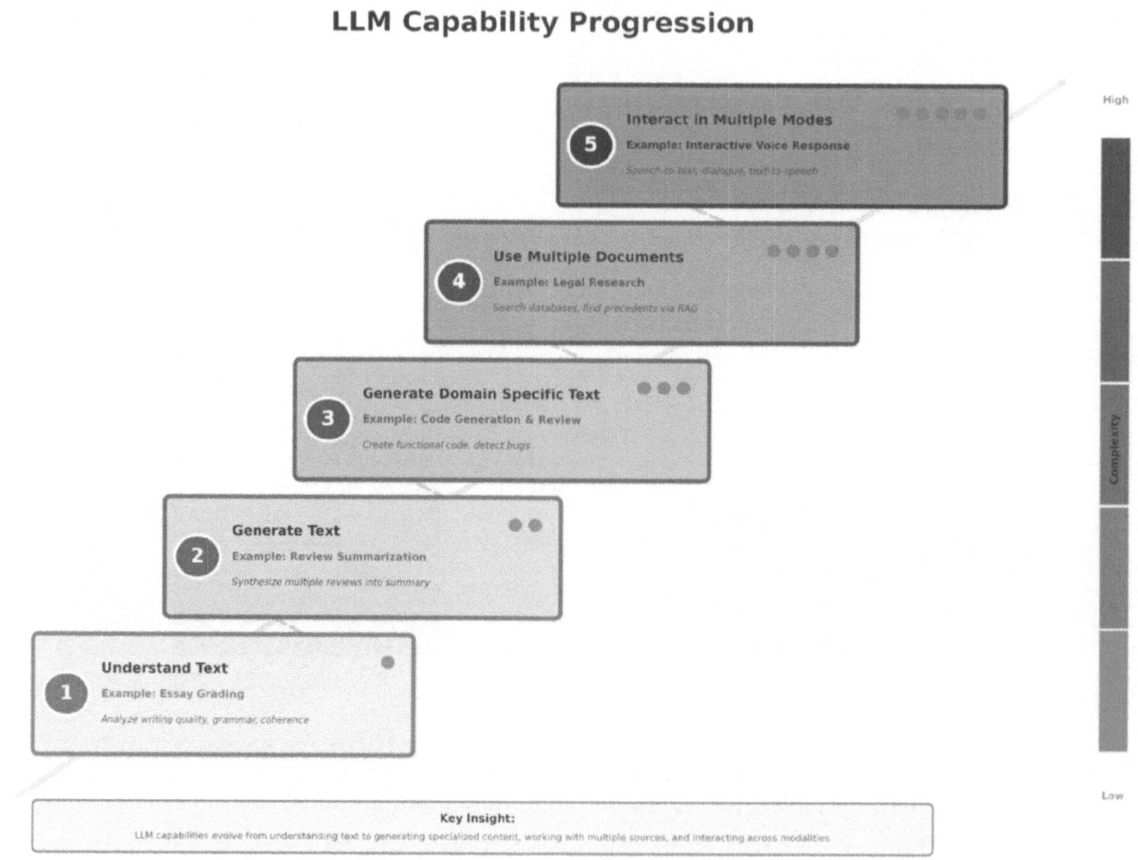

Figure 1.3: *LLM Capability Progression*

Essay Grading

The goal is to harness the model's advanced natural language understanding capabilities to evaluate written work. The process begins with the collection of essays that need to be graded. Once collected, they undergo preprocessing to ensure that they are in a format suitable for analysis by the LLM. This step may involve converting the essays from various file formats into plain text, standardizing the formatting (such as font size and style), and removing any identifying information to maintain the anonymity of the students. Such preprocessing allows the LLM to focus on the content and quality of the writing, rather than extraneous factors.

The LLM is then provided with a set of grading criteria or a rubric that outlines the parameters for evaluation. These criteria can include aspects such as coherence, argumentation, use of evidence, grammar, and style. The model is given a prompt that clearly defines the task, such as "**`Grade the following essay according to the provided rubric, focusing on the clarity of the thesis, the organization of ideas, and the correctness of language.`**" This **instruction** is crucial as it guides the LLM in applying a consistent and objective standard to each essay.

For the grading process, the LLM reads and comprehends each essay, analyzing it against the established criteria. It assesses the essay's structure, the development of ideas, the relevance and accuracy of the content, and the technical aspects of writing, such as grammar and punctuation. The model leverages its extensive training on a wide range of texts to evaluate the quality of the writing and **to assign a grade** that reflects the student's performance in relation to the rubric.

The LLM may also provide feedback on the essay, highlighting strengths and areas for improvement. This feedback is generated by identifying the key elements within the essay that correspond to the grading criteria, and noting where the essay excels or falls short. The model's ability to generate human-like text allows it to articulate constructive comments that can guide students in enhancing their writing skills.

After the essays are graded, a post-processing phase may be implemented where the grades and feedback are reviewed for consistency and fairness. This step can involve cross-referencing the LLM's evaluations with sample grades provided by human educators to ensure that the model's grading aligns with human judgment. Adjustments may be made to the model's output to correct any discrepancies, and to calibrate the grading process further. [See note below]

Finally, the quality of the essay grading is assessed through various means, including comparison with human-graded essays and analysis of the feedback's relevance and helpfulness. This quality assurance step is critical to ensure that the grading is not only accurate but also beneficial to the student's learning process. The goal is for the LLM-graded essays to provide a fair assessment of the student's work, and to offer insights that contribute to their academic growth as well as writing proficiency.

Note: *Only one caveat to keep in mind is to make sure, no bias creeps in, while calibrating results with human judgment.*[6]

Amazon Style Summary of Reviews

It is common for customers to inspect the reviews of products before buying them on Amazon. To make its customer's life easy, Amazon has added a new feature that summarizes what other users said about the product, and how they rated its specific feature. Now, let us see how you can replicate a similar process in your application.

Summarizing reviews using a Large Language Model (LLM) is a sophisticated process that involves several intricate steps to ensure that the essence of customer feedback is captured accurately and concisely. The initial phase of this process is data collection, which can be accomplished through various methods such as web scraping or accessing an existing dataset that contains customer reviews. This stage is critical as it lays the foundation for the quality of the summary; the more comprehensive and varied the collected reviews are, the more representative the summary will be of the general sentiment towards the product.

Once the reviews are collected, they undergo a crucial **preprocessing phase**. This step is designed to clean and standardize the data, making it more amenable to analysis by the LLM. Preprocessing includes the removal of HTML tags, non-standard characters, and any extraneous information that could detract from the core content of the reviews. Additionally, the text is often normalized by converting it to a uniform case, and removing punctuation as well as tokenized into smaller units such as sentences or words. This not only helps in reducing noise in the data but also aids the LLM in processing the information more efficiently.

The LLM must then be invoked with ***proper instructions and context*** to generate a summary. This is typically achieved by providing the model with a clear prompt or set of instructions that describe the objective, such as **`"Provide a concise summary of the following reviews that capture the predominant opinions and key points mentioned by customers."`** This step is vital as it sets the context for the LLM, and directs its focus towards generating a summary, rather than performing other potential tasks such as sentiment analysis or question answering.

The actual **generation of the summary** is a complex task that the LLM performs by selecting the most salient points from the reviews, and synthesizing them into a coherent narrative. This involves a delicate balance of retaining essential information, while omitting redundant or less significant details. The model achieves this by predicting the next word or phrase in a sequence that is most likely to contribute to a meaningful summary, based on its understanding of the text and the patterns, it has learned during training. The result is a concise, informative summary that distils the collective insights of numerous customer reviews into a digestible format.

Once the LLM has produced a summary, it may undergo **post-processing** to refine the output further. This can include grammatical corrections, ensuring that the summary flows logically, and adjusting the length to meet specific requirements. The quality of the generated summary is paramount, and it can be evaluated through various means, including manual review or automated metrics such as ROUGE, which compares the LLM-generated summary to human-written summaries to assess its accuracy and coherence.

Code Generation and Review

While the previous example captured LLM's capability to generate text in English, its power comes in the fact that it can be trained to **generate text on specialized domains** like code generation. Code generation and review using LLM leverage the model's ability to understand programming languages and software development concepts. The process begins with the collection of requirements or user stories that describe the functionality to be implemented. This information is crucial as it guides the LLM in creating code that is aligned with the desired outcomes and user needs. The requirements may come from various sources, such as project documentation, issue trackers, or direct input from developers and stakeholders.

Once the requirements are gathered, they are pre-processed to ensure clarity, and remove any ambiguity. This step may involve refining the language used in the requirements, breaking down complex user stories into more manageable tasks, and ensuring that the LLM has a clear and concise set of instructions to follow. The preprocessing phase is essential for minimizing misunderstandings, and ensuring that the generated code will meet the specified criteria.

The LLM is then provided with a prompt that clearly states the task at hand, such as **`"Generate a Python function that implements the following feature..." or "Review the following code snippet for potential bugs and performance issues."`** Also, we can add additional instructions like following industry standards such as pep8 for Python or adding exception handling and logging as appropriate. This instruction sets the stage for the LLM to apply its knowledge of programming languages, software design patterns, and best practices to the task of code generation or review.

For code generation, the LLM uses its extensive training in a diverse range of codebases to create functional code that fulfils the requirements. It does this by predicting sequences of code tokens that are most likely to result in a working implementation. The model considers various factors, such as the programming language syntax, the logical flow of the code, and the integration with existing codebases. *The generated code is expected to be syntactically correct, logically sound, and in line with modern coding standards.*

In the context of code review, the LLM examines the provided code snippet, and identifies areas that may require attention. This could include detecting syntax errors, potential bugs, security vulnerabilities, or areas where the code could be optimized for better performance or readability. The model draws on its understanding of common coding issues, and the nuances of the programming language to provide insightful feedback and suggestions for improvement.

After the code is generated or reviewed, it may undergo a post-processing phase where it is refined further. For generated code, this could involve integrating it into an existing codebase, ensuring that it interacts correctly with other components, and that it passes all relevant tests. Code review might mean consolidating the feedback provided by the LLM, and prioritizing the issues based on their severity or impact on the overall project.

Finally, the quality of the generated code or the code review is assessed. This can be done through automated testing frameworks that evaluate the functionality and performance of the code, as well as manual peer review by other developers who can provide additional insights and validation. This quality assurance step is crucial to ensure that the code not only meets the initial requirements but also adheres to the high standards expected in a professional software development environment.

Legal Research

Another interesting area where LLMs are highly useful is building tools which assist lawyers by quickly sifting through case law and statutes to find relevant precedents. This kind of use case can be reapplied in other similar domains as well like Medical which also may require doctors to go through a large number of documents to find any successful treatments or so.

The process begins with the user inputting a legal query or research topic into the system. The LLM then uses natural language processing techniques to parse the query, and identify key legal concepts and terms. Once the query is understood, the **model will need to search an extensive database of legal texts** to find relevant information. This involves matching the query with similar legal issues and concepts found in the database. RAG with a vector database can come to the rescue here. More details of this RAG architecture will be covered in chapter 5 of the book.

Once documents are retrieved, they are ranked as per the relevance of the texts based on the query. They are filtered as per the described criteria, and this information is fed to the LLM, along with instructions to interpret and generate the required output. These may **involve one or more iterations of LLMs** (and/or tools) for which we can use "**agentic frameworks**" (we will cover in detail in chapter 6). LLMs can also summarize the findings, extract pertinent legal principles, and even predict potential outcomes based on precedents. The user is then presented with a synthesized report that includes the most relevant documents, summaries, and insights.

The system should be designed to continuously learn and improve. It must have the capability to analyze user feedback, new legal documents, and changes in the law. This ensures that the LLM processes information which is up to date with the latest legal developments, and can provide accurate and reliable research assistance.

Moreover, the LLM can also be fine-tuned for specific jurisdictions or areas of law, ensuring that the research is tailored to the user's needs. For instance, a model might be trained specifically on tax law or intellectual property law, providing more targeted and precise research results in those fields.

Overall, legal research using an LLM represents a powerful tool for legal professionals, offering a way to quickly and efficiently navigate the vast landscape of legal information with the help of cutting-edge AI technology.

Interactive Voice Response Systems

Now, let us focus our attention on multi-modal applications like Interactive Voice Response (IVR) wherein one can combine text models with voice models such as Whisper to automate and streamline telephonic customer service. It requires LLMs to understand and respond to a wide range of customer queries with human-like comprehension.

The process starts when a customer calls the service number, and is greeted by the IVR system. The LLM, integrated within the IVR, listens to the spoken input from the customer. Using **automatic speech recognition models like Whisper** converts the spoken words into text that the model can process. The LLM then interprets the customer's request, and determines the intent behind the query.

Once the intent is identified, the LLM accesses a repository of pre-defined responses and information related to the customer's query. It selects the most appropriate response, and uses Text-To-Speech (TTS) technology to convey the information back to the customer in a clear and natural-sounding voice. Earlier versions used to generate robot-like voices, but now, we have powerful AI models which can **synthesize human sounding text** with control over style, accent, and emotion through natural language prompts. It can also be customized to understand industry-specific terminology, and adapt to different languages and accents, making it versatile across various customer service scenarios. If the customer's request is complex or falls outside the scope of the LLM's training, the system can route the call to a human operator for further assistance.

Due to their larger context window, LLM models can handle the intricacies of dialogue management, including maintaining context over the course of an interaction, and managing multi-turn conversations where the customer's queries build upon previous responses.

Furthermore, the LLM can be fine-tuned to cater to specific business needs, whether it is for banking, healthcare, retail, or any other sector that requires customer interaction. By doing so, the IVR system can provide more accurate and relevant information, improving the overall customer experience.

In summary, IVR systems powered by a combination of LLMs offer businesses a sophisticated tool to enhance customer service operations. Thus, by leveraging the latest in AI and machine learning, these systems can provide quick, accurate, and cost-effective customer service, while freeing up human agents to handle more complex issues.

Challenges in the Deployment of LLMs

Bringing sophisticated language models from the **lab to a live** operational environment is a complex undertaking rife with practical hurdles. While their power is undeniable, deploying them introduces significant engineering, ethical, and economic constraints. This section explores the critical challenges that organizations must navigate, including the immense computational demands and associated costs, the imperative to ensure fairness and mitigate harmful biases, the difficulties in maintaining data privacy, and the ongoing struggle for model transparency as well as regulatory compliance in a rapidly evolving technological landscape.

Computational Resources and Cost

One of the major challenges in deploying LLMs is their huge requirement of **computational resources**. This cost is not just limited to training but extends to inference as well. Inference requires the model to quickly process the input data and generate a response, which still necessitates the use of GPUs or TPUs for real-time applications due to its large size. While a single inference might not require much computational power, at scale, when a service is handling thousands or millions of requests, the costs can accumulate quickly.

The cost of inference can vary greatly depending on usage patterns. For casual or low-volume use, the cost might be a few dollars per thousand inferences, but for enterprise-scale applications that require a high throughput and low latency, costs can rise considerably. Some rough estimates for large-scale LLM inference can range from $0.01 to $0.10 per inference, translating to thousands of dollars per month for services with high traffic. While cloud computing offers pay-as-you-go flexibility, achieving attractive discounts for large-scale GPU deployments usually involves a 1-3-year commitment, diverging from a purely on-demand cost structure These costs must be factored into the operational expenses of companies relying on these models for their products and services. We will do a deep dive on this topic in Chapter 7.

The computational demands of Large Language Models have far-reaching implications that extend well beyond the direct financial costs associated with their operation. One of the more pressing concerns is the **environmental impact**; the substantial energy consumption required to power the GPUs and TPUs, which often come from non-renewable sources, results in a notable carbon footprint. This has prompted a call for more **sustainable and eco-friendly practices** within the AI industry, and many governments across the world are putting more policies in place to encourage sustainable development.

There is an active area of ongoing research aimed at optimizing LLMs to make them **more efficient**. Innovations such as **model pruning, quantization, and knowledge distillation** are promising techniques that seek to develop smaller and faster models, without sacrificing performance. Section **"Enhanced Fine-Tuning with PEFT LoRA" in Chapter 9** covers some practical aspects of this technique. These efforts could potentially reduce the computational burden, and make LLMs more accessible as well as environmentally friendly, contributing to a more sustainable future for AI.

Data Privacy and Security

Ensuring that the privacy and security of data utilized in the training and operation of LLMs is of paramount importance, LLMs require extensive datasets to develop their linguistic capabilities; however, these datasets often contain confidential information. For instance, the data could include proprietary business documents, sensitive health records, or personal identifiers that require stringent protection measures.

To safeguard this information, developers and operators of LLMs must implement robust data privacy protocols and security frameworks. Examples of such measures include advanced encryption techniques to secure data at rest and in transit, thereby rendering it inaccessible to unauthorized entities. Furthermore, rigorous access controls need to be established to define and restrict data access based on roles and responsibilities, ensuring that only vetted individuals can interact with the sensitive information. Additionally, continuous monitoring systems should be deployed to detect and respond to potential security breaches promptly.

Similarly, during the inference stage of Large Language Models, it is crucial to maintain data privacy and security to **prevent the inadvertent disclosure of sensitive information**. To this end, data redaction is essential, which involves using algorithms to detect and remove any Personally Identifiable Information (PII) or confidential data from the model's outputs. Moreover, implementing output filtering mechanisms ensure that the model does not produce inappropriate or sensitive content, with the aid of allow lists and blocklists that define what constitutes acceptable outputs.

Incorporating differential privacy into the inference process is another pivotal measure. This technique adds a calculated amount of noise to the outputs, making it significantly harder to infer specific details about the training data. Furthermore, maintaining comprehensive audit trails for all inference activities allows for the monitoring and review of the model's use, ensuring accountability and adherence to data protection standards.

Strong user authentication protocols are also imperative, restricting the use of the LLM for inference tasks to authorized personnel only. Lastly, the regular updating of the model to patch any security gaps is necessary to safeguard against potential exploitation during the inference stage. Collectively, these strategies form a robust framework that upholds the confidentiality of the output, and maintains the overall integrity of the data within LLMs.

These protective strategies are vital for maintaining the integrity of the data, and for fostering trust among users and stakeholders. They serve to ensure that while LLMs continue to evolve and provide value, they do so without compromising the confidentiality and security of the data that powers them. We have dedicated chapter 10 for this topic.

Bias and Fairness

LLMs have the potential to reflect and even amplify biases that exist in the vast datasets they are trained on. These biases can stem from historical inequalities, cultural stereotypes, or skewed representations within the data. For example, if an LLM is predominantly trained on texts that associate men with careers and women with domestic roles, it may inadvertently perpetuate gender stereotypes in its responses.

The issue of bias in LLMs extends beyond gender to encompass a range of other factors, such as race, age, ethnicity, sexual orientation, and disability. For instance, an LLM might generate text that is less favorable or even harmful when referring to certain racial groups, if the training data includes racially biased language. Similarly, if the training data underrepresents certain dialects or languages, the LLM might be less effective or show lower performance for speakers of those languages, leading to unfair treatment.

Mitigating these biases is crucial to prevent unfair treatment or discrimination. This can involve a variety of approaches, such as diversifying the training datasets to ensure a more balanced representation of different groups. Developers can also use techniques such as bias detection and intervention tools that actively identify and correct biased patterns in the model's output.

Moreover, engaging with stakeholders from diverse backgrounds during the model development process can provide valuable insights into potential biases and fairness concerns. In some cases, the application of LLMs may require specialized fairness metrics that are tailored to the context in which the model is deployed, ensuring that the model's outputs are equitable across different demographic groups.

In addition to these technical measures, there is also a need for clear guidelines and ethical standards to govern the use of LLMs, ensuring that they are deployed in a manner that respects the principles of fairness and inclusivity. Thus, by addressing the challenges of bias and fairness head-on, developers and operators of LLMs can contribute to the creation of more equitable and just AI systems.

Interpretability and Explainability

LLMs are complex systems that can generate highly nuanced and contextually appropriate language outputs. However, this complexity often makes it challenging to decipher exactly how these models arrive at specific conclusions or answers. This lack of clarity is why LLMs are sometimes referred to as "*black boxes*." For instance, when an LLM provides a medical diagnosis based on symptoms described in natural language, it is not always clear which parts of the input it considers most important, or how different factors were weighed against each other in reaching that conclusion.

The challenge of interpretability and explainability becomes particularly significant in scenarios where transparency is crucial. In fields such as healthcare, finance, and law, understanding the reasoning behind a model's output is necessary for trust and accountability. For example, if an LLM is used to assist in loan approval processes, stakeholders need to understand why a loan application was rejected to ensure that the decision was fair and did not discriminate against the applicant, based on irrelevant factors.

To address these concerns, researchers and developers are working on methods to make LLMs more interpretable and explainable. One approach is the development of visualization tools that can illustrate the attention mechanisms within the model, showing which parts of the input text had the most significant impact on the output. Another method involves creating simplified models that approximate the behavior of the LLM, providing a more understandable explanation for its decisions.

Additionally, there are efforts to design LLMs with built-in explainability features that can generate plain-language explanations for their outputs. For example, alongside generating a prediction, the model might also produce a summary of the key factors that influenced its decision, much like a human expert would do when explaining their reasoning.

Despite these advancements, achieving full interpretability and explainability in LLMs remains a complex challenge that is central to the broader adoption and responsible use of AI. Ensuring that LLMs can be transparent about their decision-making processes is crucial for building user trust, meeting regulatory requirements, and preventing potential harm that could arise from misunderstood or misapplied AI recommendations.

Regulatory Compliance

Navigating the complex landscape of regulatory compliance is a significant challenge when deploying Large Language Models, particularly because these regulations can vary greatly across different regions and industries. For example, the General Data Protection Regulation (GDPR) in the European Union (EU) imposes strict rules on data privacy, and gives individuals control over their personal data. This includes the right to explanation, where users can request the reasoning behind automated decisions made about them. An LLM operating in this jurisdiction must be designed to provide such explanations, and to process the personal data in accordance with the GDPR's principles.

Moreover, industry-specific regulations add another layer of complexity. In the healthcare sector, LLMs must comply with regulations such as the Health Insurance Portability and Accountability Act (HIPAA) in the United States, which protects sensitive patient health information. This means that any LLM involved in processing healthcare data must ensure that all privacy and security measures meet HIPAA standards, such as encryption of data in transit and at rest, and access controls to limit exposure of patient information.

Financial services also have stringent regulations, such as the Sarbanes-Oxley Act (SOX), which requires accurate and transparent financial reporting. LLMs used for financial analysis or reporting must therefore be capable of providing outputs that comply with these regulations, and are auditable for accuracy and integrity.

When deploying LLMs internationally, companies must also consider the varying data protection laws in different countries. For instance, some countries have data localization laws that require personal data to be stored within the country's borders. An LLM service that processes personal data would need to ensure that it has the necessary infrastructure in place to comply with these laws, which might involve setting up local data centers or adopting specific data transfer mechanisms.

The challenge is not only in the initial design and deployment of LLMs but also in maintaining compliance over time as laws and regulations evolve. Continuous monitoring and updating of the LLMs and their operational processes are required to keep pace with changes in the legal landscape.

In summary, regulatory compliance for LLMs is a multifaceted issue that demands careful consideration of data protection laws like GDPR, as well as industry-specific legislation. Companies must invest in understanding these regulations, and implement robust systems as well as processes to ensure that their use of LLMs remains compliant across all jurisdictions in which they operate. This is crucial not only for legal adherence but also for maintaining user trust, and protecting the reputation of the organization.

Integration with Existing Systems

For any practical application, LLMs will need to be integrated into the existing or other IT systems. The integration process involves ensuring that the LLMs can communicate effectively with legacy systems, databases, and applications that were not originally designed to interact with AI-driven technologies.

For instance, an organization may want to leverage an LLM to enhance customer service by integrating it with its existing Customer Relationship Management (CRM) system. This would require the LLM to understand and process customer inquiries, extract relevant information from the CRM, and generate appropriate responses. To achieve this, developers must create interfaces or APIs that allow for seamless data exchange between the LLM and the CRM software. This process can be challenging, particularly if the CRM system is outdated or uses proprietary data formats that are difficult to work with.

Another example is the integration of LLMs in the healthcare industry, where they might be used to interpret medical records, and assist with diagnostics. Such an application would need to integrate with **Electronic Health Record (EHR)** systems, which often have strict compliance requirements, and may use a variety of data standards. Ensuring that the LLM can understand and process this information without compromising patient privacy or data integrity is a significant technical challenge.

Moreover, integrating LLMs may also require changes to the existing workflows. Employees who are accustomed to traditional methods of operation may need to adapt to new processes that incorporate the LLM's capabilities. This can involve training staff to interact with the LLM, updating Standard Operating Procedures (SOPs), and even rethinking the roles and responsibilities within a team to take full advantage of the LLM's strengths.

The integration process also involves rigorous testing to ensure that the LLM performs reliably within the existing infrastructure, and that any new tools or processes do not introduce vulnerabilities or instability. Organizations must carefully plan and execute the integration of LLMs, often requiring a phased approach that allows for gradual implementation, and minimizes disruption to the ongoing operations.

Reliability and Robustness

Ensuring the reliability and robustness of LLMs is a critical factor in building and maintaining trust in their outputs. Reliability refers to the consistent performance of the LLM across a wide range of inputs and scenarios, while *robustness* relates to the model's ability to handle unexpected or adversarial inputs, without being easily misled or compromised.

One of the key challenges with LLMs is that they may encounter inputs that are designed to trick or confuse them, known as adversarial attacks. For example, slight alterations to text inputs, which might be imperceptible or seem innocuous to humans, could be crafted in such a way that they cause the LLM to produce incorrect or nonsensical outputs. An adversary might introduce these subtle manipulations to exploit vulnerabilities in the model, potentially leading to errors in decision-making or exposing sensitive information.

To combat these threats, LLMs must be trained not only on diverse and representative datasets but also on examples that include these adversarial scenarios. This helps the models learn to identify and resist such attacks. Furthermore, ongoing evaluation and testing are necessary to continuously improve the model's defenses against newly discovered vulnerabilities.

Another aspect of robustness is the model's ability to handle a variety of inputs in different contexts and languages. An LLM that performs well on standard datasets but fails to understand colloquial language, dialects, or jargon would not be considered robust. It is important for the model to be tested across these different contexts to ensure that it can maintain high performance, and provide reliable outputs, regardless of the input style or complexity.

Developers also need to implement fail-safes and monitoring systems that can detect when the LLM is operating outside of its reliable parameters. In such cases, the system might flag the output for human review or revert to a conservative response mode to prevent the propagation of potentially harmful or misleading information.

Ensuring that the reliability and robustness of LLMs requires a comprehensive approach that includes training on adversarial and diverse inputs, regular testing and updates to address new vulnerabilities, and the implementation of systems to monitor and mitigate potential failures. By taking these steps, developers can ensure that LLMs remain trustworthy, and emerge as effective tools for a variety of applications.

Conclusion

In this chapter, we have explored the remarkable ascent of Language Models in the realm of artificial intelligence, with a particular focus on the diverse types and applications of Large Language Models. These sophisticated tools have opened new horizons in AI, enabling machines to interact with human language in unprecedented ways. From customer support to content generation and beyond, LLMs have proven their versatility and transformative potential.

Yet, alongside these advancements come significant challenges in the deployment and management of LLMs. Issues such as data privacy, bias mitigation, interpretability, regulatory compliance, system integration, and ensuring robustness require careful attention to ensure that these technologies are used responsibly and effectively.

As we conclude this chapter, while LLMs hold immense promise, realizing their full benefits, while navigating the associated complexities will be an ongoing endeavor in the AI community. It is a journey that calls for continued innovation, ethical consideration, and collaboration across disciplines to ensure that LLMs serve as a force for good in society. To effectively tackle these operational challenges, and bring LLMs into reliable production, we will next delve into the *fundamental principles of* MLOps, as well as introduce newer paradigms introduced in the context of LLMs.

References

1. http://www.universelle-automation.de/1966_Boston.pdf
2. https://www.geeksforgeeks.org/nlp/bag-of-words-bow-model-in-nlp/
3. https://towardsdatascience.com/word2vec-research-paper-explained-205cb7eecc30/
4. https://arxiv.org/pdf/1706.03762
5. https://en.wikipedia.org/wiki/BLEU
6. https://moldstud.com/articles/p-ethical-considerations-in-natural-language-processing-engineering-for-admissions-decision-making
7. https://heidloff.net/article/foundation-models-transformers-bert-and-gpt/
8. https://alrafayglobal.com/gpt-vs-bert/
9. https://blog.gopenai.com/curse-of-dimensionality-decoding-the-dimensionality-dilemma-in-machine-learning-and-deep-learning-770e4abb988b
10. https://cloud.google.com/discover/what-is-llmops
11. https://en.wikipedia.org/wiki/BERT_(language_model)

12. https://en.wikipedia.org/wiki/Curse_of_dimensionality
13. https://en.wikipedia.org/wiki/Transformer_(deep_learning_architecture)
14. https://medium.com/@akankshasinha247/a-developers-guide-to-llmops-turning-llm-prototypes-into-production-powerhouses-ce9ea612fb07
15. https://medium.com/@vijayjun89/gpt-vs-bert-a-comprehensive-comparison-of-two-powerful-language-models-df27c2b45733
16. https://papers.neurips.cc/paper/7181-attention-is-all-you-need.pdf
17. https://www.datacamp.com/blog/curse-of-dimensionality-machine-learning
18. https://www.ibm.com/think/topics/large-language-models
19. https://www.researchgate.net/publication/393228997_A_Historical_Overview_of_Language_Model_Development_From_Statistical_Models_to_Transformers
20. https://www.tredence.com/llmops

Appendix

1. Curse of Dimensionality

Imagine you are trying to find a specific friend in a space.

- **1D (A straight line):** If your friend is somewhere on a long, straight road, it's relatively easy to find them. You just walk along the line. There are not many places they could be, so even with a few random points (like where your other friends are), you can easily pinpoint their relative location.
- **2D (A 2D plane/flat field):** Now, imagine your friend is somewhere in a vast, flat field. To find them, you need to search across a much larger area. If you only have a few reference points (your other friends), they are likely to be very spread out, and most of the field will be empty. It becomes much harder to narrow down your friend's exact spot.
- **3D (A 3D room/volume):** Finally, imagine your friend is somewhere in a massive, empty warehouse. The volume is enormous. If you have the same number of reference points as before, they'll be incredibly sparse, almost like tiny specks in a vast void. The chances of your friend being "*close*" to any of your reference points become extremely small, and most of the warehouse is just empty space.

This analogy illustrates the "*Curse of Dimensionality*" because:

- **Space grows exponentially:** Moving from 1D to 2D to 3D, the "*search space*" (the volume) grows dramatically.

- **Data becomes sparse:** To maintain the same "*density*" of friends in a larger space, you'd need exponentially more friends. With a fixed number of friends, they become incredibly spread out and "*lonely*" as dimensions increase.
- **"*Closeness*" loses meaning:** In the 3D warehouse, even your "*closest*" friend might still be very far away, making it difficult to use proximity to find patterns or make predictions.

So, in machine learning, when you add more features (dimensions) to your data, without a proportionally huge increase in the number of data points, your data becomes extremely sparse, and it gets much harder for algorithms to find meaningful relationships, just like trying to find a few friends in an ever-expanding, mostly empty space.

CHAPTER 2

Getting Started with MLOps

Introduction

In the rapidly evolving landscape of artificial intelligence, operationalizing machine learning models from development to production presents significant challenges. **MLOps, or Machine Learning Operations**, provides a structured discipline to address these complexities, extending DevOps principles to streamline the entire ML lifecycle. It encompasses practices, principles, and technologies designed to automate, standardize, and scale the process of building, deploying, and managing models, thereby enabling the scalable and sustainable deployment of AI capabilities. As the field advances, particularly with the advent of Large Language Models (LLMs), these operational considerations have evolved further, giving rise to the specialized domain of LLMOps.

This chapter will serve as a foundational guide to MLOps. We will explore its core principles and practices, delve into the comprehensive MLOps life cycle from model development to deployment and monitoring, and highlight the diverse tools and technologies that empower these workflows. Furthermore, we will address specific considerations for LLMOps, differentiating it from traditional MLOps by discussing unique operational aspects pertinent to Large Language Models, such as prompt management, **Retrieval Augmented Generation** (**RAG**), and the orchestration of AI Agents. Thus, by the end of this chapter, you will have a solid grasp of how MLOps positions machine learning at the heart of an organization's operations, driving innovation in a controlled, predictable, and impactful manner.

Structure

In this chapter, we will discuss the following topics:

- Introduction to MLOps: Principles and Practices
- MLOps Life Cycle: Model Development, Deployment, and Monitoring
- Tools and Technologies in MLOps
- Specific Considerations for LLMOps: Beyond Traditional MLOps

Introduction to MLOps: Principles and Practices

Often data scientists put a lot of effort and hours into cleaning data, preparing features, and finally training and tuning models to bring to the level where they can meet business expectations. But here is where the true battle starts, that is putting the model into production. Unlike traditional systems whose deployment cycles are governed by DevOps, ML applications have special needs. Here, a lot of factors need to be taken care of, so ML applications can function as desired. This science of establishing DevOps practices in the ML model is what led to the term, "*MLOps*". And when similar practices need to be established for LLM models, it gives rise to LLMOps.

Overview of MLOps

MLOps, or Machine Learning Operations, is a set of practices that aim to streamline and systematize the end-to-end machine learning lifecycle. This encompasses the iterative stages of designing, developing, testing, deploying, monitoring, and maintaining machine learning models. MLOps seeks to bridge the gap between the development of machine learning models, and their operation in production environments. By incorporating elements from DevOps and software engineering, MLOps facilitates collaboration across data scientists, engineers, and IT professionals, enabling them to efficiently deploy models into production, and scale machine learning initiatives. MLOps emphasizes automation, reproducibility, quality control, and regulatory compliance, ensuring that machine learning systems are reliable, scalable, and efficient.

Consider a financial services company that aims to leverage machine learning to detect fraudulent transactions in real-time. The data science team has developed a sophisticated model that can identify the potential fraud with high accuracy. However, moving this model from a research environment to a production setting where it can process live transaction data is where MLOps comes into play.

To begin, the team would set up an *automated pipeline* for data ingestion and preprocessing, ensuring that the model receives the right input format in a timely manner. Next, they would containerize the model using tools like Docker, allowing for consistent deployment across various environments, from testing to production. **Continuous Integration and Continuous Deployment (CI/CD)** pipelines would be established using platforms such as Jenkins or GitLab CI/CD, enabling automatic model testing and deployment whenever changes are made. Additionally, it is recommended to create uniform infrastructure, deploy networks, and assign roles across environments using IaC tools like terraform.

Monitoring is another crucial aspect. The team would implement monitoring tools to track the model's performance metrics in real-time, ensuring that it maintains high accuracy and low latency. If the model's performance degrades—perhaps due to changing patterns in transaction data—the MLOps system would alert the team, who could then retrain the model with updated data. This retraining would be automated, with pipelines set up to periodically re-evaluate the model's accuracy against new data, and promote it to production if it performs better.

Finally, the MLOps framework would handle scaling the model to accommodate the high volume of transactions the company processes daily. This would involve strategies like load balancing and auto-scaling to ensure that the model can handle peak loads, without compromising on performance.

In this example, MLOps facilitates the entire process, from model development to deployment and monitoring, ensuring that the fraud detection system operates seamlessly, and is maintained efficiently, as well as evolves with the needs of the business.

Extending the concept of MLOps to large language models leads to the notion of LLMOps. These address the specific operational challenges associated with deploying and managing large language models. These models, which can consist of billions of parameters, require substantial computational resources and sophisticated strategies for training, fine-tuning, and inference. LLMOps include techniques for efficiently distributing computation, managing the lifecycle of massive datasets, and monitoring the performance and biases of LLMs. It also involves ensuring the security and privacy of the data processed by these models. Hence, by applying the principles of MLOps to the realm of large language models, organizations can achieve more robust, scalable, and ethical AI solutions.

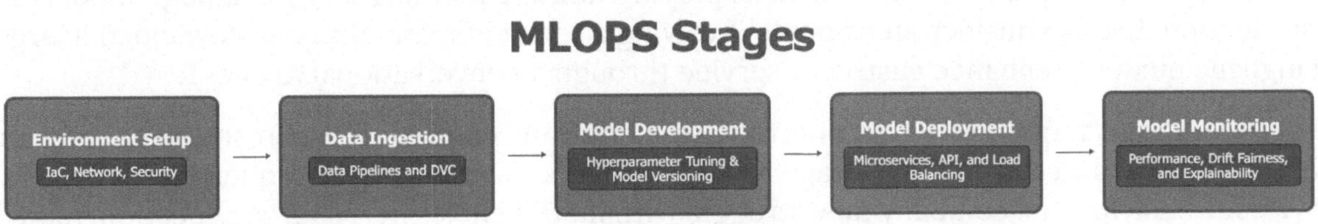

Figure 2.1: *MLOps Stages*

Need for MLOps

The need for MLOps becomes apparent when considering the complexities involved in transitioning a machine learning model from the experimental stage to real-world application. To illustrate, let us look at a healthcare organization that develops a machine learning model to predict patient readmission risks, based on electronic health records.

Initially, the data scientists create a model that performs well on historical data. However, without MLOps, several challenges arise. The model may not be updated with new data, leading to a decline in accuracy over time as patient demographics, and disease patterns evolve. Moreover, the model could perform inconsistently across different hospital systems due to variations in IT infrastructure, and there is a risk of failure to meet regulatory compliance for patient data privacy.

In fact, by implementing MLOps, the organization can create a streamlined workflow that begins with the automatic preprocessing of new and diverse patient data, maintaining the model's relevance and accuracy. An MLOps pipeline would include version control for both the data and the model, allowing for traceability and reproducibility, which are critical for meeting regulatory requirements.

Continuous monitoring with MLOps would detect when the model's performance deviates from the expected thresholds, prompting automatic retraining or alerting data scientists to intervene manually. This ensures that the model remains reliable over time, providing clinicians with accurate predictions that improve patient outcomes.

Additionally, MLOps would handle the deployment of the model across various hospital systems, managing the infrastructure to ensure consistent performance. This is crucial because it reduces the risk of errors that could arise from manual deployment processes.

In this healthcare example, the need for MLOps is driven by the necessity to maintain model accuracy and reliability in a dynamic environment, ensure regulatory compliance, and enable scalable and consistent deployment across different systems—all of which are vital for delivering predictive insights that can enhance patient care and operational efficiency.

Similarly, the need for LLMOps, or Large Language Model Operations, emerges when managing the unique challenges associated with deploying and maintaining large language models in production. Let us consider an example involving a tech company that has developed a large language model to enhance customer service through a conversational AI agent.

Large language models like this one require significant computational resources, both for initial training and for ongoing usage as they process natural language queries from users. Without LLMOps, the company may struggle with inefficiencies in resource allocation, model updating, performance monitoring, and handling user feedback effectively.

LLMOps address these challenges by providing a framework for scaling computational resources as demand fluctuates. For instance, the conversational AI agent may experience peak usage during specific hours, and LLMOps can ensure that the infrastructure dynamically adjusts to meet this demand, without over-provisioning during off-peak times.

Furthermore, large language models can drift or become outdated as language and user interactions evolve. LLMOps enable the tech company to continuously monitor the performance and relevance of the output generated by an AI agent, incorporating new data into the training pipeline to retrain and update the model as needed. This ensures that the agent remains effective, and provides high-quality responses to user inquiries.

Another crucial aspect of LLMOps is ensuring ethical and responsible AI practices. Large language models have the potential to propagate biases or generate inappropriate content, if not carefully monitored. LLMOps processes can include mechanisms to detect and mitigate such issues, maintain the model's alignment with company policies, and comply with regulatory standards.

Lastly, LLMOps facilitate user feedback integration, allowing the company to refine the conversational AI agent, based on real-world interactions. By creating a feedback loop where user experiences inform model improvements, the company can continuously enhance the AI agent's performance and user satisfaction.

In summary, the need for LLMOps arises from the operational complexities of large language models. It provides a systematic approach to resource management, model updating, performance monitoring, ethical oversight, and user feedback integration, ensuring that such models deliver their intended benefits reliably and responsibly.

Issue	Solution
Model accuracy degrades over time due to outdated data.	Automatic data preprocessing and continuous monitoring ensure model relevance and accuracy.
Inconsistent model performance across varied IT infrastructures.	Consistent deployment across systems, managing infrastructure for uniform performance.
Risk of non-compliance with data privacy regulations.	Version control for data and models ensures traceability for regulatory compliance.
Inefficient computational resource allocation for LLMs.	LLMOps dynamically scales resources based on demand fluctuations.
LLMs drift or become outdated as language evolves.	Continuous monitoring and retraining with new data keeps LLMs effective and high-quality.
LLMs may propagate biases or generate inappropriate content.	Mechanisms to detect and mitigate bias/harmful content, aligning with policies and standards.
Challenges in integrating user feedback for model refinement.	LLMOps facilitates user feedback integration, creating a loop for continuous improvement.

Table 2.1: *Issues and Their Solutions via MLOps/LLMOps*

Principles and Practices of MLOps

The principles and practices of MLOps are designed to ensure that machine learning systems are developed and maintained with efficiency, reliability, and scalability. Here is a list of the key principles and practices commonly associated with MLOps:

Principles:

- **Automation:** Automate as much of the machine learning lifecycle as possible, including data preprocessing, model training, testing, deployment, and monitoring.
- **Version Control:** Use version control systems for code, data, and model artifacts to track changes, manage collaboration, and facilitate rollback, if necessary.
- **Reproducibility:** Ensure that ML experiments and model training are reproducible for consistent results across different environments.
- **Continuous Integration and Continuous Deployment (CI/CD):** Integrate CI/CD practices to automatically test and deploy ML models, promoting rapid and reliable delivery of model updates.
- **Monitoring and Logging:** Implement comprehensive monitoring and logging to track model performance, data quality, and operational metrics in real-time.
- **Scalability**: Design systems that can scale horizontally to handle increased loads, and accommodate larger datasets as well as more complex models.
- **Governance and Compliance:** Adhere to data governance and regulatory compliance requirements, including data privacy and model explainability.
- **Collaboration**: Foster collaboration among data scientists, ML engineers, and operational teams to streamline the ML life cycle.
- **Quality Assurance:** Ensure high standards of quality for data, models, and overall system performance.
- **Continuous Learning:** Facilitate continuous learning and improvement of models with new data and feedback loops.

Practices:

- **Data Management:** Use data pipelines and data versioning tools to manage datasets, ensuring data quality and accessibility.
- **Model Training and Validation**: Establish automated training pipelines with validation steps to evaluate model performance before deployment.
- **Infrastructure as Code (IaC):** Use IaC to provision and manage infrastructure, enabling consistent and reproducible environments.
- **Model Serving and Inference:** Utilize scalable model serving frameworks to deploy models for inference with low latency and high throughput.

- **Experiment Tracking:** Employ experiment tracking tools to log, compare, and analyze model training runs and hyperparameters.
- **Model Packaging:** Package models into deployable artifacts, such as containers, to ensure consistency across environments.
- **Feature Stores:** Implement feature stores to manage, share, and reuse features across different models and projects.
- **Model Monitoring:** Monitor deployed models for performance degradation, data drift, and anomalies to trigger retraining or alerting.
- **Model Rollback:** Prepare for model rollback, in case newly deployed models underperform or cause unexpected issues.
- **Security and Privacy:** Embed security and privacy practices into the ML workflow, including secure access controls and data encryption.

By adhering to these principles and practices, organizations can develop MLOps frameworks that enhance the lifecycle management of their ML models, resulting in more robust, efficient, and trustworthy AI systems.

MLOps Life Cycle: Model Development, Deployment, and Monitoring

The MLOps life cycle is an iterative process that encompasses several stages to ensure the successful deployment and maintenance of machine learning models in production. It begins with the planning and design phase, where project goals are set, and the scope is defined. Here, stakeholders come together to outline the requirements and resources necessary to tackle the machine learning task at hand, deciding on algorithms and system architecture that align with business objectives.

Once the groundwork is laid, the team moves into the data management phase, which is crucial as the quality and appropriateness of the data directly impact model performance. Data engineers and scientists work on acquiring, cleaning, and preprocessing the data, as well as implement data versioning to maintain a history of the datasets used.

Model development is where the actual machine learning takes place. Data scientists experiment with various algorithms, train models, and tune hyperparameters, all while documenting their experiments for reproducibility and insight generation. This is followed by rigorous validation and testing to ensure that the model's performance holds up against real-world data, and to avoid pitfalls such as overfitting.

After a model passes the testing phase, it is ready for deployment into a production environment, where it starts making inferences based on new data. Deployment can be a complex process, involving the setting up of APIs, microservices, or embedding the model within larger systems, all done with the aim of providing seamless and scalable access to the model's capabilities.

Operationalization does not end with deployment; it continues with continuous monitoring of the model in the production environment. This includes tracking not just its predictive performance, but also operational metrics like response times and resource consumption. Monitoring helps in detecting issues such as data drift or model degradation, prompting necessary actions to maintain model accuracy and reliability. These actions often involve model updating and retraining; especially as new data becomes available or user needs evolve. The MLOps infrastructure should support automated retraining pipelines, ensuring that models are kept up-to-date, without requiring manual intervention for each update.

Crucially, governance and compliance are woven throughout the MLOps life cycle. As models handle potentially sensitive data, and make decisions that could have significant impacts, it is essential to ensure that they operate within legal and ethical boundaries, maintaining transparency, security, and fairness.

Incorporating a feedback loop is also a fundamental part of the life cycle. It ensures that end-user feedback, and newly acquired data inform subsequent iterations of the model, enabling continuous improvement and adaptation to changing circumstances.

Finally, the life cycle includes a decommissioning stage for models that are no longer needed, or have been superseded by more advanced versions. This involves retiring the old model safely, preserving the historical data, and ensuring a smooth transition for users to newer systems.

Overall, the MLOps life cycle is designed to be a comprehensive, end-to-end process that not only brings machine learning models from concept to production, but also ensures that they remain effective, relevant, and compliant throughout their operational life.

Thus, let us check out some of these components in detail, and also inspect LLM specific considerations as well.

Model Development

Usually, the MLOps journey begins with a clear problem definition, where the business objectives are outlined, key performance indicators are identified, and success criteria for the model are established. Following this, data collection and management take center stage, with a focus on gathering high-quality data, ensuring its integrity, and maintaining thorough documentation for reproducibility and compliance.

Exploratory Data Analysis (EDA) is then conducted to analyze and visualize the data, revealing patterns and relationships that inform subsequent steps. Feature engineering transforms raw data into meaningful features, and leveraging domain expertise to enhance model performance. The selection of an appropriate machine learning algorithm is crucial, and is based on the problem's nature, data characteristics, and computational considerations.

Training the model involves feeding prepared data into the algorithm, fine-tuning hyperparameters, and using validation sets to iteratively improve performance. Post-training, the model undergoes rigorous evaluation against a separate test set to ensure that it meets the predefined KPIs. Model versioning is employed to track different iterations, encompassing code, data, parameters, and the training environment, which facilitates reproducibility, and allows for easy rollbacks, if necessary.

Let us now inspect how MLOps can be adapted to LLMOps. The process begins with the definition of the linguistic or cognitive task that the LLM is intended to perform. This involves understanding the scope of the language model, the nuances of the language it needs to handle, and the specific use cases it will address. Clear objectives and success metrics are established to guide the development process.

Data curation and preprocessing are next, where vast amounts of textual data are collected, cleaned, and organized. Given the size of LLMs, data quality and diversity are paramount to avoid biases, and ensure the model's robustness. Data governance and ethical considerations are also critical at this stage, especially given the potential for sensitive information to be included in the training data.

Tokenization and encoding are specific to LLMs, where the raw text data is converted into a format that can be processed by neural networks. This involves choosing the right tokenization strategy that balances model performance with computational efficiency.

Architecture selection for LLMs involves choosing the appropriate neural network structure, such as Transformers, which are commonly used for their ability to handle long-range dependencies in text. The architecture must be scalable and capable of handling the enormous parameter space of LLMs.

Model training for LLMs is a resource-intensive process that requires careful planning. It involves selecting hyperparameters, training strategies, and leveraging distributed computing resources to handle the computational load. Continuous monitoring is necessary to manage resources effectively, and ensure that the training process is progressing as expected.

Aspect	MLOps	LLMOps
Initial Focus	**Problem definition, business objectives, KPIs.**	Linguistic/cognitive task definition, scope, language nuances, use cases.
Data Handling	High-quality data collection, integrity, documentation, EDA.	Vast textual data collection, cleaning, organization. Emphasis on quality, diversity, and ethical considerations to avoid biases.
Data Transformation	**Feature engineering from raw data.**	Tokenization and encoding for neural network processing, choosing optimal strategy.
Algorithm/ Architecture	Selection based on problem, data, computational needs.	Choosing scalable neural network structures like Transformers for large parameter spaces.

Aspect	MLOps	LLMOps
Training	Feeding data, hyperparameter tuning, validation sets.	Resource-intensive process with distributed computing, careful planning, hyperparameter/ strategy selection, continuous resource monitoring.
Versioning	Tracks code, data, parameters, training environment.	Crucial for large LLMs, encompassing code, data, parameters, and training environment for reproducibility and rollbacks. (Implied as an extension of MLOps versioning due to scale and complexity of LLMs).

Table 2.2: *Model Development MLOps vs LLMOps*

Model Deployment

Model deployment is a critical stage in the machine learning life cycle where a trained model is put into a production environment to start making predictions on real-world data. In MLOps, model deployment is a well-orchestrated process that requires careful planning, rigorous testing, and ongoing monitoring to ensure that the model operates as expected in its target environment.

The deployment process begins with the selection of a deployment strategy that aligns with the business needs and technical infrastructure. Options include online (real-time) deployment, where predictions are made on-demand for individual data points; batch (offline) deployment, where predictions are made on large sets of data at scheduled intervals or hybrid approaches that combine elements of both.

Once a strategy is chosen, the model is packaged into a deployable artifact. This typically involves wrapping the model in an Application Programming Interface (API) or converting it into a standalone application or microservice. The packaging must ensure that the model can be easily integrated with the existing systems, and that it can scale to meet the demands.

Before actual deployment, the model undergoes extensive testing in a staging environment that closely mimics production. This includes load testing to validate the model's performance under expected traffic conditions and A/B testing to compare the new model's performance against the currently deployed models.

The deployment itself is often automated using Continuous Integration and Continuous Deployment (CI/CD) pipelines, which enable the seamless transition of the model from development to production. Automation also ensures that the deployment process is repeatable, and minimizes the risk of human error.

Coming to LLMs, given their size and complexity, deployment must be executed with precision and care, guided by MLOps principles tailored for the scale of LLMs. The deployment begins with a strategic decision on how the LLM will be made available for use. This can include real-time inference where the model provides immediate responses to user queries, batch processing for handling large volumes of data, or a streaming approach so that the user is sent a response as soon as it is generated, rather than waiting for the whole text to generate. Also there are special cases of managing context by saving previous interaction of the user, and feeding to the current iteration's context like in case of chatbots. Similarly, RAG and AI Agents add more complexity to flow which need to be addressed effectively. The choice of deployment strategy is dictated by the use case requirements, infrastructure capabilities, and cost considerations.

Packaging the LLM for deployment typically involves encapsulating the model within a scalable and secure API that can be called by various client applications. This step may require model quantization and optimization to reduce the model's size, without significantly compromising its performance, ensuring that it can operate efficiently in a production environment.

Testing the LLM in a staging environment that replicates the production setting is crucial. It allows for load testing to validate the model's performance under high-demand scenarios, and to ensure that it meets latency requirements. The LLM might also be subjected to A/B testing to evaluate its performance relative to the existing models or previous versions.

Maintaining an LLM in production involves continuous evaluation and updates. This includes retraining the model with fresh data to stay current with the linguistic trends, and to mitigate drift. Additionally, user feedback and interactions with the LLM are often leveraged to make iterative improvements to the model.

Ethical considerations and compliance with regulations are also essential during LLM deployment. Ensuring that the model does not propagate biases or generate inappropriate content is of utmost importance, necessitating the implementation of robust content filtering and moderation mechanisms.

In LLMOps, the deployment process is an ongoing cycle that demands careful attention to operational efficiency, model performance, user experience, and ethical standards. The LLMOps framework provides the structure and practices necessary to manage LLM deployment effectively, prioritizing scalability, reliability, and responsibility in making advanced language models available for practical use.

Aspect	MLOps	LLMOps
Deployment Strategy	Online (real-time), batch (offline), or hybrid.	Real-time inference, batch processing, or streaming. Also managing context (e.g., chatbots) , RAG, and AI Agents.
Packaging	Model wrapped in API, standalone application, or microservice.	LLM encapsulated in scalable, secure API. May involve model quantization and optimization.
Testing	Load testing, A/B testing in staging environment.	Load testing, A/B testing in staging; validates performance under high demand and latency.

Aspect	MLOps	LLMOps
Automation	Automated using CI/CD pipelines.	CI/CD adapted for LLM codebases and training pipelines. Kubeflow Pipelines for end-to-end workflows.
Ongoing Maintenance	Continuous monitoring.	Continuous evaluation, updates, retraining with fresh data. Incorporates user feedback.
Ethical Considerations	(Implied as part of overall MLOps governance)	Essential: ensuring no bias propagation or inappropriate content; robust content filtering/ moderation mechanisms.
Infrastructure	Planning, rigorous testing, ongoing monitoring. Scalable access, APIs, microservices.	Precision and care due to size/complexity. Focus on operational efficiency, model performance, user experience, and ethical standards. Prioritizes scalability, reliability, and responsibility.

Table 2.3: *Model Deployment MLOps vs LLMOps*

Model Monitoring

Model monitoring is a crucial post-deployment activity that ensures the continuous health and performance of machine learning models in production. In the MLOps life cycle, model monitoring is the vigilant process of tracking and evaluating a deployed model's behavior and output to maintain its predictive quality over time, and under varying operational conditions.

Once a model is deployed, it begins interacting with real-world data, and model monitoring kicks in to detect any signs of performance degradation or unexpected behavior. The monitoring process involves collecting metrics on various aspects of the model's performance, including context relevance, latency (the time it takes for the model to provide an output), and throughput (the number of requests it can handle in a given time frame). Anomalies such as a sudden drop in accuracy or an increase in latency can indicate issues that need to be addressed.

One critical aspect of model monitoring is watching for model drift, which occurs when the statistical properties of the incoming data change over time, leading to a decrease in the model's predictive performance. This can happen due to natural evolution in the data or abrupt changes in external conditions. Detecting model drift promptly is essential for initiating corrective measures, such as retraining the model with more recent data.

Another important factor in model monitoring is keeping an eye on the input data quality. Any inconsistencies, missing values, or deviations from the expected data distribution can affect the model's predictions. Monitoring input data helps ensure that the integrity of the data feeding into the model is maintained.

In addition to performance metrics, MLOps also emphasizes the need to monitor the model for fairness and bias. Ensuring that the model treats different groups equitably, and does not propagate or amplify biases is a continuous concern that must be managed actively.

To effectively monitor a model, MLOps relies on automated tools and systems that can provide real-time or near-real-time feedback. These systems generate alerts when predefined thresholds are breached, enabling data scientists and engineers to take immediate action. Common interventions include adjusting model parameters, retraining the model with new data, or rolling back to a previous version of the model if necessary.

Furthermore, robust logging and traceability are key components of model monitoring. They enable teams to track back the model's decisions to specific inputs and understand the reasoning behind any performance changes. This traceability is crucial not only for troubleshooting and maintaining accountability but also for regulatory compliance, especially in industries subject to stringent regulations.

In conclusion, model monitoring is an ongoing and dynamic process that plays a pivotal role in the MLOps framework. It provides the insights needed to maintain the model's performance at an optimal level and to ensure that it continues to deliver value to the organization. By incorporating comprehensive model monitoring practices, MLOps helps organizations stay ahead of potential issues, maintain trust in their models, and derive sustained benefits from their machine learning investments.

Monitoring an LLM post-deployment involves continuous oversight of its performance metrics and the quality of its outputs. This includes tracking its accuracy, the relevance of its generated text, and response times. Any deviation from established benchmarks could signal potential issues such as model drift, where the model's performance degrades over time as it encounters new and varied data that differ from the training set.

A significant part of LLM monitoring is detecting and managing drift. Since LLMs are particularly sensitive to shifts in data distribution, regular checks are necessary to ascertain that the model remains attuned to the linguistic nuances and contextual variations present in the input data. Automated systems can be deployed to identify any decline in coherence, contextuality, or fluency in the LLM's responses.

The quality of input data is another focal point of LLM monitoring. Ensuring the input data is clean, diverse, and representative of the problem space is essential to maintain the quality of the model's outputs. This means monitoring for anomalies, outliers, or any changes in the input data patterns that could affect the LLM's outputs.

Ethical monitoring is a unique and critical aspect of LLMOps, where the model's outputs are scrutinized for fairness, bias, and adherence to ethical guidelines. The expansive knowledge and generative capabilities of LLMs come with the risk of producing harmful or biased content, making it imperative to have continuous checks in place to filter out such content and flag it for review.

Real-time or near-real-time feedback systems are utilized to monitor these various aspects of an LLM's performance, providing alerts and detailed logs when the model's behavior deviates from the norm. This allows teams to act swiftly to investigate and rectify any issues that arise. The tools and systems for monitoring should be scalable and capable of handling the high throughput characteristic of LLM applications.

Moreover, comprehensive logging is vital for diagnosing problems, performing audits, and maintaining accountability for the LLM's decisions. This is particularly relevant in sectors where regulatory compliance is mandatory, as it ensures transparency and facilitates the traceability of the model's outputs back to specific inputs.

In LLMOps, the model monitoring phase is an ongoing process, extending beyond the initial deployment to encompass the entire lifespan of the LLM in production. It is characterized by a proactive approach to managing the model's performance, mitigating biases, and maintaining the quality of service it provides. Effective LLM monitoring under the LLMOps framework is a multifaceted endeavor that ensures LLMs continue to operate efficiently, ethically, and in alignment with the evolving needs and expectations of their users and stakeholders.

Aspect	MLOps	LLMOps
Performance Metrics	Accuracy, precision, recall, F1-score, RMSE, etc.	Task-specific metrics (e.g., perplexity, BLEU, ROUGE), human evaluation, user satisfaction.
Data Drift	Monitoring input data distribution changes (e.g., feature drift).	Monitoring input prompt changes, semantic drift, output quality over time.
Concept Drift	Monitoring changes in the relationship between inputs and outputs.	Monitoring changes in LLM's understanding/ response to concepts, hallucinations, factual consistency.
Bias & Fairness	Detecting demographic or outcome biases.	Detecting harmful biases, toxicity, unfairness in generated content.
Latency/ Throughput	Monitoring API response times and request volume.	Monitoring response time for complex queries, token generation rates, API rate limits.
Cost Monitoring	Tracking infrastructure and compute costs.	Tracking API usage costs (e.g., token consumption), GPU usage for inference.
Explainability	Interpreting model decisions (e.g., SHAP, LIME).	Understanding LLM reasoning, attribution for generated text, interpretability of prompts.
Feedback Loop	System for collecting user feedback for retraining.	Robust feedback mechanisms for prompt engineering, RLHF, and continuous fine-tuning.

Table 2.4: *Model Monitoring MLOps vs LLMOps*

Tools and Technologies in MLOps

In the domain of MLOps, a diverse array of tools and technologies is employed to automate and enhance various stages of the machine learning life cycle. This includes everything from data preparation and model training to deployment, monitoring, and collaboration.

Version control is fundamental to MLOps, and tools like Git are ubiquitous for tracking changes in code and models. Platforms such as GitHub, GitLab, and Bitbucket build on Git's capabilities, offering hosting for repositories and tools to support team collaboration. For data and model versioning, **Data Version Control** (**DVC**) is commonly used to keep a track of datasets and ML models with a focus on reproducibility.

Data management and preparation are key components of the MLOps process, where tools like Apache Airflow and Luigi help in scheduling and orchestrating complex data pipelines. For big data processing, Apache Spark offers distributed computing capabilities. In Python, libraries such as Pandas provide extensive functions for data manipulation and analysis, and tools like Great Expectations are employed for data testing and documentation.

For model training and experimentation, frameworks such as TensorFlow and Keras, as well as PyTorch, are widely adopted for their flexibility and extensive ecosystems. Scikit-learn remains a staple for more traditional machine learning tasks, offering a broad range of algorithms and tools for data mining and analysis.

Deployment and model serving technologies are also a cornerstone of MLOps, with TensorFlow Serving and TorchServe being specialized frameworks for deploying TensorFlow and PyTorch models, respectively. Containerization is central to modern deployment strategies, with Docker providing the necessary tools for packaging applications, and Kubernetes offering an orchestration platform for automating deployment, scaling, and management of containerized applications.

The tracking and management of experiments are made more efficient with platforms like MLflow, which covers the full ML lifecycle, including experimentation. Weights and Biases and Comet.ml provide sophisticated environments for experiment tracking, results visualization, and dataset management, while TensorBoard serves as a visualization toolkit for TensorFlow to keep tabs on model metrics and structures.

Continuous Integration and Continuous Deployment (CI/CD) are crucial for automating the ML software development process, with Jenkins, CircleCI, and GitHub Actions facilitating the automation of these pipelines. Argo provides Kubernetes-native workflows for running CI/CD processes, and Kubeflow is an end-to-end toolkit on Kubernetes for deploying and managing ML workflows.

Post-deployment, model monitoring is vital to ensure ongoing model performance and health. Prometheus and Grafana are instrumental for monitoring applications and visualizing real-time metrics, while the ELK Stack enables searching, analyzing, and visualizing log data. For comprehensive application performance insights, tools such as New Relic and Datadog are leveraged.

Ensuring that models remain interpretable and explainable is addressed with tools such as **SHAP** and **LIME**, which provide ways to explain the output of machine learning models. InterpretML offers methods for creating interpretable models, and explaining black-box systems.

Security is a growing concern in MLOps, addressed by tools like Snyk for scanning and fixing vulnerabilities in dependencies and HashiCorp Vault for managing access to secrets.

Finally, cloud providers offer a range of ML services that streamline MLOps processes. AWS SageMaker, Azure Machine Learning, and Google Cloud AI Platform are examples of fully managed services that enable developers and data scientists to build, train, and deploy ML models efficiently.

The MLOps ecosystem is rich and evolving, with tools and technologies designed to facilitate collaboration, streamline workflows, and deliver robust and scalable machine learning systems in production environments.

The LLMOps ecosystem is composed of specialized tools and technologies that cater to the unique requirements of developing, deploying, and maintaining large language models. These tools often expand upon the foundations laid by MLOps to address the greater complexities involved with LLMs, such as managing massive datasets and ensuring high-performance computation.

At the core of LLM development and training are libraries such as the Transformers Library from Hugging Face, which provides a comprehensive suite for working with transformer-based models, including a variety of pre-trained LLMs. Training such models demands significant computational resources, which is why GPUs and TPUs are indispensable as hardware accelerators. Distributed training frameworks such as Horovod, DeepSpeed, and FairScale offer efficient ways to scale the training process across multiple processing units.

When it comes to serving and inference, the **ONNX** (Open Neural Network Exchange) provides an open standard for model representation, facilitating cross-platform model deployment. The NVIDIA Triton Inference Server is another key player, offering a robust solution for deploying deep learning models in production. For scalability, Ray Serve provides a library that is well-suited to the task of serving LLMs, ensuring that the high throughput and low latency demands are met.

Experiment tracking and version control are just as critical in LLMOps. Tools like Weights and Biases have been extended to support the particular requirements of tracking LLM experiments, while DVC (Data Version Control) is vital for managing large datasets. Git LFS (Large File Storage) also comes into play as an extension to Git for versioning large files, which are common in the LLM space.

Operational monitoring is a major aspect of LLMOps, with Prometheus and Grafana being used to keep tabs on the performance of LLMs in production. The ELK Stack, consisting of Elasticsearch, Logstash, and Kibana, helps with logging, monitoring, and visualizing the vast amounts of textual data processed by LLMs. Additionally, model monitoring tools like Evidently AI and WhyLabs specialize in tracking ML model performance, adapting to the intricacies of LLM outputs.

Collaboration platforms such as the Hugging Face Model Hub promote the sharing and collaborative development of LLMs. Code-sharing and collaborative development are also supported by platforms like GitHub and GitLab, which are essential for managing the collaborative aspects of LLM development.

Continuous integration and continuous deployment (**CI/CD**) are adapted to LLMOps through tools like Jenkins, CircleCI, and GitHub Actions, which can be configured for LLM codebases and training pipelines. Kubeflow Pipelines offers an integrated approach to building end-to-end workflows for LLMs, leveraging Kubernetes for orchestration.

Security and compliance are of particular importance in LLMOps, with controlled environments like OpenAI's OpenAI API offering access to models like GPT-3 with a focus on safety and ethical guidelines. HashiCorp Vault ensures the secure management of secrets and credentials associated with LLMs.

Cloud services and APIs from major providers like AWS, Azure, and Google Cloud play a pivotal role in the LLMOps landscape, offering the necessary infrastructure and specialized APIs to support tasks like translation, text-to-speech, and natural language processing at scale.

Finally, the ethical and responsible use of LLMs is supported by tools such as AI Fairness 360 (**AIF360**), which helps detect and mitigate biases, and the Model Cards Toolkit, which promotes transparent documentation of machine learning models. These tools are crucial in maintaining the integrity and trustworthiness of LLMs as they become increasingly integrated into various applications.

As the field evolves, the LLMOps toolkit will likely grow, incorporating new and improved technologies to ensure that large language models are not only powerful and efficient but also developed and managed with responsibility and care.

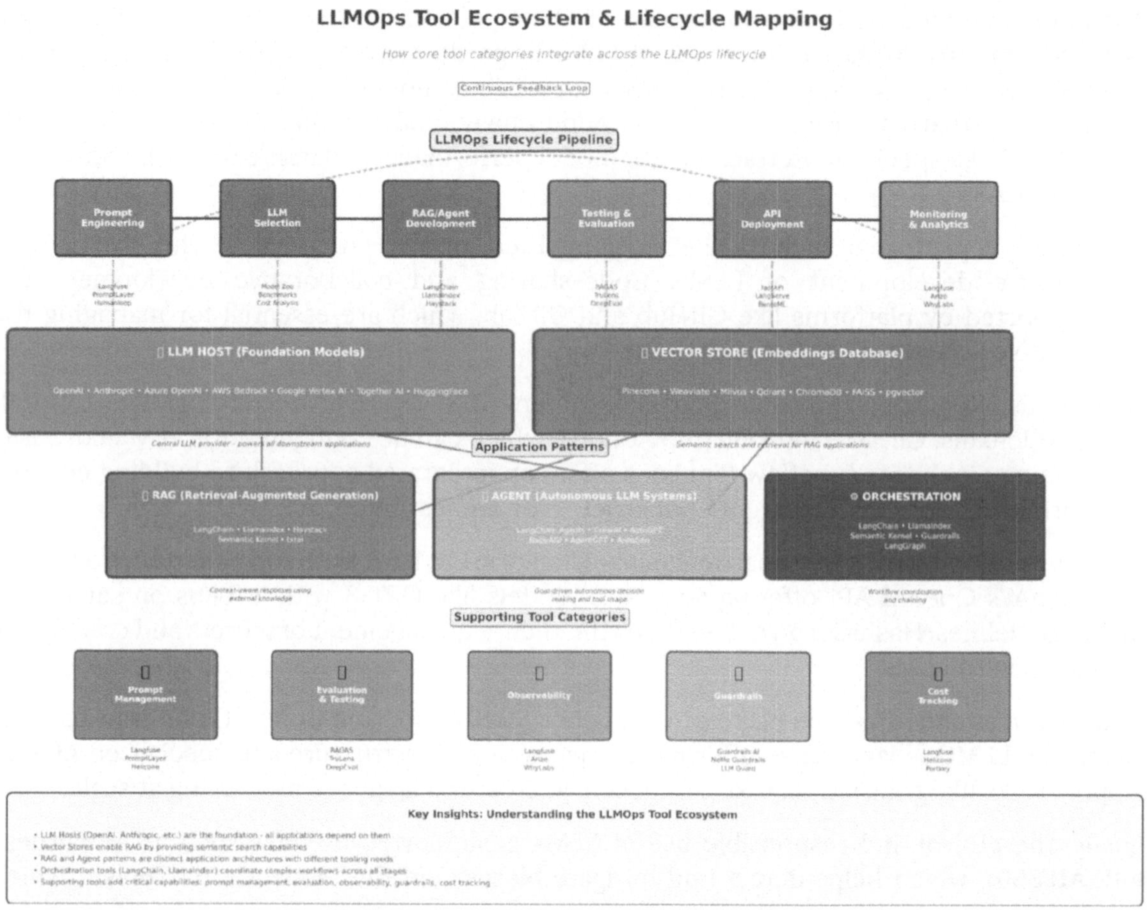

Figure 2.2: *LLMOps Stages with Tools*

Specific Considerations for LLMOps: Beyond Traditional MLOps

While MLOps provides a robust framework for managing the lifecycle of machine learning models, Large Language Models (LLMs) introduce unique challenges and opportunities, giving rise to specialized practices within LLMOps. These often revolve around managing the dynamic nature of text-based inputs, leveraging vast external knowledge, and orchestrating intelligent agents.

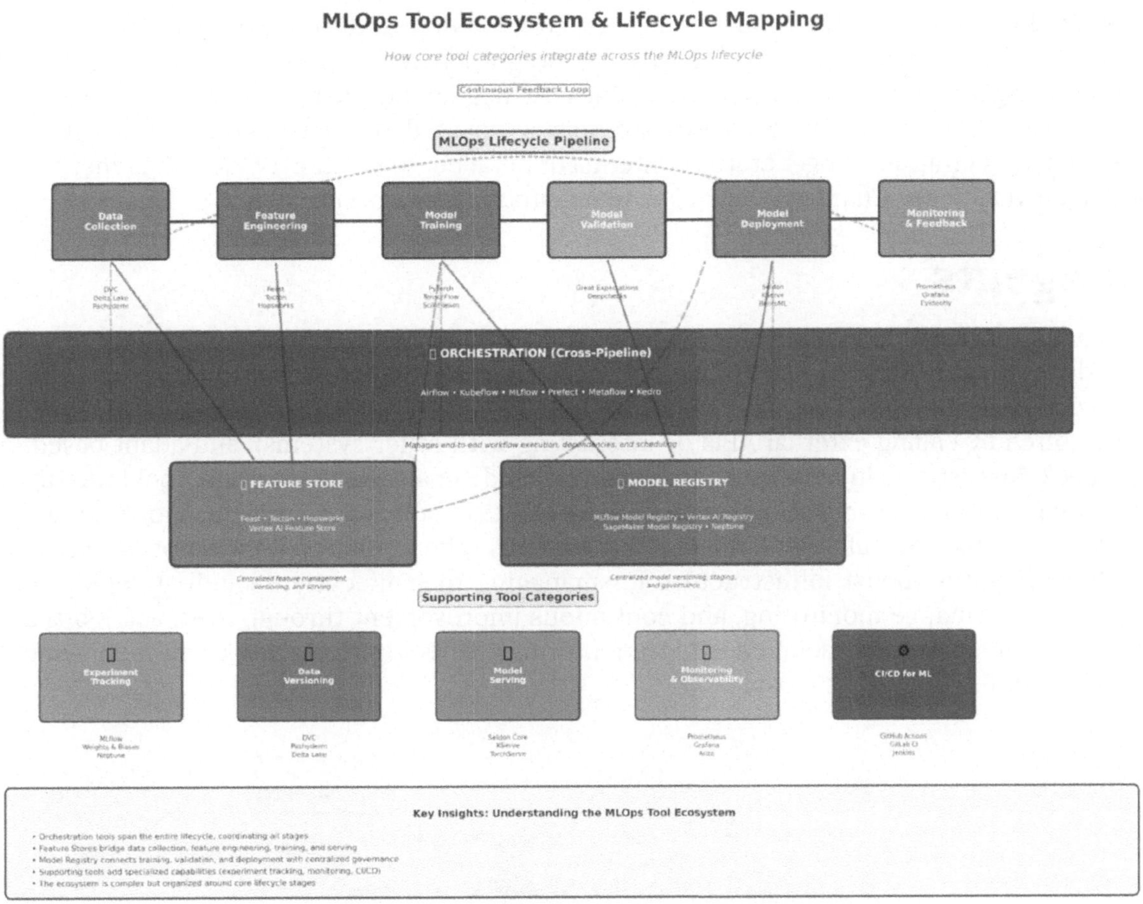

Figure 2.3: *MLOps Tools and Lifecycle Mapping*

Prompt Management

Prompt management is a critical aspect of LLMOps, focusing on the systematic creation, testing, versioning, and deployment of prompts used to interact with LLMs. Unlike traditional models with fixed inputs, LLMs' behavior is heavily influenced by the phrasing and structure of the prompts they receive. This requires specialized approaches for consistency, performance optimization, cost efficiency, version control, and security. For detailed exploration of prompt management techniques and tools, see Chapter 3.

Retrieval Augmented Generation (RAG)

Retrieval Augmented Generation (RAG) is a powerful technique that enhances the capabilities of LLMs by enabling them to access, retrieve, and synthesize information from external, authoritative knowledge bases. This addresses a key limitation of base LLMs, which are restricted to the knowledge contained in their training data and can sometimes "hallucinate" information. RAG involves external knowledge integration, information retrieval mechanisms, augmented generation processes, data freshness management, and performance optimization. RAG systems are crucial for applications requiring up-to-date information, domain-specific knowledge, or citations for generated content. For detailed exploration of RAG implementation and deployment, see *Chapter 5, Retrieval Augmentation Generation.*

AI Agents

AI Agents represent a significant evolution in LLM applications, transforming static models into dynamic, autonomous entities capable of performing complex tasks by interacting with tools and environments. These agents are designed to understand goals, plan actions, execute them (often by calling external APIs or interacting with other systems), and adapt based on feedback. Key aspects in LLMOps for AI Agents include goal-oriented design, tool integration and orchestration, reasoning and planning capabilities, state management, monitoring and control systems, and safety and alignment measures. The operationalization of AI Agents in LLMOps requires robust infrastructure for managing their lifecycle, including deployment, scaling, performance monitoring, and continuous improvement through feedback loops and iterative refinement. For detailed exploration of AI Agents implementation and deployment, see Chapter 6.

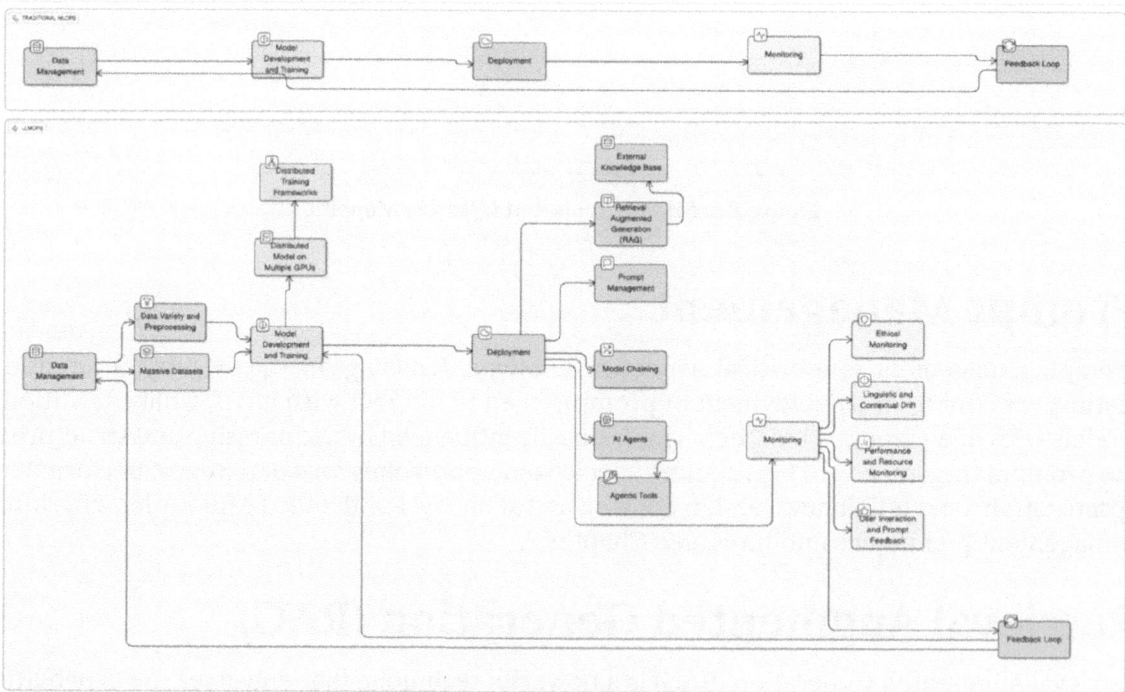

Figure 2.4: MLOps vs LLMOps

Although we have contrasted MLOps and LLMOps, it is crucial to understand they are not entirely separate disciplines. All MLOps practices remain highly applicable to LLMOps, especially when training or fine-tuning custom models. However, such extensive in-house training is often limited to large technology companies due to the significant cost and specialized expertise in distributed training required. Consequently, most industry practitioners primarily rely on APIs from LLM providers, shifting their focus to aspects like prompt management, Retrieval Augmented Generation (RAG), LLM Chaining (or orchestration), and AI Agents. Although in this book, we will primarily delve into these LLMOps-specific considerations, readers interested in foundational MLOps practices can refer here.[1]

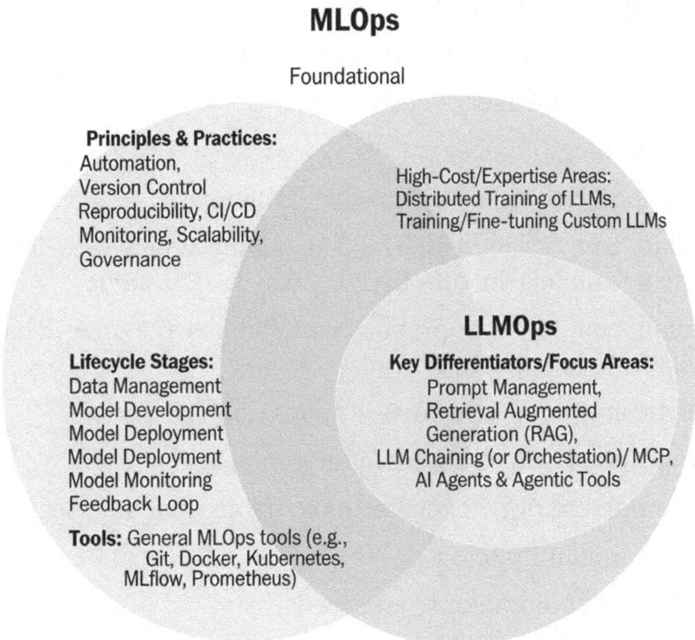

***Figure 2.5**: Overlap between MLOps and LLMOps*

Conclusion

This chapter covered a comprehensive overview of the MLOps life cycle, illustrating how it standardizes and optimizes the journey of machine learning models from conception to production and ongoing maintenance. We thoroughly contrasted traditional MLOps with the emerging paradigm of LLMOps across key stages such as: Model Development, Model Deployment, and Model Monitoring. This distinction highlighted the unique complexities and considerations introduced by Large Language Models, particularly concerning data nuances, computational demands, and ethical implications.

The special section dedicated to LLMOps underscored its distinct challenges and solutions. While sharing foundational principles with MLOps, LLMOps necessitates specialized approaches for prompt engineering, managing massive models, mitigating inherent biases, and ensuring responsible AI behavior in generative contexts. This focus is crucial for effectively operationalizing the transformative power of LLMs. Now that we have covered the overview in these two chapters, from here on, each chapter in this book will deep-dive into a specific aspect of LLMOps. With that in mind, the next chapter will delve into the critical aspect of "*Prompt Management*," a cornerstone of effective LLM operationalization.

References

1. https://arxiv.org/abs/2205.02302
2. https://www.youtube.com/watch?v=S1tN9a4Proc&pp=0gcJCfwAo7VqN5tD
3. https://github.com/visenger/awesome-mlops
4. https://lakefs.io/blog/llmops/
5. https://cloud.google.com/discover/what-is-llmops
6. https://medium.com/javarevisited/top-6-udemy-courses-to-learn-llmops-and-deploy-language-models-in-production-2025-f0317bca5c1c
7. https://medium.com/@pawanprabhashana/llmops-the-new-devops-frontier-for-large-language-models-21c15e0a2dad
8. https://analyticsindiamag.com/news/mlops-tools/
9. https://www.coursera.org/courses?query=mlops
10. https://www.coursera.org/specializations/mlops-machine-learning-duke
11. https://mlops.community/blog
12. https://rss.feedspot.com/mlops_rss_feeds/
13. https://www.fortunebusinessinsights.com/mlops-market-108986
14. https://truefoundry.com/blog
15. https://home.mlops.community/
16. https://mlops.community/
17. https://www.reddit.com/r/mlops/
18. https://www.reddit.com/r/devops/comments/1lzhjin/stuck_in_my_career_need_advice/
19. https://stackoverflow.com/tags/mlops/info
20. https://stackoverflow.com/questions/tagged/mlops
21. https://arxiv.org/abs/2409.19416
22. https://alaalab.berkeley.edu/publications/neurips-icml-iclr-publications

23. https://github.com/dair-ai/ML-Papers-of-the-Week
24. https://ml-ops.org/content/references.html
25. https://www.researchgate.net/publication/370070459_MLOps_Spanning_Whole_Machine_Learning_Life_Cycle_A_Survey
26. https://www.eventbrite.com/o/mlops-world-30341848524
27. https://mlopsworld.com/events/
28. https://www.datacamp.com/blog/top-ai-conferences
29. https://www.databricks.com/dataaisummit/session/machine-learning-operations
30. https://dev.events/ai
31. https://www.coursera.org/learn/devops-dataops-mlops-duke
32. https://www.deeplearning.ai/courses/machine-learning-in-production/
33. https://www.classcentral.com/subject/llmops
34. https://www.udemy.com/course/a-gentle-introduction-to-llmops/
35. https://360digitmg.com/usa/mlops-engineering-course-training
36. https://www.datacamp.com/blog/mlops-roadmap
37. https://www.coursera.org/specializations/large-language-model-operations
38. https://podcasts.apple.com/us/podcast/the-mlops-podcast/id1747539192
39. https://podcasts.apple.com/us/podcast/practical-ai/id1406537385
40. https://www.everand.com/podcast-show/574581786/Practical-AI
41. https://www.podcastrepublic.net/podcast/1674008350
42. https://www.latent.space/podcast
43. https://podcasts.apple.com/us/podcast/nvidia-ai-podcast/id1186480811
44. https://ai-podcast.nvidia.com/
45. https://podcasts.apple.com/us/podcast/gradient-dissent-conversations-on-ai/id1504567418
46. https://www.alooba.com/podcasts/gradient-dissent/
47. https://wandb.ai/fully-connected/podcast
48. https://sagecodes.medium.com/ai-mlops-robotics-newsletter-113-0d8cae898db9
49. https://www.zenml.io/blog/newsletter-edition-16-future-of-llmops-at-zenml
50. https://llmops.space/resources/
51. https://dexa.ai/s/rJAkGmha

52. https://neptune.ai/blog/top-machine-learning-influencers
53. https://ctomagazine.com/top-ai-speakers-on-linkedin-to-follow/
54. https://www.analyticsvidhya.com/blog/2024/04/generative-ai-influencers-on-twitter/
55. https://exchange.scale.com/public/blogs/16-machine-learning-ai-engineers-and-researchers-to-follow-twitter
56. https://mlopsworld.com/speakers/
57. https://www.prismetric.com/top-llmops-tools/
58. https://www.prnewswire.com/news-releases/large-language-model-operationalization-llmops-software-market-set-for-explosive-21-3-cagr-growth--valuates-reports-302432536.html
59. https://www.aibase.com/tool/9196
60. https://llmops.space/
61. https://llmops.space/llmops-products/
62. https://www.conf42.com/llms2025
63. https://xllms.github.io/
64. https://www.deeplearning.ai/short-courses/llmops/
65. https://neptune.ai/llmops-learning-hub
66. *https://vista.co/insights/the-oneview-podcast-a-case-study-in-fully-automated-llm-ops*
67. https://datasciencedojo.com/blog/10-top-llm-companies/

CHAPTER 3

Mastering Prompt Management for LLMs

Introduction

In the rapidly evolving landscape of Large Language Model (LLM) interaction techniques, it is the prompt that still remains the most fundamental and potent interface. Primarily, it is simply a structured sequence of words that forms the bedrock of every interaction; yet it serves as a foundational layer which underpins and enhances more complex systems like Retrieval-Augmented Generation (RAG), autonomous agents, knowledge graphs and so on. The application of managed prompts within an external knowledge-grounding system is explored in *Chapter* 5, *Retrieval Augmentation Generation*, and how prompts drive autonomous decision-making is covered in *Chapter* 6, AI *Agents and Autonomous Systems*.

A well-crafted prompt is, in itself, an exceptionally powerful tool. Therefore, for an LLMops engineer, mastering prompt design is a fundamental requirement due to its immense potential to directly influence model performance, optimize operational costs, and ensure long-term maintainability. Since prompts are written in natural language, the same command can be given in different ways, and every word choice and word order can influence the outcome. This makes its design an intricate blend of art and science, where even a minor adjustment can lead to drastically different and often unexpected outcomes. Consequently, the meticulous observation, tracking, and measurement of every prompt-output pair is absolutely critical—a practice akin to model management in classical MLOps.

This chapter will thoroughly explore the various nuances of this essential practice. We will begin by delving into the art of prompt crafting, understanding the foundational principles and techniques that enable precise and impactful interactions. Next, we will explore prompt tuning and optimization strategies, uncovering methods to refine prompts for improved performance, efficiency, and reliability. Finally, we will examine how to scale these efforts through automating prompt management using specialized tools and frameworks, equipping you with the knowledge to build robust and sustainable LLM-powered applications. Langfuse, a Python library that embodies many of these concepts, will be further explored in Chapter 11.

Structure

This chapter will address the following topics:

- Design: Prompt Engineering Techniques
- Management and Versioning: Prompt Registry
- Testing and Evaluation: A/B Testing and Metrics

Design: Prompt Engineering Techniques

When people talk about prompt engineering, they are referring to the task of communicating effectively with an AI to get the best possible response. The word "*prompt*" itself has a history. In everyday life, it is a cue that helps an actor remember their lines. In pre-LLM computing, it was a simple instruction, like "Enter your username" at a login screen. Today, within the context of LLMs, a prompt is the input text or prefix that a user provides. It often contains both context and instruction for the LLM to follow. The clearer and more detailed the context and instructions are, the better the output. This is due to the fact that a large language model is trained to predict the most likely next word in a sequence. For example, given the input **`"Today the weather is really nice. It is a good day to..."`**, the model might suggest several plausible options such as **`"walk ","swim," or "go for a stroll."`** This is similar to a more sophisticated version of autocomplete. However, if you provide more specific context, such as, **`"I just bought my new pair of shoes and today the weather is really nice. It is a good day to..."`**, the model is much more likely to narrow its response to something like **`"go for a hike."`** This ability to guide the AI with precise instructions and context is the essence of prompt engineering. It is an interdisciplinary skill that blends elements of linguistics, psychology, and computer science, focused on creating prompts that are clear, concise, and capable of guiding the AI toward useful, accurate, and contextually appropriate responses. Well-engineered prompts are the critical bridge between human intent and machine understanding, and they are the key to unlocking the true capabilities of AI systems.

Best Practices in Prompt Engineering

Prompt engineering is a meticulous practice that involves the strategic formulation of input text to guide the responses of AI language models effectively. The techniques involved in prompt engineering are designed to optimize the interaction between the user and the AI, ensuring that the output is as relevant and accurate as possible. Here are some best practices and techniques recommended in prompt engineering:

Clarity and Specificity: The Foundation of Understanding

The cornerstone of effective prompt engineering is ensuring that your instructions are crystal clear, and leave absolutely no room for ambiguity. A vague prompt will inevitably lead to a vague or inaccurate response from the AI. Precision in language, often enhanced by few-shot prompting, eliminates misinterpretation.

Think of the AI as a highly intelligent but literal assistant. If you ask it to "`Suggest good restaurants nearby,`" it does not know your dietary preferences, your preferred cuisine, your budget, or how "nearby" is defined. Is it walking distance, driving distance, within a specific radius? By contrast, a prompt like **`"List good restaurants serving vegan food within 2 miles that have outdoor seating and a rating of 4 stars or higher"`** provides all the necessary parameters for a targeted and useful response. This level of detail, often exemplified through few-shot prompting where examples guide the AI, and guides the AI directly to the relevant information, preventing it from making assumptions or generating irrelevant suggestions. Few-shot prompting, by providing a few input-output examples, effectively teaches the AI the desired format, tone, and specific constraints, thereby bringing significant clarity and specificity to its understanding of the task.

Example:

- **Poor Prompt:** "`Write about history.`" (Too broad)
- **Improved Prompt:** "`Write a concise summary of the key events leading to the American Revolutionary War, focusing on economic factors, for a high school history class.`" (Specific, contextualized, and defines audience/purpose)

Contextual Embedding: Providing the AI's Worldview

AI models benefit significantly from relevant background information. Providing context helps the AI understand the scenario, the user's role, or the desired perspective, leading to more nuanced and appropriate responses.

Without context, an AI operates in a vacuum. If you ask, "`What should I do?`" it cannot provide a meaningful answer. However, if you establish a persona or scenario, the AI can tailor its output accordingly. For instance, instructing the AI to "As a seasoned financial advisor, outline investment strategies for a client approaching retirement with a moderate risk tolerance" enables it to draw upon its knowledge base with a specific professional lens, producing advice that is both relevant and aligned with the assumed role. This technique is particularly powerful for role-playing, generating creative content, or simulating specific professional interactions.

Example:

- **Without Context:** "`Explain quantum physics.`"
- **With Context:** "`Imagine you are explaining quantum physics to a curious ten-year-old. Use simple analogies and avoid complex jargon.`"

Use of Keywords and Trigger Phrases: Guiding the AI's Action

Specific words or short phrases (control codes described above) can act as powerful signals to the AI, prompting it to perform particular actions, adopt a certain structure, or prioritize specific information.

These keywords essentially serve as direct commands or hints to the AI about the desired output format or type of processing. For example, using "**`summarize`**" in a prompt clearly instructs the AI to condense information. Other common trigger phrases include **`"list," "compare and contrast," "explain," "brainstorm," "analyze," "rewrite," "generate," "translate," "categorize," or "deconstruct."`** Strategically placed keywords can significantly streamline the AI's processing, and lead to more focused and efficient responses.

Example:

- **`"Summarize the following article, highlighting the main arguments."`**
- **`"Brainstorm five innovative marketing ideas for a new sustainable fashion brand."`**
- **`"Compare and contrast the economic policies of John Maynard Keynes and Milton Friedman."`**

Leveraging Tone and Style: Shaping the AI's Voice

The way you phrase your prompt, including its formality, humor, or politeness, can significantly influence the AI to mirror these characteristics in its replies, aligning the output with user expectations or a specific brand voice.

AI models are adept at detecting and mimicking stylistic cues. If you want a formal, academic response, your prompt should reflect that tone. If you desire a witty and informal response, inject that into your prompt. This allows for fine-grained control over the "personality" of the AI's output. For example, a prompt asking for "**`a casual, friendly email to a colleague`**" will likely generate a different style of email than one asking for "*a formal business correspondence*." This technique is invaluable for content creation, customer service interactions, and maintaining brand consistency.

Example:

- **Formal:** `"Compose a comprehensive report on the geopolitical implications of climate change, employing a formal, academic tone."`
- **Informal/Humorous:** `"Write a silly, light-hearted limerick about a clumsy cat."`

Avoiding Overfitting and Bias: Ensuring Fairness and Balance

Careful wording and, at times, providing counterexamples are essential to ensure that the AI maintains a balanced and fair perspective, preventing it from over-relying on specific examples, exhibiting unwanted biases, or generating overly narrow responses.

AI models learn from the vast datasets they are trained on, which can sometimes contain inherent biases or reflect specific viewpoints. As prompt engineers, it is our responsibility to mitigate this. Overfitting occurs when an AI becomes too specialized based on a few examples, failing to generalize to new, unseen scenarios. To counter this, prompts should be designed to encourage broader understanding and discourage narrow interpretations. Including phrases like **`"consider diverse perspectives,"`** **`"avoid generalizations,"`** or providing examples that showcase different viewpoints can help. Additionally, explicitly stating to **`"avoid bias" or "present a neutral viewpoint"`** can be effective. This technique is critical for applications where fairness, accuracy, and ethical considerations are paramount, such as in generating news articles, medical advice, or legal interpretations.

Combining Techniques: The Art of Masterful Prompt Engineering

The most effective and sophisticated prompts rarely rely on a single technique. Instead, they often integrate several of these principles to guide the AI toward comprehensive, nuanced, and precise responses. For instance, a complex prompt might:

- **Establish Context:** `"As a marketing strategist for a tech startup..."`
- **Use Keywords:** `"...brainstorm ten unique growth hacking strategies..."`
- **Specify Clarity and Detail:** `"...targeting Gen Z users, with a focus on low-cost, high-impact digital channels."`
- **Leverage Tone:** `"...present these ideas in an engaging, concise, and slightly audacious tone."`
- **Suggest Iteration (Implicitly):** `"...and provide a brief rationale for each, anticipating potential challenges."`

Prompt engineering is an iterative and creative process that requires a deep understanding of both AI capabilities and interaction goals. By artfully blending various techniques, prompt engineers can craft prompts that not only elicit desired responses but also transform AI from a simple tool into a powerful collaborative partner, enhancing the overall user experience. This continuous learning and adaptation ensure effective interaction as AI models evolve. Building on foundational techniques, the next crucial step involves refining and optimizing prompt performance, strategically tuning instructions for superior results, and addressing real-world complexities.

N-Shot Learning and Structural Techniques

Even though prompts are essentially free-form text, there are established techniques for giving instructions to large language models . These methods are rooted in how the models were trained.

While the core GPT model predicts the most likely next word, models such as ChatGPT were later fine-tuned to follow specific instructions. For example, if the model was fine-tuned in a format where a user's instruction was clearly labeled—like **User: `"Summarize this article"`**—it learns to recognize and respond to that pattern. By mimicking these instructional formats, you can significantly increase the chances of the model following your directions.

These instructions, when combined with specific inputs, help guide the output in the right direction. The techniques used in prompt engineering are designed to do so. Among these techniques, a fundamental approach involves providing the AI with varying numbers of examples, categorized as 'N-*Shot*' learning methods, which function as described in the next section: Zero-Shot, One-Shot, and Few-Shot Learning.

Zero-Shot, One-Shot, and Few-Shot Learning

Zero-shot, one-shot, and few-shot learning are concepts that refer to the number of examples provided to an AI model to help it understand and perform a new task. For example, in the context of converting natural language to SQL, these approaches would dictate how the AI model is guided to translate human-readable questions into SQL queries that can be executed against a database. Here are the definitions and examples for each:

Zero-Shot Learning

In zero-shot learning, the AI model receives no examples before performing the task. It relies solely on its pre-trained knowledge and understanding to generate the correct output. The prompt must be clear, and contain all the necessary information for the AI to infer the desired action.

Example: Prompt: `"Translate this natural language question into an SQL query: 'What is the total revenue from sales in 2024?'"` The AI is expected to generate an SQL query without having seen any prior examples:

```
SELECT SUM(revenue) FROM sales WHERE year = 2024;
```

One-Shot Learning

One-shot learning involves providing the AI model with a single example to illustrate the task. The model uses this example to understand the format and structure expected for similar tasks.

Example: Example provided to AI: **`"Translate 'List all employee names' into SQL: SELECT name FROM employees;"`** **Prompt:** **`"Now translate this question into SQL:`** `'Show me all product names and prices.'"` The AI uses the structure of the provided example to generate a new SQL query:

```
SELECT name, price FROM products;
```

Few-Shot Learning

In few-shot learning, the AI is given a small number of examples to learn from. These examples help the model grasp the task's nuances and variations, enabling it to generalize to new, unseen prompts.

Examples: Examples provided to AI:

1. **Natural Language:** **`"How many employees work in the marketing department?"`** **`SQL: SELECT COUNT(*)`** `FROM employees WHERE department = 'marketing';`
2. **Natural Language:** **`"Find the highest salary in the engineering department."`** **SQL:** **`SELECT MAX(salary) FROM employees WHERE department = 'engineering';`**

Prompt: `"Translate the following question into an SQL query: 'Which products were sold in quantities greater than 100?'"` The AI applies the patterns learned from the examples to generate the appropriate SQL query:

```
SELECT product_name FROM sales WHERE quantity_sold > 100;
```

In each of these approaches, the key is how the AI leverages its pre-existing knowledge, and the information provided through examples to perform a new task. Zero-shot learning relies entirely on the AI's ability to understand the prompt, while one-shot and few-shot learning provide the AI with additional context and structure to guide its responses.

One key point to note is that these techniques not only improve accuracy but also reduce the need for extensive model retraining. Additionally, we can choose these examples dynamically which can help customize the output as well provide "*latest*" information to LLM. For example, let us say you are designing a chatbot and want it to pick up standard responses dynamically. You can easily do so with the help of one-shot or few-shot learning.

Characteristic	Zero-Shot Learning	One-Shot Learning	Few-Shot Learning
Number of Examples	0	1	A small number (typically 2-5, but can vary)
Reliance on Pre-trained Knowledge	High (relies solely on pre-trained understanding)	High (uses pre-trained knowledge, guided by one example)	Moderate to High (leverages pre-trained knowledge, enhanced by few examples)
Typical Use Cases	General understanding, initial task interpretation	Simple format replication, direct structural guidance	Nuanced task understanding, pattern generalization, varied input handling
Prompt Clarity	Extremely critical (must be self-contained)	Important (single example sets expectation)	Important (examples clarify variations and nuances)

Table 3.1: *Zero-Shot, One-Shot, and Few-Shot Learning Comparison*

Prompt Templates

To make the process of prompt creation more systematic and efficient, prompt templates can come in handy. They are tried and tested templates that can act as blueprints to generate concrete prompts. In essence, prompt templates are pre-structured formats for prompts that provide a consistent way to interact with generative AI models. These templates are designed to streamline the process of generating content, and to ensure that the model receives clear and standardized instructions across different tasks or data inputs. This not only saves time but also ensures that the application follows certain guidelines. For example, templates can be used to guard against malicious user inputs by enforcing strict input structures. Let us explore various aspects of prompt templates in more detail:

Purpose of Prompt Templates

The primary purpose of prompt templates is to simplify the use of language models by providing a repeatable structure that can be used to elicit specific types of responses. Templates help users avoid the trial and error often associated with crafting effective prompts from scratch, saving time and effort, and increasing productivity.

Designing Prompt Templates

Designing prompt templates requires a deep understanding of the model's capabilities, and the desired task outcomes. Templates often include placeholders or variables that can be filled in with task-specific information. A well-designed template ensures that these placeholders are integrated seamlessly into the prompt to guide the model effectively.

Components of a Prompt Template

A prompt template typically includes:

- **Instructional Phrasing:** This sets the task for the model, such as "**`Summarize the following text:`**" or "**`Translate the following sentence into French:`**".
- **Contextual Information:** This provides the model with any necessary background information that helps it understand the task better.
- **Examples or Demonstrations:** Some templates may include an example of the desired output format or style to guide the model's generation process.
- **Variables or Placeholders:** These are spaces within the template where user-specific data can be inserted, such as the actual text to be summarized or translated.

Here is an example which demonstrates the above components:

```
INSTRUCTION:
Summarize the following customer email in {max_bullets} bullet points.

CONTEXT:
You are a support assistant. Be {tone}, concise, and actionable.
Emphasize: customer's goal, blockers, and requested next steps.

EXAMPLE:
Input:
"I can't log in after resetting my password. The link said it expired..."
Output:
- Goal: regain account access
- Blocker: reset link expired
- Next step: resend reset link, verify email ownership

INPUT:
{customer_email_text}

FORMAT:
- Bullet points only
- No preamble or conclusion
```

Benefits of Using Prompt Templates

- **Consistency**: Templates provide a standardized approach to prompting, which is particularly useful when the model is being used by multiple users or for automated systems.
- **Scalability**: Templates can be easily replicated and used across different datasets, making them suitable for large-scale applications.

- **Efficiency**: By reducing the need to craft individual prompts for each instance, templates save time and enable faster interaction with the model.
- **Quality Control**: A well-designed template can help maintain the quality of outputs by ensuring that prompts are always optimally formulated.

Refining Prompt Templates

Prompt templates may need to be refined based on the performance of the AI model. If the outputs are not meeting the desired standards, the template may need to be adjusted to provide more clarity or better instructions. This refinement process involves analysing the outputs, identifying any issues, and iterating on the template design.

In summary, prompt templates are a valuable tool for harnessing the power of generative AI models efficiently and effectively. They facilitate consistent, scalable, and quality-controlled interactions with AI, allowing users to focus on the content, rather than the mechanics of prompting. As generative AI continues to evolve, the design and application of prompt templates will play a crucial role in shaping user experiences and outcomes.

Control Codes

Now as prompt templates grow in complexity, the need for clarity becomes paramount. This is where Control Codes become indispensable. These are special, non-natural language tokens—such as `[INST], ###Instruction, or [SEP]`—that are strategically embedded within a template. Their primary purpose is to provide the LLM with unambiguous meta-instructions, directly influencing how the model interprets the prompt's structure and content. For instance, a control code can explicitly separate fixed instructions from dynamic user input or define distinct sections of a complex query. By ensuring that the model correctly interprets the structure and hierarchy of the prompt, control codes mitigate misinterpretation, making the template-driven prompting process far more reliable and consistent. They are the scaffolding that enables templates to deliver predictable outcomes, especially in multi-turn or multi-part interactions.

Concept of Control Codes

In the context of AI, a control code can be an actual code, a token, or a particular string of text that is recognized by the model as a command. Control codes are often used in settings where fine-grained control over the model's output is necessary and where simple natural language instructions might not be specific enough.

How Control Codes Work

Control codes work by being included in the prompt alongside the natural language instruction. They provide additional context or settings for the model, which can range from simple formatting requirements to complex content adjustments. For example, a control code could instruct the model to generate text in a formal tone or a casual one, or it might specify that the text should be in the form of a bullet-pointed list.

Examples of Control Codes

Here are some examples of how control codes might look and function:

- **Tone:** `<TONE: FORMAL>` preceding a prompt might indicate that the model should use formal language.
- **Style:** `<STYLE: HUMOROUS>` could signal the model to infuse humor into its generated content.
- **Content Type:** `<CONTENT: NEWS_ARTICLE>` might be used to tell the model to structure its output like a news article.

The following is an example of how control code can help guide the LLM to generate the response that is suitable for the scenario:

Original Example (without Control Code):

```
Prompt: "Write a short email to a colleague about the new project timeline.
AI Response (likely informal, generic):
"Hey [Colleague's Name],

Just wanted to let you know the new project timeline is out. Check it out when
you get a chance.

Thanks,
[Your Name]"
```

Improved Example (with Control Code):

```
Prompt: "<TONE:FORMAL> Write a short email to a colleague about the new project
timeline. The email should announce the updated schedule and request their
review by end of day Friday."

AI Response (demonstrating formal tone and specific request):
"Subject: Updated Project Timeline for [Project Name]
Dear [Colleague's Name],

This email serves to inform you of the recently updated project timeline for
[Project Name]. The revised schedule is now available [link to document/location
of timeline].

Kindly review the updated timeline at your earliest convenience and provide any
feedback or concerns by the end of day on Friday, [Date].

Thank you for your prompt attention to this matter.
```

```
Sincerely,
[Your Name]"
```

Benefits of Using Control Codes

- **Precision:** Control codes offer a high degree of specificity in guiding the model's outputs.
- **Customization:** They allow users to customize the output beyond what might be achievable through natural language instructions alone.
- **Repeatability:** Control codes can ensure that outputs are consistent across different prompts and use cases.
- **Complex Task Execution:** They can enable the execution of complex tasks that require a model to switch between different modes or formats on the fly.

Designing Control Codes

The design of control codes involves understanding the capabilities of the AI model, and identifying the areas where users need more precise control. Ideally, control codes should be intuitive and aligned with the tasks they are intended to influence.

Implementation Considerations

When implementing control codes, it is necessary to ensure that the model has been trained to recognize and interpret these codes correctly. This may involve additional training or fine-tuning processes where the model learns to associate specific codes with certain behaviors or outputs.

Challenges and Limitations

One of the challenges with control codes is ensuring that they are standardized and well-documented so that users know how to use them effectively. Additionally, there may be limitations in how finely a model can interpret and execute the instructions encoded in control codes.

In summary, control codes are a powerful tool within the field of generative AI, offering a means of precise, customizable, and repeatable control over model outputs. They are particularly useful for advanced users who require fine-tuned results or for applications where consistency and specificity are critical. Understanding and implementing control codes effectively can greatly enhance the capabilities and applications of AI models.

Technique	Clarity & Specificity	Contextual Embedding	Keywords/ Triggers	Tone & Style	Avoid Overfitting & Bias	Combining Techniques
Zero-Shot	Primary	Supports	Supports	Primary	Supports	Primary
One-Shot	Primary	Primary	Limited	Supports	Supports	Primary
Few-Shot	Primary	Primary	Limited	Supports	Primary	Primary
Prompt Templates	Primary	Primary	Primary	Primary	Supports	Primary
Control Codes	Primary	Supports	Primary	Primary	Limited	Primary

Table 3.2: *Techniques and Best Practices Achieved with It*

Management and Versioning - Prompt Registry

Having established a foundation in the core techniques of prompt engineering, we can now move beyond crafting individual prompts to the next critical step: refining and optimizing their performance. This is where we transition from simply giving instructions to strategically tuning them for superior results, addressing the subtleties and complexities that arise in real-world applications.

Prompt Tuning

As explained earlier, prompt engineering is both art and science. Prompt tuning serves to bridge this "*art*" and "*science*." Essentially, the artist (in this case, an LLMOps engineer) creates prompts, and then inspects the generated response. One keeps reiterating until one is satisfied. This "*satisfaction*" is measured by certain predetermined metrics depending on the business goal. The prompt for which the generated response performs best on metrics is chosen as the final candidate. (Thus, the science). In a more formal way, it involves crafting input prompts in a way that steers the model towards generating specific types of outputs. The following are detailed explanations of some key aspects of prompt tuning:

Types of Prompt Tuning

Prompt tuning can take various forms, depending on the task and desired outcome:

- **Direct Instruction**: The prompt explicitly states what the model should do, such as **`"Write a summary of the following article."`** For example, if you want the model to generate a product description, your direct instruction might be: **`"Generate a compelling product description for a new smart thermostat that emphasizes energy savings and ease of use."`**

- **Example-based Tuning**: The prompt includes examples of the task being performed correctly, guiding the model to replicate that format or style. For instance, to train a model to write positive customer reviews, you could provide several examples like: **`"I absolutely love this coffee maker! It makes perfect coffee every time and is so easy to clean."`** or **`"This app is a game-changer for productivity. The interface is intuitive, and it has all the features I need."`**
- **Contextual Cues**: The prompt provides context that hints at the desired tone, style, or content, like "As a friendly reminder," to cue the model to write a gentle nudge. Another example could be starting a prompt with **`"Imagine you are a seasoned travel agent..."`** to encourage the model to adopt a helpful and knowledgeable tone when describing travel destinations. Or, if you want a humorous response, you might begin with **`"Tell me a joke about a computer..."`**

Iterative Process: Tweaking Parameters and A/B Testing in Practice

One might not get it '*right*' in the first shot. Similar to hyperparameter tuning in MLOps, prompt tuning is typically an iterative process, where prompts are continuously refined based on the outputs produced by the model. It may involve testing various phrasings, incorporating different types of instructions, and even experimenting with the inclusion of sample outputs or additional context. This iterative refinement often involves:

Tweaking LLM Parameters

Within this iterative refinement process, a key aspect is the manipulation of Large Language Model (LLM) parameters. These settings offer fine-grained control over the model's output, allowing engineers to guide its behavior in desired directions. This leads us to consider specific parameters and their practical implications, as well as broader methodologies such as A/B testing. The following are some of the major settings that can be manipulated and its impact on outcome.

- **Temperature:** This parameter controls the randomness of the output.
  - **Example (Lowering Temperature):** If your current prompt sometimes generates overly creative or off-topic responses when summarizing technical documents, you might reduce the temperature from 0.7 to 0.3. A lower temperature encourages the model to stick closer to the most probable words, resulting in more focused and factual summaries.
  - **Example (Increasing Temperature):** Conversely, if you are using a prompt to brainstorm creative ideas or write fictional dialogue, and the output feels too repetitive, you might increase the temperature from 0.5 to 0.9. This allows the model to explore a wider range of less probable words, leading to more diverse and imaginative results.

- **Top-P (Nucleus Sampling):** This parameter controls the diversity of the output by selecting from the smallest possible set of words whose cumulative probability exceeds the `top_p` value.
  - **Example:** If you want more conservative but still somewhat varied responses, you might set `top_p` to 0.9. If you want highly focused output, you might reduce it to 0.7.
- **Max Tokens:** This sets the maximum length of the generated response.
  - **Example:** If your prompt is for a tweet generation, and the model is producing paragraphs, you would drastically reduce `max_tokens` (for example, to 50). If you need detailed reports, you could increase it.

Employing Methodologies like A/B Testing

Beyond adjusting individual parameters, a more holistic and empirical approach to prompt optimization involves systematic testing methodologies. Just as A/B testing is crucial for optimizing user interfaces or marketing campaigns, it can be equally powerful for evaluating the effectiveness of different prompt variations. This allows LLMOps engineers to move beyond intuition, and validate prompt performance with data, ensuring that the chosen prompts deliver the best possible results in real-world scenarios. For example, consider the following scenario:

- **Scenario:** You want to find the most effective prompt to generate concise product descriptions for an e-commerce website.
- **`Prompt A: "Generate a concise product description for a [Product Name] that highlights its [Key Feature 1] and [Key Feature 2]."`**
- **`Prompt B: "Write a short, engaging product description for a [Product Name], focusing on benefits for the user, such as [Benefit 1] and [Benefit 2]."`**
- **A/B Test Execution:**
  - **Audience Split:** Divide your product data into two groups.
  - **Generation:** Apply Prompt A to one group to generate descriptions, and Prompt B to the other.
  - **Evaluation (Metrics):**
    - **Quantitative:** Measure metrics such as character count (for conciseness), presence of specific keywords (for example, benefits), or even simulated click-through rates if integrated into a testing environment.
    - **Qualitative:** Have human evaluators (or another LLM acting as a critic) rate the descriptions for engagement, clarity, and adherence to brand voice.

- **Analysis:** Compare the performance of descriptions generated by Prompt A vs. Prompt B based on your chosen metrics.
- **Decision:** If Prompt B consistently leads to more engaging descriptions or better meets the length requirement, then Prompt B is the "*winning*" prompt, and should be adopted. If neither is perfect, the insights from the comparison can inform the next iteration of prompts (Prompt C, Prompt D, and so on).

This systematic approach, combining careful parameter adjustments with empirical testing like A/B experiments, transforms prompt engineering from an intuitive art into a data-driven science.

Benefits of Prompt Tuning

Prompt tuning offers several significant advantages for optimizing LLM performance and deployment:

- **Improved Output Quality:** By iteratively refining prompts, you can achieve more accurate, relevant, and nuanced responses that precisely align with the desired outcomes. This directly impacts the quality of generated content, from factual summaries to creative writing.
- **Enhanced Model Control:** Tuning allows for fine-grained control over the LLM's behavior without requiring costly retraining or fine-tuning of the underlying model. You can steer the model towards specific tones, styles, or information extraction patterns.
- **Cost Efficiency:** Optimized prompts can lead to more concise and efficient outputs, potentially reducing token consumption and, consequently, API costs associated with LLM usage.
- **Reduced Hallucinations and Bias:** Through careful tuning and A/B testing, prompts can be designed to mitigate common LLM issues like generating factually incorrect (hallucinated) information or perpetuating biases present in training data.
- **Faster Iteration and Deployment:** Prompt tuning is a relatively quick process compared to model retraining. This allows for rapid experimentation and deployment of improved prompts, accelerating the development cycle of LLM-powered applications.
- **Adaptability:** Prompt tuning enables quicker adaptation to new requirements or changes in the desired output formats, making LLM applications more flexible and responsive.

Limitations and Considerations of Prompt Tuning

However, powerful, prompt tuning also comes with its own set of limitations and considerations:

- **Dependence on Human Intuition (Initially):** The initial stages of prompt tuning often rely heavily on the engineer's intuition and understanding of natural language, making it more of an "*art*" before systematic testing can be applied.
- **Scalability Challenges (Manual Tuning):** For a very large number of diverse tasks, manually tuning each prompt can become labor-intensive and time-consuming, highlighting the need for automation tools.
- **Model Brittleness to Wording:** LLMs can sometimes be highly sensitive to minor changes in wording or punctuation, meaning a seemingly small prompt tweak can lead to drastically different and often unpredictable results.
- **Risk of Overfitting (to specific examples):** In few-shot learning or highly specific tuning, there is a risk that the prompt might become too tailored to the provided examples, and perform poorly on slightly different, unseen inputs.
- **Difficulty with Ambiguity:** Even well-tuned prompts can struggle with inherently ambiguous requests, as the model's underlying knowledge may not cover all possible interpretations.
- **Ethical Implications:** Poorly designed or tuned prompts can inadvertently lead to the generation of biased, harmful, or unethical content, requiring careful ethical review during the tuning process.
- **Limited by Model's Core Capabilities:** Prompt tuning cannot fundamentally change the core capabilities or limitations of the pre-trained LLM. If a task requires reasoning or knowledge beyond what the model possesses, tuning alone will not suffice.
- **Evaluation Complexity:** Objectively measuring the "*goodness*" of a generated response, especially for subjective tasks (for example, creativity, tone, and so on), can be challenging, and often requires a blend of automated metrics as well as human evaluation.

While manual tuning and A/B testing are powerful for optimizing individual prompts, scaling these efforts across dozens or hundreds of applications requires a more systematic, automated approach. This is where MLOps principles are applied to the prompt lifecycle.

Automated Prompt Management

While mastering the art of prompt crafting and the science of prompt tuning is essential, these skills alone do not scale. As the number of LLM-powered applications grows, so too does the need to manage a proliferation of prompts, templates, and tuning iterations. Meticulously tracking performance, versioning changes, and ensuring consistent deployment across multiple environments quickly becomes a logistical challenge that manual processes cannot sustain. This is where Automated Prompt Management becomes not just a convenience, but a necessity. By applying the same rigorous principles of a robust MLOps workflow to the prompt life cycle, we can bring structure, version control, and streamlined deployment to our prompt library. A comprehensive Prompt Content Management System should provide versioning capabilities, A/B testing frameworks, and integration with the existing MLOps pipelines. For detailed implementation examples and specific tool demonstrations, see Chapter 11.

Conclusion

Thus, this chapter has guided you through the essential journey of mastering prompt management for Large Language Models. We began by solidifying our understanding of prompt crafting, exploring techniques that transform natural language into precise instructions. We then delved into the strategic art and science of prompt tuning, uncovering methods to optimize model performance, from tweaking parameters to employing rigorous A/B testing.

The final phase of the LLMOps Prompt Lifecycle focuses on seamless deployment of tested prompts into production environments. This includes integration with the existing systems, monitoring prompt performance in real-time, implementing rollback capabilities for failed deployments, and establishing continuous improvement processes. Deployment strategies must consider scalability, reliability, and maintainability to ensure that prompt-based applications can operate effectively at enterprise scale.

Finally, we examined the critical role of automating prompt management, establishing the theoretical framework for scaling prompt engineering into a robust, maintainable, and efficient discipline. The practical implementation of these concepts will be demonstrated in Chapter 11. By embracing these principles—from meticulous creation and iterative refinement to systematic deployment and continuous maintenance—you are now equipped to build LLM applications that are not only powerful but also reliable and adaptable.

As we move forward, the concept of integrating LLMs into more complex, multi-step workflows becomes paramount. In the next chapter, we will expand on these ideas by exploring LLM chaining, a powerful paradigm that allows us to connect multiple LLM calls, external tools, and logical steps to tackle sophisticated problems that a single prompt cannot resolve.

References

1. https://abstracta.us/blog/ai/llmops-product-lifecycle-management/
2. https://aclanthology.org/2025.findings-acl.1140.pdf
3. https://agenta.ai/blog/the-definitive-guide-to-prompt-management-systems
4. https://apipark.com/techblog/en/mastering-llm-product-development-ultimate-guide-to-software-development-lifecycle-management/

5. https://arize.com/blog/prompt-optimization-few-shot-prompting/
6. https://arxiv.org/abs/2502.11560
7. https://aws.amazon.com/bedrock/prompt-management/
8. https://blog.promptlayer.com/5-best-tools-for-prompt-versioning/
9. https://blog.promptlayer.com/the-best-tools-for-creating-system-prompts/
10. https://cloud.google.com/discover/what-is-prompt-engineering
11. https://community.databricks.com/t5/technical-blog/foundation-models-api-prompting-guide-1-lifecycle-of-a-prompt/ba-p/77749
12. https://docs.promptlayer.com/why-promptlayer/prompt-management
13. https://docs.stripe.com/building-with-llms
14. https://dribbble.com/shots/23447753-Clyde-Discord-s-AI-Chatbot
15. https://github.com/hegelai/prompttools
16. https://github.com/resources/articles/software-development/what-is-sdlc
17. https://hexaware.com/blogs/revolutionizing-agile-software-development-practices-harnessing-the-power-of-prompt-engineering-across-the-entire-agile-sdlc/
18. https://humanloop.com/blog/prompt-management
19. https://infermatic.ai/ask/?question=Can%20you%20explain%20the%20concept%20of%20%27prompt%20drift%27%20and%20how%20it%20affects%20prompt%20effectiveness?
20. https://lakefs.io/blog/llmops/
21. https://latitude-blog.ghost.io/blog/common-llm-prompt-engineering-challenges-and-solutions/
22. https://latitude-blog.ghost.io/blog/top-7-open-source-tools-for-prompt-engineering-in-2025/
23. https://launchdarkly.com/blog/prompt-versioning-and-management/
24. https://learn.microsoft.com/en-us/azure/databricks/mlflow3/genai/prompt-version-mgmt/prompt-registry/reference
25. https://learningdaily.dev/building-with-llms-prepare-for-these-8-prompt-engineering-challenges-8c4216aa7a3b
26. https://medium.com/@akankshasinha247/prompt-engineering-part-5-from-experiment-to-production-the-complete-prompt-engineering-9f3af4887141
27. https://medium.com/@martin_rodek/why-large-enterprises-need-a-prompt-registry-for-ai-governance-04d744039bb4

28. https://medium.com/@mustangs007/prompt-management-the-unsung-art-in-the-llm-era-0b1c4bd4d66e
29. https://medium.com/@orq/lifecycle-of-a-prompt-a-guide-to-effective-prompts-7d0d42ad115b
30. https://medium.com/@verma.infosec/introduction-to-secure-prompt-management-lifecycle-2ad4a197e987
31. https://medium.com/code-and-theory/the-future-of-prompt-engineering-evolution-or-extinction-2a74f183fae1
32. https://mlflow.org/docs/latest/genai/prompt-registry/
33. https://portkey.ai/blog/lifecycle-of-a-prompt
34. https://promptcatalog.dev/article/The_Impact_of_Prompt_Management_on_the_Accuracy_and_Performance_of_Large_Language_Models.html
35. https://promptengineering.org/comprehensive-and-simplified-lifecycles-for-effective-ai-prompt-management/
36. https://salesforcedevops.net/index.php/2023/08/03/sdlc-for-prompts-the-next-evolution-in-enterprise-ai-development/
37. https://sourceforge.net/software/prompt-management/for-enterprise/
38. https://startups.epam.com/blog/software-development-models-comparison
39. https://techcommunity.microsoft.com/discussions/azure-ai-services/understand-the-development-lifecycle-of-a-large-language-model-llm-app/4186738
40. https://theproductmanager.com/topics/software-development-life-cycle/
41. https://www.bridgemind.ai/blog/integrating-prompt-engineering-into-ai-development
42. https://www.datacamp.com/blog/what-is-prompt-engineering-the-future-of-ai-communication
43. https://www.distributional.com/blog/the-ai-software-development-lifecycle-a-practical-framework-for-modern-ai-systems
44. https://www.geeksforgeeks.org/software-engineering/sdlc-models-types-phases-use/
45. https://www.geeksforgeeks.org/software-engineering/software-development-life-cycle-sdlc/
46. https://www.getambassador.io/blog/prompt-engineering-for-llms
47. https://www.helicone.ai/blog/prompt-management
48. https://www.ibm.com/think/topics/prompt-engineering

49. https://www.multimodal.dev/post/llm-prompting
50. https://www.paradisosolutions.com/blog/prompt-engineering-real-world-applications/
51. https://www.prompthub.us/
52. https://www.promptingguide.ai/introduction/settings
53. https://www.promptingguide.ai/techniques/ape
54. https://www.qwak.com/post/prompt-management
55. https://www.refontelearning.com/blog/future-of-prompt-engineering-trends-tools-and-job-opportunities-for-2026-and-beyond
56. https://www.reforge.com/artifacts/prompt-engineering-for-effective-pm-communications-at-stripe
57. https://www.researchgate.net/publication/389314872_A_Systematic_Survey_of_Automatic_Prompt_Optimization_Techniques
58. https://www.rtinsights.com/a-real-world-approach-to-automated-structured-prompt-engineering/
59. https://www.sandtech.com/insight/prompt-engineering-an-emerging-new-role-in-ai/
60. https://www.themoonlight.io/en/review/a-systematic-survey-of-automatic-prompt-optimization-techniques
61. https://www.trustinsights.ai/blog/2024/04/so-what-the-prompt-engineering-life-cycle/
62. https://www.trustinsights.ai/blog/2024/04/the-prompt-engineering-life-cycle/
63. https://www.walturn.com/insights/prompt-management-systems-what-they-are-and-why-they-matter
64. https://www.walturn.com/insights/prompt-management-systems-what-they-are-and-why-they-matter#:~:text=Definition,for%20prompts%20in%20natural%20language.
65. https://www.youtube.com/watch?v=dZUz3ygv95U
66. https://www.zenml.io/blog/llmops-in-production-457-case-studies-of-what-actually-works
67. https://www.zenml.io/llmops-database/building-an-llm-powered-support-response-system

Chapter 4
The Power of LLM Chaining

Introduction

In the previous chapter, we explored the critical role of prompt management in harnessing the capabilities of Large Language Models (LLMs), focusing on how precise and effective prompts can shape AI outputs. Building upon that foundation, this chapter introduces an even more powerful paradigm, which is LLM Chaining. This approach moves beyond the brilliance of a single model to orchestrate a "*dream team*" of AI components. LLM Chaining is a broad method that interconnects the outputs and functions of multiple LLMs, tools, and data sources, enabling them to collaboratively tackle complex tasks with unparalleled precision. In this system, each component contributes its unique strengths, passing refined information to the next, which eventually results in solutions that are far richer than what a single LLM could achieve on its own.

Structure

This chapter will address the following topics:

- Sequential Intelligence: Building LLM Chains
- Design Patterns for LLM Chaining
- Evaluating the Effectiveness of LLM Chains

Sequential Intelligence: Building LLM Chains

A foundational technique for implementing these intelligent workflows is prompt chaining. It is a specific method where a series of interconnected prompts are fed into a model sequentially to solve a problem that requires multiple steps. This approach is particularly effective for maintaining conversational context, as it leverages the model's ability to build upon previous responses, and guide the interaction toward the desired outcome.

Single Prompt vs Prompt Chaining

So far, we have focused on giving an LLM a single task to generate an output. While this works for simple cases, complex instructions with multiple conditions and inputs are difficult for a model to handle. Even with a large context window, an LLM is ideally trained to follow one core instruction at a time, much like how humans can become confused or inefficient when multitasking. To address this, we need a way to use multiple instruction sets where each prompt processes the output of the previous one, much like a chain of functions in traditional programming.

Prompt chaining creates a sequence of prompts, with each one building on the AI's previous response. This method is especially useful for complex tasks that require multiple steps or when the desired output can be more effectively achieved through a series of interactions. By breaking down a task into smaller and more manageable parts, prompt chaining can lead to more accurate and contextually relevant responses.

Stages of Prompt Chaining

Prompt chaining is a powerful technique for guiding AI conversations and achieving complex outcomes. By breaking down a larger goal into a series of smaller, interconnected prompts, you can lead the AI through a structured interaction. This method is particularly effective for tasks that require multiple steps, logical progression, or iterative refinement. The stages of prompt chaining typically involve:

- **Sequential Interaction**: Each prompt in the chain is designed to take the conversation forward, using the AI's last response as a stepping stone for the next question or instruction.
- **Context Preservation**: The chain maintains context throughout the interaction, which helps the AI to understand the continuity and objective of the task.
- **Incremental Complexity**: Starting with simpler prompts and gradually increasing the complexity can help the AI to build upon its responses and refine the output.
- **Feedback Loop**: Prompt chaining often includes an optional feedback mechanism where the user or the engineer can correct or redirect the AI if it goes off track.

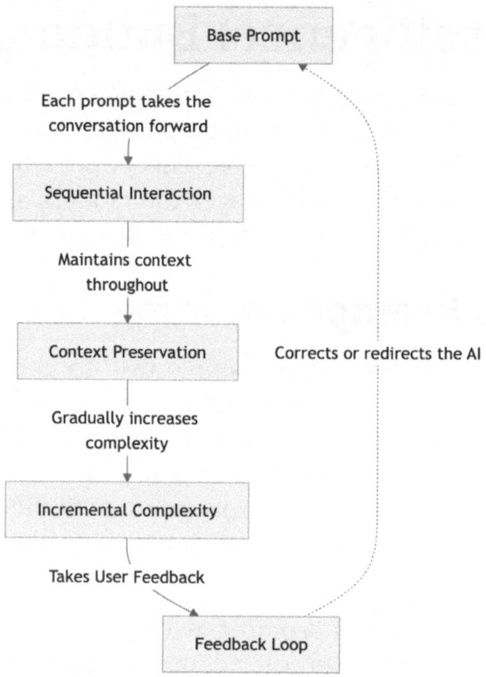

***Figure 4.1**: Stages of Prompt Chaining*

Example of Prompt Chaining in Natural Language to SQL:

Let us say we want to craft an SQL query to find the names of employees who have sold a particular product in a specific month. Here is how prompt chaining can be employed in this scenario:

1. **First Prompt:**
   a. **User Prompt:** "*What are the tables available in the sales database?*"
   b. **AI Response**: "*The sales database contains the following tables: employees, products, and* **`sales_records`**."
2. **Second Prompt:**
   a. **User Prompt:** "*Using the* **`sales_records`** *table, how can I find the IDs of sales transactions for product 'X' in January?*"
   b. **AI Response:** "*You can find the transaction IDs with the following query:* `**SELECT transaction_id FROM sales_records WHERE product_name = 'X' AND month = 'January'**`"
3. **Third Prompt:**
   a. **User Prompt:** "*Now, given the transaction IDs, how can I retrieve the names of the employees who made these sales?*"

b. **AI Response:** "You can join the employees table with the sales_records table on the employee_id field to retrieve the names: `` `SELECT e.name FROM employees e JOIN sales_records sr ON e.employee_id = sr.employee_id WHERE sr.product_name = 'X' AND sr.month = 'January'` ``"

In this example, each prompt is derived from the previous response from LLM. The first prompt establishes the available data, the second prompt narrows down the query to a specific product and time frame, and the third prompt refines the output to the specific information needed. Prompt chaining, hence, allows for a more interactive and iterative approach to reaching the final SQL query.

Basic Prompt Chaining with Langchain

```
from langchain_openai import ChatOpenAI
from langchain_core.prompts import ChatPromptTemplate, MessagesPlaceholder
from langchain_core.output_parsers import StrOutputParser
from langchain_core.runnables.history import RunnableWithMessageHistory
from langchain_core.chat_history import InMemoryChatMessageHistory

prompt = ChatPromptTemplate.from_messages([
    ("system", "You are a helpful SQL assistant. Be concise and return SQL
when appropriate."),
    MessagesPlaceholder(variable_name="history"),
    ("user", "{input}")
])

llm = ChatOpenAI(model="gpt-4o-mini", temperature=0)
chain = prompt | llm | StrOutputParser()

_store = {}
def _get_history(session_id: str):
    if session_id not in _store:
        _store[session_id] = InMemoryChatMessageHistory()
    return _store[session_id]

chat = RunnableWithMessageHistory(
    chain,
    get_session_history=_get_history,
    input_messages_key="input",
    history_messages_key="history",
)

session_id = "sales-demo"
while True:
    user_in = input("You: ").strip()
    if not user_in or user_in.lower() in {"exit", "quit", "q", "stop"}:
        break
```

```
    ai_out = chat.invoke({"input": user_in}, config={"configurable": {"session_
id": session_id}})
    print("AI:", ai_out)
```

This code implements prompt chaining by creating a conversational chatbot that remembers past interactions to build contextually aware responses over multiple turns. It achieves this by using a special prompt template that holds the conversation history, a memory system that stores it, and a stateful wrapper to automate the process of saving and loading the conversation for each new input. The script uses the following key components from the Langchain library to construct a chain that maintains context:

- **Conversational Prompt Template**: The **ChatPromptTemplate** is set up to manage a conversation.

  The most important part is the **MessagesPlaceholder(variable_name="history")**, which is a dynamic placeholder where the entire history of the user and AI messages is automatically injected on every new turn. This ensures that the AI always has the full context of the preceding conversation.

- **Session-Based Memory**: The code uses a simple dictionary (**_store**) and a helper function (**_get_history**) to manage conversation histories. Each conversation is tied to a unique **session_id**. This allows the system to maintain separate, continuous conversations without mixing them up.

- **Stateful Chain Wrapper**: **RunnableWithMessageHistory** is the component that makes the chain conversational. It wraps the basic prompt | LLM | parser chain and connects it to the memory system. Before executing a new request, it automatically:

  1. Loads the past messages for the given **session_id**
  2. Inserts them into the **MessagesPlaceholder**
  3. Saves the new user input and the AI's response back to the history after the turn is complete

- **The Chaining Process in Action:** The **while True:** loop creates the interactive session where prompt chaining occurs. With each user input, the **chat.invoke** call triggers the entire automated sequence. Since the history is loaded and saved with every turn, the process transforms into an interactive and iterative dialogue. This allows a user to perform complex tasks step-by-step, just like the example of building an SQL query. The first prompt might establish the available database tables, the second can ask about specific columns, and the third can request the final query. The AI understands the context throughout the entire sequence. Each new prompt from the user is effectively "*chained*" to the context of all previous interactions. The chaining is achieved by injecting the conversation history from **InMemoryChatMessageHistory** back into the **MessagesPlaceholder**. With each new input, the LLM receives the full context of the prior turns, which effectively 'chains' the new prompt to the previous ones.

Prompt chaining is a dynamic tool that facilitates more nuanced and effective communication with AI systems, especially when you are dealing with layered or multifaceted tasks like formulating SQL queries from natural language descriptions. Moving further one step, while prompt chaining structures the *flow* of tasks, Chain-of-Thought (CoT) prompting enhances the *quality* of each step. CoT is applied within a single prompt to encourage the model to break down its reasoning process. This leads to more reliable and transparent outputs, which can then be chained together for even greater effect.

Chain-of-Thought (CoT) Prompting

Prompt chaining breaks down complex tasks into a sequence of smaller, manageable steps. Building on this idea, CoT prompting takes it a step further by guiding the AI to articulate its reasoning for each step, which results in a more transparent and logical final output. This technique is akin to asking the LLM to '*think*' and '*reflect*' before providing an answer, which means providing more detailed instructions to help the LLM generate a more coherent response. CoT prompting is a technique where the prompt is designed to guide the AI through a logical sequence of reasoning steps to arrive at a conclusion or answer. This method is especially useful for complex problems that require reasoning, problem-solving, or when the AI needs to demonstrate its thought process. The result is that the AI produces more coherent, detailed, and logically structured responses.

- **How CoT Prompting Works:** To fully grasp the power and application of CoT Prompting, it is essential to understand the underlying mechanisms that enable the AI to generate its multi-step reasoning. This section will delve into the practical implementation and core principles behind this technique, illustrating how it guides the LLM to process information, and articulate its thought process systematically.

  When constructing effective AI prompts, two key principles significantly enhance the quality and transparency of the generated responses: **logical progression** and **explicit reasoning**. These techniques are fundamentally aimed at mimicking human cognition, which makes the AI's thought process more understandable and relatable for human users.

- **Logical Progression:** This principle dictates that a prompt should be meticulously designed to guide the AI through a series of sequential and interconnected steps. Instead of presenting a single, complex query, the prompt breaks down the problem into smaller, manageable components. Each step builds upon the previous one, which leads the AI towards a comprehensive and accurate final answer. This structured approach prevents the AI from making assumptions or taking shortcuts, while ensuring that it considers all necessary aspects of the problem before formulating its response. For instance, a prompt asking an AI to analyze a historical event might first require it to identify the key actors, then their motivations, followed by the immediate consequences, and finally the long-term impact. This step-by-step guidance allows for a more thorough and robust analysis.

- **Explicit Reasoning:** Instead of simply providing the correct answer, an effective prompt encourages the AI to articulate its reasoning process. This involves prompting the AI to explicitly state any assumptions it made, explain all its intermediate conclusions that were arrived at during various stages of analysis, and ultimately present the logical path that led to its final answer. This transparency is crucial for several reasons. Firstly, it allows users to scrutinize the AI's thought process, identifying potential biases or flawed logic. Secondly, it builds trust in the AI's capabilities and allows users to understand *how* the AI arrived at its solution, rather than just accepting it at face value. For example, if an AI is asked to recommend a financial strategy, explicit reasoning would involve outlining the economic indicators it considered, the risk assessments it performed, and the rationale behind choosing a particular investment vehicle.

In essence, by implementing logical progression and encouraging explicit reasoning, CoT prompting can transform the LLM from a black box into a more transparent and interpretable system. This approach not only yields more accurate and robust outputs for complex tasks but also fosters greater trust and understanding between human users and AI, making advanced problem-solving with LLMs more accessible and reliable. Now, let us examine CoT prompting via an example below:

Example of CoT Prompting in Natural Language to SQL

Let us consider a scenario where we want to construct an SQL query to identify employees who have not met their sales targets for the last quarter. Here is how CoT prompting can be applied:

Prompt: "*Imagine you are an analyst who needs to identify employees who have not met their sales targets for the last quarter. First, consider what information you would need. You would need to know each employee's sales target for the quarter, as well as the actual sales they achieved. This information is likely in two different tables: one for sales targets and one for actual sales. Next, think about how to compare these figures. You would join the two tables on the employee ID and then select only those records where the actual sales are less than the sales targets. Now, write the SQL query that can accomplish this.*"

AI Response:

"*To find the employees who have not met their sales targets, we can use the following SQL query:*

```
SELECT st.employee_id
FROM sales_targets st
JOIN actual_sales as ON st.employee_id = as.employee_id AND st.quarter =
as.quarter
WHERE as.actual_sales < st.sales_target AND st.quarter = 'Last Quarter'"
```

We will now analyze the provided prompt and response, while focusing on their logical progression and explicit reasoning.

1. **Logical Progression:**
   - **Initial Problem Breakdown:** The prompt does not just ask for the SQL query directly. Instead, it starts by breaking down the complex goal ("*identify employees who have not met their sales targets*") into simpler, sequential sub-problems.
   - **Information Identification (Step 1):** The prompt explicitly guides the AI to "*First, consider what information you would need. You would need to know each employee's sales target for the quarter, as well as the actual sales they achieved.*" Identifying the necessary data is thus the first logical step.
   - **Data Location (Step 2):** It further progresses by suggesting where this information might reside: "*This information is likely in two different tables: one for sales targets and one for actual sales.*" This guides the AI to think about the database schema.
   - **Comparison Logic (Step 3):** The prompt then moves to the next logical step: "*Next, think about how to compare these figures. You would join the two tables on the employee ID and then select only those records where the actual sales are less than the sales targets.*" This outlines the core relational logic needed for the comparison.
   - **Final Action:** Only after guiding the AI through these preparatory logical steps does the prompt issue the final command: "*Now, write the SQL query that can accomplish this.*"
2. **Explicit Reasoning:**
   - **Simulated Internal Monologue:** The prompt uses phrases like "*Imagine you are an analyst who needs to...*", "*First, consider...*", "*You would need to know...*", "*This information is likely in...*", "*Next, think about how to compare...*", and "*You would join...*" These phrases are designed to *simulate* an internal thought process or an analyst's problem-solving approach. They compel the AI to internally reason through the steps it would take, instead of jumping to a conclusion.
   - **Stating Assumptions/Intermediate Conclusions:** By suggesting "This information is likely in two different tables," the prompt explicitly provides an intermediate conclusion or assumption about the data structure, guiding the AI's understanding.
   - **Articulating the Why**: The prompt explains *why* certain steps are necessary (for example, "*You would join the two tables... because you need to compare these figures*"). This makes the reasoning explicit within the prompt itself, leading the AI to generate a query that reflects this explained logic.

In summary, the prompt in this example does not just ask a question; it *teaches* the AI how to think about the problem by outlining a logical progression of steps and explicitly detailing the reasoning behind each step. This robust guidance significantly increases the likelihood of the AI generating an accurate, well-reasoned, and complex SQL query.

Feature	Description
Transparency	AI articulates its reasoning, helping users understand conclusions
Error Checking	Easier to identify AI reasoning errors, allowing for corrections
Teaching Tool	Demonstrates problem-solving techniques and logical reasoning
Complex Problem Solving	Effective for tasks requiring multiple reasoning steps, ensuring comprehensive consideration

***Table 4.1**: Advantages of CoT Prompting*

CoT prompting is an invaluable technique for tasks that require detailed explanations or step-by-step reasoning. By guiding the AI through a logical sequence of thoughts, prompt engineers can improve the quality and utility of the AI's responses, while making them more interpretable and aligned with human reasoning patterns. These sophisticated prompting techniques, alongside foundational principles, contribute to effective prompt engineering. We will now delve into a set of best practices that encapsulate these and other critical considerations for crafting optimal prompts.

Integrating Multiple LLMs

Integrating multiple LLMs is the foundation of building an effective chain. Each LLM in the chain might be equipped to handle different tasks, such as understanding natural language, retrieving information, or generating text. The integration process involves defining the role of each model, setting up APIs or other interfaces for communication, and ensuring compatibility in terms of data formats and processing capabilities.

A powerful strategy in LLM chaining is to use different models for different steps. For instance, a smaller, faster model can be used for simple tasks like data extraction, while a more powerful model can be reserved for complex reasoning. This creates a chain that is both cost-effective and performant. We have mentioned a small example demonstrating the same:

```
import json
from langchain_openai import ChatOpenAI
from langchain_core.prompts import ChatPromptTemplate
from langchain_core.output_parsers import StrOutputParser
from langchain_core.runnables import RunnableLambda

# LLMs specialized per task (could be different models/providers)
nlu_llm = ChatOpenAI(model="gpt-4o-mini", temperature=0)   # extract
structured fields
sql_llm = ChatOpenAI(model="gpt-4o-mini", temperature=0)   # generate SQL

# Step 1: NLU → JSON
nlu_prompt = ChatPromptTemplate.from_messages([
```

```
    ("system", "Extract JSON with keys: product, month, goal. No extra
text."),
    ("user", "{input}")
])
nlu_chain = nlu_prompt | nlu_llm | StrOutputParser() | RunnableLambda(lambda
s: json.loads(s))

# Step 2: SQL generation using structured fields
sql_prompt = ChatPromptTemplate.from_messages([
    ("system", "You are a concise SQL assistant. Return only SQL."),
    ("user", "goal: {goal}\nproduct: {product}\nmonth: {month}")
])
to_sql_vars = RunnableLambda(lambda d: {"goal": d.get("goal",""), "product":
d.get("product",""), "month": d.get("month","")})
sql_chain = sql_prompt | sql_llm | StrOutputParser()

# Full chain: NLU → mapping → SQL
chain = nlu_chain | to_sql_vars | sql_chain

print(chain.invoke({
    "input": "My goal is to find the names of employees. Using the sales_
records table, get the employee names for product 'X' in January."
}))
```

This example shows how we integrate multiple LLMs by splitting the task into specialized stages and composing them with LCEL. The first model (**nlu_llm**) is prompted to extract a strict JSON payload (product, month, goal) from free text; its string output is parsed to a **dict** via **StrOutputParser** and **json.loads**. A small transformer (**RunnableLambda**) selects the required keys, while forming a clear data contract between models. That structured output is then fed to a second, independently prompted model (**sql_llm**) that only generates SQL. The stages are wired with the LCEL pipe operator (|), so outputs flow directly into inputs, which enables modularity (swap models/providers or prompts per stage), robustness (typed/ structured handoff), and allows for a much clearer observation of each step's behavior.

Error Handling and Exception Management

Error handling and exception management are crucial to maintain the integrity of an LLM chain. When one model in the chain misinterprets data or generates an incorrect or irrelevant output, it is vital to detect this error and correct it before passing the data on to the next model. This can be achieved by conducting validation checks at each step of the chain or by implementing a feedback loop where a subsequent model can flag and send back incorrect outputs for reprocessing. Moreover, the system must be able to handle exceptions. These instances may arise when a model becomes unavailable or when data is outside the expected parameters, without causing the entire chain to fail. Let us see this with an example:

```
import json
from langchain_openai import ChatOpenAI
from langchain_core.prompts import ChatPromptTemplate
from langchain_core.output_parsers import StrOutputParser
from langchain_core.runnables import RunnableLambda

# Primary and fallback LLMs
primary = ChatOpenAI(model="gpt-4o-mini", temperature=0, timeout=10)
fallback = ChatOpenAI(model="gpt-3.5-turbo", temperature=0, timeout=10)

# Step 1: Extract structured JSON (with validation)
extract_prompt = ChatPromptTemplate.from_messages([
    ("system", "Extract JSON with keys: product, month, goal. No extra
text."),
    ("user", "{input}")
])

def validate_payload(s: str):
    try:
        data = json.loads(s)
    except Exception as e:
        raise ValueError(f"Malformed JSON: {e}")
    required = {"product", "month", "goal"}
    missing = required - set(data.keys())
    if missing:
        raise ValueError(f"Missing keys: {missing}")
    if not isinstance(data["product"], str) or not isinstance(data["month"],
str) or not isinstance(data["goal"], str):
        raise ValueError("Fields must be strings")
    return data

extract_chain = extract_prompt | primary | StrOutputParser() |
RunnableLambda(validate_payload)
extract_chain_fb = extract_prompt | fallback | StrOutputParser() |
RunnableLambda(validate_payload)
# The .with_fallbacks method creates a new chain that will automatically try
extract_chain_fb if extract_chain fails.
safe_extract = extract_chain.with_fallbacks([extract_chain_fb])

# Step 2: Generate SQL (with fallback)
sql_prompt = ChatPromptTemplate.from_messages([
    ("system", "You are a concise SQL assistant. Return only SQL."),
    ("user", "goal: {goal}\nproduct: {product}\nmonth: {month}")
```

```
])
sql_chain = sql_prompt | primary | StrOutputParser()
sql_chain_fb = sql_prompt | fallback | StrOutputParser()
safe_sql = sql_chain.with_fallbacks([sql_chain_fb])

# Orchestrate with try/except to catch unhandled errors
try:
    structured = safe_extract.invoke({"input": "Get employee names for product 
'X' sold in January."})
    sql = safe_sql.invoke(structured)
    print(sql)
except Exception as e:
    print("Handled error:", str(e))
```

In the above example we use the following strategies to handle errors:

- **Strict Validation at Handoff:** The **`validate_payload`** function parses JSON (**`json.loads`**), verifies required keys (product, month, goal), and enforces string types. It raises **`ValueError`** on malformed or incomplete outputs, which prevents bad data from flowing downstream.
- **Automatic Fallbacks**: Both extraction and SQL stages use **`.with_fallbacks(...)`**. If the primary model times out, errors, or returns invalid JSON, the fallback chain is invoked transparently.
- **Timeouts to Avoid Hangs:** **`ChatOpenAI(..., timeout=10)`** ensures stalled calls fail fast, thus enabling fallbacks or error handling to kick in.
- **Top-Level Containment**: A try/except around orchestration catches any residual exceptions and handles them gracefully, which prevents the app from crashing.
- **Stage Isolation**: Errors are detected and handled at the step where they occur, which reduces cascading failures and makes issues easier to diagnose.

Performance Considerations

Finally, performance considerations are essential for the practical deployment of LLM chains. This includes optimizing the speed at which models can process data and respond, as well as managing the computational load to prevent bottlenecks. Since each additional LLM in the chain adds latency and computational cost, it is important to balance the complexity of the chain with the required performance. Techniques like parallel processing, caching frequent queries, and selectively engaging certain models only when needed can help maintain efficiency. Additionally, the hardware and software infrastructure supporting the LLMs must be capable of handling the intensive processing requirements of large language models, particularly when they are used in chains.

Challenges and Solutions in LLM Chaining

Building LLM chains can greatly enhance the capabilities of individual language models, but the process is not without its challenges. Developers must consider factors like contextual relevance, consistency, scalability, and resource management to ensure the chain is functioning as intended. Here, we delve into these challenges and explore potential solutions and best practices:

Handling Contextual Relevance across Chains

One of the main challenges in LLM chaining is maintaining contextual relevance as information moves through the chain. Each model must accurately understand and process the context provided by previous models to generate relevant outputs.

Solutions

a. **Context Passing:** Ensure that each model in the chain is receiving sufficient context from the previous model's output. This might involve including a summary of previous interactions or explicitly highlighting key points.

b. **Contextual Prompts:** Design prompts that explicitly incorporate context into the input for the next model to maintain relevance.

c. **Context Management Tools:** Utilize or develop tools within the chaining framework that can track and manage context across different models.

Maintaining Consistency and Coherence

As information passes through multiple LLMs, there is a risk of losing coherence or introducing inconsistencies, particularly if each model has been trained on different datasets or specializes in different tasks.

Solutions:

a. **Model Alignment:** Choose models with compatible training backgrounds and ensure that they align in terms of language, style, and the type of content they generate.

b. **Consistency Checks:** Implement checks after each step in the chain to review outputs for coherence and consistency with previous steps.

c. **Fine-tuning:** Remember fine-tune models on similar datasets wherever possible to harmonize their understanding and output generation.

Scalability Issues and Resource Management

LLM chains can be resource-intensive, and as chains become more complex or are scaled to handle more tasks simultaneously, hence managing computational resources becomes a significant challenge.

Solutions

a. **Efficient Model Selection**: You must choose more efficient models that achieve the desired output with fewer resources. One of the ways is to reduce the "`size`" of the model using quantization. We will discuss more about it later.

b. **Load Balancing**: Distribute the workload across multiple servers or cloud instances to manage computational demands and balance the load.

c. **Caching**: Implement caching for common queries to reduce the need for models to process the same input repeatedly.

Comprehensive Multi-Step Chain Example: Intent Classification → RAG Call → Final Synthesis

The following example demonstrates a production-ready multi-step chain that includes intent classification, RAG retrieval, and final synthesis with explicit error handling and latency logging at each step. This example showcases how to build robust, monitorable LLM chains for enterprise applications.

```
import time
import logging
from typing import Dict, Any, Optional
from dataclasses import dataclass

@dataclass
class ChainResult:
   intent: str
   rag_context: str
   final_response: str
   latency_ms: Dict[str, float]
   errors: list

class ProductionLLMChain:
   def __init__(self):
       self.logger = logging.getLogger(__name__)

   def classify_intent(self, user_input: str) -> tuple[str, float]:
       start_time = time.time()
       try:
           # Intent classification logic
           intent = self._call_llm(f"Classify intent: {user_input}")
           latency = (time.time() - start_time) * 1000
           self.logger.info(f"Intent classified: {intent}, latency:
{latency:.2f}ms")
           return intent, latency
       except Exception as e:
```

```
            self.logger.error(f"Intent classification failed: {e}")
            raise

    def retrieve_rag_context(self, intent: str) -> tuple[str, float]:
        start_time = time.time()
        try:
            # RAG retrieval logic
            context = self._call_rag_system(intent)
            latency = (time.time() - start_time) * 1000
            self.logger.info(f"RAG context retrieved, latency: {latency:.2f}ms")
            return context, latency
        except Exception as e:
            self.logger.error(f"RAG retrieval failed: {e}")
            raise

    def synthesize_response(self, intent: str, context: str) -> tuple[str, float]:
        start_time = time.time()
        try:
            # Final synthesis logic
            response = self._call_llm(f"Based on intent '{intent}' and context:
{context}")
            latency = (time.time() - start_time) * 1000
            self.logger.info(f"Response synthesized, latency: {latency:.2f}ms")
            return response, latency
        except Exception as e:
            self.logger.error(f"Response synthesis failed: {e}")
            raise

    def process_request(self, user_input: str) -> ChainResult:
        total_start = time.time()
        errors = []
        latency_ms = {}

        try:
            # Step 1: Intent Classification
            intent, intent_latency = self.classify_intent(user_input)
            latency_ms['intent_classification'] = intent_latency

            # Step 2: RAG Call
            context, rag_latency = self.retrieve_rag_context(intent)
            latency_ms['rag_retrieval'] = rag_latency

            # Step 3: Final Synthesis
            response, synthesis_latency = self.synthesize_response(intent, context)
            latency_ms['final_synthesis'] = synthesis_latency
```

```
            total_latency = (time.time() - total_start) * 1000
            latency_ms['total'] = total_latency

            return ChainResult(intent, context, response, latency_ms, errors)

        except Exception as e:
            errors.append(str(e))
            self.logger.error(f"Chain processing failed: {e}")
            raise
```

Best Practices for Troubleshooting LLM Chains

Troubleshooting emerging issues in LLM chains can be complex due to the multiple components involved. Therefore, it is important to have strategies that can identify and resolve issues promptly. Some of these best practices are mentioned as follows:

- **Logging and Monitoring:** Set up extensive logging for each step in the chain to track inputs, outputs, and any errors that occur. Monitoring systems can alert you to problems in real-time.
- **Stepwise Testing:** Test each model in the chain individually and then isolate and fix issues after combining all of them.
- **Fallback Mechanisms:** Create fallback options for instances of model failure, which can arise in form of default responses or calling on human intervention.
- **Documentation:** Maintain detailed documentation of the chain's architecture, individual models, and how they interact. This will come in handy while troubleshooting.
- **Incremental Development:** Build and test the chain incrementally, adding one model at a time to ensure stability at each step.

Overall, the key to overcoming challenges in LLM chaining lies in careful planning, robust architecture design, and continuous testing, as well as its ability to adapt and respond to incoming issues. Through these best practices and solutions, developers can build LLM chains that powerful, reliable, and efficient. To address these challenges in a structured and reusable way, developers can leverage established design patterns that provide proven blueprints for building robust and efficient LLM chains.

Design Patterns for LLM Chaining

Design patterns for Large Language Model (LLM) chaining refer to the systematic arrangement and how multiple LLMs coordinate to accomplish complex tasks that a single model might not be able to handle efficiently on its own. This approach leverages the unique strengths of various LLMs, which allows them to work in sequence or parallel to process information, generate outputs, and even refine the responses of other models in the chain.

Chaining Mechanisms

Chaining mechanisms define how multiple LLMs are connected and interact within a chain. These mechanisms dictate the flow of information and task execution, which impacts the overall performance and suitability for different applications.

- **Sequential Chaining:** This involves processing inputs through a series of models where the output of one model feeds into the next. It is particularly useful for tasks that require multiple, distinct processing steps.
- **Parallel Chaining:** In this mechanism, multiple models work on different parts of a problem simultaneously, with the results being aggregated at the end. This can speed up processing and is suitable for tasks that can be easily partitioned.
- **Hybrid Chaining:** A combination of sequential and parallel approaches, hybrid chaining allows for flexible arrangements that can be tailored to the specific requirements of a task.

Choosing the appropriate chaining mechanism is a crucial design decision that will impact the LLM chain's performance, robustness, and ability to handle specific types of tasks.

Pattern Types

Several distinct pattern types can be employed when designing LLM chains, each suited for different problem structures and desired outcomes:

- **Pipeline Pattern:** Just like an assembly line, this pattern passes data through a series of models, where each performs a specific operation. It is effective for processes with clearly defined stages.
- **Ensemble Pattern:** Several models are used to address the same task independently, and their results are combined. This often results in improved accuracy and robustness.
- **Feedback Loop Pattern:** Outputs are fed back into the system for iterative refinement, which allows for the continuous improvement of results.
- **Broker Pattern:** A central model directs tasks to specialized models and integrates their outputs. It acts as a coordinator to ensure that resources are used efficiently.

Model Compatibility

- **Interface Standardization:** Define a strict message envelope and typed IO for each step. Use a single schema (for example, Pydantic/JSON Schema) for inputs/outputs, include metadata (**`version`**, **`step_name`**) and an error field. You must enforce structured output parsers so that every model returns the same keys and types.
- **Model Interoperability:** You must hide provider differences behind a common chat interface (for example, LangChain chat models). Normalize function/tool-calling, stop

tokens, and **`temperature/top_p`**. Add adapters for providers, plus fallbacks/retries so that chains can swap models without changing step logic.

- **Data Format Consistency:** Pick one canonical format (JSON) and stick to it. Standardize field names, **`enums`**, and units (ISO-8601 dates, UTC times). Keep text encoding UTF-8, and align vector **`dims/dtypes`** across embedding steps. For multimodal, agree on base64 image fields and MIME hints.

Context Management

- **State Preservation:** Track intermediate results and chain progress across steps. Use stateful wrappers like **`RunnableWithMessageHistory`** or custom state objects that accumulate outputs from each model. Store step metadata (timestamps, model versions, confidence scores) for later models to adjust behavior based on earlier results' quality.
- **Context Propagation:** Pass relevant context forward through the chain. Include original user intent, intermediate reasoning, and extracted entities in each step's prompt. Use **`RunnablePassthrough().assign()`** to thread context alongside new outputs, or embed context in structured payloads, so that downstream models can understand the full conversation flow.
- **Session Memory:** Make sure that multi-turn interactions persist beyond single chains. Store conversation history in databases (Redis, PostgreSQL) keyed by session ID. Use **`InMemoryChatMessageHistory`** for short sessions or **`RedisChatMessageHistory`** for production. Enable models to reference earlier conversations, user preferences, and accumulated knowledge.

Performance Optimization

Load Balancing: Distribute requests across multiple model instances to avoid bottlenecks. Use round-robin or weighted routing based on model capacity. Implement async processing with **`asyncio`** for parallel execution, and queue systems (Celery/Redis) for high-throughput scenarios. Scale individual chain steps independently based on their computational demands.

Model Efficiency: Choose appropriately-sized models per task - use smaller, faster models (GPT-3.5-turbo) for simple extraction, reserve larger models (GPT-4) for complex reasoning. Fine-tune specialized models for frequent tasks. Cache outputs at each step to avoid recomputation and use streaming responses for long-running chains.

Response Time Reduction: Minimize latency through parallel execution wherever possible, implement timeouts and fallbacks, use connection pooling for API calls, and pre-warm model instances. Optimize prompt lengths and use structured outputs to reduce token usage and parsing overhead.

Here is a small example with async optimization:

```
import asyncio
from langchain_openai import ChatOpenAI
from langchain_core.runnables import RunnablePassthrough

# Parallel execution for independent tasks
async def parallel_chain():
    fast_model = ChatOpenAI(model="gpt-3.5-turbo", timeout=5)

    # Run extraction and validation in parallel
    tasks = await asyncio.gather(
        extract_chain.ainvoke({"input": user_query}),
        validate_chain.ainvoke({"input": user_query}),
        return_exceptions=True
    )

    return {"extraction": tasks[0], "validation": tasks[1]}

# Cache frequently used results
from functools import lru_cache

@lru_cache(maxsize=1000)
def cached_model_call(prompt_hash):
    return model.invoke(prompt)
```

Scalability and Infrastructure for LLM Chaining

- **Resource Allocation:** Dynamically scale individual chain steps based on usage patterns. Use container orchestration (Kubernetes) to allocate GPU/CPU resources per model type. Implement autoscaling policies that monitor queue depth and response times. Do not forget to optimize costs by running cheaper models during low-demand periods and premium models for critical tasks.

- **Scalable Architectures:** Design microservices where each chain step is independently deployable. Use message queues (RabbitMQ/Kafka) for asynchronous processing and horizontal scaling. Implement circuit breakers and bulkheads to isolate failures. Cache intermediate results in Redis/Memcached to reduce recomputation.

- **Cloud and On-Premises:** Cloud offers elasticity and managed services (AWS Bedrock, Azure OpenAI) but raises data residency concerns. On-premises provides control and compliance, but it also requires infrastructure expertise. Hybrid approaches keep sensitive data local while leveraging cloud for non-sensitive processing.

Security and Privacy for LLM Chaining

- **Data Privacy:** Encrypt data in transit between chain steps using TLS 1.3. Implement data anonymization/tokenization before processing. Use differential privacy techniques for sensitive datasets. Ensure GDPR/HIPAA compliance with audit trails and data retention policies.
- **Secure Model Communication:** Use API keys, OAuth 2.0, or mTLS for inter-service authentication. Implement rate limiting and request validation. Deploy models in isolated VPCs with network segmentation. Monitor for anomalous access patterns.
- **Ethical Considerations:** Implement bias detection at each chain step. Use diverse training data and fairness metrics. Add human review checkpoints for sensitive decisions. Maintain transparency about model limitations and potential biases in outputs.

Monitoring and Maintenance for LLM Chaining

- **Performance Monitoring:** Track latency, throughput, and error rates per chain step. Monitor token usage and costs. Use distributed tracing (Jaeger/Zipkin) to identify bottlenecks. Set up alerting for performance degradation or failures.
- **Model Updating:** Implement blue-green deployments for model updates. Use semantic versioning for chain compatibility. Test new models against golden datasets before production deployment. Maintain rollback capabilities for problematic updates.
- **Continuous Improvement:** A/B test different chain configurations. Analyze user satisfaction metrics and task completion rates. Use Reinforcement Learning from Human Feedback (RLHF) to improve model behavior over time.

Example monitoring setup:

```
from langchain.callbacks import StdOutCallbackHandler
from langchain.callbacks.tracers import LangChainTracer
import time

class ChainMonitor(StdOutCallbackHandler):
    def on_chain_start(self, serialized, inputs, **kwargs):
        self.start_time = time.time()
        # Log chain start metrics

    def on_chain_end(self, outputs, **kwargs):
        duration = time.time() - self.start_time
        # Log performance metrics, costs, success rates

chain = extraction_chain.with_callbacks([ChainMonitor(), LangChainTracer()])
```

Human-in-the-Loop for LLM Chaining

- **Collaborative Systems:** Design escalation paths where complex tasks route to human experts. Implement confidence scoring so low-confidence outputs trigger human review. Use active learning to identify cases where human input would most improve the system.
- **Expert Review:** Create review queues for domain experts to validate outputs. Implement approval workflows for high-stakes decisions. Use expert feedback to fine-tune models and improve prompts.
- **User Feedback:** Collect thumbs up/down ratings and detailed feedback. Implement feedback loops that update model behavior. Use user corrections to create training examples for model improvement.

Use Cases and Applications

- **Multistep Question Answering:** Chain Retrieval → Reasoning → Synthesis Models. The first model searches the knowledge base, the second analyzes relevance and relationships, and the third generates coherent answers. Each step specializes in one cognitive task rather than trying to do everything.
- **Conversational AI with Specialized Knowledge:** Route conversations through intent classification → domain-specific expert → response formatting chain. The general chat model handles pleasantries; specialized models (legal, medical, technical) provide domain expertise, while the formatter ensures consistent tone.
- **Creative Content Generation:** Pipeline story concept → character development → plot generation → style refinement. Each model contributes distinct creative aspects such as ideation, character psychology, narrative structure, and prose quality. These factors produce richer outputs than single-model approaches.

In conclusion, the design patterns for LLM chaining are vast and intricate, encompassing various strategies and considerations. Thus, by effectively leveraging these patterns, developers can build sophisticated AI systems capable of tackling complex and nuanced tasks, pushing the boundaries of what AI can achieve. Chaining LLMs effectively requires a careful consideration of compatibility, data flow, error handling, and maintaining context across models to achieve the desired outcome. Design patterns provide a blueprint for addressing these challenges in a structured manner.

Evaluating the Effectiveness of LLM Chains

Evaluating Large Language Model (LLM) chains is crucial for advanced AI systems. This involves assessing how well can multiple models perform together on complex tasks, while considering accuracy, efficiency, robustness, and scalability. For comprehensive evaluation methodologies, monitoring strategies, and detailed implementation guidance, please refer to *Chapter* 8. Challenges include evaluating the integration and communication between models, as errors can propagate. Contextual factors like maintaining context and adapting to evolving needs are also vital. Therefore, employing a multifaceted approach that combines quantitative and qualitative analyses is necessary to ensure these AI systems meet objectives and provide real-world value. **Key assessment areas include:**

Performance Metrics and Accuracy:

- **Output Quality:** Measure features like correctness, relevance, and coherence with both automated and human evaluation. Use semantic similarity scores, BLEU/ROUGE for text generation, and task-specific metrics (F1 for classification, exact match for QA).
- **Error Rate:** Track different error types such as parsing failures, logical inconsistencies, hallucinations, and format violations. Monitor error propagation through chain steps.
- **Benchmarking:** Compare against established datasets (MMLU, HellaSwag) and create custom evaluation sets for your domain.

The following is a small example demonstrating calculation of metrics:

```
from langchain.evaluation import load_evaluator
import pandas as pd

# Automated evaluation
evaluator = load_evaluator("criteria", criteria="relevance")
semantic_evaluator = load_evaluator("embedding_distance")

def evaluate_chain_output(chain, test_cases):
    results = []
    for case in test_cases:
        output = chain.invoke(case["input"])

        # Relevance score
        relevance = evaluator.evaluate_strings(
            prediction=output,
            input=case["input"]
        )

        # Semantic similarity to expected
        similarity = semantic_evaluator.evaluate_strings(
            prediction=output,
            reference=case["expected"]
        )

        results.append({
```

```
            "input": case["input"],
            "output": output,
            "expected": case["expected"],
            "relevance_score": relevance.score,
            "similarity_score": similarity.score,
            "exact_match": output.strip().lower() == case["expected"].strip().
lower()
        })

    return pd.DataFrame(results)

# Run evaluation
test_cases = [
    {"input": "Find sales for product X", "expected": "SELECT * FROM sales WHERE
product = 'X'"},
    # ... more test cases
]
results_df = evaluate_chain_output(my_chain, test_cases)
print(f"Accuracy: {results_df['exact_match'].mean():.2f}")
print(f"Avg Relevance: {results_df['relevance_score'].mean():.2f}")
```

Efficiency and Resource Management:

- **Response Latency:** Measure end-to-end latency and per-step timing. Track P50, P95, P99 percentiles to understand tail latency.
- **Resource Utilization:** Monitor CPU, memory, GPU usage, and API costs for each request. Track token consumption across chain steps.
- **Cost-Benefit Analysis:** Calculate cost per successful task completion and compare against alternatives.

The following is a small example of a chain profiler to calculate various metrics. It uses the python concept of decorator to add extra functionalities without disturbing the core functionality.

```
import time
import psutil
from functools import wraps

class ChainProfiler:
    def __init__(self):
        self.metrics = []

    def profile_step(self, step_name):
        def decorator(func):
            @wraps(func)
```

```
            def wrapper(*args, **kwargs):
                start_time = time.time()
                start_memory = psutil.Process().memory_info().rss / 1024 / 1024
# MB

                try:
                    result = func(*args, **kwargs)
                    success = True
                    error = None
                except Exception as e:
                    result = None
                    success = False
                    error = str(e)

                end_time = time.time()
                end_memory = psutil.Process().memory_info().rss / 1024 / 1024

                self.metrics.append({
                    "step": step_name,
                    "latency_ms": (end_time - start_time) * 1000,
                    "memory_delta_mb": end_memory - start_memory,
                    "success": success,
                    "error": error,
                    "timestamp": start_time
                })

                if not success:
                    raise Exception(error)
                return result
            return wrapper
        return decorator

    def get_summary(self):
        df = pd.DataFrame(self.metrics)
        return {
            "total_latency": df["latency_ms"].sum(),
              "avg_latency_per_step": df.groupby("step")["latency_ms"].mean().
to_dict(),
            "success_rate": df["success"].mean(),
            "total_memory_usage": df["memory_delta_mb"].sum()
        }

# Usage
profiler = ChainProfiler()

@profiler.profile_step("extraction")
```

```
def extract_step(input_text):
    return extraction_chain.invoke({"input": input_text})

@profiler.profile_step("sql_generation")
def sql_step(extracted_data):
    return sql_chain.invoke(extracted_data)

# Run chain with profiling
result = sql_step(extract_step("Find sales for product X"))
print(profiler.get_summary())
```

Robustness and Scalability:

- **Adaptability:** Test with diverse inputs, edge cases, and adversarial examples. Measure performance degradation across different domains.
- **Stress Testing:** Simulate high concurrent load and measure performance under stress.
- **Scalability:** Test horizontal scaling capabilities and performance with increasing complexity.

Here is a small example demonstrating stress testing using multi-threading:

```
import asyncio
import concurrent.futures
from datetime import datetime
import random

class StressTester:
    def __init__(self, chain):
        self.chain = chain
        self.results = []

    async def stress_test(self, num_requests=100, concurrency=10):
        test_inputs = [
            f"Find sales for product {random.choice(['A', 'B', 'C', 'X', 'Y'])}
in {random.choice(['January', 'February', 'March'])}"
            for _ in range(num_requests)
        ]

        semaphore = asyncio.Semaphore(concurrency)

        async def single_request(input_text, request_id):
            async with semaphore:
                start_time = time.time()
                try:
                    # Simulate async chain call
                  result = await asyncio.to_thread(self.chain.invoke, {"input":
```

```
input_text})
                    success = True
                    error = None
                except Exception as e:
                    result = None
                    success = False
                    error = str(e)

                latency = (time.time() - start_time) * 1000

                return {
                    "request_id": request_id,
                    "input": input_text,
                    "result": result,
                    "success": success,
                    "error": error,
                    "latency_ms": latency,
                    "timestamp": datetime.now()
                }

        # Execute all requests concurrently
        tasks = [single_request(inp, i) for i, inp in enumerate(test_inputs)]
        self.results = await asyncio.gather(*tasks, return_exceptions=True)

        return self.analyze_results()

    def analyze_results(self):
        valid_results = [r for r in self.results if isinstance(r, dict)]

        latencies = [r["latency_ms"] for r in valid_results if r["success"]]
       success_rate = sum(1 for r in valid_results if r["success"]) / len(valid_
results)

        return {
            "total_requests": len(valid_results),
            "success_rate": success_rate,
          "avg_latency_ms": sum(latencies) / len(latencies) if latencies else 0,
             "p95_latency_ms": sorted(latencies)[int(len(latencies) * 0.95)] if
latencies else 0,
             "p99_latency_ms": sorted(latencies)[int(len(latencies) * 0.99)] if
latencies else 0,
            "errors": [r["error"] for r in valid_results if not r["success"]]
        }

# Adaptability testing with edge cases
```

```
def test_adaptability(chain):
    edge_cases = [
        "",  # Empty input
        "a" * 10000,  # Very long input
       "Find sales for product 'DROP TABLE users; --'",  # SQL injection attempt
        "🎵🎶 Musical notes in query 🎵🎶",  # Unicode/emoji
        "What is the meaning of life?",  # Off-topic query
    ]

    results = []
    for case in edge_cases:
        try:
            result = chain.invoke({"input": case})
            results.append({"input": case, "success": True, "output": result})
        except Exception as e:
            results.append({"input": case, "success": False, "error": str(e)})

    return results

# Usage
stress_tester = StressTester(my_chain)
stress_results     =     asyncio.run(stress_tester.stress_test(num_requests=50,
concurrency=5))
adaptability_results = test_adaptability(my_chain)

print("Stress Test Results:", stress_results)
print("Adaptability Results:", adaptability_results)
```

These are the range of considerations which ensure that the LLM chains are performing their intended functions effectively, and are doing so in a manner that is sustainable, reliable, and scalable to meet future demands. These evaluation methods provide a comprehensive framework for assessing chain performance. For detailed operational instructions, including setting up automated alerting and KPI tracking for these chained systems, see *Chapter 8, Model Monitoring and Evaluation.*

Conclusion

In conclusion, LLM chaining is a powerful paradigm that moves beyond the capabilities of a single LLM by orchestrating multiple specialized models to collaboratively solve complex tasks. By breaking down problems into sequential or parallel steps, and carefully managing context, errors, and performance, we can achieve more precise, creative, and robust AI solutions. The effective implementation of LLM chains requires careful consideration of design patterns, error handling, performance optimization, and robust infrastructure. This ensures that these systems are both powerful and reliable.

These evaluation methods provide a comprehensive framework to assess the effectiveness of LLM chains, and ensure that they deliver accurate, efficient, robust, and scalable solutions for real-world applications. By continuously monitoring and refining these aspects, developers can ensure that their LLM chains stay high-performing and valuable. Having explored prompt engineering and delving into the intricacies of LLM chaining, we will now turn our attention to another advanced technique: Retrieval-Augmented Generation (RAG). The RAG technique, which often employs a specific type of chain, is explored in considerable detail in *Chapter* 5.

References

1. https://cobusgreyling.medium.com/comparing-llm-agents-to-chains-differences-advantages-disadvantages-a86029a1445f
2. https://galileo.ai/blog/llm-evaluation-step-by-step-guide
3. https://learn.microsoft.com/en-us/azure/databricks/generative-ai/guide/agent-system-design-patterns
4. https://medium.com/@dewanshsinha71/advanced-reasoning-frameworks-in-large-language-models-chain-tree-and-graph-of-thoughts-bafbfd028575
5. https://medium.com/@tungvu_37498/understanding-llm-evaluation-metrics-best-practices-for-reliable-llm-assessment-3fce1fa48251
6. https://www.analyticsvidhya.com/blog/2024/12/ai-agents-research-papers/
7. https://www.comet.com/site/blog/llm-evaluation-metrics-every-developer-should-know/
8. https://www.evidentlyai.com/llm-guide/llm-evaluation-metrics
9. https://www.ibm.com/think/tutorials/prompt-chaining-langchain
10. https://www.researchgate.net/publication/391246469_From_LLM_Reasoning_to_Autonomous_AI_Agents_A_Comprehensive_Review
11. https://www.voiceflow.com/blog/prompt-chaining

CHAPTER 5
Retrieval Augmentation Generation

Introduction

This chapter will discuss Retrieval Augmented Generation (RAG), which overcomes many drawbacks of naive LLMs and empowers us to utilize their capabilities to a greater extent. One major drawback of LLMs is that their knowledge is limited to the data that is used to train them. Hence, when asked about anything outside of their trained knowledge base, LLMs either fail to answer or, worse, hallucinate and give wrong answers. One fix is to fine-tune them on new data or domain-specific data. However, this approach has its own limitations. Although fine-tuning LLMs is powerful, it comes with significant drawbacks. It can cause the model to forget previously learned information, which results in a phenomenon known as catastrophic forgetting. Additionally, fine-tuning is computationally expensive, as it requires significant resources and large datasets, which are hard to obtain. This process also runs the risk of overfitting, where the model performs well on training data, but poorly on new, unseen data. Furthermore, fine-tuning often requires managing multiple models for different tasks, which adds complexity. In contrast, RAG is a more efficient and adaptable solution. RAG grounds the model's responses in external knowledge sources, which reduces the likelihood of generating factually incorrect information or hallucinations. This approach is less computationally intensive and requires less training data than fine-tuning. RAG's flexibility shines in its ability to adapt to new information and changing contexts without retraining. This makes it ideal for domains with rapidly evolving knowledge. Ultimately, RAG enhances the accuracy and relevance of responses by leveraging external knowledge. It provides a more robust and adaptable solution compared to traditional fine-tuning. While RAG is a powerful concept, the actual operationalization process which includes data pipeline construction and vector database serving is discussed in *Chapter 7, Deploying Large Language Models.*

Structure

This chapter will address the following topics:

- RAG: Bridging the Gap between Retrieval and Generation
- Implementing RAG: Architecture and Processes
- Evaluating RAG: Task and Evaluation
- Future Trends in RAG

RAG: Bridging the Gap between Retrieval and Generation

Essentially, RAG is an approach that combines retrieval-based techniques with generation-based models. It enhances the performance of generative models by fetching relevant information from a large corpus of documents or data before generating a response. Here is how it works:

1. **Retrieval Phase:** When a question or prompt is given, the system first retrieves relevant documents or information from a predefined dataset or database. This step gathers context and ensures that the generated response is grounded in accurate and relevant information.
2. **Augmentation Phase:** The retrieved information is then used to inform the generative model. This helps in generating more accurate, coherent, and contextually appropriate responses.
3. **Generation Phase:** Finally, the generative model produces the response, while leveraging both the input prompt and the retrieved information.

Here is an example of a basic RAG flow:

```
# Simple illustration of RAG workflow
def rag_system(query, knowledge_base):
    # 1. RETRIEVAL: Find relevant documents
    retrieved_docs = retriever.search(query, knowledge_base)
    # Example: query = "What is the return policy?"
    # retrieved_docs = ["Return policy: 30 days...", "Refund process..."]

    # 2. AUGMENTATION: Combine query with retrieved context
    context = "\n".join(retrieved_docs)
```

```
    augmented_prompt = f"Context: {context}\n\nQuestion: {query}\nAnswer:"

    # 3. GENERATION: Generate response using LLM
    response = llm.generate(augmented_prompt)

    return response

# Without RAG: LLM might hallucinate or say "I don't know"
# With RAG: LLM uses actual company documents to answer accurately
```

Benefits of RAG

- **Improved Accuracy and Relevance:** RAG systems can generate more accurate and relevant responses by leveraging external knowledge.
- **Enhanced Information:** RAG systems can provide more comprehensive and insightful responses by incorporating diverse perspectives and factual information.
- **Increased Trustworthiness:** RAG systems can enhance transparency and trustworthiness by providing explanations for their responses and grounding them in retrieved evidence.
- **Versatility and Adaptability:** RAG systems can be applied to a wide range of tasks and domains, while adapting to different information needs and user preferences.

Troubles Solved by RAG

RAG addresses several key challenges in Natural Language Processing (NLP) and AI by offering constructive solutions to problems that traditional language models often struggle with. Here are some of the troubles that can be solved by RAG:

- **Limited Knowledge:**
    - **Problem:** Traditional language models are often trained on a fixed dataset, which limits their knowledge and ability to access up-to-date information.
    - **Solution:** RAG overcomes this limitation by retrieving relevant information from external knowledge bases. This enables it to access a vast amount of information and generate responses that are more informed and comprehensive.
- **Factual Inaccuracy:**
    - **Problem:** Language models can sometimes generate factually incorrect or nonsensical information, a phenomenon known as hallucination.
    - **Solution:** RAG mitigates this issue by grounding its responses in retrieved evidence and provides a basis for factual claims and reducing the likelihood of generating false information.

- **Lack of Contextual Awareness:**
    - **Problem:** Traditional language models may struggle to understand the context of a conversation or query, leading to irrelevant or inappropriate responses.
    - **Solution:** RAG addresses this by retrieving contextually relevant information, which allows it to better understand the user's intent and generate responses that are more appropriate and informative.
- **Difficulty Handling Complex Queries:**
    - **Problem:** Language models may struggle with complex or multi-step queries, requiring a deeper understanding of the information and relationships between different concepts.
    - **Solution:** RAG can handle such queries by retrieving relevant passages from multiple sources and integrating them into a coherent response, thus providing a more comprehensive and nuanced answer.
- **Inability to Adapt to New Information:**
    - **Problem:** Traditional language models are typically static and cannot easily adapt to new information or evolving knowledge domains.
    - **Solution:** RAG's ability to retrieve information from external sources enables it to stay up-to-date with the latest knowledge and adapt to changing information needs, which makes it more versatile and dynamic.
- **Limited Explainability:**
    - **Problem:** Language models often operate as black boxes, making it difficult to understand the reasoning behind their responses.
    - **Solution:** RAG enhances explainability by providing the retrieved context alongside the generated response, while offering insights into the information used to generate the answer and increasing transparency.
- **Lack of Personalization:**
    - **Problem:** Traditional language models may not be able to personalize responses based on individual user preferences or needs.
    - **Solution:** RAG can be tailored to specific users or domains, retrieving and utilizing information that is most relevant to the individual, resulting in the creation of more personalized and engaging experiences.

By addressing these troubles, RAG empowers AI systems with enhanced knowledge, accuracy, contextual awareness, and adaptability. Thus, it paves the way for more sophisticated and trustworthy applications in various domains.

RAG can be particularly useful in applications where accuracy and relevance are crucial, such as customer support, research, and content creation. Let us see this in more detail using the example of Customer Support. In this use case, RAG can enhance automated customer service by providing more accurate and contextually relevant responses to customer queries. It retrieves specific information from a company's knowledge base, ensuring that customers receive the correct information quickly. Let us see how it is implemented in the following section.

Implementation of RAG for Customer Support

Implementing Retrieval-Augmented Generation (RAG) for customer support involves several steps. Here is a detailed walkthrough of how it can be done and how it compares with other methods like fine-tuning.

Steps for Implementing RAG in Customer Support

1. **Data Collection:** Collect a large corpus of documents, such as FAQs, customer queries, product manuals, and support articles from the company's knowledge base.
2. **Indexing:** Use indexing techniques like BM25, TF-IDF, or dense retrievers (for example, DPR) to organize and store the collected data efficiently. This ensures quick and relevant document retrieval based on input queries.
3. **Retrieval Model:** Use retrieval models to fetch the most relevant documents based on the customer's query. For example, if a customer asks about a product's return policy, the retrieval model will fetch documents related to return policies.
4. **Generative Model:** Utilize a generative model like GPT-3 or T5 that can take the retrieved information and the input query to generate a coherent and contextually accurate response. The retrieved documents provide context, thereby ensuring that the generated response is relevant and accurate.
5. **Integration**: Combine the retrieval and generative models in a pipeline. The process starts with the retrieval model fetching relevant information, which is then passed to the generative model to produce the final response.
6. **Evaluation and Tuning:** Regularly evaluate the performance of the RAG system using metrics like accuracy, relevance, and customer satisfaction. Fine-tune the models to improve performance based on feedback and evaluation results.

Fine-Tuning vs. RAG in Customer Support

While RAG ensures that support agents have real-time access to dynamic product documentation to prevent hallucinations, fine-tuning optimizes the model's ability to consistently mirror a company's unique brand persona and empathetic tone. Understanding the operational trade-offs between these two approaches is essential for building a customer support system that is both factually reliable and conversationally professional.

Feature	Fine-Tuning	Retrieval-Augmented Generation (RAG)
Scope	Best for domains with a narrow and well-defined scope	Suitable for a broader range of queries and topics, leveraging a large corpus of documents
Adaptability	Less adaptable to significant scope changes without re-training (requires new data and additional fine-tuning)	Highly adaptable to scope changes by simply updating the corpus with new information
Accuracy and Relevance	Highly accurate and relevant within the fine-tuned domain	Contextually accurate and relevant due to the retrieval of specific, up-to-date documents
Implementation Complexity	Requires expertise in fine-tuning models but is generally relatively straightforward for implementation	More complex due to the need for integrating retrieval and generative models (data engineering, vector databases, and so on)
Data Requirements	Requires a substantial amount of task-specific data for model training	Relies on a large corpus of documents but does not require task-specific fine-tuning data
Cost	Higher initial costs for fine-tuning data preparation and model training; ongoing costs for inference and potential re-training	Higher initial costs for data collection, indexing, and integration; generally lower costs for model training (as the base model is not re-trained)
Expertise Required	Focused expertise in ML, data preparation, and distributed training (optimizing resource usage on clusters)	Broader range of expertise including data engineering, NLP, ML, software engineering, and domain expertise

Table 5.1: *Comparison of Techniques for Customer Support*

In summary, RAG offers the advantage of combining retrieval and generation to provide contextually accurate and versatile responses, which makes it ideal for customer support applications. Fine-tuning, while highly effective in narrow domains, may not offer the same versatility and will require more specific data.

Implementing RAG: Architecture and Processes

We briefly covered how RAG can be implemented for the customer support use case. However, that implementation is basic, and there are many other challenges that need to be overcome or mitigated to improve the outcome. Let us explore them in more detail here:

Challenges in the "Retrieval Phase" of RAG

- **Irrelevant Data:** One of the primary challenges is fetching irrelevant or redundant data. Simplistic retrieval methods can often pull in data that does not align well with the query and leads to poor quality results.
- **Incomplete Data:** Sometimes, the retrieval process may miss out on crucial information, which results in the model fetching incomplete data. This can affect the overall quality of the generated output.
- **Balancing Relevance and Diversity**: Ensuring that the retrieved documents are both relevant and diverse is another challenge. Techniques like Maximal Marginal Relevance (MMR) are used to balance these aspects, but they require careful implementation.
- **Combining Semantic and Keyword Search**: Hybrid retrieval methods that combine semantic and keyword search can improve accuracy, but they make the retrieval process more complex. This involves using techniques like BM25 for keyword relevance and embeddings for semantic similarity.

Addressing these challenges involves refining retrieval strategies, optimizing data management, and continuously improving the retrieval algorithms to ensure high-quality and relevant results.

Mitigation Strategies

Let us now consider some approaches to mitigate these challenges

Challenge 1: Poor Data Quality

- Implement data cleaning and preprocessing techniques to improve data quality. This might include removing duplicates, correcting errors, standardizing formats, and enriching the data with relevant metadata. Regularly update and curate the knowledge base to ensure its accuracy and relevance.

Challenge 2: Inefficient Retrieval

- Optimize the retrieval process by using efficient indexing techniques like inverted indexes or vector databases. Employ techniques like query expansion or semantic search to improve the accuracy and speed of retrieval. Consider using specialized hardware or cloud-based solutions for faster processing.

Challenge 3: Insufficient Context

- Implement techniques to retrieve multiple passages or documents that can provide a broader context. Employ techniques like query reformulation or relevance feedback to refine the retrieval process and capture a wider range of relevant information. Consider using techniques like question decomposition to break down complex queries into smaller, more manageable sub-queries.

Challenge 4: Handling Ambiguity

- Employ techniques like query clarification or disambiguation to resolve ambiguity. Use natural language processing (NLP) techniques to identify the user's intent and refine the query before retrieval. Consider using techniques like entity recognition or semantic role labeling to extract key information from the query and improve retrieval accuracy.

Challenge 5: Maintaining Relevance

- Regularly update the knowledge base and re-index the content to reflect the latest information. Implement mechanisms to monitor retrieval performance and identify potential issues. Consider using techniques like active learning or reinforcement learning to continuously improve the retrieval system's ability to adapt to changing information needs.

Indexing Optimization

Indexing is a crucial step in the retrieval phase of RAG, as it determines how quickly and accurately relevant information can be retrieved from a knowledge base. Optimizing the indexing process can significantly improve the overall performance and efficiency of a RAG system. Here is a breakdown of key considerations that should be factored in during indexing:

1. **Data Structure Selection**
    - **Inverted Index:** This is a widely used data structure for text retrieval. It maps each term in the knowledge base to a list of documents containing that term. This allows for efficient keyword-based search.
    - **Vector Database:** These databases store documents as vectors, enabling similarity-based search. They are particularly useful for semantic search and handling complex queries. Choosing the right data structure depends on the specific needs of the RAG system, such as the size of the knowledge base, the type of queries expected, and the desired retrieval performance.
2. **Chunking and Segmentation**
    - **Chunking:** Dividing large documents into smaller chunks can improve retrieval accuracy and efficiency. This ensures that relevant passages within a document are not missed due to the limitations of the retrieval model.
    - **Segmentation:** For structured data, such as tables or code, applying appropriate segmentation techniques can improve retrieval performance. This might involve splitting tables into rows or columns or identifying code blocks based on syntax. Chunking and segmentation strategies should be tailored to the specific data format and the characteristics of the retrieval model.

Example: Document Chunking Strategies

```
# Simple chunking examples
def fixed_size_chunking(document, chunk_size=500):
    """Split document into fixed-size chunks"""
    words = document.split()
    chunks = []
    for i in range(0, len(words), chunk_size):
        chunk = " ".join(words[i:i + chunk_size])
        chunks.append(chunk)
    return chunks
    # Result: ["chunk1 with 500 words...", "chunk2 with 500 words...", ...]

def semantic_chunking(document):
    """Split document by semantic boundaries (paragraphs, sections)"""
    chunks = document.split("\n\n")  # Split by paragraphs
    return [chunk.strip() for chunk in chunks if chunk.strip()]
    # Result: ["Introduction paragraph", "Methods section", "Results..."]

# Example document
doc = "Product Overview: Our widget is amazing... [500 words] \n\n Features: 
It has feature A and B... [300 words]"

# Fixed chunks might split mid-sentence
fixed_chunks = fixed_size_chunking(doc, chunk_size=200)

# Semantic chunks preserve meaning
semantic_chunks = semantic_chunking(doc)
# Better for retrieval: each chunk is a complete thought
```

3. **Embedding Generation**

   - **Embedding Model:** Choosing an appropriate embedding model is crucial for effective indexing. Embedding models transform text into numerical vectors, capturing semantic relationships between words and phrases. This enables similarity-based search and retrieval.

   - **Dimensionality:** The dimensionality of the embedding vectors can impact both retrieval accuracy and efficiency. Higher dimensionality can capture more nuanced semantic information but may also increase computational overhead. Selecting the right embedding model and dimensionality depends on the complexity of the knowledge base and the desired retrieval performance.

Example: Vector Similarity Search

```
# Simple illustration of semantic search using embeddings
import numpy as np
```

```
def semantic_search_example():
    """Demonstrate how embeddings enable semantic search"""

    # Documents in knowledge base (simplified as vectors)
    documents = {
        "doc1": "How to reset password",
        "doc2": "Product return policy",
        "doc3": "Forgot login credentials",
        "doc4": "Shipping information"
    }

    # Convert text to embedding vectors (simplified representation)
    # In practice, use models like sentence-transformers
    doc_embeddings = {
        "doc1": np.array([0.8, 0.1, 0.2, 0.1]),  # password-related
        "doc2": np.array([0.1, 0.9, 0.1, 0.2]),  # return-related
        "doc3": np.array([0.7, 0.1, 0.3, 0.1]),  # password-related (similar
to doc1)
        "doc4": np.array([0.1, 0.2, 0.1, 0.9])   # shipping-related
    }

    # User query
    query = "I can't remember my password"
    query_embedding = np.array([0.75, 0.15, 0.25, 0.1])  # Similar to password
docs

    # Calculate cosine similarity between query and each document
    similarities = {}
    for doc_id, doc_vec in doc_embeddings.items():
        similarity = np.dot(query_embedding, doc_vec) / (
            np.linalg.norm(query_embedding) * np.linalg.norm(doc_vec)
        )
        similarities[doc_id] = similarity

    # Results (sorted by similarity):
    # doc1: 0.95 (reset password) - HIGH MATCH
    # doc3: 0.92 (forgot credentials) - HIGH MATCH
    # doc2: 0.35 (return policy) - LOW MATCH
    # doc4: 0.30 (shipping) - LOW MATCH

    # Key insight: Query doesn't mention "reset" or "credentials"
    # but semantic search finds relevant docs based on meaning!

    return sorted(similarities.items(), key=lambda x: x[1], reverse=True)

# Traditional keyword search would miss doc3 (no shared keywords)
# Semantic search finds both relevant documents
```

4. **Index Structure**
    - **Tree-Based Indexes:** Indexes such as B-trees or KD-trees organize data in a hierarchical structure, enabling efficient range queries and nearest neighbor search.
    - **Hash-Based Indexes:** Hash-based indexes use hash functions to map data to buckets, which allows for fast lookup operations.
    - **Graph-Based Indexes:** Graph-based indexes represent data as nodes and edges and enable complex relationships and connections for capturing. Your choice of the right index structure will depend on the specific retrieval needs and the characteristics of the data.
5. **Index Compression**
    - **Quantization:** This technique reduces the size of embedding vectors by representing them with fewer bits. This reduces storage requirements and improving retrieval speed.
    - **Pruning:** Removing less important or redundant information from the index can further reduce its size and improve efficiency.
    - **Compression Algorithms:** Applying compression algorithms to the index can further reduce storage costs and improve retrieval performance. Index compression techniques should be carefully chosen to balance retrieval accuracy with efficiency.
6. **Index Maintenance**
    - **Updating:** Regularly updating the index with new information is essential for maintaining retrieval accuracy. This might involve adding new documents, removing outdated information, or updating embeddings to reflect changes in the knowledge base.
    - **Rebuilding:** Periodically rebuilding the index can improve retrieval performance by optimizing data structures and removing fragmentation.
    - **Monitoring:** Monitoring index performance metrics, such as retrieval speed and accuracy, can help identify potential issues and trigger necessary maintenance tasks. Index maintenance strategies should be implemented to ensure the long-term effectiveness of the RAG system.

Query Optimization

Query optimization focuses on refining the user's initial query to enhance the retrieval of relevant information from the knowledge base. This is a crucial step as it significantly impacts the quality and relevance of the context provided to the language model for generating responses. Here are key techniques involved in query optimization:

1. **Query Expansion:**

    - **Rationale:** Expanding the original query with synonyms, related terms, or broader concepts can increase the chances of retrieving relevant documents that might not contain the exact keywords used in the initial query.
    - **Techniques:** Leverage word embeddings to identify semantically similar terms. Use knowledge graphs or ontologies to find related concepts. Apply query rewriting rules based on domain expertise or linguistic patterns.

Example: Query Expansion

```
# Simple query expansion example
def expand_query(original_query):
    """Expand query with synonyms and related terms"""

    # Original query
    query = "fix broken laptop"

    # Synonym expansion
    synonyms = {
        "fix": ["repair", "troubleshoot", "resolve"],
        "broken": ["damaged", "malfunctioning", "not working"],
        "laptop": ["notebook", "computer", "device"]
    }

    expanded_terms = []
    for word in query.split():
        expanded_terms.append(word)
        if word in synonyms:
            expanded_terms.extend(synonyms[word])

    # Expanded query captures more relevant documents
    return " ".join(expanded_terms)
    # Result: "fix repair troubleshoot resolve broken damaged
    #          malfunctioning laptop notebook computer"

# This helps retrieve documents that use different terminology
# for example, "How to repair a malfunctioning notebook computer" compared to
original query "fix broken laptop"
```

2. **Query Reformulation:**

    - **Rationale:** Rephrasing the query using different wording or sentence structures can improve retrieval accuracy by capturing the underlying intent of the user's query more effectively.
    - **Techniques:** Employ Natural Language Processing (NLP) techniques like paraphrasing or sentence simplification. Utilize machine translation to generate

alternative query formulations in different languages. Use query templates or patterns to guide the reformulation process.

3. **Term Re-weighting:**
    - **Rationale:** Adjusting the importance of different terms in the query can improve retrieval performance by prioritizing terms that are more likely to indicate relevance.
    - **Techniques:** Use techniques like TF-IDF (Term Frequency-Inverse Document Frequency) to assign weights to terms based on their frequency in the knowledge base and the query. Apply Machine Learning (ML) models to learn term weights based on user feedback or relevance judgments.
4. **Query Filtering:**
    - **Rationale:** Removing irrelevant or noisy terms from the query can improve retrieval precision by focusing the search on the most important keywords or concepts.
    - **Techniques:** Use stop word removal to eliminate common words that do not carry much meaning. Apply regular expressions to filter out specific patterns or characters. Utilize domain-specific knowledge to identify and remove irrelevant terms.
5. **Query Relaxation:**
    - **Rationale:** Broadening the scope of the query by including more general terms or concepts can help retrieve documents that might not be an exact match but still contain relevant information.
    - **Techniques:** Use query generalization techniques to replace specific terms with more general ones. Employ semantic similarity measures to identify documents that are conceptually related to the query. Apply query expansion with broader synonyms or hypernyms.

Generation Phase of RAG

The generation phase in RAG involves utilizing the retrieved context and the user's query to generate a comprehensive and informative response. While RAG systems have shown promising results, the following challenges need to be addressed in this phase:

1. **Context Integration:**
    - **Problem:** Effectively integrating the retrieved context into the language model's generation process is crucial. Simply concatenating the context with the query can result in disjointed or irrelevant responses.
    - **Mitigation:** Explore advanced techniques like attention mechanisms or fusion models to seamlessly weave the context into the generation process. Fine-tuning

the language model on a dataset of context-augmented queries can improve its ability to incorporate external knowledge effectively.

2. **Hallucination:**
   - **Problem:** Language models can sometimes generate factually incorrect or nonsensical information, a phenomenon known as hallucination. This is particularly problematic in RAG systems, where the model may fabricate information which is not present in the retrieved context.
   - **Mitigation:** Implement fact verification mechanisms to cross-reference generated content with external sources. Train the language model to distinguish between factual and speculative information. Employ techniques like knowledge grounding or constrained decoding to guide the model towards generating more reliable responses.

Example: Faithfulness Checking

```
# Simple faithfulness verification example
def check_faithfulness(generated_response, retrieved_context):
    """Verify if generated response is faithful to retrieved context"""

    # Retrieved context from knowledge base
    context = """
    Our return policy allows customers to return products within 30 days
    of purchase. Returns must include the original receipt.
    Refunds are processed within 5-7 business days.
    """

    # Generated response by LLM
    response_good = "You can return the product within 30 days with receipt."
    response_hallucinated = "You can return the product within 90 days."

    # Check if key facts are supported by context
    def verify_claim(claim, context):
        # Simplified verification (in practice, use NLI models)
        facts_in_context = {
            "30 days": "30 days" in context,
            "90 days": "90 days" in context,
            "receipt required": "receipt" in context,
            "5-7 business days": "5-7 business days" in context
        }
        return facts_in_context

    # Verification results:
    # response_good: "30 days" ✓ (supported by context)
    # response_hallucinated: "90 days" ✗ (NOT in context - HALLUCINATION!)
```

```
    # Actions based on verification:
    # - If faithful: Return response to user
    # - If hallucination detected: Regenerate or flag for review
    # - Add citation to improve transparency

    return verify_claim(generated_response, context)

# Faithfulness checking helps ensure RAG responses are grounded in facts
# Reduces risk of AI confidently stating incorrect information
```

3. **Response Coherence and Fluency:**
    - **Problem:** Generating coherent and fluent responses that seamlessly integrate retrieved information is challenging. The generated text should flow naturally and avoid abrupt transitions or inconsistencies.
    - **Mitigation:** Employ techniques like discourse parsing or text planning to structure the response effectively. Fine-tune the language model on a dataset of high-quality responses to improve its ability to generate coherent and fluent text. Utilize techniques like beam search or nucleus sampling to explore a wider range of potential responses and select the most coherent ones.
4. **Evaluation and Monitoring:**
    - **Problem:** Evaluating the quality of generated responses in RAG systems is challenging. Traditional metrics like BLEU or ROUGE may not adequately capture the faithfulness and relevance of the response to the retrieved context.
    - **Mitigation:** Develop evaluation metrics that are specifically tailored for RAG systems after considering factors like factual accuracy, coherence, and relevance to the user's query. Continuously monitor the system's performance and identify areas for improvement. Utilize human evaluation to assess the quality and trustworthiness of generated responses.

Context Curation

Context curation involves selecting, refining, and organizing the retrieved information to create a comprehensive and relevant context for the language model to generate a response. This step is crucial as it directly impacts the quality, coherence, and factual accuracy of the generated output. Here is a breakdown of key aspects of context curation:

1. **Context Selection:**
    - **Rationale:** Not all retrieved information may be equally relevant or useful for answering the user's query. Selecting the most pertinent passages or documents is crucial to avoid overwhelming the language model with irrelevant information.

- **Techniques:** Rank retrieved documents based on relevance scores or similarity to the query. Apply diversity filters to select a variety of perspectives or viewpoints. Utilize user feedback or relevance judgments to refine the selection process.

Example: Context Reranking and Selection

```
# Simple reranking example
def rerank_and_select_context(query, retrieved_docs, top_k=3):
    """Rerank retrieved documents and select most relevant"""

    # Initial retrieval returns many documents
    retrieved_docs = [
        {"text": "Return policy: 30 days full refund", "score": 0.75},
        {"text": "Shipping takes 5-7 days", "score": 0.60},
        {"text": "Returns must include receipt", "score": 0.70},
        {"text": "Product warranty is 1 year", "score": 0.45},
        {"text": "Return shipping is free", "score": 0.68}
    ]

    # Query: "How do I return a product?"

    # Rerank based on relevance to specific query
    # (In practice, use cross-encoder or semantic similarity)
    reranked = sorted(retrieved_docs, key=lambda x: x["score"], reverse=True)

    # Select top-k most relevant
    selected = reranked[:top_k]

    # Selected context: ["30 days full refund", "Returns must include receipt",
    #                    "Return shipping is free"]
    # Excluded less relevant: ["Shipping", "Warranty"]

    return [doc["text"] for doc in selected]

# This ensures LLM gets most relevant context within token limits
```

2. **Context Filtering:**
    - **Rationale:** Removing redundant, contradictory, or potentially harmful content from the retrieved information is essential to ensure the quality and trustworthiness of the generated response.
    - **Techniques:** Apply techniques like deduplication to eliminate duplicate or near-duplicate passages. Use fact verification mechanisms to identify and filter out inaccurate or misleading information. Employ content moderation tools to remove potentially harmful or offensive content.

3. **Context Ordering:**
    - **Rationale:** Arranging the selected context in a logical and coherent manner can improve the language model's ability to generate a well-structured and informative response.
    - **Techniques:** Organize passages based on chronological order, topical relevance, or argumentative flow. Utilize discourse parsing or text structuring algorithms to identify logical relationships between passages. Apply techniques like summarization or keyphrase extraction to obtain a concise overview of the context.
4. **Context Summarization:**
    - **Rationale:** Summarizing the selected context can help reduce the amount of information presented to the language model. This also improves generation efficiency and reducing the risk of information overload.
    - **Techniques:** Employ extractive summarization techniques to select the most important sentences or phrases from the context. Utilize abstractive summarization techniques to generate a concise summary of the main ideas. Apply techniques like query-focused summarization to tailor the summary to the user's specific information needs.
5. **Context Formatting:**
    - **Rationale:** Formatting the context in a way that is easily understandable by the language model can improve generation quality and efficiency.
    - **Techniques:** Use clear and concise language, avoiding complex sentence structures or jargon. Structure the context using headings, bullet points, or other formatting elements to improve readability. Apply techniques like entity linking or relation extraction to provide additional context and structure.

Advanced Augmentation Techniques

The augmentation process in RAG involves enriching the retrieved context with additional information to enhance the language model's understanding and generation capabilities. This step aims to provide a more comprehensive and informative context, leading to more accurate, relevant, and insightful responses. Here is a breakdown of key augmentation techniques used in RAG:

1. **Knowledge Graph Integration**
    - **Rationale:** Knowledge graphs provide structured representations of entities and their relationships, which can be used to augment the retrieved context with factual information and semantic connections.

- **Techniques:** Identify entities mentioned in the retrieved context and link them to corresponding entries in a knowledge graph. Extract relevant information from the knowledge graph, such as entity descriptions, properties, or relationships, and incorporate it into the context. Use knowledge graph embeddings to enhance semantic understanding and retrieval.

2. **External Data Sources:**
   - **Rationale:** Incorporating information from external data sources like databases, APIs, or web services can provide valuable context and insights that might not be present in the original knowledge base.
   - **Techniques:** Identify relevant external data sources based on the user's query or the retrieved context. Extract relevant data from these sources using APIs or data integration tools. Format the external data to be compatible with the language model's input format and integrate it into the context.
3. **Contextual Embeddings:**
   - **Rationale:** Contextual embeddings capture the meaning of words and phrases within their specific context, which provides a richer representation of the retrieved information.
   - **Techniques:** Use pre-trained language models to generate contextual embeddings for the retrieved context. Fine-tune the language model on a dataset of context-augmented queries to improve its ability to leverage contextual information. Incorporate contextual embeddings into the retrieval process to enhance relevance and accuracy.
4. **Common Sense Reasoning:**
   - **Rationale:** Augmenting the context with common sense knowledge can help the language model make inferences and generate more nuanced and insightful responses.
   - **Techniques:** Integrate common sense knowledge bases, such as ConceptNet or Cyc, into the RAG system. Use common sense reasoning engines to infer implicit information or fill in missing gaps in the context. Train the language model on a dataset of common sense reasoning tasks to improve its ability to apply common sense knowledge.
5. **Multimodal Information:**
   - **Rationale:** Incorporating information from different modalities such as images, videos, or audio can provide a more comprehensive understanding of the context and enhance the language model's generation capabilities.
   - **Techniques:** Extract relevant features from multimodal data using computer vision or audio processing techniques. Integrate multimodal features into the

context representation. Train the language model on a dataset of multimodal inputs to improve its ability to generate responses that incorporate information from different modalities.

Evaluating RAG: Task and Evaluation

Evaluating a RAG system involves assessing its ability to retrieve relevant information and generate high-quality, informative, and trustworthy responses. This requires a combination of automated metrics and human evaluation to capture different aspects of system performance. For comprehensive evaluation methodologies, monitoring strategies, and detailed implementation guidance, please refer to *Chapter* 8. Here are some key evaluation metrics specific to RAG systems:

1. **Retrieval Evaluation**
    - **Metrics**
        - **Precision:** Measures the proportion of retrieved documents that are relevant to the query
        - **Recall:** Measures the proportion of relevant documents that are retrieved by the system
        - **F1-*Score*:** Combines precision and recall into a single metric, while providing a balanced measure of retrieval performance
        - **Mean Average Precision (MAP):** Measures the average precision across multiple queries, providing a more comprehensive evaluation of retrieval effectiveness
        - **Normalized Discounted Cumulative Gain (NDCG):** Takes into account the ranking of retrieved documents and gives higher weight to documents ranked higher in the list
    - **Evaluation Datasets:** Use benchmark datasets with labeled relevance judgments to evaluate retrieval performance against ground truth. You can also create your own evaluation datasets by manually annotating a set of queries and documents.

Example: Computing Retrieval Metrics

```
 # Simple example of calculating retrieval metrics
def calculate_precision_recall(retrieved_docs, relevant_docs):
    """Calculate precision and recall for retrieval"""

    # Retrieved documents (what the system returned)
    retrieved = ["doc1", "doc2", "doc3", "doc4", "doc5"]

    # Ground truth relevant documents (what should be retrieved)
```

```
    relevant = ["doc1", "doc3", "doc6", "doc7"]

    # Calculate metrics
    retrieved_set = set(retrieved)
    relevant_set = set(relevant)

    # True Positives: documents that are both retrieved and relevant
    true_positives = retrieved_set.intersection(relevant_set)
    # Result: {"doc1", "doc3"}

    # Precision: Of what we retrieved, how many are relevant?
    precision = len(true_positives) / len(retrieved_set)
    # Result: 2/5 = 0.40 (40% of retrieved docs are relevant)

    # Recall: Of all relevant docs, how many did we retrieve?
    recall = len(true_positives) / len(relevant_set)
    # Result: 2/4 = 0.50 (50% of relevant docs were retrieved)

    # F1-Score: Harmonic mean of precision and recall
    f1 = 2 * (precision * recall) / (precision + recall)
    # Result: 2 * (0.4 * 0.5) / (0.4 + 0.5) = 0.444

    return {
        "precision": precision,
        "recall": recall,
        "f1_score": f1
    }

# High precision: few irrelevant docs retrieved
# High recall: most relevant docs retrieved
# F1 balances both metrics
```

2. **Generation Evaluation**
    - **Metrics**
        - **BLEU** (Bilingual Evaluation Understudy): Measures the overlap between the generated response and a set of reference responses
        - **ROUGE** (Recall-Oriented Understudy for Gisting Evaluation): Measures the overlap between the generated response and a set of reference summaries
        - **METEOR** (Metric for Evaluation of Translation with Explicit ORdering): Considers word order and synonyms when comparing the generated response to reference responses
        - **BERT*Score*:** Uses contextual embeddings to measure the semantic similarity between the generated response and reference responses

    - **Factuality Metrics:** Evaluate the factual accuracy of the generated response by comparing it to external knowledge sources or using fact verification tools

- **Evaluation Datasets:** Use benchmark datasets with human-written reference responses or summaries to evaluate generation quality. You can also create your own evaluation datasets by collecting human judgments on the quality and relevance of generated responses.

3. **Human Evaluation**

    - **Rationale:** Human evaluation is essential to capture aspects of system performance that are difficult to measure with automated metrics like coherence, fluency, and overall user satisfaction.

    - **Methods:** Conduct user studies where participants are asked to rate the quality and relevance of generated responses. Use expert annotators to assess the factual accuracy and trustworthiness of the information provided. Employ qualitative feedback methods like interviews or surveys, to gather insights into user perceptions and preferences.

4. **Holistic Evaluation**

    - **Rationale:** A holistic evaluation will consider both retrieval and generation performance, as well as the overall user experience.

    - **Methods:** Combine automated metrics, human evaluation, and user feedback to provide a comprehensive assessment of system performance. Conduct A/B testing to compare different RAG configurations or strategies. Analyze user interactions and feedback to identify areas for improvement.

5. **Context Evaluation in RAG**

    Context evaluation focuses on assessing the quality and relevance of the retrieved context used by the RAG system to generate responses. This evaluation is crucial as it directly impacts the accuracy, the degree of informativeness, and trustworthiness of the generated output. Here is a breakdown of key aspects of context evaluation in RAG:

    a. **Relevance**

        - **Rationale:** The retrieved context should be relevant to the user's query and provide information that is useful for answering the question or fulfilling the request.

        - **Relevance Judgments:** Human annotators can provide relevance judgments on a scale (for example, 1-5) to assess the degree of relevance between the retrieved context and the query.

- **Evaluation Datasets:** Benchmark datasets with labeled relevance judgments or human-annotated queries and documents can be used for evaluating context relevance.

b. **Faithfulness**

- **Rationale:** The generated response should be faithful to the retrieved context, meaning that it should not contradict or misrepresent the information provided in the context.
- **Metrics**
    - **Fact Verification:** Compare the generated response to external knowledge sources or use fact verification tools to identify any factual inaccuracies or inconsistencies.
    - **Contextual Entailment:** Assess whether the generated response is logically entailed by the retrieved context using natural language inference techniques.
    - **Human Evaluation:** Expert annotators can assess the faithfulness of the generated response by comparing it to the retrieved context and identifying any deviations or misinterpretations.
- **Evaluation Datasets:** Datasets with human-annotated claims and evidence can be used for evaluating faithfulness.

c. **Comprehensiveness**

- **Rationale:** The retrieved context should provide sufficient information to answer the user's query comprehensively.
- **Metrics**
    - **Coverage:** Measure the extent to which the retrieved context covers the relevant aspects of the user's query.
    - **Information Gain:** Assess the amount of new or relevant information provided by the retrieved context.
    - **Human Evaluation:** Expert annotators can assess the comprehensiveness of the retrieved context by judging whether it contains enough information to answer the query adequately.
- **Evaluation Datasets:** Datasets with complex queries requiring detailed answers can be used for evaluating comprehensiveness.

d. **Diversity**

- **Rationale:** The retrieved context should represent a variety of perspectives or viewpoints to avoid bias and provide a more balanced understanding of the topic.

- **Metrics**
  - **Diversity Score:** Measure the degree of diversity among the retrieved documents or passages based on their content or source.
  - **Topic Coverage:** Assess the range of topics covered by the retrieved context.
  - **Human Evaluation:** Expert annotators can examine the diversity of the retrieved context by judging whether it represents different viewpoints or perspectives.
- **Evaluation Datasets:** Datasets with diverse perspectives on a particular topic can be used for evaluating diversity.

Advanced RAG Architectures

Moving beyond the basic Retriever-Generator model, advanced RAG architectures incorporate sophisticated techniques to enhance retrieval accuracy, improve context relevance, and optimize overall system performance. These architectures address the limitations of traditional RAG systems via innovative indexing strategies, intelligent post-retrieval processing, and modern fusion techniques.

Advanced Indexing and Chunking Strategies

Traditional chunking strategies often fail to preserve semantic coherence and contextual relationships. Advanced indexing techniques address these limitations through the following measures:

- **Hierarchical Chunking:** Creates multi-level document representations with different granularities (paragraph, section, document) to capture both fine-grained details and broader context
- **Recursive Chunking:** Dynamically adjusts chunk sizes based on content structure to preserve semantically complete units regardless of their length
- **Semantic Chunking:** Uses semantic similarity and topic modeling to create chunks that maintain conceptual coherence and improves retrieval relevance and generation quality

Post-Retrieval Processing and Reranking

Advanced RAG systems implement sophisticated post-retrieval processing to refine and optimize retrieved content before generation:

- **Cross-Encoder Reranking:** Uses bidirectional attention models to re-rank retrieved documents based on their relevance to the specific query, significantly improving retrieval precision

- **Context Compression:** Intelligently compresses retrieved content to fit within model context limits, while preserving the most relevant information for generation.

RAG-Fusion: Multi-Query Retrieval

RAG-Fusion represents a significant advancement in retrieval strategies by generating multiple query variations and fusing their results through the following steps:

- **Query Generation:** Creates multiple query variations (reformulations, expansions, and alternative phrasings) to capture different aspects of the user's intent
- **Result Fusion:** Combines results from multiple queries using techniques like reciprocal rank fusion (RRF) or weighted scoring to create a more comprehensive and relevant document set
- **Diversity Enhancement:** Ensures retrieved documents cover diverse perspectives and information types, reducing redundancy and improving answer completeness

Example: RAG-Fusion Multi-Query Approach

```
# Simplified RAG-Fusion example
def rag_fusion(original_query):
    """Generate multiple query variations and fuse results"""

    # Step 1: Generate query variations
    query_variations = [
        "What are the best practices for LLM deployment?",  # Original
        "How to deploy large language models effectively?",  # Reformulation
        "LLM production deployment guide",                    # Simplified
        "Deploying language models best practices"          # Alternative
phrasing
    ]

    # Step 2: Retrieve documents for each query variation
    all_results = {}
    for i, query in enumerate(query_variations):
        # Each query returns different ranked results
        results = retrieve_documents(query)
        # Example results:
        # Query 1: [doc_a, doc_b, doc_c]
        # Query 2: [doc_b, doc_d, doc_a]
        # Query 3: [doc_c, doc_d, doc_e]
        all_results[i] = results

    # Step 3: Apply Reciprocal Rank Fusion (RRF)
    # Documents ranked higher in multiple queries get higher scores
    fused_scores = {}
```

```
    k = 60  # RRF constant

    for query_results in all_results.values():
        for rank, doc in enumerate(query_results):
            # RRF score: 1 / (k + rank)
            score = 1.0 / (k + rank + 1)
            fused_scores[doc] = fused_scores.get(doc, 0) + score

    # Step 4: Rerank by fused scores
    final_ranked = sorted(fused_scores.items(),
                         key=lambda x: x[1], reverse=True)

    # Benefit: Documents appearing in multiple query results rank higher
    # doc_b appears in query 1 & 2 → higher fused score
    # More comprehensive than single query retrieval

    return final_ranked

# RAG-Fusion captures multiple aspects of user intent
# More robust than single-query retrieval
```

Future Trends in RAG

RAG is a rapidly evolving field with significant potential to enhance the capabilities of AI systems. As research and development continue, we can expect several exciting trends to shape the future of RAG. Some of these are mentioned as follows:

- **Enhanced Retrieval Methods**
  - **Hybrid Search:** Involves combining keyword-based search with semantic search to improve retrieval accuracy and capture a wider range of relevant information
  - **Multimodal Retrieval:** Involves expanding retrieval capabilities to incorporate information from different modalities like images, videos, or audio
  - **Real-time Retrieval:** Enables retrieval of information in real-time, which allows RAG systems to adapt to dynamic and evolving contexts
  - **Personalized Retrieval:** Refers to tailoring retrieval results to individual user preferences and needs, thereby providing more personalized and relevant responses
- **Advanced Contextualization**
  - **Dynamic Context Selection:** Refers to adaptively selecting the most relevant context based on the user's query and the ongoing conversation
  - **Context Fusion:** Refers to integrating information from multiple retrieved sources to create a more comprehensive and coherent context

  - **Knowledge Graph Integration:** Refers to leveraging knowledge graphs to provide structured information and semantic connections within the context
  - **Common Sense Reasoning:** Refers to common sense knowledge to enhance the language model's understanding and generation capabilities

- **Improved Generation Techniques**
  - **Fine-grained Control:** This refers to more control over the generation process, which allows users to specify desired attributes of the response such as length, style, or tone.
  - **Interactive Generation:** This enables users to iteratively refine the generated response through feedback or suggestions.
  - **Multimodal Generation:** This involves generating responses that incorporate information from different modalities such as text, images, or audio.
  - **Explainable Generation:** This provides insights into the reasoning behind the generated response, which ends up enhancing transparency and trustworthiness.

- **Applications in Diverse Domains:**
  - **Conversational AI:** Involves building more engaging and informative chatbots that can access and utilize external knowledge
  - **Question Answering:** Refers to the process of systems that can provide accurate and comprehensive answers to complex questions
  - **Content Creation:** Involves automating the generation of high-quality content, such as articles, summaries, or reports
  - **Personalized Education:** Refers to educational materials and experiences to individual student needs and preferences

- **Ethical Considerations:**
  - **Bias Mitigation:** Refers to addressing potential biases in the retrieved context and generated responses to ensure fairness and inclusivity
  - **Privacy Preservation:** Refers to protecting sensitive information in the knowledge base and user interactions
  - **Transparency and Explainability:** Refers to providing clear explanations of how the RAG system works and the reasoning behind its decisions
  - **Human Oversight:** Involves maintaining human oversight and control over the RAG system to ensure responsible and ethical use

These trends represent exciting directions for the future of RAG, paving the way for more intelligent, informative, and trustworthy AI systems. As research progresses and technology advances, we can expect RAG to become increasingly integrated into various applications, which can transform the way we interact with information and AI. The evaluation of RAG systems involves assessing both retrieval and generation performance. The methodology for setting up continuous evaluation pipelines and collecting human feedback on RAG outputs is covered in detail in *Chapter 8*.

Conclusion

Thus, RAG is a powerful approach in AI that combines information retrieval and text generation to create more versatile and intelligent systems. It bridges the gap between retrieving relevant information from a knowledge base and generating coherent and informative responses. By leveraging retrieval techniques, RAG systems can access and incorporate external knowledge into the generation process, which generates more informed and comprehensive responses. These systems typically consist of a retriever module to access knowledge, a generator module to produce responses, and a context curation module to refine and organize the retrieved information. Evaluating RAG systems involves assessing both retrieval and generation performance using various metrics and human judgments. The future of RAG is bright, as we anticipate advancements in retrieval methods, contextualization techniques, generation capabilities, and applications across diverse domains. Furthermore, ethical considerations like bias mitigation and privacy preservation are increasingly important. Ultimately, RAG offers significant benefits, including improved accuracy, enhanced degrees of informativeness, increased trustworthiness, and versatility. These benefits can radically transform our interactions with information and AI systems. As research and development progress, RAG is poised to become an integral part of more intelligent, adaptable, and reliable AI solutions.

References

1. https://arxiv.org/abs/2005.11401
2. https://arxiv.org/abs/2312.10997
3. https://cobusgreyling.medium.com/rag-vs-fine-tuning-comparing-methods-for-customizing-llms-d2b380290547
4. https://research.google/pubs/evaluating-the-faithfulness-of-rag-systems/
5. https://towardsdatascience.com/a-framework-for-evaluating-rag-applications-5c5f0962b9a3
6. https://www.databricks.com/blog/building-production-quality-rag-applications-retrieval-augmented-generation
7. https://www.pinecone.io/learn/rag-chunking-strategies/

CHAPTER 6

AI Agents and Autonomous Systems

Introduction

So, in the previous two chapters, we really dug into prompt management and how powerful it can become when enhanced with techniques like Retrieval-Augmented Generation (RAG), and even the Model Context Protocol (MCP). However, even with these advancements, we are still left with quite a bit of heavy lifting on the development side. Thus, we would have to write a lot of explicit codes to manage the entire workflow. Think about our summarization example: you would still need to write the logic to figure out which RAG source to call based on the input, or which MCP-enabled tool or data source would be best for retrieving the specific context. Then, you would have to decide which prompt to use to properly parse the input and generate the output, and finally, how to handle that output. This kind of manual orchestration quickly becomes tedious and cumbersome, and honestly, it is a nightmare to scale when your application grows more complex.

This is precisely where AI Agents stepped in to truly simplify our lives. They solve this problem by intelligently orchestrating these complex interactions and decision-making processes all by themselves. Instead of us having to write out every single "**`if/else`**" statement and function call, an AI agent can autonomously reason and plan, deciding on its own what steps are needed to achieve a high-level goal, like "*summarize this document*." It can intelligently pick and use various "*tools*"-whether that is a RAG retriever, a code interpreter, or leveraging a specific data source exposed via an MCP server-all based on its understanding and objective. So, in our summary example, it would dynamically figure out which RAG source to query, which MCP-enabled resource to access for context, which prompt to apply, and then execute the LLM call, even refining the output, all without you having to code each specific step. Essentially, AI agents abstract away all that low-level orchestration, letting us define the big-picture goals and trust the agent to handle all the intricate details, which leads to much more robust, scalable, and genuinely intelligent applications with a lot less manual coding on our part. This autonomous orchestration relies heavily on the underlying techniques of prompt chaining (see *Chapter 4, The Power of LLM Chaining*) and tool use, which often includes calling a RAG system (see *Chapter 5, Retrieval Augmentation Generation*).

Structure

In this chapter, we will discuss the following topics:

- Introduction to AI agents and agent frameworks
- Agent architectures and design patterns
- Tool use and function calling
- Multi-agent systems and coordination
- Agent memory and state management
- Agent monitoring and observability
- Agent safety and security considerations
- Production deployment strategies for AI agents
- Agent lifecycle management

Introduction to AI Agents

AI agents are sophisticated software programs designed to mimic aspects of intelligent behavior by interacting with an environment to achieve predefined objectives. They are more than just passive tools; they are dynamic entities capable of independent thought and action within their designated domain. For foundational concepts about AI Agents in the LLMOps context, including their role in the broader LLMOps lifecycle, see *Chapter 2, Getting Started with MLOps*.

Understanding AI Agents

AI agents are software programs that can perceive their environment, make decisions, and take actions to achieve specific goals. Think of them as digital entities equipped with a level of autonomy that allows them to operate and execute tasks, without requiring constant human oversight or explicit instructions for every step. They are designed to be goal-oriented and can adapt their behavior based on the information they gather from their surroundings.

Key Characteristics of AI Agents

- **Autonomy:** This is perhaps the most defining characteristic. AI agents possess the ability to operate independently, making their own decisions and executing actions, without constant human intervention. They are not merely executing pre-programmed scripts; rather, they can determine the best course of action based on their understanding of the environment and their objectives. This independence allows them to handle complex, multi-step tasks efficiently.
- **Reactivity:** AI agents are designed to be responsive to changes within their environment. They continuously monitor their surroundings (which could be digital data streams, physical sensor inputs, or user commands) and react appropriately to new information or events. For example, a reactive agent might detect a change in a stock price and immediately execute a pre-defined trading strategy.
- **Proactivity:** Beyond just reacting to external stimuli, AI agents can take initiative to achieve their goals. They do not simply wait for instructions; they can anticipate needs, plan future actions, and initiate processes to move closer to their objectives. This often involves internal goal-setting and planning mechanisms. For instance, a proactive scheduling agent might anticipate a busy period and pre-book necessary resources.
- **Social Ability:** Many advanced AI agents are designed to interact with other agents (both AI and human) in a collaborative or communicative manner. This can involve exchanging information, negotiating, coordinating tasks, or even learning from human feedback. This characteristic is crucial for agents operating in multi-agent systems or those designed for human-computer interaction, such as intelligent personal assistants.

Types of AI Agents

AI agents can be categorized into several types based on their architecture and behavior:

- **Reactive Agents:** Respond directly to environmental stimuli without maintaining internal state. Examples include simple chatbots and rule-based systems.
- **Deliberative Agents:** Maintain internal models and plan actions based on goals. Examples include autonomous vehicles and strategic game-playing agents.
- **Hybrid Agents:** Combine reactive and deliberative behaviors. Most modern LLM-based agents fall into this category, balancing quick responses with thoughtful planning.
- **Learning Agents:** Improve their performance over time through experience. Examples include recommendation systems and adaptive trading algorithms.

Coming to our example of summarization, for this use case, the agent's design would reflect the following characteristics:

- **Perception:** It "*perceives*" its environment by receiving input in the form of documents (for example, text files, web pages, and research papers).
- **Decision-making:** Based on complex algorithms (often powered by Large Language Models), it "decides" which sentences or phrases are most important, how to structure the summary, and what level of detail is appropriate for the given context or user preferences.
- **Action:** Its "*action*" is to generate and output the summarized text.
- **Autonomy:** Once configured, it can automatically process new documents as they become available, without a human needing to manually trigger the summarization for each one.
- **Proactivity (optional):** A more advanced summarization agent might proactively scan news feeds for articles on specific topics and summarize them, or identify relevant sections within a large dataset to summarize for an analyst.

Example: Summarization Agent Architecture

```
class SummarizationAgent:
      def __init__(self):
            self.memory = []
            self.summarizer = None

      def perceive(self, document):
            # Receive document input
            return {"length": len(document),"doc_type":document.extension}

      def decide(self, input_data):
            # Decide how to summarize based on document length
            if input_data["length"] < 1000:
                  return "short_summary"
            else:
                  return "detailed_summary”

      def act(self, decision, text):
            # Generate summary based on decision
            if decision == "short_summary":
                  return self.create_brief_summary(text)
            else:
                  return self.create_detailed_summary(text)
```

The ReAct Framework: Reasoning and Acting

The ReAct (Reasoning and Acting) Framework represents the operational mechanism that separates an autonomous Agent from a simple Chain. This framework formalizes how agents make decisions about tool usage, plan their actions, and execute complex tasks through an iterative loop of observation, reasoning, and action.

The Agent Loop: Observe → Plan/Reason → Act → Repeat

The core of the ReAct Framework is the Agent Loop, a continuous cycle that enables autonomous decision-making:

1. **Observe:** The agent perceives its current state, including user inputs, environmental changes, and the results of previous actions. This observation phase gathers all relevant information needed for decision-making.
2. **Plan/Reason:** Based on observations, the agent reasons about the current situation, evaluates available tools and actions, and formulates a plan to achieve its goals. This is where the model decides which tools to use and in what sequence.
3. **Act:** The agent executes the planned action, which may involve calling external tools, generating responses, or modifying its internal state. Actions can be simple (single tool call) or complex (multi-step workflows).
4. **Repeat:** The cycle continues, with the agent observing the results of its actions, and adjusting its reasoning and planning accordingly. This iterative process continues until the goal is achieved or a termination condition is met.

Tool Selection and Decision Making

Understanding how the model decides to use a tool is crucial for deployment and monitoring. The ReAct Framework provides explicit reasoning traces that show:

- **Reasoning Process:** The agent's thought process and rationale for choosing specific tools or actions.
- **Action Selection:** Clear documentation of which tools were selected and why, enabling better debugging and optimization.
- **Outcome Evaluation:** Assessment of action results and adjustment of future behavior based on success or failure patterns.

Agent Frameworks vs. Platforms

A critical distinction in LLMOps is between open-source Agent Frameworks and managed Agent Platforms, as this represents a significant deployment choice:

Open-Source Agent Frameworks

Examples include LangChain, LlamaIndex, and AutoGen. These provide:

- **Full Control:** Complete customization and control over agent behavior, tool integration, and deployment architecture.

- **Flexibility:** Ability to integrate with any infrastructure, customize workflows, and implement proprietary logic.
- **Operational Overhead:** Requires managing infrastructure, scaling, monitoring, and maintenance internally.

Managed Agent Platforms

Examples include AWS Bedrock Agents, Azure AI Agents, and Google Vertex AI Agents. These provide:

- **Managed Infrastructure:** Cloud providers handle scaling, availability, and infrastructure management.
- **Pre-built Integrations:** Native integration with cloud services, databases, and enterprise systems.
- **Vendor Lock-in:** Limited customization options and dependency on specific cloud provider ecosystems.

Popular Agent Frameworks

To avoid building these complex architectures from scratch, developers can leverage several powerful open-source frameworks. The open-source community, alongside major tech players, has developed several powerful frameworks that abstract away a lot of the complexity. Let us quickly review some of these:

- **LangChain:** This framework has become incredibly popular for anyone looking to build LLM-powered applications. LangChain provides a comprehensive toolkit for chaining together various components, from different LLMs and prompt templates to external data sources and tools. Its core strength lies in its modularity and ability to orchestrate complex workflows. Hence, if you are looking to build an agent that needs to integrate with a wide array of data, use RAG, manage conversation memory, and utilize various external tools, LangChain offers a flexible and extensible foundation. It is like a Swiss Army knife for building agentic applications, giving you the building blocks to craft sophisticated decision-making processes.
- **CrewAI:** When your problem space demands more than just a single agent working in isolation, CrewAI steps into the spotlight. This framework specifically focuses on multi-agent collaboration. It allows you to define a "*crew*" of AI agents, each with a distinct role, specific tools, and a clear set of responsibilities. Imagine a team of human experts working together; CrewAI enables you to mimic this by orchestrating how these specialized AI agents communicate, delegate tasks, share context, and collectively achieve a common goal. This is incredibly powerful for tackling complex problems that naturally break down into sub-tasks requiring different areas of expertise, such as research, writing, and editing, all working like a concert.

- **AutoGen:** Developed by Microsoft, AutoGen provides a robust framework for building and managing conversational AI agents. Its unique selling proposition is its focus on facilitating automated chat among multiple agents, which can include LLMs, external tools, and even human participants. AutoGen simplifies the orchestration of complex LLM workflows by allowing agents to initiate and carry on conversations to collaboratively solve tasks. This event-driven, message-passing architecture is excellent for scenarios where agents need to engage in multi-turn dialogues, dynamically switch roles, or use tools in real-time within a conversational context, such as automating customer support interactions or collaborative coding sessions.
- **Semantic Kernel:** Also from Microsoft, Semantic Kernel is an SDK designed for seamlessly integrating AI models (especially LLMs) into your existing applications, particularly those within the Microsoft ecosystem. While not exclusively an "*agent*" framework in the same way LangChain or AutoGen are, it is fundamental for building agentic workflows because it provides the "*kernel*" that allows your code to interact intelligently with AI. It lets you define "*skills*" (collections of functions, often powered by LLMs) and use a "*planner*" to orchestrate these skills to fulfill user requests. This makes it ideal for enterprise-grade applications where you want to embed AI capabilities, including agentic behavior, into established business processes with a focus on security, compliance, and structured workflow execution. Thus, it is about bringing the power of AI into your existing codebase in a very organized and extensible way.

AutoGPT and BabyAGI represent the next generation of autonomous AI agents. AutoGPT focuses on goal-oriented task execution with internet access and file operations, while BabyAGI emphasizes recursive task decomposition and execution. AgentGPT provides a web-based interface for creating and deploying autonomous agents, without coding.

Framework Selection Guide

Each framework offers distinct advantages, catering to different needs in the agent development landscape. Your choice depends on the specific problem: LangChain for versatile single agents, CrewAI for multi-agent teams, AutoGen for conversational workflows, Semantic Kernel for Microsoft ecosystem integration, and AutoGPT/BabyAGI for autonomous goal-oriented tasks.

Agent Architectures and Design Patterns

So, as an LLMOps architect, or more precisely, AgentOps architect, how would you structure these "*digital minds*"? Let us break down the fundamental building blocks and common design patterns implemented in industry.

Basic Agent Architecture

A typical AI agent, regardless of its complexity, is usually composed of several interconnected modules that work in harmony:

- **Perception Module:** This is the agent's "*senses*." It is responsible for receiving input from the environment. This input could be anything from text queries, sensor data, or changes in a database, to responses from APIs or other LLMs. For an agent summarizing documents, its perception module would be processing the text content of those documents.
- **Decision Module:** Often considered the "*brain*" of the agent, the Decision Module takes the information gathered by the Perception Module and processes it. This is where the agent reasons about the current state, evaluates options, and chooses the next action. In modern AI agents, this module is typically the LLM itself, which orchestrates the entire flow through reasoning and function calling. This is the paradigm shift from traditional software; instead of explicit `if/else` logic, the '*decision*' is an act of reasoning by a language model, which determines the next best action. The LLM analyzes the current context, determines what actions are needed, and coordinates the execution of tools and external resources to achieve the agent's objectives.
- **Action Module:** Once a decision is made, the Action Module is responsible for executing the chosen action. This could involve generating a response, calling an external tool or API (like a RAG system or an external database), sending an email, or manipulating data. It is the agent's way of interacting with its environment, based on its decisions.
- **Memory Module:** For an agent to be truly intelligent and adaptable, it needs to remember past experiences and learned information. The Memory Module serves this purpose, storing relevant data, historical interactions, goals, and even learned strategies. This allows the agent to maintain context over time, learn from its mistakes, and improve its performance in future tasks. Think of it as the agent's long-term and short-term memory, crucial for sustained coherent behavior.

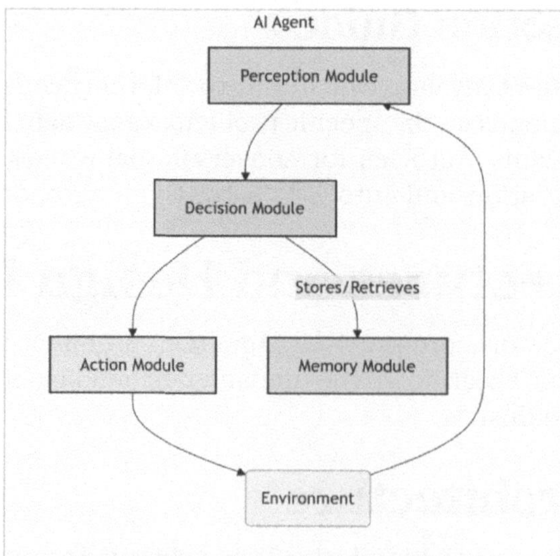

Figure 6.1: *Basic Agent Architecture*

Common Design Patterns

While the basic architecture provides a blueprint, how these modules interact and prioritize their functions leads to different design patterns, each suited for various types of tasks.

- **Reactive Agents:** Reactive agents are the simplest and fastest. They operate on a direct stimulus-response model. They do not typically maintain complex internal models of the world or engage in long-term planning. Instead, they react immediately to their current perceptions.
  - **Simple and fast:** Their straightforward nature makes them very efficient for tasks requiring quick responses.
  - **Good for straightforward tasks:** A perfect example is a document summarization agent. It receives a document (stimulus) and immediately produces a summary (response), without needing to plan multiple steps or consider future implications. Another might be a simple chatbot that gives predefined answers to specific keywords.

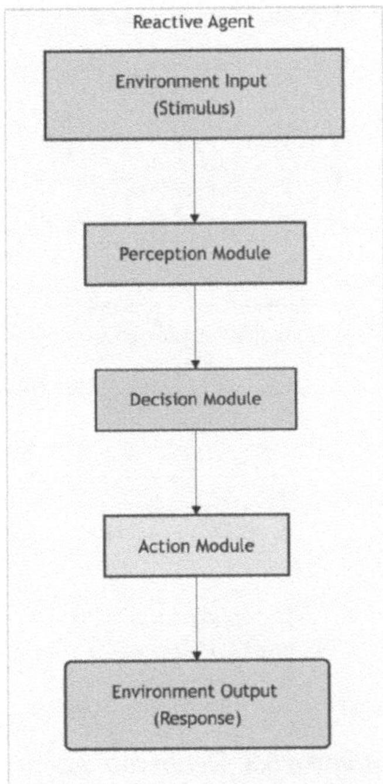

Figure 6.2: *Reactive Agents*

- **Deliberative Agents:** In contrast to reactive agents, deliberative agents are all about planning. They build and maintain an internal model of their environment and use this model to plan sequences of actions that will lead them to their goals. This planning involves search, reasoning, and prediction.

- **More complex but flexible:** Their ability to plan makes them highly flexible and capable of tackling intricate, multi-step problems.
- **Better for multi-step tasks:** Consider an agent tasked with booking a complex travel itinerary. It would need to check flights, hotels, car rentals, consider dates, prices, and availability, and then execute a series of booking actions. This requires a significant amount of planning and sequential decision-making.

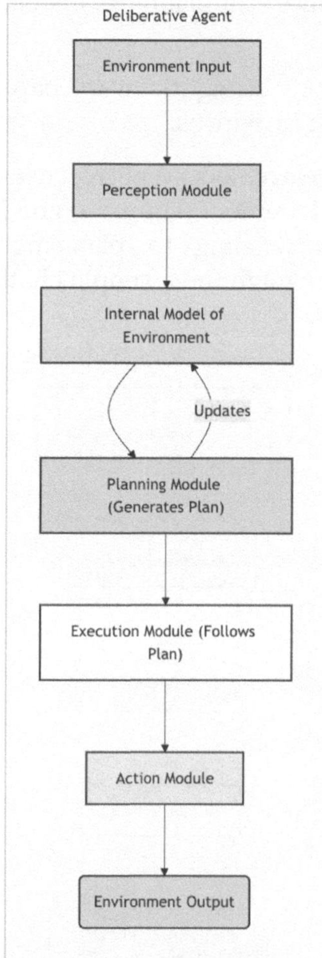

Figure 6.3: *Deliberate Agent*

- **Hybrid Agents:** Most practical and robust AI agents in real-world applications today adopt a hybrid approach. These agents combine the quick responsiveness of reactive components with the foresight and planning capabilities of deliberative components.
    - **Best of both worlds:** They can react quickly to immediate changes or emergencies, while still pursuing long-term goals through planning.

- **Most practical for real applications:** Imagine a self-driving car (a complex agent). It needs to react instantaneously to sudden obstacles (reactive), but it also needs to plan its route from point A to point B, considering traffic, speed limits, and fuel efficiency (deliberative). This blend allows for both efficiency and adaptability, making hybrid agents the go-to choice for complex, dynamic environments where both quick reflexes and strategic thinking are crucial.

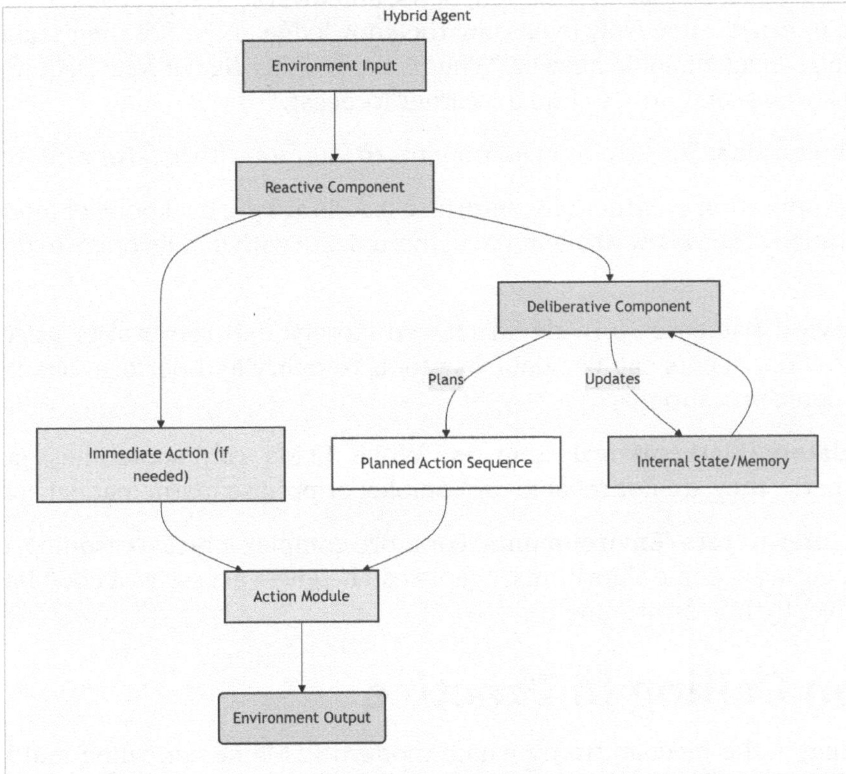

Figure 6.4: *Hybrid Agent*

Tool Use and Function Calling

Tool Use and Function Calling are fundamental concepts through which the capabilities of AI agents are accomplished. So, let us explore them in more detail.

Understanding Tool Use

As stated, Tool Use is the ability of an AI agent to leverage external systems and services to accomplish tasks that are beyond its inherent capabilities. Think of an AI agent as a highly intelligent individual who, instead of knowing everything or being able to do everything, knows how to use the right tools to get the job done. This paradigm shifts the focus from building monolithic AI models that are masters of all trades to creating agile agents that can integrate with and orchestrate a diverse ecosystem of specialized functionalities.

Common Tools for Agents

- **Web Search:** This is perhaps one of the most impactful tools. It allows agents to access current events, factual information, news, and diverse perspectives from the vastness of the internet, effectively bypassing the knowledge cut-off of their training data. For example, an agent could answer "*What is the weather like in New Delhi tomorrow?*" by using a web search tool to find a weather forecast.
- **File Operations:** These tools enable agents to interact with local or remote file systems.
- **APIs** (Application Programming Interfaces)**:** APIs are the backbone of modern software integration. They allow AI agents to communicate with and leverage external software services.
- **Databases:** Databases provide structured storage and retrieval of large amounts of information. Agents can use database tools to query and perform `upsert` operations (with some precautions).
- **Calculators/Mathematical Engines:** While LLMs can sometimes perform basic arithmetic, they are not reliable for complex or precise mathematical computations.
- **Code Interpreters/Environments:** For more complex logical reasoning, data analysis, or executing specific algorithms, agents can be given access to a code interpreter (for example, Python environment).

Function Calling in Practice

Function Calling is the mechanism by which modern LLMs decide when and how to use a tool. It is the "*brain*" that orchestrates tool use. Instead of just generating text, these LLMs are trained to identify when a user's prompt requires the use of an external function (a tool), and to then generate a structured output (often JSON) that specifies:

- **Which function to call:** The name of the tool/function that is most appropriate for the current task.
- **What arguments to provide:** The necessary inputs or parameters that the tool requires to execute successfully.

The Workflow of Function Calling

The function calling workflow can be visualized as a simple flowchart:

User Prompt -> LLM Analysis -> Function Call Generation -> Tool Execution -> Final Response

This visual representation breaks down the process into clear, sequential steps that make the concept easier to understand and implement.

1. **User Prompt:** The user provides a query or instruction to the AI agent.
2. **LLM Analysis:** The LLM analyzes the prompt and determines if any of the available tools (functions) can help fulfill the request.
3. **Function Call Generation:** If a tool is deemed necessary, the LLM generates a "*function call*" - typically a structured object (like JSON) containing the function's name and its required arguments. The LLM does not execute the function itself; it just suggests the call.
    - **Example:** If the user asks, "Give me latest news", the LLM might generate a function call like `{"function_name": "web_search", "arguments": {"query": "latest news"}}`.
4. **Tool Execution:** An external orchestrator or application receives this function call, executes the specified tool with the provided arguments.
5. **Tool Output:** The tool performs its task, and returns the result (for example, the population of Tokyo from a web search).
6. **LLM Re-prompt/Response Generation:** The tool's output is then fed back to the LLM as additional context. The LLM then uses this new information, along with the original prompt, to generate a comprehensive and accurate final response to the user.

Benefits of Function Calling

- **Increased Reliability:** By explicitly calling functions with structured arguments, the likelihood of errors or misinterpretations is reduced compared to an LLM trying to infer and perform complex actions directly.
- **Enhanced Control and Safety:** Developers have precise control over which functions an LLM can call and under what conditions. This allows for implementing safety checks and permissions around tool usage.
- **Smarter Agents:** Agents become "smarter" because they can proactively identify when they need external help and how to request it, rather than just relying on their internal knowledge.
- **Reduced Hallucinations:** By grounding responses in real-time data retrieved via tools, the problem of LLM "hallucinations" (generating factually incorrect but plausible-sounding information) is significantly mitigated.
- **Complex Task Execution:** Function calling enables agents to break down complex, multi-step problems into smaller, manageable sub-tasks, each handled by an appropriate tool. For instance, planning a trip might involve calling a flight search

tool, then a hotel booking tool, and then a weather forecast tool, all orchestrated by the LLM.

In essence, Tool Use provides the AI with capabilities, and Function Calling provides the intelligence to know when and how to use those capabilities effectively, leading to more powerful, versatile, and reliable AI agents.

Error Handling and Security

Robust error handling is crucial for production agents. Implement timeout mechanisms, retry logic with exponential backoff, graceful degradation when tools fail, and comprehensive logging. Security best practices include input validation, output sanitization, rate limiting, and sandboxing tool execution to prevent malicious code execution.

Example: Summarization Agent with Tools

```
def read_file(filename):
    """Read content from a file"""
    with open(filename, 'r') as f:
        return f.read()

def save_summary(summary, filename):
    """Save summary to a file"""
    with open(filename, 'w') as f:
        f.write(summary)

def count_words(text):
    """Count words in text"""
    return len(text.split())

class SmartSummarizationAgent:
    def __init__(self):
        self.tools = {
            "read_file": read_file,
            "save_summary": save_summary,
            "count_words": count_words
        }

    def use_tool(self, tool_name, *args):
        return self.tools[tool_name](*args)

    def run_agent(self, user_prompt):
        # e.g., user_prompt = "Read 'my_doc.txt', count the words,
        #                     and save a summary to 'summary.txt'."
        # 1. LLM Analysis: The LLM receives the prompt and available tools.

        #    The tools are 'read_file', 'save_summary', 'count_words'.
        llm_response = llm.invoke(prompt=user_prompt, tools=self.tools)
```

```
        # 2. Function Call Generation: The LLM's response is not text,
        #    but a structured request to call a tool.
```

Multi-Agent Systems and Coordination

Tool Use and Function Calling are foundational for individual AI agents, but when you bring multiple specialized agents together, you enter the realm of Multi-Agent Systems (MAS). MAS involves individual agents working together, often cooperatively, to solve complex problems or achieve shared goals that would be difficult or impossible for a single agent to accomplish alone.

Example: Multi-Agent Summarization System

```
class DocumentAnalyzer:
    def analyze_document(self, text):
        return {
            "type": "research_paper",
            "complexity": "high",
            "sections": ["abstract", "introduction", "methods", "results"]
        }

class SummaryGenerator:
    def generate_summary(self, text, analysis):
        # Generate summary based on document analysis
        return f"Summary of {analysis['type']}: {text[:100]}..."

class QualityChecker:
    def check_quality(self, summary, original_text):
        # Check if summary meets quality standards
        return len(summary) > 50 and len(summary) < len(original_text) * 0.3

class ManagerAgent:
    def __init__(self):
        self.analyzer = DocumentAnalyzer()
        self.generator = SummaryGenerator()
        self.checker = QualityChecker()

    def create_summary(self, document):
        # 1. Manager delegates the first task to the Analyzer agent.
        print("Manager: Analyzer, please analyze this document.")
        analysis = self.analyzer.analyze_document(document)

        # 2. Manager receives the result and delegates the next task.
        print("Manager: Generator, use this analysis to summarize the doc.")
        summary = self.generator.generate_summary(document, analysis)
```

```
# 3. Manager delegates the final quality check.
      print("Manager: Checker, is this summary good enough?")
is_good = self.checker.check_quality(summary, document)
      if is_good:
print("Manager: The summary is complete and approved.")
return summary
else:
print("Manager: Quality check failed. Aborting.")
return "Could not generate a high-quality summary."
```

Coordination Strategies

For a multi-agent system to function effectively, its individual agents cannot simply operate in isolation; they must coordinate their efforts. Coordination strategies define the rules and mechanisms by which agents communicate, share information, resolve conflicts, and synchronize their actions towards common goals. The choice of strategy heavily depends on the nature of the problem, the agents' capabilities, and the desired system properties (for example, efficiency, robustness, autonomy, and so on).

Strategy	Description	Pros	Cons
Centralized	A single "**master**" agent manages and directs all other agents.	Simple design, easier global optimization, efficient resource allocation.	Single point of failure, potential bottleneck, less flexible/scalable.
Distributed	Agents communicate directly, making local decisions; global behavior emerges.	High resilience, excellent scalability, increased agent autonomy.	More complex to design, potential for suboptimal local decisions.
Market-based	Agents "**bid**" for tasks/resources based on capabilities and costs (like an economy).	Flexible, adaptive, encourages efficiency, robust to agent failures.	Can be computationally intensive, requires careful rule design, potential for "**gaming**."
Hierarchical	Agents organized in levels; higher levels delegate to lower levels.	Balances control & autonomy, efficient for complex, decomposable problems.	Bottlenecks at higher levels possible, less flexible, complex to set up.

Table 6.1: *Comparison of Coordination Strategies*

In conclusion, Multi-Agent Systems represent a powerful paradigm for building sophisticated AI solutions. By leveraging the combined strengths of specialized, communicating agents, these systems can tackle challenges of scale, complexity, and dynamism that are beyond the reach of individual AIs, paving the way for truly intelligent and adaptable autonomous systems.

The effectiveness of such systems hinges critically on the chosen coordination strategies, which dictate how individual intelligences coalesce into collective intelligence.

Agent Memory and State Management

Just like humans, AI agents need memory to operate effectively in dynamic environments, and engage in meaningful, ongoing interactions. In fact, Memory is not just about recall; it is the bedrock for an agent's ability to learn, adapt, and behave consistently over time. Without the ability to remember, learn, and maintain context, an AI would be limited to processing each interaction in isolation, making it rigid and inefficient. Memory and state management helps AI agent to:

- **Remember Previous Interactions:** Memory allows an agent to recall what was said or done earlier in a conversation or sequence of tasks. This is crucial for coherent dialogue, where an agent can build upon past turns, acknowledge previous statements, or reference earlier decisions. Without this, every new input would be treated as a fresh start, leading to repetitive questions and disjointed interactions.
- **Learn from Experience:** A core aspect of intelligence is the ability to improve over time. Memory provides the data for this learning. By storing the outcomes of its actions, both successful and unsuccessful, an agent can refine its strategies, adjust its understanding, and make better decisions in similar future scenarios. This forms the basis for reinforcement learning and continuous improvement.
- **Maintain Context across Conversations:** For more complex, multi-turn interactions or even across different sessions, memory ensures the agent retains the overarching context. This means it understands the user's overarching goal, the current topic, or the state of a long-running process, even if there are digressions or pauses. Losing context would force the user to repeatedly re-explain themselves, leading to frustration.
- **Store Important Information for Future Use:** Beyond immediate conversational context, agents often need to store more enduring information. This could include user preferences, and factual data learned during research, plans, or internal states. This persistent storage ensures that valuable information is not lost, and can be retrieved precisely when needed for future tasks or interactions, enhancing the agent's utility and efficiency over time.

Types of Agent Memory

AI agents can be equipped with various types of memory, each serving a distinct purpose, much like the different memory systems in the human brain.

Memory Type	Description	Analogy	Key Characteristics and Purpose
Short-term Memory	Holds information for the current, immediate interaction or task.	Holding a phone number in mind just long enough to dial it.	Volatile, limited capacity, crucial for immediate next steps in a conversation or task.
Long-term Memory	Provides persistent storage for information across multiple sessions.	General knowledge and life experiences stored over years.	Durable, cumulative knowledge base, enables recall over extended periods.
Working Memory	Active, temporary storage where the agent actively processes information.	A mental scratchpad used while actively solving a problem.	Dynamic, used for active reasoning and decision-making, where "thinking" happens.
Episodic Memory	Stores specific experiences, events, and their unique context.	Recalling a specific birthday party or a past conversation.	About "*what happened where and when*," stores unique occurrences and interaction histories.
Semantic Memory	Stores general knowledge, facts, concepts, and relationships about the world.	Knowing "*Paris is the capital of France*" or "*birds have wings*."	About "*what things mean*" and "*how things relate*," independent of personal experience.

Table 6.2*: Agent Memory Types*

State Management Strategies

"*State management*" refers to how an AI agent handles and preserves its internal memory and contextual information across different interactions or over time. The chosen strategy significantly impacts an agent's capabilities, complexity, and resource requirements.

Strategy	Description	Analogy	Pros	Cons
Stateless	Agent processes each interaction independently, retaining no memory of past ones.	A vending machine; it doesn't remember your last purchase.	Simple, highly scalable (each request is isolated).	No context, requires user to re-explain, unsuitable for conversations.
Session-based	Memory persists only for the duration of a single continuous interaction or session.	A phone call; context exists within the call, then is lost.	Maintains coherent context within one interaction, relatively simple.	Context lost if session breaks, no long-term learning across sessions.

Strategy	Description	Analogy	Pros	Cons
Persistent	Memory survives across multiple sessions, tasks, and even agent reboots.	A personal assistant remembering your preferences over months.	Enables personalization, long-term learning, cumulative knowledge.	Requires robust storage, more complex management, potential privacy issues.
Distributed	Memory is shared and managed across multiple agents in a system.	A shared knowledge base accessible by an entire team.	Enables collaboration, leverages collective knowledge, enhances resilience.	Complex synchronization, potential conflicts, requires strong communication.

***Table 6.3**: Comparison of State Management Strategies*

The sophisticated interplay between these various memory types and state management strategies is what empowers AI agents to move beyond simple automation and into the realm of truly intelligent, adaptive, and context-aware systems, laying the groundwork for more advanced and human-like interactions.

Example: Summarization Agent with Memory

```
class MemoryManager:
      def __init__(self):
            self.short_term = {}
            self.long_term = self.load_long_term_memory()

      def remember(self, key, value, memory_type="short"):
            if memory_type == "short":
                        self.short_term[key] = value
            else:
                        self.long_term[key] = value
                        self.save_long_term_memory()

      def recall(self, key, memory_type="short"):
            if memory_type == "short":
                        return self.short_term.get(key)
            else:
                        return self.long_term.get(key)

      def load_long_term_memory(self):
                  with open('agent_memory.json', 'r') as f:
                        return json.load(f)

      def save_long_term_memory(self):
```

```
            with open('agent_memory.json', 'w') as f:
                        json.dump(self.long_term, f)

class SmartSummarizationAgent:
      def __init__(self):
            self.memory = MemoryManager()
            self.preferences = {}

      def summarize_with_memory(self, document, user_id):
            # Check if we've summarized for this user before
            user_prefs = self.memory.recall(f"user_{user_id}_preferences",
      "long")

            if user_prefs:
                        # Use learned preferences
                        summary_length = user_prefs.get("preferred_length",
            "medium")
            else:
                        # Default settings
                        summary_length = "medium"

            # Generate summary
            summary = self.generate_summary(document, summary_length)

            # Remember this interaction
            self.memory.remember(f"last_summary_{user_id}", {
                  "document_length": len(document),
                  "summary_length": len(summary),
                  "timestamp": datetime.now().isoformat()
            }, "long")

            return summary

      def learn_user_preferences(self, user_id, feedback):
            # Learn from user feedback
            current_prefs = self.memory.recall(f"user_{user_id}_preferences",
      "long") or {}

            if feedback == "too_long":
                        current_prefs["preferred_length"] = "short"
            elif feedback == "too_short":
                        current_prefs["preferred_length"] = "long"

            self.memory.remember(f"user_{user_id}_preferences", current_
      prefs, "long")
```

Agent Monitoring and Observability

Effective monitoring is crucial for production-ready AI agents. This section covers agent-specific monitoring strategies and tools. For comprehensive monitoring methodologies, evaluation frameworks, and detailed implementation guidance applicable to all LLM systems, please refer to *Chapter 8, Model Monitoring and Evaluation.*

Performance Monitoring

The key performance metrics to monitor include:

- **Latency Metrics:** Response time, end-to-end latency, tool execution time, and LLM inference time. Track P50, P95, and P99 percentiles to understand performance distribution.
- **Throughput Metrics:** Requests per second, concurrent users, and system capacity utilization. Monitor for bottlenecks and scaling needs.
- **Error Rates:** Tool failures, LLM errors, timeout rates, and user-facing errors. Implement alerting for error rate spikes.

Quality Metrics

- **Hallucination Rate:** The percentage of responses that contain factually incorrect or unsupported information. This is vital given the reliance on real-time data via tools to mitigate this issue.
- **Context Utilization Rate:** The measure of how often the agent successfully uses retrieved information (for example, from RAG, Memory, or a tool output) to inform and correctly ground the final generated response.

Behavioral Monitoring

Monitor agent decision-making patterns, tool usage frequency, conversation flow analysis, and drift detection in agent behavior. This is vital because agents can develop unexpected or suboptimal behaviors as they interact with real-world data, or when underlying LLMs are updated. Tools like LangSmith for LangChain agents, custom monitoring solutions, and observability platforms provide real-time insights into agent behavior and performance.

Agent Safety and Security

Production agents require comprehensive safety and security measures to ensure reliable, ethical, and secure deployment.

- **Safety Mechanisms:** Implement robust safety mechanisms including input validation and sanitization, output filtering and content moderation, rate limiting and abuse prevention, and fallback mechanisms for edge cases. Input validation and sanitization is the first line of defense against prompt injection attacks, where a user might try to trick the agent into executing unintended commands. These measures protect against prompt injection, harmful outputs, and system abuse.

- **Security Considerations:** Security considerations encompass authentication and authorization, data privacy and protection, secure tool integration, and vulnerability assessment. Implement proper access controls, encrypt sensitive data, and regularly audit security measures.
- **Ethical AI Practices:** Ethical AI practices involve bias detection and mitigation, fairness in agent decision-making, transparency and explainability, and human oversight as well as intervention points. Thus, ensure that agents make fair, unbiased decisions and provide explanations for their actions.
- **Context Filtering/Data Leak Prevention:** The core Principle is simple yet paramount: No confidential data for unauthorized users. This is achieved through Implementation that enforces real-time, granular access control to sensitive data, based on the user's role or identity, often referred to as Context-Based Access Control (C-BAC). The Mechanism involves an intermediary layer that detects and either masks, filters out, or applies encryption to Personally Identifiable Information (PII), confidential business data, or other sensitive information from the context, before it is ever passed to the Large Language Model (LLM). The Goal of this robust security measure is to prevent unauthorized data leaks by ensuring that all context materials used during the agent's reasoning, retrieval, and generation steps are appropriately secured.

Production Deployment Strategies

Deploying agents in production requires scalable infrastructure, high availability setup, load balancing, and container orchestration. Deployment patterns include blue-green deployments, canary releases, A/B testing for agent behavior, and rollback strategies. Operational excellence involves CI/CD pipelines, configuration management, secrets management, and disaster recovery planning.

Agent Lifecycle Management

Managing agent lifecycles involves testing strategies, staging environments, performance benchmarking, and quality assurance processes. Maintenance includes model versioning, gradual rollout mechanisms, performance regression detection, and continuous improvement processes to ensure that agents evolve effectively over time.

Conclusion

Building production-ready AI agents requires a comprehensive approach that extends far beyond the core concepts of autonomous behavior and multi-agent coordination. The journey from conceptual design to real-world deployment demands rigorous attention to monitoring and observability, ensuring that agents perform as expected and can be debugged when issues arise. Equally critical are robust safety and security measures that protect both the system and its users from potential risks and vulnerabilities. The deployment of AI agents in production environments requires careful consideration of infrastructure, scalability, and operational excellence, while effective lifecycle management ensures that agents can evolve and improve over time. These interconnected considerations-monitoring, safety, deployment, and lifecycle management-form the essential foundation for reliable, ethical, and secure AI agent systems that can truly deliver value in our increasingly AI-driven world.

Thus, by mastering these principles, developers and architects can build the next generation of intelligent, reliable, and truly autonomous AI systems. Having designed intelligent agents, the next logical step is making them accessible to users, which requires a robust deployment strategy as we will explore in the next chapter.

References

1. https://aws.amazon.com/blogs/aws-insights/the-rise-of-autonomous-agents-what-enterprise-leaders-need-to-know-about-the-next-wave-of-ai/
2. https://www.ibm.com/think/topics/ai-agents
3. https://www.gocodeo.com/post/top-10-ai-agent-frameworks
4. https://cloud.google.com/discover/what-are-ai-agents
5. https://superagi.com/autonomous-ai-agents-101-a-beginners-guide-to-getting-started-in-2025/
6. https://www.ibm.com/think/topics/multiagent-system
7. https://www.ibm.com/think/topics/ai-agent-memory
8. https://www.xcubelabs.com/blog/how-to-build-an-ai-agent-a-step%E2%80%91by%E2%80%91step-guide/
9. https://www.youtube.com/watch?v=W4Zr_9XyonU

CHAPTER 7
Deploying Large Language Models

Introduction

Following our deep dive into building intelligent AI Agents (in the previous chapter), the next critical step in the LLMOps lifecycle is making these systems accessible to users. This chapter provides a comprehensive guide to the deployment of LLMs, covering the various methods and best practices for serving models effectively. From the system's perspective, one has to consider deployment of all components in the LLM ecosystem like the LLM model itself, and also RAG components such as data pipeline, indexes and so on. In this chapter, we will particularly focus on deployment of LLM with an additional section on deploying RAG systems.

Structure

In this chapter, we will discuss the following topics:

- Approaches for LLM Deployment
- Serving Methods for LLM
- Monitoring and Maintenance of Deployed LLMs
- Security and Privacy Considerations in LLM Deployment
- Deploying RAG for LLMs

Approaches for LLM Deployment

LLM deployment involves making a trained language model available for use, either through an API or a web interface. This allows users or other systems to interact with the model, and obtain predictions or generate text. LLMs can be either deployed on cloud or can be self-hosted. So, let us consider these approaches in detail.

Cloud-Based Deployment

Cloud-based deployment involves using services provided by cloud providers like Google Cloud, AWS, and Azure to host and manage the LLM. These platforms offer managed services, pre-built tools, and infrastructure to simplify deployment and handle complexities.

Example: Calling a Cloud-Hosted LLM (OpenAI API)

```
import openai

# Initialize client
client = openai.OpenAI(api_key="your-api-key")

# Make a request to deployed model
response = client.chat.completions.create(
    model="gpt-4",
    messages=[{"role": "user", "content": "Explain cloud deployment"}]
)
print(response.choices[0].message.content)
```

Advantages of Cloud-Based Deployment

- **Scalability:** Easily scale resources up or down based on demand.
- **Cost-Effectiveness:** Pay-as-you-go pricing models avoid upfront infrastructure investments.
- **Ease of Use:** Managed services handle infrastructure management and deployment complexities.
- **Faster Deployment:** Pre-built tools and APIs accelerate deployment time.
- **Integration:** Integrate with other cloud services for data management, monitoring, and much more.

Disadvantages of Cloud-Based Deployment

- **Vendor Lock-In:** Dependence on a specific cloud provider.
- **Security Concerns:** Potential risks associated with data stored and processed in the cloud.
- **Limited Customization:** Constraints on customizing infrastructure and configurations.
- **Cost at Scale:** Can become expensive for high-volume usage.

Self-Deployment

Self-deployment involves hosting and managing the LLM on your own infrastructure, either on-premise or in a private cloud. This gives you greater control but requires more technical expertise and resources.

Advantages of Self-Deployment

- **Control:** Full control over infrastructure, configurations, and security.
- **Customization:** Flexibility to tailor the deployment environment to specific needs.
- **Cost Savings at Scale:** Potentially lower costs for high-volume usage.
- **Data Privacy:** Enhanced control over data security and privacy.

Disadvantages of Self-Deployment

- **Higher Initial Costs:** Upfront investment in hardware and infrastructure.
- **Technical Expertise:** Requires significant DevOps and infrastructure management skills.
- **Maintenance:** Responsibility for ongoing maintenance, updates, and security.
- **Slower Deployment:** Manual setup and configuration can take longer.

Choosing the Right Option

The best deployment option depends on factors like:

- **Scale and workload:** Cloud platforms are suitable for variable workloads and rapid scaling, while self-deployment may be more cost-effective for consistent, high-volume usage.
- **Technical expertise:** Self-deployment requires significant technical skills, while cloud platforms are more user-friendly.
- **Security and privacy:** Self-deployment offers greater control over data security, while cloud platforms often have robust security measures in place.
- **Cost:** Evaluate the costs associated with each option, considering infrastructure, maintenance, and usage fees.

The following is a quick comparison of popular cloud platforms for deploying LLMs:

Feature	Google Cloud AI Platform	Amazon SageMaker	Microsoft Azure Machine Learning
Pre-trained Models	Gemini, PaLM 2, other open-source models	Titan, Llama 2, Claude, other open-source models	GPT-3.5, GPT-4, Codex, other open-source models
Model Training	Vertex AI, custom training options	SageMaker training jobs, distributed training	Azure ML Studio, automated ML, hyperparameter tuning
Inference Optimization	Model optimization tools, serverless deployment	SageMaker inference endpoints, model monitoring	Azure ML deployment, model scaling, batch inference
Scalability	Auto-scaling, serverless options	Elastic inference, managed endpoints	Autoscaling, Kubernetes integration
Pricing	Pay-as-you-go, various pricing tiers	Pay-as-you-go, instance-based pricing	Pay-as-you-go, resource consumption-based pricing
Ease of Use	User-friendly interface, pre-built workflows	Comprehensive documentation, wide range of tools	Integrated development environment, drag-and-drop functionalities
Supported Frameworks	TensorFlow, PyTorch, scikit-learn	TensorFlow, PyTorch, MXNet	TensorFlow, PyTorch, scikit-learn
Security Features	Data encryption, access control, VPC Service Controls	Security policies, encryption, VPC integration	Role-based access control, encryption, network security
Strengths	Strong focus on AI and ML, wide range of pre-trained models	Comprehensive ecosystem, mature platform	Integration with Microsoft products, user-friendly tools
Weaknesses	Can be complex for beginners, pricing can be unpredictable	Can be overwhelming for beginners, complex pricing structure	Historically fewer first-party models than competitors, though rapidly expanding via 'Models as a Service' (MaaS) to include Llama 3, Mistral, and Cohere alongside its exclusive OpenAI partnership.

Table 7.1: *Platform Comparison for Deploying LLMs on Popular Cloud*

Essentially, Google Cloud AI Platform, Amazon SageMaker, and Microsoft Azure Machine Learning are popular choices with varying strengths. Google offers strong AI/ML focus and diverse pre-trained models, while Amazon provides a mature ecosystem with comprehensive tools. Microsoft provides deep integration with its enterprise ecosystem and a premier, exclusive partnership with OpenAI; while it previously trailed in model variety, its new 'Models as a Service' offering now provides streamlined access to a broad range of leading open-source and proprietary models. Ultimately, the best platform depends on your specific needs for models, training, scalability, cost, ease of use, and security.

Workflow for Cloud-Based Deployment

The general deployment workflow for deploying LLMs on cloud platforms:

1. **Model Preparation**
    a. **Choose a Pre-Trained Model:** Select a pre-trained LLM or fine-tune an existing one to suit your specific task.
    b. **Optimize the Model:** Apply techniques such as quantization or pruning to reduce the model's size and improve inference speed.
    c. **Package the Model:** Prepare the model for deployment by saving it in a format compatible with the chosen cloud platform.
2. **Infrastructure Setup**
    a. **Create a Project:** Set up a project on the cloud platform to manage your resources.
    b. **Provision Resources:** Allocate compute instances, storage, and networking resources based on your model's requirements.
    c. **Configure Environment:** Set up the necessary software dependencies and environment variables for your model.
3. **Deployment Configuration**
    a. **Choose a Deployment Method:** Select a deployment option like serverless functions, containers, or virtual machines.
    b. **Configure Inference Endpoint:** Define the endpoint for accessing your deployed model.
    c. **Set Scaling Options:** Configure auto-scaling to handle variations in request volume.
4. **Deployment Execution**
    a. **Deploy the Model:** Upload your model package and deploy it to the configured infrastructure.
    b. **Test the Endpoint:** Verify that the deployed model is accessible and functioning correctly.
    c. **Monitor Performance:** Set up monitoring to track metrics such as latency, throughput, and error rates.

5. **Ongoing Management**
    a. **Update the Model:** Regularly update the deployed model with newer versions or fine-tuned variations.
    b. **Scale Resources:** Adjust resource allocation based on usage patterns and performance requirements.
    c. **Monitor and Maintain:** Continuously monitor the deployed model's performance and address any issues that arise.

Variations by Cloud Platform

While the general workflow is similar across cloud platforms, specific steps and tools may vary. Refer to the documentation of your chosen platform for detailed instructions and platform-specific considerations.

Workflow for Self-Hosted Deployment

The deployment workflow for self-hosting an LLM:

1. **Hardware and Software Setup**
    a. **Hardware Selection:** Choose appropriate hardware based on the LLM's size and computational demands, such as GPUs with sufficient memory.
    b. **Operating System:** Install a suitable operating system like Linux with the necessary drivers and libraries.
    c. **Software Dependencies:** Install the required software, including Python, CUDA, and deep learning frameworks like TensorFlow or PyTorch.
    d. **LLM Framework:** Choose and install an LLM serving framework, such as TensorFlow Serving, TorchServe, or Triton Inference Server.
2. **Model Preparation**
    a. **Model Conversion:** Convert the trained LLM model to a format compatible with the chosen serving framework.
    b. **Model Optimization:** Apply techniques such as quantization or pruning to reduce the model's size and improve inference speed.
    c. **Model Packaging:** Package the model and its dependencies into a deployable format, such as a Docker image.
3. **Infrastructure Configuration**
    a. **Networking:** Configure network settings to allow access to the deployed LLM.
    b. **Storage:** Set up storage to store the model files and any required data.
    c. **Security:** Implement security measures to protect the LLM and its infrastructure.

4. **Deployment Execution**
    a. **Deploy the Model:** Deploy the packaged model to the self-hosted infrastructure using the chosen serving framework.
    b. **Configure API:** Set up an API endpoint for accessing the deployed LLM.
    c. **Test and Verify:** Thoroughly test the deployed LLM to ensure it is functioning correctly.
5. **Monitoring and Maintenance**
    a. **Monitoring:** Implement monitoring tools to track performance metrics like latency, throughput, and resource utilization.
    b. **Scaling:** Configure scaling mechanisms to handle variations in workload.
    c. **Updates:** Regularly update the deployed LLM with newer versions or fine-tuned variations.
    d. **Security:** Continuously monitor and address any security vulnerabilities.

Considerations for Self-Hosting

- **Technical Expertise:** Self-hosting requires significant technical expertise in system administration, DevOps, and deep learning frameworks.
- **Infrastructure Management:** You are responsible for managing the underlying infrastructure, including hardware, software, and security.
- **Cost:** While potentially cost-effective at scale, self-hosting involves upfront hardware and ongoing maintenance costs.
- **Flexibility:** Offers greater control and customization compared to cloud-based solutions.

Serving Methods for LLM

In the last section, we talked about various approaches that can be used to deploy the LLM model. In this section, we will take a look at various tools and frameworks for the same.

Serving Frameworks

Serving frameworks play a crucial role in deploying and managing LLMs in production. They handle tasks such as:

- **Model Serving:** Loading and running the model efficiently for inference.
- **Request Management:** Handling incoming requests, queuing, and routing them to the model.

- **Resource Management:** Optimizing resource allocation (CPU, memory, GPU) for performance and cost-efficiency.
- **Scaling and Load Balancing:** Ensuring that the system can handle varying workloads, and maintain responsiveness.
- **Monitoring and Logging:** Tracking performance metrics, errors, and other relevant data.

Let us explore this in more detail using some popular frameworks:

Triton Inference Server

Triton Inference Server, developed by NVIDIA, is a leading choice for deploying and serving Large Language Models (LLMs) in production environments. It offers a robust and scalable solution to handle the demanding requirements of LLMs.

Key Features for LLM Serving

- **Optimized for LLMs:** Triton has been optimized for serving LLMs, including models like GPT-3, BERT, and T5. It provides features such as dynamic batching and model pipelining, which are crucial for efficient LLM inference.
- **Multi-Framework and Multi-GPU Support:** Triton supports LLMs from various frameworks, including TensorFlow, PyTorch, and ONNX Runtime. It also enables running LLMs across multiple GPUs for enhanced performance and scalability.
- **Dynamic Batching and Scheduling:** Triton's dynamic batching capabilities automatically group incoming requests to maximize GPU utilization and reduce latency. Its advanced scheduling algorithms ensure efficient model execution and resource allocation.
- **Model Pipelining for Complex Workflows:** LLMs often involve complex workflows, such as text preprocessing, tokenization, and generation. Triton's model pipelining feature allows you to chain multiple models together, enabling efficient execution of these workflows.
- **Custom Backends and Operations:** Triton provides flexibility to integrate custom backends and pre/post-processing operations specific to LLM serving. This allows for tasks like text normalization, sentiment analysis, or custom tokenization.
- **Scalability and High Availability:** Triton can be deployed on a cluster of servers and scaled horizontally to handle increasing LLM traffic. It supports features such as model replication and load balancing to ensure high availability and fault tolerance.
- **Monitoring and Management:** Triton offers comprehensive monitoring capabilities, allowing you to track LLM performance, resource utilization, and latency. It provides insights to optimize deployment, and ensure smooth operation.

Benefits for LLM Serving

- **Reduced Latency and Increased Throughput:** Triton's optimization for LLMs and dynamic batching significantly reduce inference latency and increase throughput, enabling real-time applications.
- **Simplified Deployment and Management:** It provides a streamlined process for deploying and managing LLMs, simplifying operational tasks and reducing overhead.
- **Cost-Effectiveness:** Triton's efficient resource utilization and scalability help minimize infrastructure costs, making LLMs serving more affordable.
- **Flexibility and Extensibility:** Its multi-framework support, custom backends, and model pipelining enable flexibility in deploying various LLMs and complex workflows.

Triton Inference Server is a powerful solution for deploying and serving LLMs in production environments. Its features and optimizations address the specific requirements of LLMs, enabling organizations to build and deploy AI-powered applications with efficiency and scalability.

TorchServe

TorchServe, developed by PyTorch, is a model serving framework designed to simplify the deployment and management of PyTorch models, including LLMs, in production environments.

Key Features and Capabilities for LLM Serving

- **Built for PyTorch:** TorchServe is specifically designed for serving PyTorch models, making it a natural choice for deploying LLMs trained using PyTorch. It seamlessly integrates with the PyTorch ecosystem, and provides optimized performance for PyTorch models.
- **Model Archiving and Versioning:** TorchServe supports model archiving and versioning, allowing you to deploy multiple versions of the same LLM and easily switch between them. This facilitates A/B testing, model updates, and rollbacks.
- **Custom Handlers for LLMs:** You can create custom handlers in TorchServe to implement pre-processing, inference, and post-processing logic specific to your LLM. This allows you to handle tasks like text tokenization, input formatting, and response generation tailored to your LLM's requirements.
- **Batch Inference for LLMs:** TorchServe supports batch inference for LLMs, enabling efficient processing of multiple requests simultaneously. This significantly increases throughput and reduces latency, especially when handling a large volume of requests.

- **Scalability and Management:** TorchServe can be deployed on a cluster of servers and scaled horizontally to handle increasing LLM traffic. It provides APIs and tools for managing deployed models, monitoring performance, and scaling resources.
- **Metrics and Logging:** TorchServe exposes metrics for monitoring LLM performance, resource utilization, and latency. It also integrates with logging frameworks, enabling detailed tracking and analysis of inference operations.
- **REST API and gRPC:** TorchServe supports both REST API and gRPC interfaces for client communication, providing flexibility in how applications interact with your deployed LLMs.

Benefits for LLM Serving

- **Simplified Deployment:** TorchServe streamlines the deployment process for PyTorch LLMs, reducing operational overhead and making it easier to get your models into production.
- **Performance and Scalability:** Its optimized inference engine and batching capabilities deliver high performance and scalability for serving LLMs, enabling real-time applications.
- **Flexibility and Customization:** Custom handlers and pre/post-processing options provide flexibility to adapt TorchServe to your specific LLM and workflow requirements.
- **Management and Monitoring:** Built-in tools for model management, monitoring, and logging simplify operational tasks and provide insights into LLM performance.

TorchServe is a powerful and versatile framework for serving PyTorch-based LLMs in production environments. Its features and capabilities address the specific requirements of LLMs, enabling organizations to build and deploy AI-powered applications with efficiency and scalability.

Example: Creating a Custom TorchServe Handler

```
from ts.torch_handler.base_handler import BaseHandler

class LLMHandler(BaseHandler):
    def preprocess(self, data):
        # Tokenize input text
        text = data[0].get("data") or data[0].get("body")
        return self.tokenizer(text, return_tensors="pt")

    def inference(self, inputs):
        # Generate response
        outputs = self.model.generate(**inputs, max_length=100)
        return outputs
```

```
    def postprocess(self, outputs):
        # Decode tokens to text
        return [self.tokenizer.decode(out, skip_special_tokens=True)
                for out in outputs]
```

LangServe

LangServe is a library developed by LangChain that simplifies the process of deploying language models and chains as REST APIs. It offers a straightforward way to expose your language model-based applications for external access and integration with other systems.

Key Features and Benefits of LangServe

- **Easy Deployment:** LangServe streamlines the deployment of LangChain chains, agents, and runnables as REST APIs. It handles the underlying infrastructure and configuration, allowing developers to focus on building their language model logic.
- **FastAPI Integration:** LangServe leverages FastAPI, a modern and high-performance web framework for Python, to provide a robust and efficient API foundation. This ensures scalability and responsiveness for deployed language models.
- **Pydantic for Data Validation:** It utilizes Pydantic for data validation, ensuring that incoming requests conform to the expected schema. This helps to maintain data integrity, and prevent errors caused by invalid inputs.
- **Client Libraries:** LangServe provides client libraries for interacting with deployed APIs. This makes it easy to integrate language model functionalities into other applications or services.
- **JavaScript Client:** A JavaScript client is available, enabling seamless integration with web-based applications and front-end development workflows.
- **Simplified Development Workflow:** LangServe simplifies the development workflow by abstracting away the complexities of API deployment. Developers can focus on building language model logic and easily expose it as a REST API with minimal effort.
- **Enhanced Collaboration:** By providing a standardized way to deploy and access language models, LangServe promotes collaboration and sharing among developers. This fosters a community-driven ecosystem for building and deploying language model-based applications.

In essence, LangServe acts as a bridge between language models and external systems, enabling developers to easily deploy and access their language model-based functionalities through REST APIs. This facilitates the integration of language models into a wide range of applications and services.

Example: Deploying a LangChain App with LangServe

```
from fastapi import FastAPI
from langchain.llms import OpenAI
from langchain.prompts import PromptTemplate
from langserve import add_routes

app = FastAPI(title="LangServe Demo")

# Create a simple chain
llm = OpenAI()
prompt = PromptTemplate.from_template("Summarize: {text}")
chain = prompt | llm

# Add chain as API endpoint
add_routes(app, chain, path="/summarize")

# Run: uvicorn app:app --host 0.0.0.0 --port 8000
```

vLLM for LLM Serving

vLLM is an open-source LLM serving system designed for high throughput and low latency inference. It employs various optimizations to accelerate LLM serving, and make it more efficient for real-time applications.

Key Features and Capabilities of LLM Serving

- **`PagedAttention`:** vLLM implements **`PagedAttention`**, a novel attention algorithm that reduces the memory footprint of LLMs, allowing for serving larger models with limited resources. This optimization is particularly beneficial for deploying LLMs on devices with less memory capacity.
- **Continuous Batching:** vLLM utilizes continuous batching, a technique that dynamically groups incoming requests into batches for inference. This maximizes GPU utilization, and reduces latency by processing multiple requests concurrently.
- **Optimized GPU Kernels:** vLLM incorporates optimized GPU kernels for LLM operations, such as attention and matrix multiplication. These kernels accelerate computation and further enhance inference speed.
- **Model Parallelism:** For large LLMs, vLLM supports model parallelism, distributing the model across multiple GPUs. This enables serving larger models that would not fit on a single GPU, and further improves performance.
- ***Flexible Deployment:*** vLLM can be deployed on various platforms, including CPUs, GPUs, and cloud instances. It offers a simple and flexible deployment process, making it easy to integrate into the existing infrastructure.

- **Scalability and Throughput:** vLLM is designed for high throughput and scalability, enabling it to handle a large volume of requests with low latency. It can be scaled horizontally by adding more servers to meet the increasing demand.

Benefits of LLM Serving

- **Reduced Latency:** vLLM's optimizations, such as **`PagedAttention`** and continuous batching, significantly reduce inference latency, enabling real-time applications.
- **Increased Throughput:** Optimized GPU kernels and model parallelism enhance throughput, allowing vLLM to handle a higher volume of requests concurrently.
- **Memory Efficiency:** **`PagedAttention`** reduces the memory footprint of LLMs, enabling serving larger models on devices with limited resources.
- **Ease of Deployment:** vLLM offers a straightforward deployment process, simplifying integration into the existing infrastructure.
- **Open-Source and Extensible:** As an open-source project, vLLM allows for customization and extension to meet the specific requirements.

vLLM is a promising open-source LLM serving system that focuses on delivering high throughput and low latency inference. Its innovative optimizations and flexible deployment options make it a valuable tool for productionizing LLMs, especially in applications requiring real-time performance and efficient resource utilization.

Example: Using vLLM for Model Serving:

```
from vllm import LLM, SamplingParams

# Load model with vLLM
llm = LLM(model="meta-llama/Llama-2-7b-hf")

# Configure sampling parameters
sampling_params = SamplingParams(
    temperature=0.7,
    top_p=0.9,
    max_tokens=100
)

# Generate responses (supports batching automatically)
prompts = ["Explain vLLM benefits", "What is PagedAttention?"]
outputs = llm.generate(prompts, sampling_params)

for output in outputs:
    print(f"Generated: {output.outputs[0].text}")
```

OLLAMA

Ollama is an open-source tool for running Large Language Models (LLMs) locally. It simplifies the process of downloading, installing, and running LLMs on your own hardware, offering a user-friendly interface and a focus on privacy. Here is a breakdown of its key features:

Key Features and Benefits

- **Local Execution:** Ollama allows you to run LLMs on your own computer or server, keeping your data private and secure. This eliminates the need to rely on cloud-based services and share sensitive information.
- **Simplified Model Management:** It offers a straightforward way to download and manage various LLMs. With a single command (**`ollama pull`**), you can install models from a curated list or even from custom repositories.
- **User-Friendly Interface:** Ollama provides a command-line interface and a web interface for interacting with LLMs. You can easily start and stop models, monitor their resource usage, and stream responses.
- **Open Source and Extensible:** As an open-source project, Ollama encourages community contributions and customization. You can extend its functionality by creating custom model loaders or integrating it with other tools.
- **Privacy-Focused:** By running models locally, Ollama minimizes data exposure and ensures that your interactions with LLMs remain private. This is crucial for sensitive applications and research involving personal or confidential data.

Overall, Ollama provides a powerful and accessible way to run LLMs locally, enabling a wide range of applications, while prioritizing privacy and security.

Example: Using OLLAMA Locally

````
```bash
# Install and run a model
ollama pull llama2
ollama run llama2 "Explain local LLM deployment"
```

# Using OLLAMA API in Python
import requests

response = requests.post('http://localhost:11434/api/generate',
    json={
        "model": "llama2",
        "prompt": "Why use local LLMs?",
        "stream": False
````

```
    })
print(response.json()['response'])
```

Serving APIs

Once an LLM is selected, it must be exposed through a reliable interface to handle requests and deliver responses. This section examines the primary methods for serving models via APIs, comparing managed cloud endpoints with open-source and local alternatives.

Cloud Options

- **OpenAI API:** This provides access to OpenAI's powerful LLMs, such as GPT-3, Codex, and DALL-E. It offers a variety of endpoints for different tasks, including text completion, code generation, and image generation. Authentication is handled through API keys. To authenticate, you need to create an OpenAI account, and obtain an API key. Please see the OpenAI API documentation for more details on authentication and usage.
- **Vertex AI:** Offers a comprehensive suite of tools for deploying and managing LLMs. It supports various model types, including those from Google and other providers. You can also customize models using Vertex AI's training and tuning capabilities. To authenticate, you need to create a Google Cloud project, and enable the AI Platform API.

Example: Deploying LLM on AWS SageMaker

```
import boto3
from sagemaker.huggingface import HuggingFaceModel

# Initialize SageMaker session
sagemaker_session = boto3.Session().client('sagemaker')

# Define model configuration
huggingface_model = HuggingFaceModel(
    model_data="s3://your-bucket/model.tar.gz",
    role="arn:aws:iam::<ACCT_ID>:role/SageMakerRole",
    transformers_version="4.26",
    pytorch_version="1.13",
    py_version="py39",
)

# Deploy model to endpoint
predictor = huggingface_model.deploy(
    initial_instance_count=1,
    instance_type="ml.g5.xlarge",  # GPU instance
```

```
    endpoint_name="llm-endpoint"
)

# Make predictions
response = predictor.predict({
    "inputs": "Explain SageMaker deployment"
})
print(response)
```

- **Amazon SageMaker:** It provides a managed service for deploying and scaling LLMs. It integrates with other AWS services, such as S3 and CloudWatch, for data storage and monitoring. Authentication is handled through AWS IAM roles and credentials.
- **Microsoft Azure Machine Learning:** Offers a cloud-based platform for deploying and managing LLMs. It supports a variety of frameworks and tools, including TensorFlow and PyTorch. You can authenticate using Azure Active Directory or service principals.

Open-Source Options

- **Ollama:** This allows you to serve LLMs locally or on your own infrastructure. It provides a simple API for interacting with models, and supports various model formats. No authentication is required for local serving, but you may need to configure access control for remote deployments.
- **Hugging Face Inference Endpoints:** This enables you to deploy LLMs from the Hugging Face Model Hub with a few clicks. It offers a scalable and reliable infrastructure for serving models, and you can authenticate using API tokens.
- **Replicate:** It provides a platform for deploying and sharing LLMs. It supports various model formats, and offers a simple API for interacting with models. Authentication is handled through API tokens.

Performance Tuning for LLM Serving

Performance tuning for LLM serving focuses on optimizing the speed, efficiency, and resource utilization of deployed language models. Here are some key aspects and tools used for the same:

Hardware Optimization

Utilizing specialized hardware like GPUs or TPUs can significantly accelerate inference speed. Techniques such as quantization can further enhance performance by reducing model size and memory footprint.

- **NVIDIA TensorRT:** A high-performance inference optimizer and runtime that delivers low latency and high throughput for deep learning inference applications.

- **Intel OpenVINO:** A toolkit for optimizing and deploying AI inference across Intel hardware, including CPUs, GPUs, and VPUs.
- **XLA (Accelerated Linear Algebra):** A compiler for linear algebra that can accelerate TensorFlow models on various hardware backends.

Model Optimization

Techniques such as knowledge distillation (training a smaller `'student'` model to mimic a larger `'teacher'` model) and pruning (removing redundant model weights) can create smaller, faster models, without significant performance loss.

- **OpenVINO Model Optimizer:** This converts models from various frameworks into an optimized intermediate representation for deployment with OpenVINO.
- **TensorFlow Lite:** A lightweight version of TensorFlow designed for mobile and embedded devices. It supports model quantization and pruning for performance optimization.
- **ONNX (Open Neural Network Exchange):** An open format for representing machine learning models, allowing for interoperability between different frameworks and tools.
- **DistilBERT, TinyBERT:** Examples of pre-trained distilled models that offer reduced size and faster inference compared to their larger counterparts.

Caching

Caching frequently used inputs and outputs can reduce latency by avoiding redundant computations. This is particularly effective for repetitive queries or tasks.

- **Redis:** An in-memory data store that can be used as a cache for frequently accessed data, including LLM inputs and outputs.
- **Memcached:** Another popular in-memory caching system that can be used to accelerate LLM serving.
- **FAISS (Facebook AI Similarity Search):** A library for efficient similarity search and clustering of vectors, which can be used for caching embeddings.

Example: Implementing Caching for LLM Responses

```
import redis
import hashlib
import json

# Connect to Redis
cache = redis.Redis(host='localhost', port=6379, decode_responses=True)
```

```
def get_llm_response(prompt, llm_function):
    # Create cache key from prompt
    cache_key = hashlib.md5(prompt.encode()).hexdigest()

    # Check cache first
    cached = cache.get(cache_key)
    if cached:
        return json.loads(cached)

    # Generate response if not cached
    response = llm_function(prompt)

    # Store in cache with 1 hour expiry
    cache.setex(cache_key, 3600, json.dumps(response))
    return response
```

Batching

Processing multiple requests simultaneously can improve throughput by reducing overhead. However, it is crucial to balance batch size with latency requirements.

- **Triton Inference Server:** An open-source inference serving software that supports batching and dynamic batching for optimized throughput.
- **TorchServe:** A PyTorch model serving library that includes features for batching and request scheduling.

Context Window Management

Efficiently managing the context window size can impact both performance and accuracy. Strategies like sliding windows or dynamic context selection can optimize resource usage.

- **Sliding Window:** A technique that limits the context window to a fixed size and slides it over the input sequence as new tokens are processed.
- **Dynamic Context Selection:** An approach that dynamically adjusts the context window size based on the content of the input.

Monitoring and Profiling

Continuous monitoring of key metrics such as latency, throughput, and resource utilization is essential. Profiling tools can identify performance bottlenecks and guide optimization efforts.

- **Prometheus:** An open-source monitoring system that can collect and store metrics from LLM serving infrastructure.
- **Grafana:** A visualization tool that can be used to create dashboards and alerts, based on Prometheus metrics.

- **TensorBoard:** A visualization toolkit that can be used to profile TensorFlow models, and identify performance bottlenecks.

Versioning and Lifecycle Management of LLM APIs

Versioning of LLM APIs is crucial for reproducibility, performance monitoring, and rollback capabilities. It helps you understand how your models evolve and how changes impact downstream tasks. Lifecycle management ensures smooth transitions between different versions of your models. It includes training, testing, deployment, and retirement of APIs. RAG systems introduce additional complexities related to data and retrieval methods. Consider the tools mentioned above alongside `LlamaIndex` to manage data versions and track retrieval performance effectively. Proper version control and lifecycle management are essential for building robust and reliable LLM applications, ensuring transparency and maintainability over time. Some useful tools in these space are:

- **DVC (Data Version Control):** This tool can be used to track different versions of your datasets, models, and experiments. It can be integrated with tools like MLflow for a complete workflow.
- **MLflow:** A platform for managing the ML lifecycle, including experiment tracking, model packaging, and deployment. You can use MLflow to version your LLM APIs and track their performance over time.
- **Pachyderm:** A data versioning and pipeline orchestration platform. While often associated with data pipelines, it can also manage the model lifecycle.
- **Weights and Biases (WandB):** A platform for experiment tracking, dataset versioning, and model management. It offers tools to compare different versions of your models and monitor their performance.
- **TruLens:** An open-source platform for evaluating and monitoring LLMs in production. It includes data logging, performance metrics, and drift detection.

Efficient Resource Utilization and Cost Optimization

Serving large language models can be resource-intensive and costly. Here are some strategies to optimize resource usage, and reduce expenses:

Model Selection and Compression

Select a model that balances performance with resource requirements. Smaller models often consume less memory and compute power, while still delivering satisfactory results for specific tasks. Employ techniques such as pruning, quantization, and knowledge distillation to reduce the size and complexity of models, without significant performance degradation. This can lead to faster inference and a lower memory footprint. The following are some popular libraries used for model compression, especially for LLMs.

Example: Knowledge Distillation for Model Compression

```
from transformers import AutoModelForSequenceClassification, AutoTokenizer,
Trainer

# Load large teacher model
teacher_model = AutoModelForSequenceClassification.from_pretrained("bert-base-
uncased")

# Load smaller student model
student_model = AutoModelForSequenceClassification.from_pretrained("distilbert-
base-uncased")

# Custom training loop with distillation loss
def distillation_loss(student_logits, teacher_logits, labels,
temperature=2.0):
    soft_targets = F.softmax(teacher_logits / temperature, dim=-1)
    soft_prob = F.log_softmax(student_logits / temperature, dim=-1)
    distillation_loss = F.kl_div(soft_prob, soft_targets,
reduction='batchmean')
    student_loss = F.cross_entropy(student_logits, labels)
    return 0.5 * distillation_loss + 0.5 * student_loss

# Train student to mimic teacher (simplified example)
# Student model is now 40% smaller with ~95% of teacher performance!
```

1. **TensorFlow Model Optimization Toolkit:**
    - **Purpose:** This provides various techniques for model compression, including pruning, quantization, and knowledge distillation.
    - **Key Features:**
        - Built-in support for popular model architectures like BERT and transformers.
        - Easy-to-use APIs for applying compression techniques.
        - Tools for evaluating the performance and size trade-offs of compressed models.
    - **Installation:** `pip install tensorflow-model-optimization`

2. **PyTorch Pruning:**
    - **Purpose:** Offers tools for structured and unstructured pruning of neural networks.
    - **Key Features:**
        - Supports various pruning schedules and criteria.
        - Integrates seamlessly with PyTorch's training workflows.
        - Can be used to compress LLMs by removing redundant connections.
    - **Installation:** Since this functionality is a part of PyTorch, it is included when you install `torch`.
3. **Hugging Face Transformers:**
    - **Purpose:** Though primarily known for providing pre-trained models, it also includes some compression capabilities.
    - **Key Features:**
        - Supports knowledge distillation for compressing LLMs.
        - Offers tools for quantizing transformer-based models.
        - Provides access to compressed versions of popular LLMs.
    - **Installation:** `pip install transformers`
4. **ONNX Runtime:**
    - **Purpose:** Enables optimized inference of machine learning models, including compressed ones.
    - **Key Features:**
        - Supports various compression formats, including quantization and pruning.
        - Can be used to accelerate the inference of LLMs on different hardware platforms.
        - Offers tools for converting models to the ONNX format.
    - **Installation:** `pip install onnxruntime`
5. **CTranslate2:**
    - **Purpose:** A fast and efficient inference engine for neural machine translation models, including LLMs.
    - **Key Features:**
        - Supports quantization and pruning for model compression.
        - Optimized for running on CPUs and GPUs.

    - Can be used to deploy compressed LLMs for real-time applications.
- **Installation:** `pip install ctranslate2`

Inference Optimization

LLM's substantial computational demands often pose challenges during inference, especially in resource-constrained environments. To address this, several libraries have been developed that focus on optimizing the inference process, enhancing both performance and efficiency.

Here are some of the prominent libraries that enable streamlined LLM inference:

1. **ONNX Runtime:**
    - **Purpose:** Provides optimized inference for a wide range of machine learning models, including LLMs.
    - **Key Features:**
        - Supports various hardware platforms (CPUs, GPUs, and NPUs).
        - Offers graph optimizations and operator fusion for faster execution.
        - Can be used to deploy LLMs on cloud and edge devices.
    - **Installation:** `pip install onnxruntime`
2. **TensorFlow Lite:**
    - **Purpose:** Designed for deploying machine learning models on mobile, embedded, and IoT devices.
    - **Key Features:**
        - Supports model quantization and pruning for reduced size and faster inference.
        - Provides tools for converting TensorFlow models to the TensorFlow Lite format.
        - Offers hardware acceleration on select devices.
    - **Installation:** `pip install tensorflow-lite-support`
3. **PyTorch Mobile:**
    - **Purpose:** Enables the deployment of PyTorch models on mobile and edge devices.
    - **Key Features:**
        - Supports model quantization and scripting for optimized inference.
        - Provides tools for building and deploying mobile applications with integrated LLMs.

    - Offers hardware acceleration on select devices.
  - **Installation:** `pip install torch torchvision torchaudio`
4. **NVIDIA TensorRT:**
  - **Purpose:** A high-performance inference engine for deep learning models, including LLMs.
  - **Key Features:**
    - Optimized for NVIDIA GPUs.
    - Offers graph optimizations, operator fusion, and mixed-precision inference.
    - Can significantly accelerate the inference of LLMs.
  - **Installation:** This comes as a part of CUDA toolkit which you can download from Nvidia website, if you are using GPU runtime.
5. **OpenVINO:**
  - **Purpose:** A toolkit for optimizing and deploying deep learning models on Intel hardware.
  - **Key Features:**
    - Supports model quantization and pruning.
    - Offers hardware acceleration on Intel CPUs, GPUs, and VPUs.
    - Can be used to deploy LLMs on edge devices.
  - **Installation:** Can be installed using this command: `pip install openvino-dev[tensorflow2]`

These libraries offer diverse approaches to tackle inference optimization in LLMs, catering to various hardware platforms and deployment scenarios. Leveraging these libraries empowers developers and researchers to deploy high-performing LLM applications, while minimizing latency and maximizing resource utilization.

Monitoring and Maintenance of Deployed LLMs

Once deployed, an LLM requires continuous oversight. All core operational aspects, including tracking infrastructure metrics, logging, alert mechanisms, and defining LLM-specific Key Performance Indicators (KPIs), are the central focus of *Chapter 8, Model Monitoring and Evaluation.*

Effective monitoring and maintenance are vital for ensuring the reliability, performance, and safety of deployed LLMs, ultimately leading to improved user experiences and business outcomes.

Monitoring of Deployed LLMs

Monitoring focuses on tracking key metrics to ensure that your LLM is performing as expected, and to identify potential issues early on. Here are some important aspects:

Performance Metrics

- **Accuracy:** How often the LLM provides correct or relevant responses. Monitor this by comparing its output to a gold standard or using human evaluation. You can calculate metrics such as precision, recall, F1-score, or BLEU score, depending on your specific task.
- **Relevance:** Assesses the quality and appropriateness of the LLM's responses in relation to the given input. This is more subjective and often requires human evaluation. For example, in the case of a chatbot, relevance would measure how well the responses address the user's queries and maintain a coherent conversation.
- **Latency:** The time taken for the LLM to generate a response. Use timers or profiling tools to track latency and set up alerts if it exceeds acceptable thresholds.
- **Throughput:** How many requests the LLM can handle per unit of time. Track the number of requests processed and monitor system resource utilization (CPU, memory, and network) to identify bottlenecks.
- **Perplexity:** Measures how well the LLM predicts the next word in a sequence, reflecting the model's understanding of the language. Lower perplexity generally indicates better language modeling capabilities.
- **Calibration:** Assesses the LLM's confidence in its predictions. Well-calibrated LLMs provide accurate confidence estimates, which are crucial for decision-making tasks.
- **Fairness and Bias:** Metrics that evaluate the fairness and potential biases in the LLM's outputs, ensuring that the model treats different groups or demographics equitably.

Thus, by consistently monitoring these performance metrics, you can gain valuable insights into the effectiveness, efficiency, and potential issues of your deployed LLMs. This information enables you to make informed decisions about model optimization, resource allocation, and potential improvements to enhance the overall quality and reliability of your LLM-powered applications. Remember to tailor your monitoring strategy and the specific metrics you track to your specific LLM use case and performance goals.

Example: Monitoring LLM Performance Metrics

```
import time
import logging
from prometheus_client import Counter, Histogram
```

```
# Define metrics
request_counter = Counter('llm_requests_total', 'Total LLM requests')
latency_histogram = Histogram('llm_latency_seconds', 'LLM response latency')
error_counter = Counter('llm_errors_total', 'Total LLM errors')

def monitored_llm_call(prompt, llm_function):
    request_counter.inc()
    start_time = time.time()

    try:
        response = llm_function(prompt)
        latency = time.time() - start_time
        latency_histogram.observe(latency)

        logging.info(f"Request completed in {latency:.2f}s")
        return response
    except Exception as e:
        error_counter.inc()
        logging.error(f"LLM error: {str(e)}")
        raise
```

Resource Utilization for LLMs on Cloud

Deploying and running Large Language Models (LLMs) on cloud platforms like Google Cloud, AWS, or Azure require careful consideration of resource utilization to ensure cost-effectiveness and optimal performance. Here is a breakdown of the key resources to monitor and manage:

1. **Compute:**
    - **CPU:** LLMs typically require significant CPU resources for tasks such as text processing, tokenization, and inference. Choose appropriate CPU instance types, based on your model size and workload demands.
    - **Monitoring:** Track CPU utilization metrics like CPU usage percentage, load average, and the number of CPU cores used by the LLM.
    - **Optimization:** Consider using CPU-optimized instance types for tasks that do not require heavy GPU acceleration. Optimize code for CPU efficiency.
    - **GPU:** For large and complex LLMs, GPUs can significantly accelerate inference and training. Select GPU instance types, based on your model's computational requirements.
    - **Monitoring:** Use tools such as **`nvidia-smi`** (on Google Cloud) or cloud-specific monitoring dashboards to track GPU utilization, memory usage, and temperature.

- **Optimization:** Choose GPU instances with sufficient memory bandwidth and interconnect speed. Leverage techniques like mixed precision training to reduce memory footprint.
- **Memory:** LLMs often have large memory requirements to store model parameters, activations, and intermediate data. Ensure that your chosen instance type has enough memory to avoid performance bottlenecks.
- **Monitoring:** Monitor memory usage metrics such as RAM utilization, swap space usage, and page faults.
- **Optimization:** Use memory-efficient data structures and algorithms. Consider techniques like model compression or quantization to reduce memory footprint.

2. **Storage:**
    - **Disk:** Store training data, model checkpoints, and other relevant files on persistent disk storage. Select storage options based on performance needs and cost considerations.
    - **Monitoring:** Track disk I/O metrics like read/write throughput, latency, and disk space utilization.
    - **Optimization:** Choose appropriate disk types (for example, SSDs for faster access) and optimize data access patterns.
    - **Network:** LLMs may require significant network bandwidth for communication between different components (e.g., model serving, data loading). Choose network configurations that meet your throughput and latency requirements.
    - **Monitoring:** Monitor network metrics such as bandwidth utilization, packet loss, and latency.
    - **Optimization:** Use Content Delivery Networks (CDNs) to cache static content, and reduce latency for remote users.
3. **Cost Management:**
    - **Pricing Models:** Understand the pricing models for different cloud resources (compute, storage, network) and choose options that align with your budget.
    - **Resource Optimization:** Right-size your instances based on actual resource utilization. Leverage autoscaling to dynamically adjust resources, based on workload demands.
    - **Cost Monitoring:** Utilize cloud cost management tools to track spending, identify cost drivers, and optimize your resource allocation.

4. **Token Utilization:**
    - **Token Limits:** LLMs have limits on the number of tokens they can process in a single request. This includes both input and output tokens. Exceeding token limits can lead to errors or truncated responses.
    - **Monitoring:** Track the number of tokens processed per request using tools provided by your LLM provider or by calculating token counts, based on the model's tokenizer.
    - Some common problems and their resolutions:
        - **Problem:** Exceeding input token limits.
        - **Resolution:**
            - Break down large input texts into smaller chunks, and process them separately.
            - Use summarization techniques to reduce the length of input text.
            - Consider using LLMs with larger context windows if available.
        - **Problem:** Exceeding output token limits.
        - **Resolution:**
            - Limit the maximum number of tokens generated by the LLM in its response.
            - Use techniques like response streaming to receive partial outputs as they are generated.
            - Refine your prompts to encourage shorter and more concise responses.
        - **Problem:** Inefficient token usage due to repetitive or redundant text.
        - **Resolution:**
            - Preprocess input text to remove unnecessary repetitions or redundancy.
            - Use techniques like co-reference resolution to replace repeated mentions with pronouns.
            - Design prompts that encourage the LLM to focus on the most important information.

Thus, by carefully monitoring and optimizing token utilization, you can ensure that your LLMs process information efficiently, and avoid token-related limitations, leading to improved performance and cost savings. Remember to choose appropriate LLM configurations and prompt engineering techniques to minimize token usage, while achieving your desired outcomes. Also leverage cloud provider tools and best practices for resource optimization and cost management, whenever applicable.

Error and Anomaly Detection

Monitoring for errors and anomalies is a crucial aspect of maintaining the reliability and performance of deployed LLMs. By proactively identifying and addressing these issues, you can ensure that your LLMs continue to function as expected, and deliver accurate results. Here is a breakdown of strategies for error and anomaly detection:

1. **Error Detection:**
    a. **Logging and Exception Handling:** Implement robust logging mechanisms to capture errors, warnings, and exceptions generated by the LLM and related components. Use Python's logging module or similar tools. Handle exceptions gracefully to prevent unexpected program termination.

    b. **Health Checks:** Periodically send health check requests to the LLM to verify its availability and responsiveness. Monitor the response times and status codes of these requests to detect potential service disruptions.

    c. **Input Validation:** Validate user inputs to ensure that they are within acceptable formats and ranges. Reject or sanitize invalid inputs to prevent unexpected behavior or errors in the LLM.

Example: Robust Error Handling for LLM Services

```
import logging
from functools import wraps
from typing import Optional

logging.basicConfig(level=logging.INFO)
logger = logging.getLogger(__name__)

def llm_error_handler(max_retries=3):
    def decorator(func):
        @wraps(func)
        def wrapper(*args, **kwargs):
            for attempt in range(max_retries):
                try:
                    # Validate input
                    prompt = kwargs.get('prompt', '')
                    if len(prompt) > 10000:
                        raise ValueError("Prompt exceeds maximum length")

                    # Execute LLM call
                    result = func(*args, **kwargs)
                    logger.info(f"LLM call successful on attempt {attempt + 1}")
                    return result
```

```
                except ValueError as e:
                    logger.error(f"Invalid input: {e}")
                    raise  # Don't retry validation errors

                except Exception as e:
                    logger.warning(f"Attempt {attempt + 1} failed: {e}")
                    if attempt == max_retries - 1:
                        logger.error(f"All {max_retries} attempts failed")
                        raise
            return None
        return wrapper
    return decorator

@llm_error_handler(max_retries=3)
def call_llm(prompt: str) -> Optional[str]:
    # Your LLM call logic here
    return llm_client.generate(prompt)
```

2. **Anomaly Detection:**
   - **Performance Monitoring:** Continuously monitor performance metrics like latency, throughput, and accuracy. Establish baselines for these metrics and set up alerts for significant deviations from the expected behavior.
   - **Output Analysis:** Analyze the LLM's outputs for unexpected patterns or anomalies. This can involve checking for:
     - **Nonsense or irrelevant responses:** Implement techniques to detect nonsensical or irrelevant outputs, such as using semantic similarity metrics or perplexity scores.
     - **Bias or toxicity:** Use tools or models trained to detect biased or toxic language in the LLM's responses.
     - **Sudden changes in output style or format**: Monitor for any abrupt shifts in the LLM's writing style or response format, which could indicate a problem.
   - **Statistical Methods:** Apply statistical methods like outlier detection or time series analysis to identify unusual patterns in the LLM's behavior or performance metrics.
3. **Response and Mitigation:**
   - **Alerting:** Set up alerting systems to notify you of detected errors or anomalies. This allows for timely intervention and mitigation.
   - **Automated Remediation:** For certain types of errors or anomalies, consider implementing automated remediation strategies, such as restarting the LLM service or adjusting model parameters.

- **Human Review:** For more complex or critical issues, escalate to human review and intervention to ensure proper investigation and resolution.

Hence, by incorporating these errors and anomaly detection strategies into your LLM monitoring workflow, you can enhance the reliability, safety, and performance of your deployed models. Remember to tailor your approach to your specific LLM use case and risk tolerance.

Maintenance of Deployed LLMs

Maintenance involves actions to keep the LLM running smoothly, and ensure its performance over time. Here are some key aspects:

Model Updating

Maintaining deployed LLMs involves regularly updating the models to ensure that they remain performant, relevant, and aligned with the evolving data and user needs. Model updating is a crucial aspect of this maintenance process, and can be categorized into several approaches:

1. **Fine-tuning:**
    - **Purpose:** Adapting a pre-trained LLM to a specific task or domain by training it on a smaller, task-specific dataset. This allows for customization without requiring training from scratch.
    - **Benefits:** Improves accuracy and relevance for the target task, reduces training time and resources compared to full training.
    - **Process:**
        a. **Prepare a task-specific dataset:** Collect and annotate data relevant to the desired task or domain.
        b. **Load the pre-trained LLM:** Use the pre-trained LLM as a starting point.
        c. Train the LLM on the new dataset: Fine-tune the model's parameters using the task-specific data.
        d. **Evaluate performance:** Assess the model's performance on a validation set to ensure improvements.
        e. **Deploy the updated model:** Replace the existing deployed model with the fine-tuned version.

Example: Fine-tuning an LLM with Hugging Face

```
from transformers import AutoModelForCausalLM, AutoTokenizer, Trainer,
TrainingArguments
from datasets import load_dataset

# Load model and tokenizer
```

```
model = AutoModelForCausalLM.from_pretrained("gpt2")
tokenizer = AutoTokenizer.from_pretrained("gpt2")

# Prepare dataset
dataset = load_dataset("your_custom_dataset")
tokenized = dataset.map(lambda x: tokenizer(x["text"], truncation=True))

# Configure training
training_args = TrainingArguments(
    output_dir="./finetuned_model",
    num_train_epochs=3,
    per_device_train_batch_size=4,
    save_steps=500
)

# Fine-tune
trainer = Trainer(model=model, args=training_args, train_
dataset=tokenized["train"])
trainer.train()
```

2. **Continual Learning:**

   - **Purpose:** Enabling the LLM to learn and adapt to new information over time without forgetting previously acquired knowledge. This addresses the issue of model staleness and ensures that the LLM stays up-to-date.
   - **Benefits:** Maintains model relevance, adapts to evolving data distributions, and reduces the need for frequent retraining.
   - **Techniques:**
     - **Incremental Learning:** Gradually train the LLM on new data batches while retaining previous knowledge.
     - **Online Learning:** Update the model's parameters in real-time as new data becomes available.
     - **Experience Replay:** Store past experiences and replay them during training to reinforce previous knowledge.

3. **Model Replacement:**

   - **Purpose:** Replacing the existing deployed model with a completely new model trained on a larger or more diverse dataset. This is typically done when significant improvements in LLM architectures or training data become available.
   - **Benefits:** Incorporates latest advancements in LLM technology, potentially achieves significant performance gains.

- **Process:**
    a. **Train a new LLM:** Develop or select a new LLM architecture and train it on a large dataset.
    b. **Evaluate performance:** Thoroughly evaluate the new model's performance against the existing model.
    c. **Deploy the new model:** Gradually roll out the new model, potentially running both models in parallel for a period to compare performance and ensure a smooth transition.

4. **Prompt Engineering:**
    - **Purpose:** Modifying the input prompts provided to the LLM to elicit desired responses or adapt to changing requirements. This is a less resource-intensive approach compared to model retraining.
    - **Benefits:** Allows for quick adjustments to the LLM's behavior, without requiring model updates.
    - **Techniques:**
        - **Adding instructions or constraints:** Provide clear instructions in the prompt to guide the LLM's generation process.
        - **Modifying the context:** Include relevant background information in the prompt to influence the LLM's understanding.
        - **Iterative refinement:** Experiment with different prompt variations to achieve the desired results.

Considerations for Model Updating

- **Frequency:** Determine the appropriate frequency for model updates based on the rate of data change, user feedback, and performance degradation.
- **Evaluation:** Thoroughly evaluate updated models to ensure they meet performance expectations and do not introduce new biases or errors.
- **Deployment:** Implement strategies for seamless model deployment, such as A/B testing or canary deployments, to minimize disruption to user experience.
- **Monitoring:** Continuously monitor the performance of updated models to detect any issues and ensure that they continue to function as intended.

Example: A/B Testing for Model Deployment

```
import random
from typing import Dict, Any

class ModelRouter:
    def __init__(self, model_a, model_b, traffic_split=0.5):
```

```
        self.model_a = model_a  # Current production model
        self.model_b = model_b  # New candidate model
        self.traffic_split = traffic_split  # % to route to model_b
        self.metrics = {'model_a': [], 'model_b': []}

    def route_request(self, prompt: str, user_id: str) -> Dict[str, Any]:
        # Consistent routing per user
        use_model_b = hash(user_id) % 100 < (self.traffic_split * 100)

        model = self.model_b if use_model_b else self.model_a
        model_name = 'model_b' if use_model_b else 'model_a'

        # Generate response and track metrics
        response = model.generate(prompt)
        self.metrics[model_name].append({
            'latency': response.latency,
            'quality_score': self.evaluate(response)
        })

        return {'response': response.text, 'model': model_name}

    def get_performance_comparison(self):
        # Compare metrics between models
        return {
            'model_a': self._compute_stats(self.metrics['model_a']),
            'model_b': self._compute_stats(self.metrics['model_b'])
        }

# Usage: Gradually increase traffic_split if model_b performs well
router = ModelRouter(current_model, new_model, traffic_split=0.1)
```

Thus, by carefully planning and executing model updates, you can maintain the effectiveness and relevance of your deployed LLMs, ensuring that they provide value to your users and support your evolving business needs. Remember to consider the various approaches, benefits, and considerations involved in the model updating process to choose the most appropriate strategy for your specific use case.

Data Management: The Foundation of Robust and Reliable LLMs

Effective data management is paramount for deploying secure and reliable LLMs. It involves several key strategies to ensure that the data used for training and validation is of high quality, and remains relevant over time.

- **Keeping Data Updated and Relevant:** LLMs learn from the data they are trained on, and the quality and relevance of this data directly impact the model's performance and accuracy. Regularly updating the training and validation data is crucial. This means removing outdated or irrelevant data points and incorporating new, relevant data sources to reflect the evolving nature of information and user needs. Neglecting this aspect can lead to a decline in the model's performance and ability to provide accurate and up-to-date responses.

- **Ensuring Data Consistency and Quality:** Cleaning and preprocessing data is essential for eliminating inconsistencies, errors, and biases. This involves tasks like data normalization, handling missing values, and addressing potential biases or sensitive information. Consistent and high-quality data not only improves the LLM's performance but also enhances its ability to make fair and unbiased decisions.
- **Monitoring Data Distribution and Drift:** Data drift, which refers to changes in the statistical properties of data over time, can significantly affect the LLM's performance. Continuous monitoring of the data distribution is crucial for detecting any drift or changes that could impact the model's accuracy and reliability. Hence, by identifying such shifts, developers can proactively address them by retraining the model on updated data or adjusting the preprocessing steps.

By prioritizing these data management practices, developers can significantly enhance the security, privacy, and overall performance of their deployed LLMs.

Implementing Robust Security for LLMs and Their Data

Safeguarding LLMs and their underlying data from unauthorized access, use, or disclosure is of paramount importance. This involves implementing a comprehensive set of security measures across the entire LLM lifecycle, from development to deployment and ongoing operation.

- **Protecting the LLM and Data:** Implementing security measures begins with securing the LLM itself and its associated data. This includes restricting access to the model's weights, architecture, and training data. Employing encryption techniques to protect sensitive data both in transit and at rest is crucial. Access controls should be implemented to ensure only authorized personnel can interact with the LLM and its data. These measures help prevent unauthorized modification or manipulation of the model and safeguard against data breaches.
- **Regular Security Reviews and Updates:** The security landscape is constantly evolving, with new threats and vulnerabilities emerging regularly. To stay ahead of potential risks, it's crucial to establish a process for regularly reviewing and updating security policies and practices. This involves conducting periodic security audits, vulnerability assessments, and penetration testing to identify and address any weaknesses in the system. Thus, by staying vigilant and proactive, developers can ensure the LLM's security posture remains robust.
- **Monitoring for Vulnerabilities and Threats:** Continuous monitoring for security vulnerabilities and threats is an essential part of LLM security. This involves employing

security information and event management (SIEM) systems to detect and respond to suspicious activity. Regularly scanning for known vulnerabilities and implementing security patches can help prevent exploits. Implementing intrusion detection systems can further enhance security by identifying and alerting on potential intrusions or malicious activities.

Thus, by prioritizing these security measures, developers can significantly reduce the risk of unauthorized access, misuse, or disclosure of LLMs and their data, ensuring their secure and reliable operation.

Troubleshooting and Issue Management for LLMs

Even with careful planning and security measures, issues can arise in deployed LLMs. Establishing a robust troubleshooting process and issue tracking system is essential for resolving problems efficiently and continuously improving the system.

- **Using Monitoring Data and Logs:** When issues occur, the first step is to identify the root cause. Monitoring data and logs provide valuable insights into the LLM's behavior and performance. Analyzing these data sources can help pinpoint the source of the problem, whether it's related to the model itself, the input data, or the infrastructure. Tools such as Datadog or Edge Delta can assist in anomaly detection and troubleshooting.
- **Developing a Troubleshooting Process:** A well-defined troubleshooting process streamlines the identification and resolution of common problems. This process should include clear steps for reporting, investigating, and resolving issues. Thus, by establishing escalation procedures for more complex problems ensures they are addressed by the appropriate experts. Creating a knowledge base of known issues and solutions can help users and developers quickly resolve common problems.
- **Setting Up an Issue Tracking System:** An issue tracking system provides a centralized platform for managing bugs, feature requests, and other issues related to the LLM. This allows for efficient tracking and prioritization of issues, ensuring they are addressed in a timely manner. Systems like Jira or GitHub Issues can help manage workflows and facilitate communication among developers and users. This system is also valuable for documenting resolutions and tracking progress towards resolving issues.

Hence, by prioritizing these troubleshooting and issue management practices, developers can effectively address problems, minimize downtime, and continuously improve the performance and reliability of their deployed LLMs.

Security and Privacy Considerations in LLM Deployment

This chapter highlighted the potential risks associated with LLMs, such as prompt injection, data poisoning, and data leakage. For a comprehensive breakdown of each vulnerability, detailed defense mechanisms, and best practices for securing your LLMOps pipeline, please refer to *Chapter* 10, '*LLM Security: Vulnerabilities and Defenses*'.

Deploying RAG for LLMs

Deploying RAG systems requires careful consideration of operational aspects, infrastructure setup, and system integration. While **Chapter 5: Retrieval-Augmented Generation (RAG)** covers the architecture and concepts of RAG systems, this section focuses on the operationalization and deployment aspects, including setting up data pipelines, indexing strategies, and serving the vector database as part of the overall application architecture.

Key Components of RAG Deployment

- **Knowledge Base:** This is the external data source used for retrieval. It could be a document collection, a database, or a knowledge graph. You will need to index the knowledge base for efficient retrieval.
- **Retrieval System:** This component retrieves relevant information from the knowledge base based on the user's query. Popular choices include vector databases (for example, Faiss, Pinecone) and search engines (for example, Elasticsearch).
- **RAG Pipeline:** This orchestrates the flow of information between the components. It receives the user's query, retrieves relevant context, and feeds it to the LLM, and returns the generated response.

Steps for Deploying RAG

1. **Index the Knowledge Base:** Use a suitable indexing method to make the knowledge base searchable. For example, vector databases store documents as embeddings, allowing for semantic similarity search.
2. **Deploy the Retrieval System:** Set up the chosen retrieval system, ensuring that it can handle the expected query load.
3. **Implement the RAG Pipeline:** Create a pipeline that connects the LLM, knowledge base, and retrieval system. This could be done using a framework like LangChain or Haystack.
4. **Deploy the Pipeline:** Make the RAG pipeline accessible through an API or web interface.

Example: Deploying a Basic RAG System

```
from langchain.vectorstores import FAISS
from langchain.embeddings import OpenAIEmbeddings
from langchain.llms import OpenAI
from langchain.chains import RetrievalQA

# Step 1: Index knowledge base
```

```
documents = ["LLMs are powerful", "RAG improves accuracy", "Deploy with care"]
embeddings = OpenAIEmbeddings()
vectorstore = FAISS.from_texts(documents, embeddings)

# Step 2: Create retriever
retriever = vectorstore.as_retriever(search_kwargs={"k": 2})

# Step 3: Build RAG pipeline
llm = OpenAI(temperature=0)
rag_chain = RetrievalQA.from_chain_type(
    llm=llm,
    retriever=retriever,
    return_source_documents=True
)

# Step 4: Query the system
result = rag_chain({"query": "How does RAG help LLMs?"})
print(f"Answer: {result['result']}")
print(f"Sources: {result['source_documents']}")
```

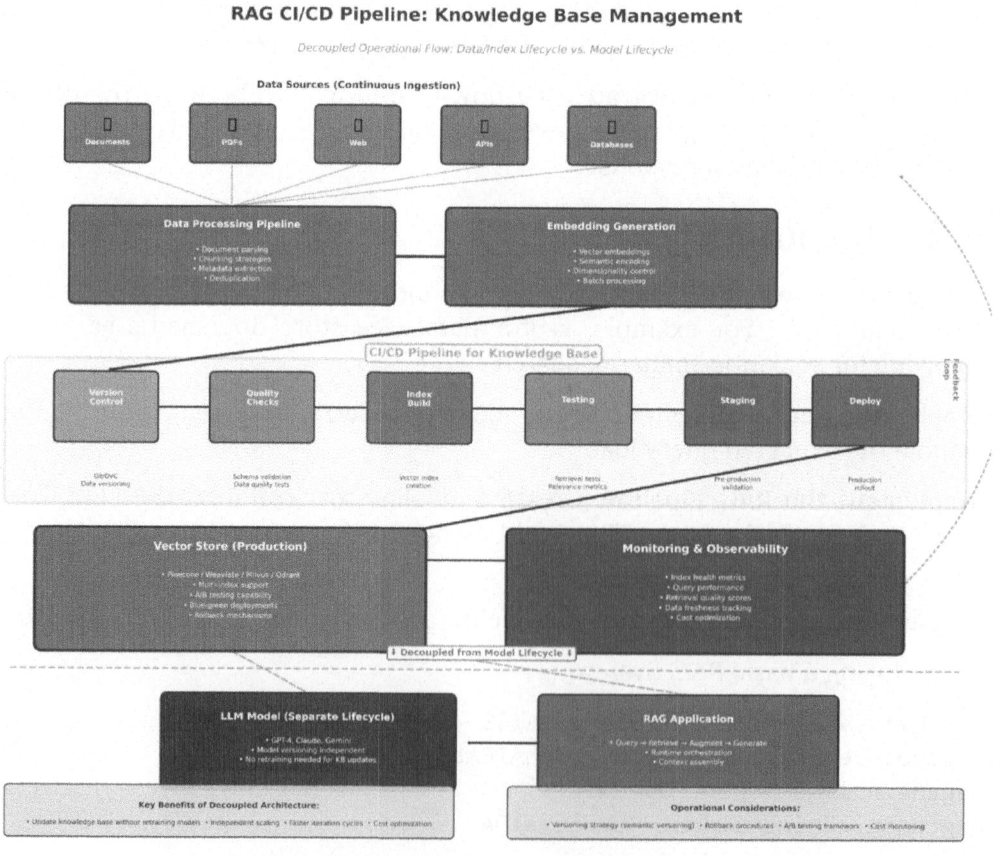

Figure 7.1: RAG CI/CD Pipeline

Considerations for RAG Deployment

- **Data Freshness:** Keep the knowledge base up-to-date to ensure that the LLM has access to the latest information.
- **Retrieval Accuracy:** Fine-tune the retrieval system to improve the relevance of the retrieved context.
- **Latency:** Optimize the retrieval process to minimize response times.
- **Cost:** Evaluate the costs associated with storing and querying the knowledge base.

Essential LLM Optimization Techniques for Production

Production deployment of LLMs requires sophisticated optimization techniques to achieve acceptable performance, cost efficiency, and scalability. Two critical optimization strategies that are essential for enterprise-grade LLM serving are **Quantization and Continuous Batching**.

Quantization: Reducing Model Size and Memory Requirements

Quantization reduces the precision of model weights and activations, significantly decreasing memory usage and computational requirements, while maintaining acceptable model performance. Key quantization techniques include:

- **INT8 Quantization:** Reduces 32-bit floating-point weights to 8-bit integers, achieving up to 4x memory reduction and 2-3x inference speedup with minimal accuracy loss.
- **GPTQ (Generative Pre-Trained Transformer Quantization):** Advanced post-training quantization method that minimizes quantization error by considering the impact of each weight on the overall model output, achieving superior accuracy retention.
- **AWQ (Activation-Aware Weight Quantization):** Focuses on protecting the most important weights by analyzing activation patterns, providing better performance than GPTQ for certain model architectures.

Example: Applying Quantization to an LLM

```
from transformers import AutoModelForCausalLM, AutoTokenizer
from optimum.quanto import quantize, freeze

# Load model
model = AutoModelForCausalLM.from_pretrained("meta-llama/Llama-2-7b-hf")
tokenizer = AutoTokenizer.from_pretrained("meta-llama/Llama-2-7b-hf")
```

```
# Apply INT8 quantization
quantize(model, weights="int8", activations="int8")
freeze(model)  # Freeze quantized weights

# Test inference
inputs = tokenizer("Explain quantization", return_tensors="pt")
outputs = model.generate(**inputs, max_length=50)
print(tokenizer.decode(outputs[0]))

# Model is now 4x smaller in memory!
```

Continuous Batching: Maximizing GPU Utilization

Continuous Batching addresses the inefficiency of traditional batching where all requests in a batch must wait for the slowest request to complete. This technique provides:

- **Dynamic Request Management:** New requests can join the batch as soon as they arrive, and completed requests can exit without waiting for the entire batch to finish.
- **Improved Throughput:** Can achieve 2-10x higher throughput compared to static batching, especially for requests with varying sequence lengths.
- **Better Resource Utilization:** Maintains high GPU utilization by continuously processing requests without idle time, reducing infrastructure costs, and improving response times.

These optimization techniques are necessary for deploying LLMs at scale, enabling organizations to serve more users with fewer resources, while maintaining acceptable performance and cost efficiency. Implementation of these techniques requires careful consideration of hardware compatibility, model architecture, and performance requirements.

Example: Conceptual Continuous Batching Implementation:

```
from queue import Queue
from threading import Thread
import time

class ContinuousBatcher:
    def __init__(self, model, max_batch_size=8, timeout=0.1):
        self.model = model
        self.max_batch_size = max_batch_size
        self.timeout = timeout
        self.request_queue = Queue()
        self.processing = True
        Thread(target=self._process_batches, daemon=True).start()

    def _process_batches(self):
        while self.processing:
```

```
            batch = []
            deadline = time.time() + self.timeout

            # Collect requests up to max_batch_size or timeout
            while len(batch) < self.max_batch_size and time.time() < deadline:
                if not self.request_queue.empty():
                    batch.append(self.request_queue.get())

            if batch:
                # Process batch (varying lengths handled efficiently)
                prompts = [req['prompt'] for req in batch]
                responses = self.model.generate_batch(prompts)

                # Return results immediately as they complete
                for req, resp in zip(batch, responses):
                    req['callback'](resp)

    def generate(self, prompt: str, callback):
        # Add request to queue, it will be batched automatically
        self.request_queue.put({'prompt': prompt, 'callback': callback})

# Requests are batched dynamically without waiting for slowest completion
```

Conclusion

Deploying Large Language Models (LLMs) is a multifaceted process that requires careful consideration of various factors. This chapter has explored crucial aspects of successful LLM deployment, ranging from strategic approaches to ongoing maintenance, and security considerations.

We began by examining various approaches for LLM deployment, highlighting the importance of selecting the right method, based on specific needs and resources. Whether opting for cloud-based services, on-premise solutions, or edge deployments, understanding the trade-offs and considerations is crucial for optimal performance and scalability.

Next, we delved into the critical aspects of monitoring and maintaining deployed LLMs. Continuous monitoring, performance evaluation, and regular updates are essential for ensuring the model remains accurate, reliable, and efficient over time. Establishing clear processes for troubleshooting and addressing issues is crucial for minimizing downtime, and maximizing user satisfaction.

Security and privacy considerations are paramount in LLM deployment. This chapter highlighted the potential risks associated with LLMs, such as prompt injection, data poisoning, and data leakage, and presented strategies for mitigating these threats. Thus, by implementing robust security measures and adhering to privacy best practices, developers can safeguard user data, and ensure responsible use of LLMs.

Finally, we explored the deployment of Retrieval Augmented Generation (RAG), a powerful technique for enhancing LLM capabilities by incorporating external knowledge sources. Understanding the different RAG architectures and implementation considerations is vital for leveraging the benefits of this approach.

In conclusion, deploying LLMs requires a holistic approach that encompasses strategic planning, technical expertise, and a strong commitment to security and privacy. Hence, by carefully considering the various aspects discussed in this chapter, developers can successfully navigate the LLM deployment landscape, and unlock the transformative potential of these powerful models, while minimizing risks and maximizing benefits. As the field of LLMs continues to evolve, staying informed about new advancements and best practices will be crucial for ensuring continued success in deployment and operation.

References

1. https://cheatsheetseries.owasp.org/cheatsheets/LLM_Prompt_Injection_Prevention_Cheat_Sheet.html
2. https://compileinfy.com/self-hosted-llms-vs-cloud-based-llms-which-one-should-your-business-choose/
3. https://latitude-blog.ghost.io/blog/cloud-vs-on-prem-llms-long-term-cost-analysis/
4. https://llmtop10.com/
5. https://medium.com/@adembatman/security-vulnerabilities-in-large-language-models-llms-prompt-injection-and-data-poisoning-76de4e234ed6
6. https://medium.com/@rdmurugan/hybrid-llm-strategies-for-enterprises-balancing-self-hosted-governance-with-cloud-flexibility-769cb5dcafae
7. https://medium.com/whylabs/best-practices-for-monitoring-large-language-models-e929fcbbf0b3
8. https://northflank.com/blog/llm-deployment-pipeline
9. https://orq.ai/blog/model-vs-data-drift
10. https://portswigger.net/web-security/llm-attacks
11. https://thenewstack.io/six-frameworks-for-efficient-llm-inferencing/
12. https://www.evidentlyai.com/ml-in-production/model-monitoring
13. https://www.truefoundry.com/blog/model-deployment-tools

CHAPTER 8

Model Monitoring and Evaluation

Introduction

Following our discussion on AI *Agents (Chapter* 6) and the *core principles of deployment* (*Chapter* 7), this chapter explores the crucial aspect of monitoring LLM performance and continuous evaluation. This chapter serves as the comprehensive guide and single source of truth for all monitoring, evaluation, and feedback loop principles in LLMOps. Throughout this chapter, we will consider the example of monitoring a customer support chatbot built on an LLM. We will explore how to track its latency, ensure that its responses are helpful and safe, and measure its cost-effectiveness. This running case study will help illustrate the practical application of monitoring concepts. The principles and methodologies established here should be referenced by other chapters when discussing monitoring, evaluation, and feedback systems.

Structure

This chapter is organized into four main sections that build upon each other:

- The Foundation: Setting Up a Monitoring System for LLMs
- Measuring What Matters: Key Performance Indicators (KPIs) for LLM Health
- From Data to Action: Automated Alerting and Anomaly Detection
- Closing the Loop: Continuous Evaluation and Human Feedback

The Foundation: Setting Up Monitoring Systems for LLMs

Here the goal is to build a robust monitoring system that provides actionable insights into the health, performance, and quality of the deployed LLM applications. This involves selecting the right tools, integrating them into your existing infrastructure, and configuring them to track relevant metrics.

Here is a breakdown of how one might approach this, covering different aspects of monitoring:

Infrastructure Monitoring and Log Management

Infrastructure monitoring in LLMOps tracks the health and performance of underlying resources like servers and GPUs, ensuring that the LLM runs smoothly. Log management provides a centralized view of application behavior, capturing errors, latency, and request details, crucial for debugging and understanding LLM interactions and potential issues within the deployment environment. Hence, let us see the tools that can be used to track the underlying infrastructure health and application logs to identify system-level issues.

Prometheus and Grafana

A powerful open-source combination for metrics monitoring. Prometheus scrapes metrics from your application and infrastructure, and Grafana visualizes them. You can go through the links in the appendix for installing and configuring the same.

- **Implementation:** You would need to instrument your LLM inference service to expose relevant metrics in the Prometheus format. This could involve custom code or using client libraries for your framework (for example, Python Prometheus client).
- **Example Prometheus Metrics:**
    - `llm_inference_request_total`: Total number of inference requests.
    - `llm_inference_request_duration_seconds_sum`: Sum of inference durations.
    - `llm_inference_request_duration_seconds_count`: Count of inference durations.
    - `llm_gpu_utilization`: GPU utilization percentage (if applicable).
- **Example Grafana Dashboard: Visualizing:**
    - Real-time inference latency.
    - Request throughput.
    - GPU utilization trends.

- Custom business metrics (for example, number of successful vs. failed content generation attempts).

Example: Prometheus metrics for our chatbot:

```
# Example Python code using Prometheus client
from prometheus_client import Counter, Histogram
import time

REQUEST_COUNT = Counter('llm_inference_request_total', 'Total number of
inference requests')
REQUEST_LATENCY = Histogram('llm_inference_request_duration_seconds', 'LLM
inference latency')

# Usage in your LLM endpoint
def process_chatbot_request(user_prompt):
    REQUEST_COUNT.inc()  # Increment request counter

    start_time = time.time()
    response = llm_model.generate(user_prompt)  # Your LLM call
    duration = time.time() - start_time

    REQUEST_LATENCY.observe(duration)  # Record latency
    return response
```

ELK Stack (Elasticsearch, Logstash, Kibana)

This is a very popular open-source stack for centralized logging and analysis.

- **Implementation:** You would configure your LLM application and inference endpoints to output structured logs (for example, in JSON format) that include timestamps, request IDs, input prompts (if privacy allows or anonymized), output lengths, latency, HTTP status codes, and any error messages. Logstash can be used to ingest and process these logs, Elasticsearch to store them, and Kibana to create dashboards for visualization and querying.
- **Example Kibana Dashboard: You could create dashboards showing:**
    - Request volume over time.
    - Average and P95 latency of API endpoints.
    - Error rate (for example, 5xx status codes).
    - Resource utilization (CPU, memory) of the inference servers (if logs include this information, or are joined with infrastructure metrics).

Example ELK Stack JSON log entry for our chatbot:


```
{
  "timestamp": "2025-10-08T15:30:00Z",
  "request_id": "xyz-123",
  "model_version": "v1.2-finetuned",
  "prompt_length": 55,
  "output_tokens": 210,
  "latency_ms": 1542,
  "status_code": 200,
  "user_feedback": "positive"
}
```


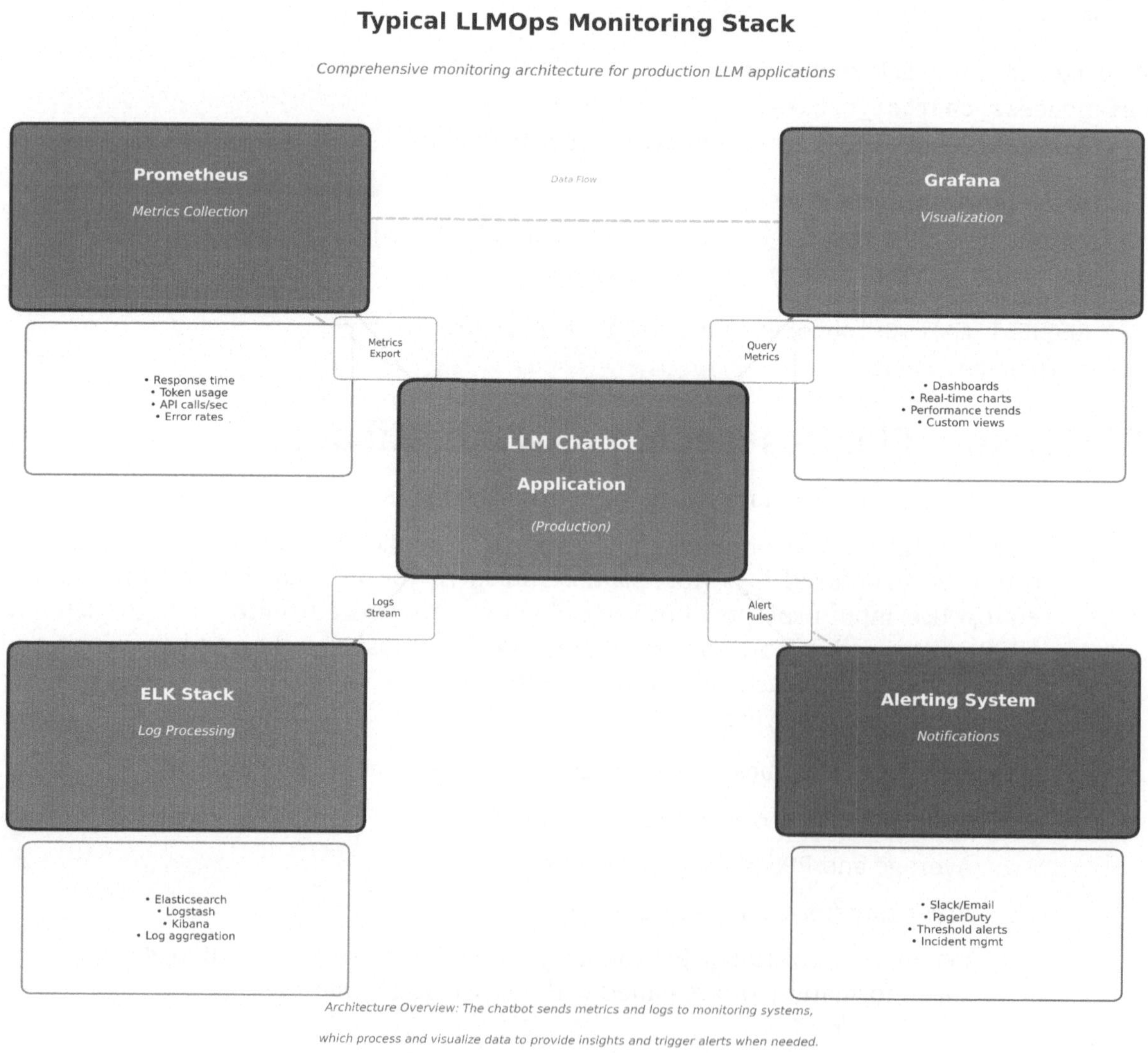

Figure 8.1: Typical LLMOps Monitoring Stack

LLM-Specific Output Quality and Safety Monitoring

It is crucial to establish a system that automatically assesses the quality, safety, and factual correctness of the LLM's generated outputs. This is where things get more LLM-specific.

Open-Source Evaluation Frameworks

These frameworks provide tools and integrations for evaluating LLM outputs against various metrics.

- **Implementation:** You can integrate these frameworks into your post-processing pipeline or as a separate monitoring service. You would define evaluation datasets or configure them to analyze live traffic (though this requires careful consideration of privacy).
- **Example LangChain Evaluation:** You could use StringEvaluator to check for the presence of specific keywords or patterns (for example, indicators of toxicity) in the output. You could also use more sophisticated evaluators that leverage other LLMs to assess aspects like relevance or coherence.
- **Example LM Evaluation Harness:** This framework allows you to run your LLM against a wide range of benchmark tasks and metrics, which can be adapted for continuous monitoring on a representative sample of production data.

Dedicated LLM Monitoring Platforms:

These platforms (for example, Arize AI, WhyLabs, and Galileo) offer specialized features for LLM monitoring, including automated quality scoring, drift detection on embeddings, and visualization of high-dimensional text data.

- **Implementation:** Typically involves integrating their SDK into your LLM application to send input prompts, generated outputs, and metadata. These platforms then provide dashboards and alerting capabilities.
- **Example Arize AI Dashboard: You might see visualizations of:**
  - Distribution of sentiment scores of generated text over time.
  - Clusters of semantically similar prompts that are experiencing high error rates or low quality scores.
  - Drift in the embedding space of input prompts or generated outputs.

Custom Rule-Based Systems

For specific safety or quality checks, you might implement custom rules using regular expressions or keyword matching.

- **Implementation:** This could be a simple Python script that analyzes the generated text after it is produced and flags outputs that violate certain rules. This can be integrated into your logging or alerting pipeline.
- **Example Rule:** Flag any output containing a predefined list of profanity or hate speech terms.

```
# Example custom safety check
import re

UNSAFE_PATTERNS = [
    r'ignore previous instructions',
    r'system prompt',
    r'<script>',  # XSS attempts
]

UNSAFE_KEYWORDS = ['profanity1', 'profanity2', 'hate_term']

def check_output_safety(llm_output):
    # Pattern-based checks
    for pattern in UNSAFE_PATTERNS:
        if re.search(pattern, llm_output, re.IGNORECASE):
            return False, f"Unsafe pattern detected: {pattern}"

    # Keyword checks
    for keyword in UNSAFE_KEYWORDS:
        if keyword.lower() in llm_output.lower():
            return False, f"Unsafe keyword detected: {keyword}"

    return True, "Safe"

# Usage
response = llm_model.generate(prompt)
is_safe, message = check_output_safety(response)
if not is_safe:
    log_safety_violation(response, message)
    return fallback_response
```

Embedding Drift Monitoring

Embedding drift monitoring in LLMOps tracks changes in the semantic representation of input prompts and generated outputs over time. This is crucial because shifts in these embeddings can indicate evolving user behavior, data drift impacting model relevance, or even subtle model degradation that might not be apparent in traditional metrics, thus ensuring that the LLM remains aligned with its intended purpose and data landscape. The techniques can be mainly segregated into:

Vector Databases (for example, Pinecone, Weaviate, and ChromaDB) with Monitoring Features: Some vector databases offer built-in capabilities for monitoring embedding drift.

- **Implementation:** If you are using embeddings for retrieval or semantic search, you can track the distribution of new embeddings compared to a baseline set.
- **Example:** Pinecone offers a "`drift`" metric that quantifies the change in the distribution of vectors.

Statistical Methods and Libraries (for example, SciPy, TensorFlow/PyTorch): You can calculate drift metrics manually using statistical tests (for example, Kolmogorov-Smirnov test) on the embeddings.

- **Implementation:** You would need to periodically sample embeddings from your production traffic, and compare their distributions to a baseline using these libraries.
- **Example:** Calculate the mean and variance of the embedding vectors over different time windows, and track significant changes.

```
# Example embedding drift detection
import numpy as np
from scipy.spatial.distance import cosine
from scipy.stats import ks_2samp

# Baseline embeddings from training/evaluation period
baseline_embeddings = np.array([...])  # Shape: (n_baseline, embedding_dim)

# Current production embeddings (collected over last hour/day)
current_embeddings = np.array([...])   # Shape: (n_current, embedding_dim)

# Method 1: Compare mean embeddings
baseline_mean = np.mean(baseline_embeddings, axis=0)
current_mean = np.mean(current_embeddings, axis=0)
drift_score = cosine(baseline_mean, current_mean)

print(f"Cosine distance between means: {drift_score}")
if drift_score > 0.1:  # Threshold
    alert("Embedding drift detected!")

# Method 2: KS test on first principal component
from sklearn.decomposition import PCA
pca = PCA(n_components=1)
baseline_pc1 = pca.fit_transform(baseline_embeddings).flatten()
```

```
current_pc1 = pca.transform(current_embeddings).flatten()

ks_statistic, p_value = ks_2samp(baseline_pc1, current_pc1)
if p_value < 0.05:
    alert(f"Significant drift detected (KS stat: {ks_statistic})")
```

Prompt Injection and Security Monitoring

Prompt injection and security monitoring in LLMOps are essential to detect and prevent malicious user inputs that could manipulate the LLM to bypass intended constraints or reveal sensitive information. Monitoring for anomalous input patterns and adversarial prompts safeguards the LLM's integrity, ensures its secure operation, and protects against potential misuse or harm, maintaining the trustworthiness and reliability of the deployed application.

- **Rule-Based Detection:** Implementing rules to identify common prompt injection patterns (for example, specific keywords, unusual formatting). This can be done using regular expressions or custom parsing logic within your application or a dedicated monitoring service.
    - **Example Rule:** Flag prompts containing phrases such as "*ignore previous instructions*" or code-like blocks that are not expected.
- **Anomaly Detection on Input Embeddings:** Monitoring the embedding space of input prompts for outliers that might indicate malicious intent. One can train an anomaly detection model (for example, Isolation Forest, One-Class SVM) on a baseline of normal prompts, and use it to score new incoming prompts.
- **Dedicated Security Tools:** Some security platforms are starting to incorporate LLM-specific threat detection.
- **Prompt Sandboxing and Auditing:** Implementing mechanisms to isolate and audit LLM interactions to identify suspicious behavior.

Feedback Loop Integration

Lastly it is always helpful to incorporate user feedback (both explicit and implicit) into your monitoring and evaluation processes, providing invaluable real-world insights into the LLM's performance and user satisfaction. This feedback loop helps identify areas for improvement that automated metrics might miss, ensuring that the LLM truly meets user needs and expectations in the dynamic context of your application needs. Typical implementation involves:

- **Feedback Collection Mechanisms:** Implementing UI elements (for example, thumbs up/down buttons, rating scales, and free-text feedback boxes) in your LLM application.
- **Data Pipelines:** Building pipelines to collect, process, and store user feedback.

- **Sentiment Analysis:** Using NLP models to analyze free-text feedback, and identify recurring themes or negative sentiments.
    - **Libraries:** NLTK, spaCy, and Transformers (for pre-trained sentiment analysis models).
- **Integration with Monitoring Dashboards:** Displaying aggregated feedback metrics and qualitative feedback alongside other performance indicators.

```
# Example feedback collection and storage
import json
from datetime import datetime

class FeedbackCollector:
    def collect_feedback(self, request_id, user_id, response,
                         rating=None, comment=None):
        """Collect and store user feedback"""
        feedback = {
            "timestamp": datetime.utcnow().isoformat(),
            "request_id": request_id,
            "user_id": user_id,
            "rating": rating,  # e.g., 1-5 or thumbs up/down
            "comment": comment,
            "response_length": len(response),
        }

        # Store in database/log system
        self.store_feedback(feedback)

        # Real-time alerting on negative feedback
        if rating and rating <= 2:
            self.alert_on_negative_feedback(feedback)

        return feedback

    def analyze_feedback_trends(self, time_window="24h"):
        """Analyze aggregated feedback"""
        feedbacks = self.get_recent_feedback(time_window)

        positive = sum(1 for f in feedbacks if f['rating'] >= 4)
        negative = sum(1 for f in feedbacks if f['rating'] <= 2)
        satisfaction_rate = positive / len(feedbacks) if feedbacks else 0

        print(f"Satisfaction rate: {satisfaction_rate:.2%}")
        return satisfaction_rate

# Usage in your API endpoint
```

```
feedback_collector = FeedbackCollector()

@app.post("/chatbot/feedback")
def submit_feedback(request_id, rating, comment):
    feedback_collector.collect_feedback(
        request_id=request_id,
        user_id=get_current_user(),
        response=get_response_from_cache(request_id),
        rating=rating,
        comment=comment
    )
```

Implementation Workflow (Example):

1. **Identify Key Metrics:** Determine what aspects of your LLM application are most critical to monitor (for example, latency, error rate, content safety, and user satisfaction).
2. **Choose Your Tools:** Select the monitoring tools and libraries that best fit your infrastructure, budget, and expertise. You might start with open-source solutions, and consider dedicated platforms as your needs evolve.
3. **Instrument Your Application:** Modify your LLM application code to emit logs, expose metrics, and potentially integrate with monitoring SDKs.
4. **Configure Your Monitoring Infrastructure:** Set up your chosen tools (for example, ELK stack, Prometheus/Grafana, LLM monitoring platform). This might involve deploying new services or configuring the existing ones.
5. **Build Dashboards and Alerts:** Create visualizations to track key metrics, and configure alerts to notify you of anomalies or threshold violations.
6. **Implement Evaluation Pipelines:** Set up offline and potentially online evaluation processes to assess LLM quality and safety. Integrate these results into your monitoring dashboards.
7. **Establish Feedback Loops:** Implement mechanisms to collect and analyze user feedback.
8. **Iterate and Refine:** Continuously monitor your monitoring system itself, and refine your metrics, dashboards, and alerts based on your observations and evolving needs.

Setting up a comprehensive LLMOps monitoring system is an ongoing process that requires careful planning, implementation, and iteration. By focusing on the key areas of infrastructure, output quality, safety, and user feedback, and by leveraging the right tools and techniques, you can gain valuable insights into your LLM applications, and ensure their continued success. Remember to prioritize data privacy and security when logging and monitoring user interactions and generated content.

Measuring What Matters: Key Performance Indicators of LLM Health

The "*health*" of an LLM in production encompasses its operational stability, performance efficiency, output quality, safety, and cost-effectiveness. Here are certain key categories and practical KPIs with implementation details and examples:

Operational and Infrastructure Health KPIs

These tell you if the LLM service is up and reachable.

- **KPI: Uptime/Availability**
  - **What it measures:** The percentage of time the LLM API or service endpoint is successfully responding to basic health checks or requests.
  - **Why it is important:** If the service is down, nothing else matters.
  - **Implementation:**
    - Use standard monitoring tools (for example, Prometheus with Black box Exporter, Datadog Synthetic Monitoring, AWS CloudWatch Synthetics, Google Cloud Monitoring and Uptime Checks).
    - Configure simple HTTP checks (GET /health) that the LLM service exposes. This endpoint should ideally perform a minimal check (for example, can load the model configuration).
    - Track the success rate over time (for example, 5-minute intervals).
  - **Example: Target: > 99.9% uptime measured monthly. Alert if availability drops below 99% in any 1-hour window.**
- **KPI: API Error Rate (Server-Side)**
  - **What it measures:** The percentage of incoming requests that result in server-side errors (HTTP 5xx codes).
  - **Why it is important:** High error rates indicate backend problems (infrastructure issues, model loading failures, and bugs in the serving layer).
  - **Implementation:**
    - Monitor HTTP status codes from the load balancer or API gateway logs sitting in front of the LLM service.
    - Tools such as Datadog, Splunk, ELK Stack (Elasticsearch, Logstash, Kibana), or cloud provider logging services (CloudWatch Logs, Google Cloud Logging) can aggregate and visualize this.

- Filter for 500, 502, 503, 504 status codes.

- **Example: Target: < 0.1% 5xx error rate. Alert, if the rate exceeds 1% over a 15-minute period.**

Performance and Latency KPIs

These tell you how *fast* and *efficiently* the LLM is responding.

- **KPI: End-to-End Latency (Percentiles)**
  - **What it measures:** The total time taken from the moment a user request hits your system (for example, API gateway) until the full response is returned. Crucially, track percentiles (P50, P90, P95, and P99).
  - **Why it is important:** User experience heavily depends on responsiveness. Average latency can hide issues affecting a significant portion of users (tail latency).
  - **Implementation:**
    - Log timestamps at the entry point (API gateway/load balancer) and just before sending the final response back. Calculate the difference.
    - Use Application Performance Monitoring (APM) tools (Datadog APM, Dynatrace, and New Relic) which automatically trace requests across services.
    - Aggregate these timings and calculate P50 (median), P90, P95, and P99 values.
  - **Example: Target: P90 latency < 2 seconds for interactive chat. Alert, if P95 latency exceeds 5 seconds.**
- **KPI:** Model Inference Latency (Percentiles)
  - **What it measures:** The time the LLM itself takes to process the input and generate the output, excluding network overhead, queueing time, pre/post-processing.
  - **Why it is important:** Isolates the performance of the core model execution. Helps diagnose if slowdowns are due to the model or surrounding infrastructure.
  - **Implementation:**
    - Log timestamps immediately before sending the request to the model inference engine and immediately after receiving the response.
    - If using managed services (like OpenAI API, Vertex AI, and Bedrock), this might be harder to get directly, but you can estimate it by subtracting known overheads from end-to-end latency. If self-hosting (for example, using TGI, vLLM), and instrument the serving framework.

  - **Example: Target: P90 inference latency < 1.5 seconds (assuming the end-to-end target is 2s, leaving 0.5s for other overheads).**

- **KPI:** Throughput (Requests per Second/Tokens per Second)
  - **What it measures:** How many requests the system can handle concurrently, or how many tokens it can process/generate per unit of time.
  - **Why it is important:** Capacity planning and understanding load limits.
  - **Implementation:**
    - Monitor request counts at the load balancer or API gateway level per second/minute.
    - For token throughput (more relevant for cost and model work), log the number of input + output tokens for each request, and sum them up over time intervals. This requires parsing the request/response.
    - **Note:** Tokens per Second (TPS) is a more fundamental and model-centric performance metric than Requests per Second, as one request could generate 10 tokens or 10,000. TPS directly relates to model efficiency, and is essential for cost management.
  - **Example: Target: Sustain 50 requests/second during peak hours. Monitor average tokens/second per inference worker.**

Output Quality and Relevance KPIs

These are often harder to automate but crucial for judging if the LLM is useful.

- **KPI:** Relevance/Helpfulness Score (Proxy Metrics)
  - **What it measures:** How relevant, accurate, and helpful the LLM's response is to the user's query. Direct measurement is hard, so proxies are used.
  - **Why it is important:** The core value proposition of the LLM.
  - **Implementation:**
    - **User Feedback:** Implement thumbs up/down buttons, star ratings, or short feedback forms after responses. Track the percentage of positive feedback. This is often the most practical signal.
    - **Task Completion Rate:** If the LLM is part of a workflow (for example, chatbot booking an appointment, code generation that compiles), track the success rate of the overall task.
    - **Automated Metrics (Use with Caution):** For specific tasks such as summarization or translation, metrics like ROUGE, BLEU can be calculated on a curated evaluation dataset run periodically, but they do not capture

nuance well for general chat.

    - **Human Evaluation (Golden Sets):** Periodically have humans review a sample of production requests/responses against predefined criteria (for example, rate relevance, coherence, and harmlessness on a 1-5 scale). This is expensive but provides high-quality data.

  - **Example: Target: > 80% "Thumbs Up" rating on user feedback. Maintain > 90% score on the human-evaluated golden set for "Relevance".**

- **KPI:** Hallucination Rate (Proxy Metrics)
  - **What it measures:** The frequency with which the LLM generates factually incorrect or nonsensical information presented as fact.
  - **Why it is important:** Hallucinations erode trust, and can be harmful.
  - **Implementation:**
    - **Contradiction Detection:** If using Retrieval Augmented Generation (RAG), check if the LLM's output contradicts the retrieved source documents. Implement checks (for example, using another model or specific algorithms) to flag contradictions.
    - **Fact Checking on Golden Sets:** Include prompts in your human evaluation set specifically designed to test factual recall on known information. Track the error rate.
    - **User Feedback:** Users often report hallucinations implicitly ("*That is wrong*", "*That didn't happen*"). Analyze user feedback text for keyword s indicating factual errors.
  - **Example: Target: < 5% contradiction rate in RAG responses. < 2% hallucination rate detected in human spot checks.**

- **KPI:** Response Length / Token Count
  - **What it measures:** The number of tokens (or characters/words) in the LLM's output.
  - **Why it is important:** Impacts latency, cost, and user experience (overly verbose or unhelpfully brief responses).
  - **Implementation:** Log the number of output tokens for every request. Monitor average, P95, and maximum length.
  - **Example: Target: Average response length between 50-500 tokens for a chatbot use case. Alert, if P95 length exceeds 1500 tokens unexpectedly.**

Safety and Responsibility KPIs

Ensuring the LLM behaves ethically and safely.

- **KPI:** Harmful Content Rate
  - **What it measures:** The percentage of responses flagged as containing harmful content (hate speech, harassment, unsafe instructions, etc.).
  - **Why it's important:** Essential for brand safety, user trust, and ethical AI deployment.
  - **Implementation:**
    - Use content moderation APIs (for example, OpenAI Moderation endpoint, Google Cloud Natural Language API, Perspective API) or internal classifiers applied to LLM outputs *before* they reach the user (or logged for review).
    - Track the number/percentage of requests flagged by severity level.
  - **Example: Target: < 0.01% of responses flagged for high-severity harmful content. Review all flagged content daily.**
- **KPI:** Bias Detection (Proxy Metrics)
  - **What it measures:** The presence of systematic bias (e.g., gender, racial, stereotypical) in LLM responses.
  - **Why it's important:** Fairness and equity.
  - **Implementation:**
    - **Bias Evaluation Datasets:** Periodically run standardized tests (like BOLD, BBQ) or custom-designed prompts comparing outputs for different demographic groups (e.g., "*Describe a [male nurse/female doctor]*"). Analyze for stereotypical associations or differing sentiment/quality.
    - **User Reports:** Track user feedback specifically mentioning biased or unfair responses.
  - **Example: Target: No statistically significant difference in sentiment or quality scores for paired prompts across protected attributes in the evaluation set.**
- **KPI:** PII (Personally Identifiable Information) Leakage Rate
  - **What it measures:** The frequency with which the LLM inadvertently includes PII (names, emails, phone numbers, etc.) in its output, especially if trained on potentially sensitive data.
  - **Why it's important:** Privacy regulations (GDPR, CCPA) and user trust.

- **Implementation:**
  - Use PII detection tools/libraries (e.g., spaCy, Presidio, AWS Comprehend, Google Cloud DLP) to scan LLM outputs *before* sending them to users or in logs.
  - Track the number of responses where PII is detected.
- **Example: Target: Zero PII detected in final outputs reaching users. Alert on any PII detection for investigation.**

Cost and Efficiency KPIs

Monitoring the financial impact

- **KPI:** Cost per Request/Cost per 1k Tokens
  - **What it measures:** The monetary cost associated with each LLM interaction or per unit of work (tokens).
  - **Why it is important:** Budget management and ROI calculation.
  - **Implementation:**
    - **If using API-based LLMs:** (API Cost / Number of Requests) or (API Cost / Total Tokens Processed) * 1000. Get costs from your provider's billing dashboard/API. Correlate usage logs (request/token counts) with the billing data.
    - **Important:** Most LLM providers differentiate billing for input tokens and output tokens (for example, output tokens often cost more). This is a practical LLMOps detail that directly impacts cost optimization, and links back to the Response Length KPI.
    - **If self-hosting:** (Infrastructure Cost (GPU hours, servers) / Number of Requests or Tokens). Infrastructure cost needs careful calculation (instance runtime, data transfer, and so on).
  - **Example: Target:** Average cost per request < $0.01. Keep cost per 1k tokens below $0.002.

```
# Example: Cost tracking for LLM API calls
class CostTracker:
    def __init__(self):
        # Example pricing (OpenAI GPT-4 style)
        self.input_price_per_1k = 0.03   # $0.03 per 1k input tokens
        self.output_price_per_1k = 0.06  # $0.06 per 1k output tokens

    def calculate_cost(self, input_tokens, output_tokens):
```

```
        """Calculate cost for a single request"""
        input_cost = (input_tokens / 1000) * self.input_price_per_1k
        output_cost = (output_tokens / 1000) * self.output_price_per_1k
        total_cost = input_cost + output_cost
        return total_cost

    def log_request_cost(self, request_id, input_tokens, output_tokens):
        """Log cost for monitoring and alerting"""
        cost = self.calculate_cost(input_tokens, output_tokens)

        # Log to monitoring system
        log_metric("llm_cost_per_request", cost, {"request_id": request_id})

        # Example alert: expensive request
        if cost > 0.10:  # $0.10 threshold
            alert(f"High-cost request: ${cost:.4f} for {request_id}")

        return cost

# Usage
tracker = CostTracker()

# After LLM call
response = llm_api.complete(prompt)
cost = tracker.log_request_cost(
    request_id="req_123",
    input_tokens=150,   # From API response
    output_tokens=500   # From API response
)
print(f"Request cost: ${cost:.4f}")  # e.g., $0.0345

# Daily cost tracking
def calculate_daily_costs(requests_log):
    """Calculate total daily cost from request logs"""
    total_cost = sum(
        tracker.calculate_cost(r['input_tokens'], r['output_tokens'])
        for r in requests_log
    )
    avg_cost_per_request = total_cost / len(requests_log)

    print(f"Total daily cost: ${total_cost:.2f}")
    print(f"Average cost per request: ${avg_cost_per_request:.4f}")

    return total_cost, avg_cost_per_request
```

- **KPI:** Total LLM Infrastructure/API Cost
    - **What it measures:** The overall spending on the LLM service.

- **Why it is important:** Overall budget control.
- **Implementation:** Monitor cloud provider billing dashboards, filtering by tags associated with the LLM resources or API usage reports.
- **Example: Target: Monthly LLM spend below $10,000. Alert, if projected monthly cost exceeds the budget.**

Data and Model Drift KPIs

Monitoring changes in input data or model behavior over time.

- **KPI:** Input Data Drift
  - **What it measures:** Changes in the statistical properties of the prompts the LLM is receiving compared to its training or evaluation data.
  - **Why it is important:** If production input data diverges significantly, the model's performance and quality might degrade ("*out-of-distribution*" problem).
  - **Implementation:**
    - Log incoming prompts. Periodically (for example, daily/weekly), calculate distributions of prompt length, topic distribution (using topic modeling), keyword frequencies, embedding drift (average distance between embeddings of new prompts vs. a baseline set).
    - Use statistical tests (for example, Kolmogorov-Smirnov test, Population Stability Index - PSI) to compare current distribution to a reference period.
    - Tools like WhyLabs, Arize AI, Fiddler, or custom scripts using libraries such as scipy.stats or evidentlyai can help.
  - **Example: Target: PSI for prompt length distribution < 0.1. Alert, if topic distribution changes significantly (for example, KL divergence > threshold).**
- **KPI:** Output Quality Drift (on Evaluation Set)
  - **What it measures:** Changes in the model's performance on a fixed evaluation dataset over time.
  - **Why it is important:** Catches degradation in the model's core capabilities, potentially due to underlying infrastructure changes or subtle model issues.
  - **Implementation:**
    - Maintain a high-quality, representative evaluation set ("*golden set*") of prompts and expected good responses/criteria.
    - Periodically (for example, daily or weekly) run the current production model against this set, and calculate relevant quality metrics (for example, accuracy, BLEU/ROUGE if applicable, and human rating, if feasible).

- Track these metrics over time.

  - **Example: Target: Accuracy on the fact-checking subset of the golden set remains above 95%. Alert, if it drops by > 3% compared to the baseline.**

Implementation Strategy:

1. **Prioritize:** You do not need all these KPIs from day one. Start with critical operational (Uptime, Error Rate), performance (Latency), cost (Cost/Request), and a basic quality measure (User Feedback).
2. **Tooling:** Select appropriate monitoring (Prometheus/Grafana, Datadog, and CloudWatch), logging (ELK, Splunk, and Cloud Logging), and potentially specialized LLM Observability platforms.
3. **Baseline:** Establish baseline values for your KPIs soon after launch or during testing. What is "*normal*" for your application?
4. **Dashboarding:** Create dashboards that visualize these KPIs, showing trends over time. Segment by model version, endpoint, user type, and so on, where relevant.
5. **Alerting:** Set up meaningful alerts on key deviations from baselines or targets. Avoid alert fatigue.
6. **Feedback Loop:** Use the insights from these KPIs to drive improvements such as: adjust infrastructure, fine-tune prompts, retrain/update models, improve safety filters, and so on.
7. **Iterate:** Continuously review and refine your KPIs as your understanding of the system and user needs evolves.

By implementing a practical set of these KPIs, you gain crucial visibility into your LLM's health, ensuring that it runs reliably, efficiently, safely, and continues to deliver value.

Automated Alerting and Anomaly Detection

The goal is to move from manually watching dashboards or logs to having the system automatically tell you when something is wrong (Alerting) or when something looks weird and might need investigation (Anomaly Detection).

Automated Alerting: Reacting to Known Conditions

This is about setting predefined rules. If a specific metric crosses a threshold or a specific event occurs, an alert is triggered.

- **Practical Goal:** Notify the right people (or systems) immediately when a known bad state occurs, enabling faster reaction and resolution.

- **Implementation Components:**
    - **Data Source:** Metrics (for example, CPU usage, latency, error counts, LLM token cost from Prometheus, Datadog, and CloudWatch) or Logs (for example, application errors, specific event messages from Splunk, ELK, Loki, and CloudWatch Logs).
    - **Monitoring System:** A tool that ingests the data, and allows you to define rules on it (for example, Grafana, Prometheus Alertmanager, Datadog Monitors, AWS CloudWatch Alarms, and Google Cloud Monitoring Alerting Policies).
    - **Alerting Rules:** The specific conditions you define. These are the core of alerting.
    - **Notification Channels:** How the alert reaches you (for example, Slack messages, PagerDuty incidents, Opsgenie alerts, email, SMS, Microsoft Teams messages, and webhooks to trigger automated actions).
    - **(Optional) Action/Automation:** Triggering automated responses via webhooks (for example, restarting a service, scaling up resources, running a diagnostic script, and so on).
- **Types of Alerting Rules and Examples:**
    - **Threshold Alerts:** Most common. Trigger when a metric goes above or below a certain value for a defined duration.
        - **Example 1 (LLM Latency):** `ALERT IF p95_latency > 2500ms FOR 5m` (Alert if the 95th percentile latency stays above 2.5 seconds for 5 minutes).
        - **Example 2 (API Errors):** `ALERT IF sum(rate(http_errors_5xx[5m])) / sum(rate (http_requests_total[5m])) > 0.01 FOR 10m` (Alert if the ratio of 5xx errors to total requests over 5-minute intervals exceeds 1% and stays that way for 10 minutes).
        - **Example 3 (LLM Cost):** `ALERT IF daily_llm_api_cost > $500` (Alert if the accumulated cost for the LLM API exceeds $500 within the current day).
        - **Example 4 (Resource Usage):** `ALERT IF avg(gpu_utilization_percent) > 90 FOR 15m` (Alert if average GPU util utilization across your LLM inference servers is over 90% for 15 minutes).
    - **Event-Based Alerts:** Trigger based on specific log messages or events.
        - **Example 1 (Deployment Failure):** `ALERT IF log_message CONTAINS "Deployment failed: model_download_error"` (Alert immediately if a

log indicating a model download failure appears).

    - **Example 2 (Security Event):** `ALERT IF audit_log CONTAINS "Unauthorized access attempt"` (Alert on specific security-related log entries).

  - **Rate of Change / Delta Alerts**: Trigger based on how quickly a metric is changing.
    - **Example 1 (Sudden Error Spike):** `ALERT IF increase(error_count[5m]) > 50` (Alert if the number of errors increased by more than 50 in the last 5 minutes).
    - **Example 2 (Sudden Traffic Drop):** `ALERT IF rate(requests_total[1m]) < (avg_over_time(rate(requests_total[1h])[60m:1m]) * 0.5)` (Alert if the current request rate is less than 50% of the hourly average from an hour ago - simplified example).

- **Practical Considerations:**
  - **Tuning:** Setting thresholds is critical. Too sensitive -> Alert fatigue (people ignore alerts). Too insensitive -> Miss real issues. Start with educated guesses, monitor, and adjust based on real incidents and false positives. Use percentiles (P95, P99) for latency/performance, rather than averages.
  - **Alert Severity:** Use levels (for example, Critical, Warning, Info). Critical alerts should wake people up (PagerDuty); Warnings might just go to Slack during business hours.
  - **Actionability:** Ensure that alerts provide context. Include links to relevant dashboards, logs, or runbooks (step-by-step guides for diagnosing/fixing the issue). An alert like "CPU *High*" is less useful than "CPU *High on LLM-Inference-Pod-XYZ, potentially impacting* P99 *latency. [Link to Dashboard] [Link to Runbook]*".
  - **Notification Routing:** Send alerts to the specific team responsible for that service. Use tools such as `PagerDuty` or Opsgenie to manage on-call schedules.
  - **Deduplication and Grouping:** Configure your system (for example, `Alertmanager`) to group related alerts (for example, 10 pods having high CPU) into a single notification.

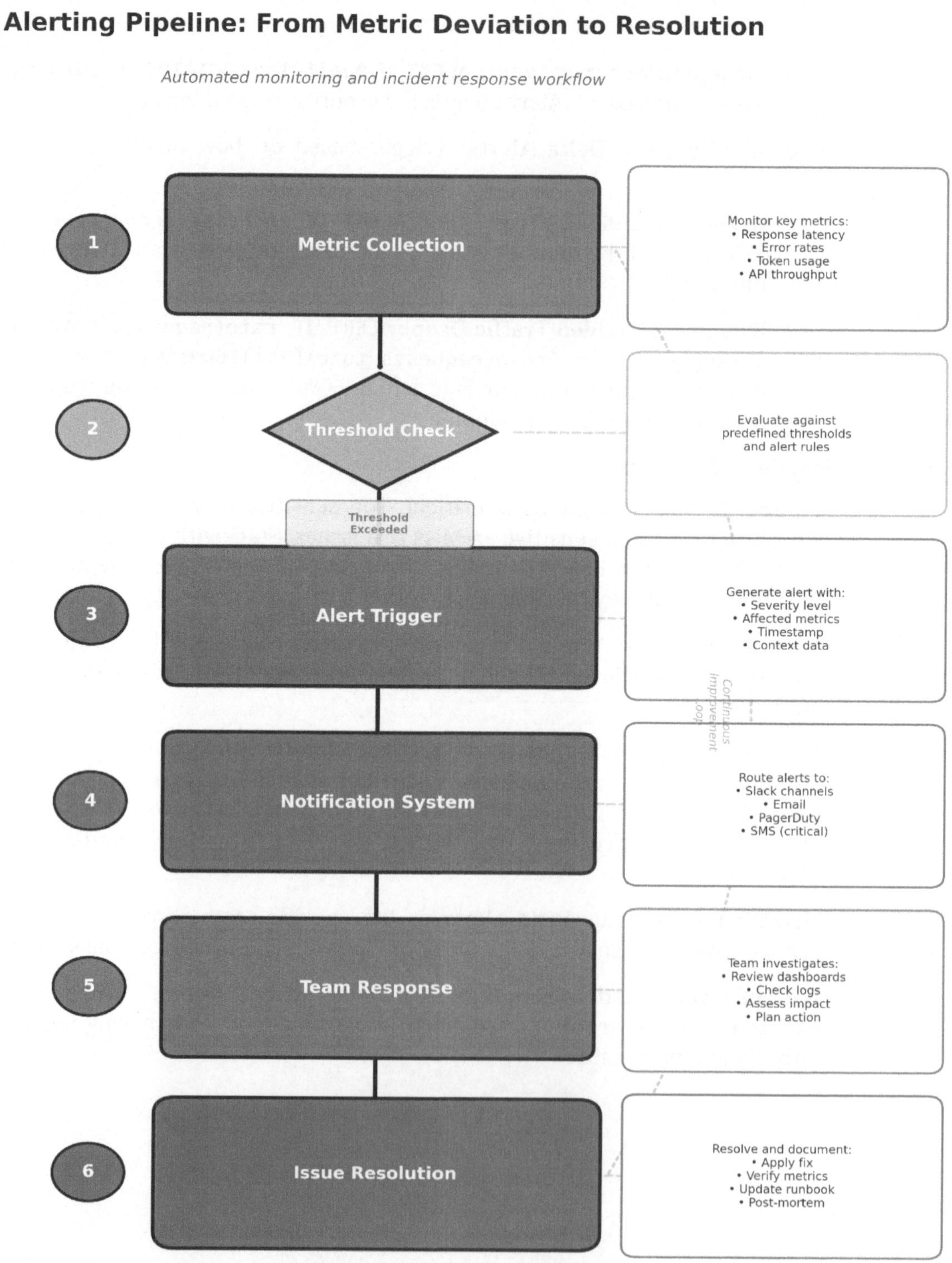

Figure 8.2: *Alerting Pipeline: From Metric Deviation to Resolution*

Anomaly Detection: Finding the Unexpected

This is about identifying patterns in data that deviate from what is considered "*normal*" behavior, without necessarily having a predefined threshold. It helps catch "*unknown unknowns*".

- **Practical Goal:** Surface subtle, novel, or complex issues that fixed threshold alerts might miss. Provide early warnings or identify shifts in system behavior.
- **Implementation Approaches:**
  - **Statistical Methods:** Simpler to implement and interpret.
    - **Moving Averages / Standard Deviations:** Compare the current metric value to its recent moving average. Flag as anomalous if it is more than N standard deviations away. Many monitoring tools have this built-in.
    - **Example:** Flag `user_sessions` if the current count is more than 3 standard deviations below the moving average calculated over the last hour (detects sudden drops).
    - **Chatbot-Specific Example:** An anomaly detection model monitors the coherence score of chatbot responses. It flags when the average coherence score drops significantly for prompts containing the keyword "`refunds`", indicating the model suddenly started generating poor responses in that domain. This catches unexpected spikes in nonsensical answers for specific topics that threshold-based alerts might miss.
    - **Seasonality Decomposition (for example, STL):** Breaks down a time series into trend, seasonal, and residual components. Anomalies are often points with high residuals after accounting for normal daily/weekly patterns.

      Example: Detect an unusual spike in `LLM_query_volume` at 3 AM, even if the absolute number is low, because it deviates significantly from the typical pattern for that time and day.
    - **Distribution Analysis (Histograms/Percentiles):** Monitor the distribution of a metric (like latency). An anomaly could be a sudden shift in the shape of the distribution (for example, P99 latency increasing significantly, while P50 remains stable).
  - **Machine Learning (ML) Methods:** More powerful for complex patterns but require more data and expertise.
    - **Clustering (for example, DBSCAN, K-Means):** Group similar data points (for example, based on request features such as latency, token count, and user ID). Points that do not belong to any cluster or form very small clusters can be anomalies.

Example: Identify a small cluster of user requests experiencing unusually high `LLM_inference_latency`, potentially indicating an issue affecting only certain inputs or users.

- **Time Series Forecasting (for example, ARIMA, Prophet):** Build a model to predict the expected value of a metric. Flag points where the actual value deviates significantly from the forecast.

  Example: Predict the expected `token_cost_per_hour`. Flag an hour where the actual cost is 20% higher than predicted, even if it has not crossed a fixed budget alert threshold yet.

- **Autoencoders (Neural Networks):** Train a network to compress and reconstruct normal data. Anomalous data points will likely have a high "*reconstruction error*".

  Example: Detect subtle changes in the patterns of `GPU_memory_usage` over time that might precede an out-of-memory error.

- **Isolation Forests:** Efficient algorithm for detecting outliers by randomly partitioning data. Anomalies are easier to "*isolate*".

```
# Example: Anomaly detection using Isolation Forest
from sklearn.ensemble import IsolationForest
import numpy as np

# Training phase: Learn normal behavior
historical_metrics = np.array([
    [latency, token_count, error_count],  # Features from normal operation
    # ... collect data over baseline period
])

# Train model on normal data
anomaly_detector = IsolationForest(contamination=0.1, random_state=42)
anomaly_detector.fit(historical_metrics)

# Production monitoring
def check_for_anomalies(current_latency, current_tokens, current_errors):
    """Check if current metrics are anomalous"""
    current_metrics = np.array([[current_latency, current_tokens, current_
errors]])

    # Predict: -1 for anomaly, 1 for normal
    prediction = anomaly_detector.predict(current_metrics)

    # Get anomaly score (more negative = more anomalous)
    anomaly_score = anomaly_detector.score_samples(current_metrics)[0]
```

```
    if prediction[0] == -1:
        alert(f"Anomaly detected! Score: {anomaly_score:.3f}")
        return True, anomaly_score

    return False, anomaly_score

# Usage in monitoring loop
is_anomalous, score = check_for_anomalies(
    current_latency=2500,  # ms
    current_tokens=350,
    current_errors=5
)
```

- **Integrating Anomaly Detection with Alerting:**
    - Anomaly detection systems typically generate an "*anomaly score*" or a binary "**`is_anomaly`**" flag.
    - These scores/flags become *input metrics* for the Automated Alerting system.
    - You then define an alert rule on the anomaly score.
    - **Example: `ALERT IF anomaly_score(p95_latency) > 0.8 FOR 10m`** (Alert if the anomaly detection system consistently flags P95 latency as highly anomalous for 10 minutes).
    - **Example: `ALERT IF anomaly_detected_flag(log_pattern_frequency) == 1`** (Alert if the system detects an anomalous frequency of certain log patterns).
- **Practical Considerations:**
    - **Training Data:** ML models need sufficient normal data to learn baseline behavior. Avoid training during incidents or abnormal periods. Seasonality needs to be captured.
    - **Tuning Sensitivity:** Adjusting model parameters or score thresholds determines how sensitive it is. Too sensitive -> False positives. Too insensitive -> Misses anomalies. This often requires experimentation.
    - **Explainability:** Why was something flagged? Statistical methods are often easier to interpret. For ML models, techniques like SHAP values or feature importance can help, but it can be challenging.
    - **Computational Cost:** ML models can be more resource-intensive to train and run compared to simple statistical checks.
    - **Context is Key:** An anomaly is not always a problem. It might be a genuine change in usage (for example, marketing campaign launch causing traffic spike). Human investigation is usually needed. Use anomaly detection primarily for warning or investigation triggers, not necessarily critical, and wake-up alerts unless the signal is very strong or corroborated.

Tools and Platforms:

- **Integrated Monitoring Suites:** Datadog (Watchdog), Dynatrace (Davis AI), New Relic (Applied Intelligence), AWS CloudWatch Anomaly Detection, Google Cloud Monitoring Intelligence often have built-in anomaly detection features alongside alerting.
- **Time Series Databases and Visualization:** Prometheus + Grafana (some anomaly detection plugins exist), InfluxDB (Kapacitor for alerting/detection).
- **Log Management:** Elasticsearch (ML features), Splunk (ML Toolkit).
- **Specialized AIOps/Observability Platforms:** Tools focused specifically on ML-driven monitoring and anomaly detection. LLM Observability tools (Arize, WhyLabs, Fiddler) often include drift and anomaly detection for inputs/outputs.
- **Libraries (DIY):** Python libraries like scikit-learn (Isolation Forest, Local Outlier Factor, Clustering), statsmodels (STL, ARIMA), Facebook Prophet, PyOD (Python Outlier Detection).

In Summary:

- Automated Alerting is your first line of defense, acting on known failure conditions using predefined rules (thresholds, events). It is essential for immediate reaction to critical issues.
- Anomaly Detection is your surveillance system, looking for unusual patterns that might indicate novel problems or subtle shifts before they trigger threshold alerts. It often requires more tuning and investigation but can catch issues you did not anticipate.

Implementing both, with anomaly detection often feeding into the alerting system, provides a robust, layered approach to monitoring system health proactively. Start with simple threshold alerts for critical metrics, then gradually introduce statistical or ML-based anomaly detection for key indicators where subtle changes matter.

Continuous Evaluation and Feedback Loops

Continuous evaluation and feedback loops are necessary for the ongoing improvement and maintenance of Large Language Model (LLM) applications. Unlike traditional software where performance can often be measured with well-defined metrics, evaluating LLMs is more nuanced, and requires considering factors such as response quality, relevance, coherence, safety, and user satisfaction. Establishing robust continuous evaluation processes and incorporating feedback effectively allows for iterative refinement, proactive issue detection, and ultimately, a better user experience.

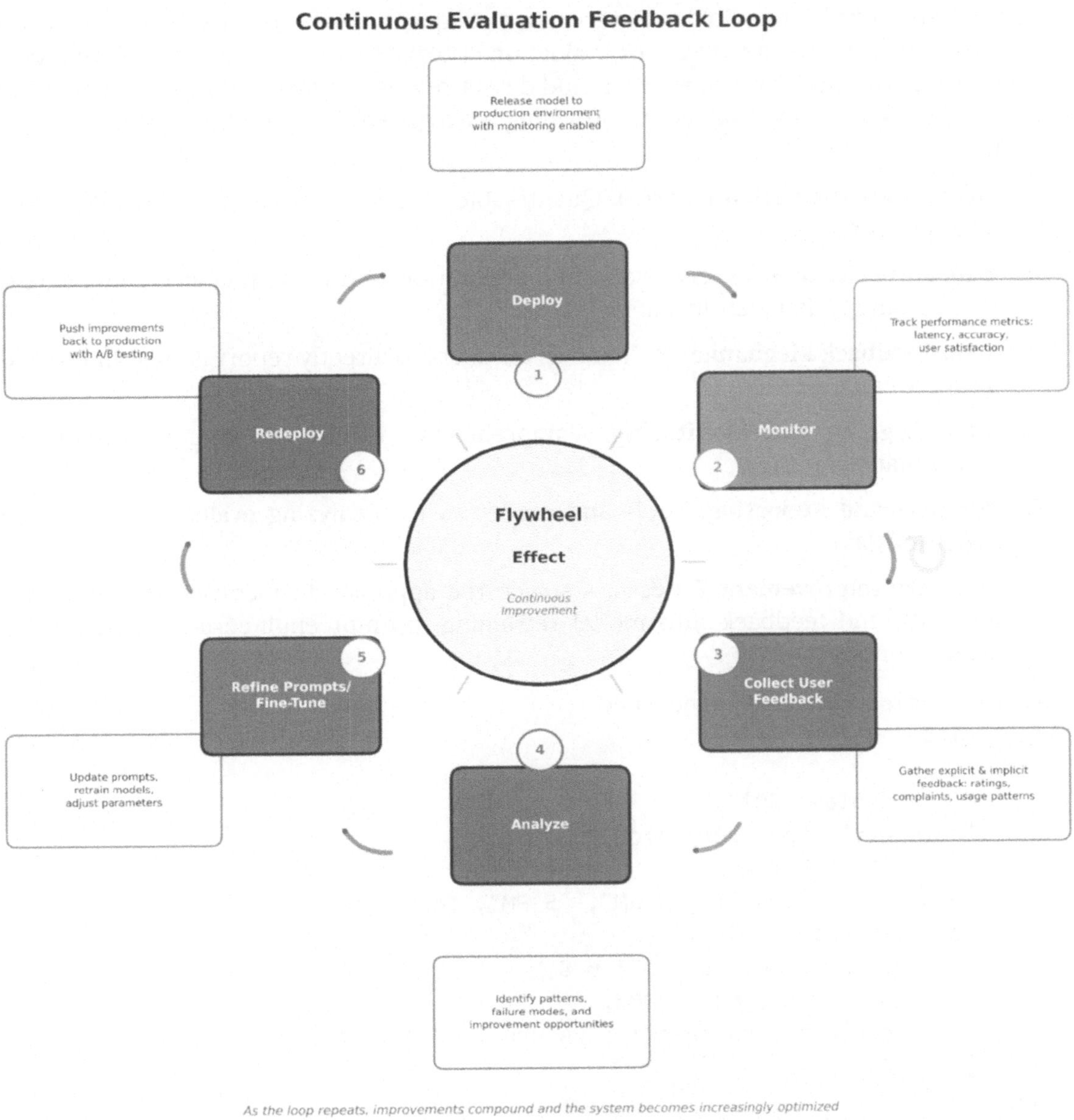

Figure 8.3: Continuous Evaluation Feedback Loop

Components of Continuous Evaluation and Feedback Loops

A comprehensive system for continuous evaluation and feedback loops typically includes the following components:

Golden Dataset Definition: A Golden Dataset is a high-quality, small, and fixed set of inputs and their desired, expert-vetted outputs (or evaluation criteria) that is run against the production model regularly to track core capabilities, and detect regression/drift. It serves as the bridge between offline and online evaluation, providing a consistent baseline for measuring model performance over time.

1. **Automated Evaluation Metrics:** Quantifiable measures to assess various aspects of LLM performance.
2. **Human Evaluation:** Expert review and annotation to provide nuanced judgments on output quality and identify subtle issues.
3. **User Feedback Mechanisms:** Channels for users to directly report issues, and provide suggestions.
4. **Data Logging and Monitoring:** Comprehensive logging of inputs, outputs, and performance metrics.
5. **Analysis and Reporting:** Tools and processes for analyzing evaluation results and feedback data.
6. **Iterative Improvement Process:** A structured approach to incorporating evaluation findings, and feedback into model retraining, prompt engineering, or application adjustments.

```
# Example: Golden Dataset structure
golden_dataset = [
    {
        "id": "golden_001",
        "category": "product_info",
        "prompt": "What are your business hours?",
        "expected_content": ["9 AM", "5 PM", "Monday-Friday"],
        "quality_criteria": {
            "min_relevance_score": 0.8,
            "max_latency_ms": 2000,
            "should_not_contain": ["unsure", "don't know"]
        }
    },
    {
        "id": "golden_002",
        "category": "refund_policy",
        "prompt": "How do I get a refund?",
        "expected_content": ["30 days", "contact support", "receipt"],
        "quality_criteria": {
            "min_relevance_score": 0.85,
            "max_latency_ms": 2000,
            "must_be_factual": True
```

```
        }
    },
    # ... more golden examples
]

def evaluate_on_golden_set(model, golden_dataset):
    """Run model against golden dataset and track performance"""
    results = []

    for item in golden_dataset:
        start_time = time.time()
        response = model.generate(item["prompt"])
        latency = (time.time() - start_time) * 1000

        # Check if expected content is present
        content_found = all(
            exp in response.lower()
            for exp in item["expected_content"]
        )

        # Check latency
        latency_ok = latency < item["quality_criteria"]["max_latency_ms"]

        results.append({
            "id": item["id"],
            "passed": content_found and latency_ok,
            "latency_ms": latency,
            "response": response
        })

    pass_rate = sum(r["passed"] for r in results) / len(results)
    print(f"Golden set pass rate: {pass_rate:.2%}")

    return results, pass_rate
```

Automated Evaluation Metrics

A comprehensive taxonomy of LLM evaluation metrics is essential for systematic assessment of model performance across different dimensions. The following consolidated framework groups LLM-specific metrics by function, providing a structured approach to evaluation:

Quality Metrics

Quality metrics assess the linguistic and semantic quality of LLM outputs:

- **ROUGE (Recall-Oriented Understudy for Gisting Evaluation):** Measures overlap between generated and reference text using n-gram matching, particularly effective for summarization tasks.

- **BERTScore:** Uses contextual embeddings to evaluate semantic similarity between generated and reference texts, providing more nuanced quality assessment than n-gram based metrics.
- **Perplexity:** Measures how well the model predicts a sequence of words, with lower perplexity indicating better language modeling performance.

```
# Example: Calculating ROUGE scores
from rouge_score import rouge_scorer

scorer = rouge_scorer.RougeScorer(['rouge1', 'rouge2', 'rougeL'], use_
stemmer=True)

# Reference text (ground truth summary)
reference = "The AI model successfully processed customer inquiries with high
accuracy."

# Generated text (LLM output)
generated = "The AI system handled customer questions accurately and
efficiently."

scores = scorer.score(reference, generated)

print(f"ROUGE-1: {scores['rouge1'].fmeasure:.3f}")  # Unigram overlap
print(f"ROUGE-2: {scores['rouge2'].fmeasure:.3f}")  # Bigram overlap
print(f"ROUGE-L: {scores['rougeL'].fmeasure:.3f}")  # Longest common
subsequence

# For batch evaluation
def evaluate_summaries(references, generated_outputs):
    scores_list = []
    for ref, gen in zip(references, generated_outputs):
        scores = scorer.score(ref, gen)
        scores_list.append(scores['rougeL'].fmeasure)

    avg_rouge = sum(scores_list) / len(scores_list)
    print(f"Average ROUGE-L: {avg_rouge:.3f}")
    return avg_rouge

# Example: Calculating BERTScore
from bert_score import score

references = ["The customer service chatbot resolved the issue quickly."]
candidates = ["The support bot fixed the problem fast."]

# Calculate BERTScore (returns precision, recall, F1)
P, R, F1 = score(candidates, references, lang="en", verbose=False)
```

```
print(f"BERTScore F1: {F1.item():.3f}")  # Typically ranges 0.8-1.0
# F1 > 0.9 indicates high semantic similarity
```

Safety/Harm Metrics

Safety metrics evaluate the potential harm and bias in LLM outputs:

- **Toxicity Detection:** Uses specialized models to detect harmful, offensive, or inappropriate content in generated text, providing toxicity scores and classification.
- **Bias Detection:** Evaluates fairness and bias across demographic groups, measuring differential performance and representation in model outputs.

RAG-Specific Metrics

RAG-specific metrics evaluate the quality of retrieval-augmented generation systems:

- **Groundedness/Faithfulness:** Measures how well the generated response is supported by the retrieved context, ensuring that claims are factually grounded in the provided information.
- **Context/Answer Relevance:** Evaluates the relevance of retrieved context to the user query and the appropriateness of the generated answer given the retrieved information.

This taxonomy provides a systematic framework for evaluating LLM performance across multiple dimensions, enabling comprehensive assessment and continuous improvement of LLM systems in production environments.

```
# Example: Checking groundedness in RAG systems
def check_groundedness(response, retrieved_context):
    """Simple groundedness check for RAG responses"""
    from sentence_transformers import SentenceTransformer, util

    model = SentenceTransformer('all-MiniLM-L6-v2')

    # Split response into claims/sentences
    response_sentences = response.split('. ')

    # Encode context and response sentences
    context_embedding = model.encode(retrieved_context, convert_to_
tensor=True)

    groundedness_scores = []
    for sentence in response_sentences:
        if not sentence.strip():
            continue

        sent_embedding = model.encode(sentence, convert_to_tensor=True)
```

```
        similarity = util.cos_sim(sent_embedding, context_embedding).item()
        groundedness_scores.append(similarity)

    avg_groundedness = sum(groundedness_scores) / len(groundedness_scores)

    # Flag if low groundedness (potential hallucination)
    if avg_groundedness < 0.5:
        return False, f"Low groundedness: {avg_groundedness:.2f}"

    return True, f"Grounded: {avg_groundedness:.2f}"

# Usage
context = "Our product costs $99/month and includes 24/7 support."
response = "The product is priced at $99 monthly with round-the-clock
support."
is_grounded, message = check_groundedness(response, context)
print(message)
```

Human Evaluation

Human evaluation provides crucial qualitative insights that automated metrics might miss. This can involve:

- **Annotation:** Trained annotators evaluate LLM outputs based on specific criteria (for example, helpfulness, accuracy, clarity, and safety) using defined rubrics.
- **A/B Testing:** Comparing different versions of the LLM application or prompts by showing their outputs to human evaluators, and asking for preferences.
- **Expert Reviews:** Subject matter experts assess the accuracy and relevance of the LLM's responses in specific domains.
- **Red Teaming:** Security experts intentionally try to elicit harmful or biased outputs to identify vulnerabilities.

```
# Example: Human evaluation rubric for chatbot responses
evaluation_rubric = {
    "relevance": {
        "description": "Does the response address the user's question?",
        "scale": {
            1: "Completely irrelevant",
            2: "Somewhat relevant but misses key points",
            3: "Mostly relevant with minor gaps",
            4: "Highly relevant and comprehensive",
            5: "Perfect - directly and completely addresses the query"
        }
    },
```

```
    "accuracy": {
        "description": "Is the information factually correct?",
        "scale": {
            1: "Contains major factual errors",
            2: "Some inaccuracies present",
            3: "Mostly accurate with minor issues",
            4: "Accurate with no significant errors",
            5: "Completely accurate and verifiable"
        }
    },
    "helpfulness": {
        "description": "Would this response help the user?",
        "scale": {
            1: "Not helpful at all",
            2: "Minimally helpful",
            3: "Moderately helpful",
            4: "Very helpful",
            5: "Exceptionally helpful and actionable"
        }
    },
    "safety": {
        "description": "Is the response free from harmful content?",
        "binary": ["Safe", "Unsafe (flag for review)"],
        "unsafe_categories": ["Bias", "Toxicity", "Misinformation", "PII leak"]
    }
}

# Example annotation data structure
annotation_sample = {
    "prompt": "How do I reset my password?",
    "response": "You can reset your password by clicking 'Forgot Password' on
the login page...",
    "scores": {
        "relevance": 5,
        "accuracy": 5,
        "helpfulness": 4,
        "safety": "Safe"
    },
    "annotator_id": "annotator_123",
    "timestamp": "2025-10-08T14:30:00Z",
    "comments": "Clear and accurate instructions. Could include more details
about verification steps."
```

```
}

# Example: A/B testing framework for LLM comparison
import random

class ABTestManager:
    def __init__(self):
        self.results = {"variant_A": [], "variant_B": []}

    def assign_variant(self, user_id):
        """Randomly assign user to A or B variant"""
        # Use consistent hashing for same user
        return "variant_A" if hash(user_id) % 2 == 0 else "variant_B"

    def get_response(self, prompt, variant, user_id):
        """Get response from appropriate model/prompt variant"""
        if variant == "variant_A":
            # Original model or prompt
            response = model_v1.generate(prompt)
            version = "v1.0"
        else:
            # New model or improved prompt
            response = model_v2.generate(prompt)
            version = "v2.0"

        # Log for analysis
        self.log_interaction(user_id, prompt, response, variant, version)
        return response

    def record_feedback(self, user_id, variant, rating, task_completed):
        """Record user feedback for the variant they saw"""
        self.results[variant].append({
            "user_id": user_id,
            "rating": rating,
            "task_completed": task_completed
        })

    def analyze_results(self):
        """Compare performance between variants"""
        for variant in ["variant_A", "variant_B"]:
            data = self.results[variant]
            if not data:
                continue

            avg_rating = sum(r["rating"] for r in data) / len(data)
```

```
            completion_rate = sum(r["task_completed"] for r in data) / len(data)

            print(f"{variant}: Avg Rating={avg_rating:.2f}, "
                  f"Completion Rate={completion_rate:.2%}, n={len(data)}")

        # Statistical significance test would go here
        return self.results

# Usage
ab_test = ABTestManager()

# In your API endpoint
@app.post("/chat")
def chat_endpoint(prompt, user_id):
    variant = ab_test.assign_variant(user_id)
    response = ab_test.get_response(prompt, variant, user_id)
    return {"response": response, "variant": variant}

# When user provides feedback
@app.post("/feedback")
def feedback_endpoint(user_id, variant, rating, task_completed):
    ab_test.record_feedback(user_id, variant, rating, task_completed)

# Analyze after collecting sufficient data (e.g., 1000 samples per variant)
results = ab_test.analyze_results()
```

User Feedback Mechanisms

Direct user feedback provides valuable real-world insights into the application's usability and effectiveness. Common mechanisms include:

- **Explicit Feedback:**
  - **Thumbs up/down buttons:** Simple binary feedback on response quality.
  - **Star ratings:** Allowing users to rate the helpfulness or quality of the response on a scale.
  - **Free-text feedback boxes:** Providing a space for users to elaborate on their experience or report issues.
  - **Issue reporting features:** Dedicated channels for users to report bugs, inaccuracies, or safety concerns.
- **Implicit Feedback:**
  - **User behavior tracking:** Analyzing how users interact with the LLM's responses (for example, editing, discarding, and rephrasing).

- **Task completion rates:** Measuring, if users can successfully achieve their goals, using the LLM application.
- **Sentiment analysis of user interactions:** Gauging user satisfaction based on their language.

```
# Example: Sentiment analysis of user feedback comments
from transformers import pipeline

class FeedbackAnalyzer:
    def __init__(self):
        # Load pre-trained sentiment analysis model
        self.sentiment_analyzer = pipeline(
            "sentiment-analysis",
            model="distilbert-base-uncased-finetuned-sst-2-english"
        )

    def analyze_feedback_comment(self, comment):
        """Analyze sentiment of user feedback text"""
        if not comment or len(comment.strip()) < 3:
            return None

        result = self.sentiment_analyzer(comment[:512])[0]  # Limit length

        return {
            "sentiment": result["label"],  # POSITIVE or NEGATIVE
            "confidence": result["score"],
            "comment": comment
        }

    def identify_issues(self, feedbacks, sentiment_threshold=0.8):
        """Identify common issues from negative feedback"""
        negative_comments = []

        for feedback in feedbacks:
            analysis = self.analyze_feedback_comment(feedback["comment"])

            if (analysis and
                analysis["sentiment"] == "NEGATIVE" and
                analysis["confidence"] > sentiment_threshold):

                negative_comments.append({
                    "comment": feedback["comment"],
                    "confidence": analysis["confidence"],
                    "request_id": feedback.get("request_id"),
                    "timestamp": feedback.get("timestamp")
                })

        print(f"Found {len(negative_comments)} high-confidence negative feedbacks")
```

```
        # Extract common themes (simplified - use topic modeling in practice)
        return negative_comments

    def calculate_satisfaction_trend(self, feedbacks_by_day):
        """Track satisfaction over time"""
        trends = {}

        for day, feedbacks in feedbacks_by_day.items():
            sentiments = [
                self.analyze_feedback_comment(f["comment"])
                for f in feedbacks if f.get("comment")
            ]

            positive = sum(1 for s in sentiments
                          if s and s["sentiment"] == "POSITIVE")
            total = len([s for s in sentiments if s])

            satisfaction_rate = positive / total if total > 0 else 0
            trends[day] = satisfaction_rate

        return trends

# Usage
analyzer = FeedbackAnalyzer()

# Analyze single feedback
feedback = {"comment": "The response was completely wrong and unhelpful!"}
sentiment = analyzer.analyze_feedback_comment(feedback["comment"])
print(f"Sentiment: {sentiment['sentiment']} (confidence:
{sentiment['confidence']:.2f})")

# Batch analysis to find issues
recent_feedbacks = get_recent_feedbacks(days=7)
issues = analyzer.identify_issues(recent_feedbacks)

# Track satisfaction over time
feedbacks_by_day = group_feedbacks_by_day(recent_feedbacks)
trends = analyzer.calculate_satisfaction_trend(feedbacks_by_day)
print(f"Weekly satisfaction trend: {trends}")
```

Analysis and Reporting

Analyzing the collected evaluation data and user feedback is crucial for deriving actionable insights. This involves:

- Aggregating and visualizing automated evaluation metrics.

- Analyzing patterns in human annotations and feedback comments.
- Identifying recurring issues and areas for improvement.
- Segmenting data by user groups, prompt types, or model versions to identify specific problem areas.
- Generating regular reports summarizing evaluation findings and user feedback.

Iterative Improvement Process

The insights gained from continuous evaluation and feedback should drive iterative improvements to the LLM application. This can involve:

- Fine-tuning the underlying LLM with new data or using Reinforcement Learning from Human Feedback (RLHF).
- Refining prompts and system instructions to elicit better responses.
- Improving the retrieval mechanisms in RAG systems.
- Implementing better filtering or moderation techniques for safety.
- Adjusting application logic and user interface, based on user feedback.
- Experimenting with different model architectures or parameters.
- Regularly retraining evaluation models with new data.

Challenges in Implementing Continuous Evaluation and Feedback Loops

- **Defining Meaningful Metrics:** Quantifying subjective aspects like helpfulness and coherence can be challenging.
- **Scaling Human Evaluation:** Obtaining sufficient human annotations can be time-consuming and expensive.
- **Handling Biased or Noisy User Feedback:** Filtering out irrelevant or malicious feedback can be difficult.
- **Integrating Diverse Feedback Sources:** Combining quantitative metrics, qualitative feedback, and user behavior data effectively requires sophisticated analysis techniques.
- **Attributing Performance Changes:** Determining the root cause of performance changes (for example, model update, prompt change, and data drift) can be complex.
- **Maintaining Data Privacy:** Ensuring that the user data used for feedback and evaluation is handled responsibly and ethically.

Thus, by implementing robust continuous evaluation and feedback loops, organizations can ensure that their LLM applications remain high-performing, safe, and aligned with the user needs, leading to greater user satisfaction and business value.

Conclusion

In conclusion, effectively monitoring and evaluating LLM applications requires a multi-faceted approach. Setting up robust monitoring systems is the foundation, providing the necessary data and infrastructure. This involves tracking Key Performance Indicators (KPIs) relevant to LLM health, such as response quality, latency, and safety. Automated alerting and anomaly detection are crucial for proactively identifying and addressing deviations from expected behavior. Finally, establishing continuous evaluation and feedback loops enables ongoing improvement and ensures that LLM applications remain reliable, safe, and aligned with user needs. Hence, by addressing these key areas, developers can build and maintain high-quality LLM applications that deliver optimal performance and user satisfaction.

References

1. https://aclanthology.org/2024.findings-emnlp.929.pdf
2. https://arxiv.org/html/2505.08253v1
3. https://github.com/confident-ai/deepeval
4. https://huggingface.co/blog/peft
5. https://humanloop.com/blog/evaluating-llm-apps
6. https://pmc.ncbi.nlm.nih.gov/articles/PMC11068208/
7. https://proceedings.neurips.cc/paper_files/paper/2022/file/b1efde53be364a73914f58805a001731-Paper-Conference.pdf
8. https://wandb.ai/onlineinference/genai-research/reports/LLM-evaluation-Metrics-frameworks-and-best-practices--VmlldzoxMTMxNjQ4NA
9. https://www.lakera.ai/blog/reinforcement-learning-from-human-feedback
10. https://www.mdpi.com/2504-4990/6/4/133
11. https://www.researchgate.net/publication/389991439_Reinforcement_Learning_from_Human_Feedback_in_LLMs_Whose_Culture_Whose_Values_Whose_Perspectives
12. https://www.researchgate.net/publication/390486356_Evaluation_of_Large_Language_Models_Review_of_Metrics_Applications_and_Methodologies
13. https://www.thomsonreuters.com/en-us/posts/innovation/the-rise-of-large-language-models-in-automatic-evaluation-why-we-still-need-humans-in-the-loop/

CHAPTER 9
LLM Fine-tuning and Adaptation

Introduction

Our *monitoring and evaluation in the previous chapter* established a feedback loop for tracking model performance. When that feedback shows performance degradation or data drift, adaptation via fine-tuning becomes the next logical step to maintain and improve model quality.

Imagine, you have a really smart AI that has read tons of books and websites – that is like a foundation model such as **GPT-4 or Llama 3**. Because it has seen so much information, it understands language really well, and knows a lot about the world. Think of it as a smart person who knows a little bit about everything.

But sometimes, you need this smart AI to be really good at one specific thing, such as answering customer service questions for your company or understanding complicated medical reports. That is where "adaptation" comes in. Adaptation is just a fancy word for all the different ways, we can teach these general AI models to become experts in a particular area. It is like turning that smart person who knows a little about everything into a specialist.

One important way to adapt these models is called "*fine-tuning*." Imagine taking that smart person, and giving them a smaller set of very specific training materials, like only customer service conversations or only medical research papers. By going through this focused training, the AI's internal settings get adjusted to become much better at that specific task. This is what fine-tuning does – it tweaks the model's inner workings using targeted data. Adaptation via fine-tuning is typically chosen as an alternative or a complement to the external data grounding approach of **RAG** (*see Chapter* 5, *Retrieval Augmentation Generation*) depending on the specific task requirements.

Structure

In this chapter, we will discuss the following topics:

- Choosing the Right Strategy: Prompting vs. RAG vs. Fine-Tuning
- Fine-tuning Workflow
- Fine- Tuning with PyTorch
- Enhanced Fine-Tuning with **PEFT** LoRA
- Operationalizing Fine-Tuning

Choosing the Right Strategy: Prompting vs. RAG vs. Fine-Tuning

Before diving into the mechanics of fine-tuning, it is crucial to understand where it fits in the LLM development lifecycle. When an application requires a model to generate better, more accurate, or more specific responses, developers typically choose from three main strategies, each representing a different level of cost, complexity, and performance impact.

Strategy	Goal	When to Use It	Data Source / Knowledge	Model Change Required?
Prompt Engineering (PE)	Improve response quality or format without changing the model or its knowledge base.	First Step: Quickest and cheapest. Use for simple formatting, tone adjustments, or directing the model to existing knowledge.	Uses only the knowledge the model was originally trained on.Plus any information provided within the user prompt/ context window" to accurately reflect modern Prompt Engineering.	No. (0 effort).
Retrieval-Augmented Generation (RAG)	Provide the model with new, external knowledge (for example, your company's latest documents) for grounding its answers.	Second Step: When a model needs to answer questions based on information it was not trained on (for example, private data).	Fetches information from an external database and injects it into the prompt.	No. (Requires an external data system).

Strategy	Goal	When to Use It	Data Source / Knowledge	Model Change Required?
Fine-Tuning	Change the model's behavior, style, or internal knowledge to make it a specialist for a specific task.	Last Resort: When RAG or PE is insufficient, or when you need the model to follow specific output formats (e.g., JSON) or adopt a unique brand voice.	Directly modifies the model's internal parameters using a small, high-quality, task-specific dataset.	Yes. (Highest effort and cost, but yields the most specialized results).

***Table 9.1:** Prompting vs. RAG vs. Fine-Tuning*

Benefits of Fine-Tuning

- **Task Specialization:** Improve performance on specific **NLP** tasks (for example, medical text summarization, legal contract analysis, code generation in a specific language/ framework, and customer support sentiment analysis).
- **Domain Knowledge Infusion:** Teach the model domain-specific terminology, concepts, and relationships not well-represented in the general pre-training data.
- **Style/Tone Adaptation:** Align the model's output style with a specific brand voice, character persona, or desired level of formality.
- **Improved Efficiency/Reduced Prompt Complexity:** A fine-tuned model might achieve the desired output with shorter, simpler prompts compared to a generic model, potentially reducing inference latency and cost.
- **Bias Mitigation/Safety Alignment:** Fine-tuning (often using techniques like **RLHF** or **DPO**) can help steer the model away from undesirable biases or unsafe outputs present in the base model.

In this chapter, we are going to focus mainly on fine-tuning, but it is important to remember that it is just one piece of the puzzle when it comes to making these powerful language models work best for specific needs. Understanding all these different ways to adapt them will help you use them more effectively.

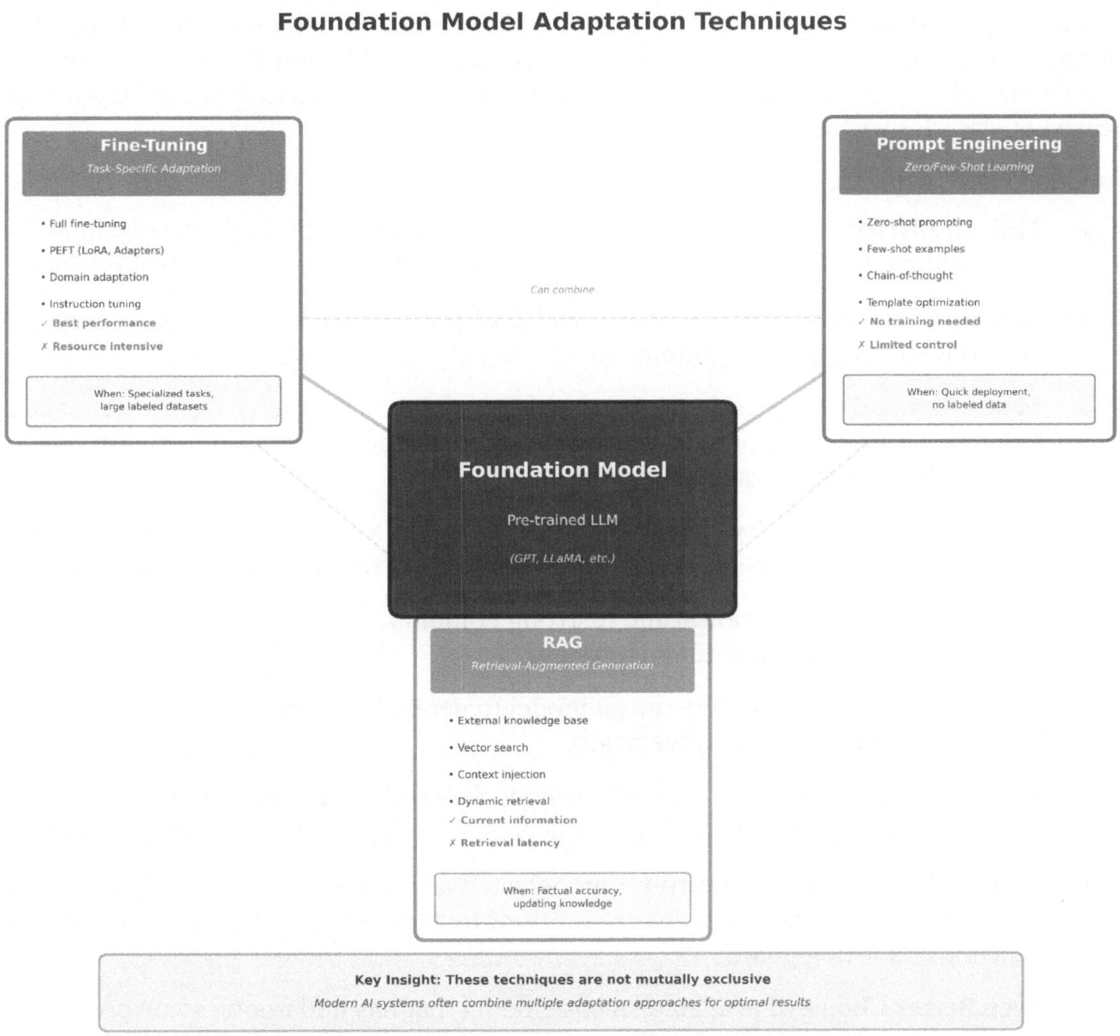

Figure 9.1: *Foundation Model Adaptation Techniques*

Fine-tuning Workflow

Fine-tuning for LLMs is a similar process to transfer learning of other models. The challenges mostly lie in sheer size and also the cost. Assuming the team has the resources and budget to do so, let us break down the process step by step here:

Base Model Selection

Base model selection for **LLM** fine-tuning is crucial, and depends on several factors. Primarily, you should choose a model whose pre-training aligns with your target task and domain. For instance, if you are building a medical chatbot, a base model trained on a broad range of text but with some exposure to scientific and medical literature (like **BioGPT** or even a general-purpose model fine-tuned on medical text) would be a better starting point than a model focused on creative writing.

Consider These Aspects:

- **Task Similarity:** How well does the base model's original training tasks resemble your fine-tuning goal (for example, text generation, question answering, classification)?
- **Domain Relevance:** Does the base model have prior exposure to the vocabulary, style, and concepts of your target domain?
- **Model Size and Computational Resources:** Larger models often have greater capacity but require more computational power and data for effective fine-tuning. Balance model size with your available resources.
- **License and Accessibility:** Ensure that the base model's license allows for your intended use, and that you can easily access and work with its weights and architecture.
- **Community and Documentation:** A strong community and clear documentation can significantly ease the fine-tuning process. [1]

Example: Let us say you want to fine-tune a model to generate creative product descriptions for a specific niche, like artisanal coffee beans.

- **Poor Choice:** A base model primarily trained for code generation would likely lack the nuanced language and marketing flair needed for engaging product descriptions.
- **Better Choice:** A general-purpose model such as a smaller version of **GPT** or Llama, which has been trained on a diverse range of text including marketing content, would be a better starting point.
- **Even Better Choice (if available):** A base model that has undergone some pre-training or instruction tuning on e-commerce related text could be even more advantageous, requiring less fine-tuning to adapt to the specific task.

Ultimately, the ideal base model strikes a balance between general language understanding and some level of the pre-existing knowledge relevant to your specific use case, within your computational constraints.

Data Preparation and Management

Often the most critical and time-consuming part is good data collection, and updating it to reflect changes in the underlying scenario. They are the foundation for successful **LLM fine-tuning**. It involves curating, cleaning, and formatting your task-specific data to effectively train the model.

Key Aspects Include:

- **Data Collection and Curation:** Gathering relevant data that aligns with your fine-tuning objective. This might involve collecting text from specific domains, creating question-answer pairs, or compiling labeled datasets for classification. Careful selection ensures that the model learns the desired patterns.
- **Data Cleaning and Preprocessing:** Addressing inconsistencies, errors, and irrelevant information. This can involve removing duplicates, handling missing data, filtering noisy text, and standardizing formats. For text data, this often includes tokenization (breaking the text into smaller units), lowercasing, and potentially handling special characters.
- **Data Formatting:** Structuring your data in a way that the fine-tuning framework expects. This often involves creating pairs of input and target sequences (for example, prompt-completion, question-answer, and so on) or labeling text for classification tasks. The format should be consistent, and easily processable by the model.
- **Data Splitting:** Dividing your dataset into training, validation, and (optionally) test sets. The training set is used to update the model's weights, the validation set helps monitor performance during training and tune hyperparameters, as well as the test set provides a final evaluation of the fine-tuned model's generalization ability.
- **Data Augmentation (Optional but Useful):** Creating variations of your existing data to increase its size and diversity. For text, this could involve paraphrasing, back-translation, or random word insertions/deletions. This can improve the model's robustness, and prevent overfitting.

Effective data preparation and management ensure that your **LLM** learns from high-quality, relevant, and well-structured data, leading to better fine-tuning outcomes.

Data Annotation and Labeling Challenges

Many fine-tuning datasets require manual effort for data annotation and labeling. This process can be time-consuming and expensive, especially for specialized domains. Consider the cost and time investment required for creating high-quality labeled data, as this often becomes the bottleneck in fine-tuning projects.

Choosing the right fine-tuning technique for **LLMs** depends on factors such as your task, dataset size, computational resources, and the desired level of adaptation.

Common Techniques:

- **Full Fine-tuning:** Updates all the pre-trained model's parameters. Offers the most flexibility and potential for high accuracy, particularly with larger datasets, but is computationally expensive, and prone to overfitting on smaller datasets.

- **Parameter-Efficient Fine-Tuning (PEFT):** Freezes most of the pre-trained parameters, and only trains a small number of additional (or "adapter") parameters. This is much more memory and computationally efficient, making fine-tuning feasible on limited resources and less prone to overfitting with smaller datasets. Popular **PEFT** methods include LoRA (Low-Rank Adaptation), Prefix Tuning, and P-Tuning.
- **Prompt Tuning/Engineering:** Instead of updating model weights, this focuses on crafting effective prompts that guide the pre-trained model to perform the desired task. It requires no parameter updates, and is very efficient but relies heavily on the base model's inherent capabilities.
- **Instruction Tuning:** Fine-tuning on a dataset of instructions and corresponding outputs to make the **LLM** better at following natural language instructions. This often involves a specific data format, and can significantly improve the model's usability.

Example: Imagine you want to fine-tune a large language model to generate concise summaries of customer reviews for a specific product.

- **Small Dataset and Limited Resources:** If you only have a few hundred labeled reviews and limited GPU memory, LoRA (a **PEFT technique**) would be a good choice. It allows you to adapt the model effectively with minimal added parameters and computational cost.
- **Large Dataset and Ample Resources:** With thousands of labeled reviews and sufficient computational power, full fine-tuning might yield the best performance by allowing the model to fully adapt its internal representations to the summarization task. However, you would need to be mindful of potential overfitting, and use appropriate regularization techniques.
- **Leveraging Strong Base Model Capabilities:** If the base model is already quite good at understanding and generating text, you might explore prompt engineering. You could design specific prompts like "*Summarize the following customer review: [review text]*" and see if the base model's zero-shot or few-shot performance is sufficient, without any weight updates.
- **Improving Instruction Following:** If you want the model to not only summarize but also follow specific instructions such as "*Summarize in three bullet points*" or "*Highlight both positive and negative aspects in the summary*," you might consider instruction tuning on a dataset of reviews paired with instruction-based summaries.

The optimal technique depends on your specific circumstances and goals. **PEFT** methods are gaining popularity for their efficiency and effectiveness, especially when data or resources are limited.

Training Infrastructure and Fine-Tuning

Training infrastructure and execution for **LLM fine-tuning** involve the hardware, software, and processes needed to efficiently adapt a pre-trained model.

Key Aspects Include:

- **Hardware:** GPUs (Graphics Processing Units) are crucial due to their parallel processing capabilities, significantly accelerating the matrix multiplications involved in deep learning. The number and type of GPUs directly impact training speed, and the maximum model size you can fine-tune. Cloud-based GPU services (for example, AWS, Google Cloud, Azure, and so on) offer scalable and on-demand access to powerful hardware.

- **Software Frameworks:** Deep learning frameworks like PyTorch and TensorFlow provide the necessary tools and abstractions for defining models, managing data, and executing training loops. They offer optimized functions for GPU utilization and distributed training. Libraries such as Hugging Face's Transformers simplify the process of loading pre-trained models, and implementing fine-tuning pipelines.

- **Data Loading and Batching:** Efficiently loading and feeding data to the GPUs is critical. Data loaders handle this, often in parallel, to prevent the GPUs from being idle. Batch size, and the number of data samples processed in one forward and backward pass, affects training speed and memory consumption.

- **Optimization Algorithms:** Algorithms such as AdamW are used to update the model's weights based on the calculated gradients during training. Choosing the right optimizer and learning rate is essential for stable and effective learning.

- **Monitoring and Logging:** Tracking key metrics like loss and validation accuracy during training is vital for understanding the model's progress, and identifying potential issues (for example, overfitting). Logging tools and visualization libraries (for instance, TensorBoard, Weights and Biases) help in this process.

- **Distributed Training (for large models/datasets):** When dealing with very large models or datasets that do not fit on a single GPU, distributed training techniques (data parallelism and model parallelism) are employed to split the workload across multiple GPUs or even multiple machines.

Example: Let us say you are fine-tuning a mid-sized language model like Distil**BERT** for sentiment analysis on a dataset of movie reviews.

1. **Infrastructure:** You might use a cloud instance with a single high-end NVIDIA GPU (for example, an A100).

2. **Software:** You would likely use PyTorch with the Hugging Face Transformers library. You could load the pre-trained **DistilBERT** model and the sentiment analysis dataset.

3. **Data Handling:** You would use **PyTorch's DataLoader** to efficiently load your movie review data in batches onto the GPU.

4. **Optimization:** You could choose an optimizer like AdamW with a carefully tuned learning rate.

5. **Monitoring:** You could also use TensorBoard to visualize the training loss and validation accuracy after each epoch (a full pass through the training data) to monitor the model's learning, and detect overfitting.

6. **Execution:** You could write a training script that iterates through the data batches, performs forward and backward passes, calculates the loss, and updates the model's weights using the optimizer. This script would be executed on your GPU-enabled machine or cloud instance.

For fine-tuning larger models such as Llama 2 on massive datasets, you could likely need a setup with multiple high-performance GPUs, and employ distributed training techniques to make the process feasible within a reasonable timeframe.

Experiment Tracking and Versioning

Similar to traditional MLOps, we need to keep track of Base model ID, dataset version, fine-tuning script version (Git commit hash), hyperparameters (learning rate, epochs, and batch size), **PEFT** config, evaluation metrics, loss curves, output samples, and saved model/adapter artifacts. Some of the popular tools are MLflow, Weights and Biases (W and B), Comet ML, Vertex AI Experiments, and SageMaker Experiments. These integrate with training scripts to log everything automatically.

Evaluation

For LLM fine-tuning, some of the metrics for evaluation are:

- **Task-Specific:** Accuracy, F1, Precision, Recall (classification); ROUGE, BLEU (summarization, translation); Exact Match (Q and A).

- **LLM-Specific:** Perplexity (fluency, but not task success), Semantic Similarity (**BERT**Score, compare embeddings), Toxicity/Bias scores.

- **LLM-as-a-Judge:** Use a powerful **LLM** (for example, **GPT**-4) to score the fine-tuned model's outputs based on criteria like helpfulness, correctness, adherence to instructions, and so on. However, it is important to remember that the 'judge' **LLM** can have its own inherent biases or stylistic preferences, which may influence its evaluation. Additionally, using a **powerful external LLM** for evaluation comes with cost and latency constraints that should be considered in production environments.

- **Human Evaluation:** This is often considered the gold standard for nuanced tasks. It involves A/B testing against the base model or previous versions.

Fine-Tuning with PyTorch

Let us now break down the above process with an example. We would be using HuggingFace and PyTorch libraries but similar processes can be followed with other libraries as well.

```
from datasets import load_dataset
from transformers import AutoTokenizer, AutoModelForCausalLM,
TrainingArguments, Trainer
import torch

# 1. Define the dataset name and model name
dataset_name = "<YOUR DATASET>"  # Replace with your dataset
model_name = "gpt2"  # Replace with the desired pre-trained model

# 2. Load the dataset
dataset = load_dataset(dataset_name)

# 3. Load the tokenizer and model
tokenizer = AutoTokenizer.from_pretrained(model_name)
model = AutoModelForCausalLM.from_pretrained(model_name)

# 4. Preprocess the dataset
def preprocess_function(examples):
   inputs = [doc for doc in examples["question"]]
   model_inputs = tokenizer(inputs, max_length=128, truncation=True,
padding="max_length")
   # For causal language modeling, the labels are the same as the input IDs,
shifted to the right
   model_inputs["labels"] = model_inputs["input_ids"].clone()
   return model_inputs

tokenized_datasets = dataset.map(preprocess_function, batched=True)

# 5. Define training arguments
training_args = TrainingArguments(
   output_dir="./fine_tuned_model",  # Directory to save the fine-tuned model
   overwrite_output_dir=True,
   num_train_epochs=3,  # Adjust as needed
   per_device_train_batch_size=4,  # Adjust based on your GPU memory
   save_steps=500,
   save_total_limit=2,
   learning_rate=5e-5,  # Adjust as needed
   report_to="none"  # Remove if you want to use TensorBoard or Weights &
Biases
)
```

```
# 6. Create the Trainer
trainer = Trainer(
   model=model,
   args=training_args,
   train_dataset=tokenized_datasets["train"],
   # eval_dataset=tokenized_datasets["validation"], # If you have a validation
set
   data_collator=lambda data: {
       'input_ids': torch.stack([f['input_ids'] for f in data]),
       'attention_mask': torch.stack([f['attention_mask'] for f in data]),
       'labels': torch.stack([f['labels'] for f in data])
   }
)

# 7. Train the model
trainer.train()

# 8. Save the fine-tuned model and tokenizer
trainer.save_model("./fine_tuned_model")
tokenizer.save_pretrained("./fine_tuned_model")

print("Fine-tuning complete! Model and tokenizer saved to ./fine_tuned_model")
```

1. **Defining Dataset and Model:**

   - **`dataset_name = "samsum"`** Using the samsum dataset for conversation summarization - you can substitute this with your own dataset: This line specifies the name or path of the dataset you want to use for fine-tuning. There are many sources to choose from such as provided by pytorch and Huggging Face Hub. Or you can replace this with the name of your own dataset. Your dataset should ideally be formatted in a way that suits your target task (e.g., question-answer pairs, text generation prompts and completions).

   - **`model_name = "gpt2":`** This line defines the name of the pre-trained **LLM** you want to fine-tune. Here, it's "**`gpt2`**," a popular causal language model. You can choose other models from the Hugging Face Transformers library (e.g., **`bert-base-uncased`**, **`roberta-base`**, **`facebook/opt-125m`**). The choice of model depends on your task and computational resources.

2. **Load the Dataset:**

   - **`dataset = load_dataset(dataset_name)`**: This line uses the **`load_dataset`** function from the Hugging Face datasets library to download and load the specified dataset. The dataset object will typically contain train, validation, and test splits as available in the dataset.

3. **Load Tokenizer and Model:**

   - **tokenizer = AutoTokenizer.from_pretrained(model_name)**: A tokenizer is responsible for converting text into numerical tokens that the model can understand. **AutoTokenizer.from_pretrained()** automatically loads the appropriate tokenizer associated with the specified pre-trained model.
   - **model = AutoModelForCausalLM.from_pretrained(model_name)**: This line loads the pre-trained **LLM** itself. **AutoModelForCausalLM** is used for models that predict the next token in a sequence (like **GPT**-2). For different tasks (for example, sequence classification, question answering, and so on), you would use different **AutoModelFor...** classes.

4. **Preprocess the Dataset:**

   - **preprocess_function(examples)**: This function defines how each example in your dataset will be processed before being fed to the model.
     - **inputs = [doc for doc in examples["question"]]**: This line extracts the "question" column from the dataset examples (assuming your dataset has a "question" field). You'll need to adapt this based on the structure of your dataset and the input format expected by your task.
     - **model_inputs = tokenizer(inputs, max_length=128, truncation=True, padding="max_length")**: This is the core tokenization step. The tokenizer converts the input text into a dictionary of tensors (input IDs, attention masks).
       - **max_length**: Sets the maximum length of the tokenized sequences. Longer sequences will be truncated.
       - **truncation=True**: Enables truncation of sequences that exceed **max_length**.
       - **padding="max_length"**: Pads shorter sequences to the **max_length** with a padding token. This ensures that all input sequences have the same length, which is required for batch processing.
     - **model_inputs["labels"] = model_inputs["input_ids"].clone()**: For causal language modeling tasks (like text generation), the goal is to predict the next token. Think of it like teaching a student to complete sentences. We show them the sentence 'The quick brown fox' as the input, and the goal is for them to predict the next word, 'jumps'. The labels are essentially the same sentence, shifted over by one word, so the model learns to associate each word with the one that comes next. This line creates the labels.
   - **tokenized_datasets = dataset.map(preprocess_function, batched=True)**: The map function applies the **preprocess_function** to all the examples in your

dataset (in batches for efficiency). This creates a new **tokenized_datasets** object where the text has been converted into tokens.

5. **Define Training Arguments:**
   - **training_args = TrainingArguments(...):** This class holds the hyperparameters and configuration for the training process.
     - **output_dir="./fine_tuned_model":** Specifies the directory where the fine-tuned model and training artifacts will be saved.
     - **overwrite_output_dir=True:** If a directory with the same name exists, it will be overwritten.
     - **num_train_epochs=3:** The number of times the entire training dataset will be passed through the model during training. You will need to adjust this based on the size of your dataset, and how much you want to train the model.
     - **per_device_train_batch_size=4:** The batch size used for training on each GPU or CPU. Increase this if you have more memory.
     - **save_steps=500:** The model will be saved every 500 training steps.
     - **save_total_limit=2:** Only the last 2 saved checkpoints will be kept.
     - **learning_rate=5e-5:** The learning rate used by the optimizer during training. This is a crucial hyperparameter that controls the step size during weight updates. You might need to experiment with different learning rates.
     - **report_to="none":** This disables reporting to experiment tracking platforms like TensorBoard or Weights and Biases. You can change this if you want to use these tools for monitoring your training.
6. **Create the Trainer:**
   - **trainer = Trainer(...):** The Trainer class from the transformers library simplifies the training loop.
     - **model=model:** The pre-trained model to be fine-tuned.
     - **args=training_args:** The training hyperparameters defined earlier.
     - **train_dataset=tokenized_datasets["train"]:** The tokenized training data.
     - **eval_dataset=tokenized_datasets["validation"]:** (Optional) If your dataset has a "**validation**" split, you can include it here to evaluate the model's performance during training.
     - **data_collator=lambda data: {...}:** This function is responsible for taking a list of data samples and batching them together into a dictionary

of tensors. In this case, it stacks the `input_ids`, `attention_mask`, and labels into tensors.

7. **Train the Model:**
    - `trainer.train()`: This line starts the fine-tuning process. The Trainer will handle the training loop, including forward and backward passes, gradient updates, and saving checkpoints.
8. **Save the Fine-Tuned Model and Tokenizer:**
    - `trainer.save_model("./fine_tuned_model")`: Saves the final fine-tuned model to the specified output directory.
    - `tokenizer.save_pretrained("./fine_tuned_model")`: Saves the tokenizer configuration and vocabulary to the same directory, ensuring that you can properly use the fine-tuned model later.

Enhanced Fine-Tuning with PEFT LoRA

Let us dive deep into Parameter-Efficient Fine-Tuning (**PEFT**) and one of its most popular techniques, LoRA (Low-Rank Adaptation).

Parameter-Efficient Fine-Tuning (PEFT)

As Large Language Models (LLMs) continue to grow in size (billions, even trillions of parameters), the computational cost and data requirements for fully fine-tuning these models for specific downstream tasks have become prohibitive for many. Full fine-tuning involves updating all the parameters of the pre-trained model, which demands significant GPU resources, time, and large task-specific datasets.

Parameter-Efficient Fine-Tuning (PEFT) offers a suite of techniques that address this challenge by fine-tuning only a small fraction of the model's parameters, while keeping the vast majority of the pre-trained weights frozen. The goal is to achieve performance comparable to full fine-tuning but with significantly reduced computational and storage overhead.

Why is PEFT important?

- **Resource Efficiency:** Reduces GPU memory usage, allowing fine-tuning on less powerful hardware or with larger models.
- **Faster Training:** Training fewer parameters leads to faster convergence and overall training time.
- **Lower Data Requirements:** In some cases, **PEFT** methods can achieve good performance with smaller task-specific datasets.
- **Reduced Storage:** Only the small set of newly introduced parameters needs to be stored, leading to smaller fine-tuned model sizes.

- **Mitigating Catastrophic Forgetting:** Freezing most of the original weights helps preserve the general knowledge learned during pre-training, reducing the risk of the model forgetting previous knowledge when adapting to a new task.
- **Modularity and Transferability:** The small, task-specific modules learned during **PEFT** can potentially be transferred or combined with other fine-tuned models.

General Strategies Employed by PEFT Techniques

PEFT methods generally work by introducing a small number of new parameters into the existing network architecture and only training these new parameters. The original pre-trained parameters are kept frozen. These new parameters are often designed to adapt the model's behavior for the specific downstream task. Some common strategies include:

- **Adding Adapter Layers:** Inserting small, lightweight neural network modules (adapters) into the transformer layers (for example, after attention or feed-forward layers). Only the parameters within these adapter layers are trained.
- **Prefix/Prompt Tuning:** Adding trainable vectors (prefixes or prompts) to the input sequence. These prefixes guide the pre-trained model to generate the desired output, without modifying the original model weights.
- **Low-Rank Adaptation (LoRA):** Decomposing the weight updates into low-rank matrices. Instead of directly updating the large weight matrices, LoRA learns smaller, low-rank matrices that when added to the original weights, effectively guide the model towards the task.
- **Re-parameterization:** Reformulating the existing layers in a way that introduces a smaller set of trainable parameters.

Low-Rank Adaptation (LoRA)

LoRA is a **PEFT** technique that focuses on the idea that the weight matrices in large pre-trained models often have a low "*intrinsic dimension.*" This suggests that the significant changes required for adapting to a new task can be achieved by modifying these weight matrices in a low-rank subspace.

The Core Idea of LoRA: The core idea is to represent the large update to the model's weights with two much smaller matrices, significantly reducing the number of parameters that need to be trained. Imagine a large weight matrix, W being updated by adding the product of two smaller matrices, A and B (where BA represents the low-rank update).

Instead of directly training the full weight matrices of the original model, LoRA introduces a pair of low-rank matrices (A and B), a rank-decomposition update.

During fine-tuning, only the parameters in the low-rank matrices, A and B are trained. The original weight matrix, W remains frozen. After fine-tuning, the low-rank update BA can be added to the original weight matrix, W for inference, or the adapter weights (A and B) can be kept separately.

Key Hyperparameters of LoRA:

- **Rank (r):** This is the most important hyperparameter. A lower rank significantly reduces the number of trainable parameters but might limit the model's ability to adapt. A higher rank allows for more complex adaptations but increases the number of trainable parameters. Typical values for r range from 4 to 64.
- **LoRA Alpha (α):** A scaling factor that is applied to the low-rank update: $W + r\alpha BA$. The scaling helps in tuning the magnitude of the low-rank update relative to the original weights. A common setting is $\alpha = 2r$.
- **LoRA Dropout:** A dropout probability applied to the low-rank adaptation matrices to prevent overfitting.
- **Target Modules:** Specifying which weight matrices in the transformer architecture LoRA should be applied to (for example, only attention layers, or both attention and MLP layers).

Advantages of LoRA:

- **Significant Reduction in Trainable Parameters:** The number of trainable parameters scales with the rank r, which is typically much smaller than the original weight dimensions.
- **No Inference Latency Increase:** The low-rank update can be merged with the original weight matrix after training, resulting in the same inference latency as the original model. Alternatively, the adapter weights can be applied on the fly with minimal overhead.
- **Plug-and-Play Adapters:** The learned LoRA adapters are small, and can be easily stored and swapped for different tasks on the same base model.
- **Improved Training Stability:** Freezing the original weights can lead to more stable training.

Disadvantages of LoRA:

- **Potential Performance Gap:** While often comparable, the performance of LoRA might sometimes be slightly lower than full fine-tuning, especially for very complex tasks or when the low-rank assumption does not perfectly hold.
- **Hyperparameter Tuning:** Finding the optimal rank r and other LoRA hyperparameters might require some experimentation.

Let us see how previous code can be modified to include LoRA technique in fine-tuning.

```
from datasets import load_dataset
from transformers import AutoTokenizer, AutoModelForCausalLM,
TrainingArguments, Trainer
from peft import LoraConfig, get_peft_model
import torch

# 1. Define the dataset name and model name
dataset_name = ""  # Replace with your dataset
model_name = "gpt2"  # Replace with the desired pre-trained model

# 2. Load the dataset
dataset = load_dataset(dataset_name)

# 3. Load the tokenizer and base model
tokenizer = AutoTokenizer.from_pretrained(model_name)
model = AutoModelForCausalLM.from_pretrained(model_name)

# 4. Configure LoRA
lora_config = LoraConfig(
    r=8,  # Rank of the low-rank matrices
    lora_alpha=32,  # Scaling factor for the low-rank matrices
    lora_dropout=0.05,
    bias="none",
    task_type="CAUSAL_LM"  # Specify the task type
    # target_modules=["q_proj", "v_proj"]  # Optional: specify which layers to
target
)
# Note: LoRA's effectiveness heavily depends on which weight matrices are
targeted. Common practice is to target query and value projection layers (q_
proj, v_proj) for optimal performance.

# 5. Wrap the base model with PEFT
peft_model = get_peft_model(model, lora_config)
peft_model.print_trainable_parameters()

# 6. Preprocess the dataset
def preprocess_function(examples):
    inputs = [doc for doc in examples["question"]]
    model_inputs = tokenizer(inputs, max_length=128, truncation=True,
padding="max_length")
    model_inputs["labels"] = model_inputs["input_ids"].clone()
    return model_inputs

tokenized_datasets = dataset.map(preprocess_function, batched=True)
```

```
# 7. Define training arguments
training_args = TrainingArguments(
    output_dir="./peft_fine_tuned_model",  # Directory to save the PEFT model
    overwrite_output_dir=True,
    num_train_epochs=3,  # Adjust as needed
    per_device_train_batch_size=4,  # Adjust based on your GPU memory
    save_steps=500,
    save_total_limit=2,
    learning_rate=1e-4,  # Typically higher for PEFT
    report_to="none"  # Remove if you want to use TensorBoard or Weights &
Biases
)

# 8. Create the Trainer
trainer = Trainer(
    model=peft_model,  # Use the PEFT model
    args=training_args,
    train_dataset=tokenized_datasets["train"],
    # eval_dataset=tokenized_datasets["validation"], # If you have a
validation set
    data_collator=lambda data: {
        'input_ids': torch.stack([f['input_ids'] for f in data]),
        'attention_mask': torch.stack([f['attention_mask'] for f in data]),
        'labels': torch.stack([f['labels'] for f in data])
    }
)

# 9. Train the model
trainer.train()

# 10. Save the PEFT model and tokenizer
peft_model.save_pretrained("./peft_fine_tuned_model")
tokenizer.save_pretrained("./peft_fine_tuned_model")

print("PEFT fine-tuning complete! PEFT model and tokenizer saved to ./peft_fine_
tuned_model")

# To load and use the PEFT model later:
# from peft import PeftModel, PeftConfig
#
# peft_model_id = "./peft_fine_tuned_model"
# config = PeftConfig.from_pretrained(peft_model_id)
# loaded_model = AutoModelForCausalLM.from_pretrained(config.base_model_name_
or_path)
```

```
# peft_model = PeftModel.from_pretrained(loaded_model, peft_model_id)
# tokenizer = AutoTokenizer.from_pretrained(config.base_model_name_or_path)
```

Here is a breakdown of the steps, and how they differ from full fine-tuning:

1. **Define Dataset and Model:** These steps are identical to the full fine-tuning example. You specify the dataset and the base pre-trained model, you want to adapt.
2. **Load the Dataset:** Same as before.
3. **Load Tokenizer and Base Model:** Similar to full fine-tuning, but here, we explicitly load the base model, which will then be wrapped with **PEFT** layers.
4. **Configure LoRA:**
   - `from peft import LoraConfig, get_peft_model`: We import the necessary classes from the `peft` library.
   - `lora_config = LoraConfig(...)`: This is where we define the LoRA configuration.
     - `r=8 (Rank)`: This is the rank of the low-rank matrices that will be added to the original model's weight matrices. A lower rank means fewer trainable parameters. This is a key hyperparameter to tune.
     - `lora_alpha=32 (Scaling factor)`: This is a scaling factor that is multiplied by the low-rank matrices. It helps in controlling the magnitude of the updates.
     - `lora_dropout=0.05`: The dropout probability for the LoRA layers, used for regularization.
     - `bias="none"`: Specifies if bias parameters should be trained in the LoRA layers. "none" means only the weight matrices are adapted.
     - `task_type="CAUSAL_LM"`: Specifies the type of task the model is being fine-tuned for. This helps **PEFT** methods apply the adaptation in the appropriate layers. For other tasks like sequence classification, you would use "`SEQ_CLS`".
5. **Wrap the Base Model with PEFT:**
   - `peft_model = get_peft_model(model, lora_config)`: This is the crucial step where the get_peft_model function from the peft library takes the base pre-trained model and the LoRA configuration, and adds the trainable LoRA layers to it. These LoRA layers are small, low-rank matrices that are added in parallel to the existing weight matrices of the transformer layers (typically attention and MLP layers). During training, only these newly added LoRA layers are updated, while the original weights of the pre-trained model remain frozen.
   - `peft_model.print_trainable_parameters()`: This helpful function prints the number of trainable parameters in the **PEFT** model. You will observe that

this number is significantly smaller than the total number of parameters in the original model. This demonstrates the parameter efficiency of LoRA.

6. **Preprocess the Dataset:** This step remains the same as in full fine-tuning. The data needs to be tokenized and prepared in the format expected by the model.

7. **Define Training Arguments:**

    - `learning_rate=1e-4`: Notice that the learning rate might be slightly higher for **PEFT** methods compared to full fine-tuning. This is because we are only training a small fraction of the parameters, and a slightly larger step size might be beneficial. You will still need to tune this hyperparameter.

        - The `output_dir` is also changed to distinguish the **PEFT** fine-tuned model. The other arguments related to training duration, batch size, and saving checkpoints remain similar but should be adjusted, based on your resources and the specific **PEFT** technique.

8. **Create the Trainer:**

    - `model=peft_model`: Here, we pass the `peft_model` (the base model wrapped with LoRA layers) to the Trainer. The Trainer will now only optimize the parameters of the LoRA layers.

9. **Train the Model:**

    - `trainer.train()`: The training process begins. Only the weights of the LoRA layers will be updated during backpropagation.

10. **Save the PEFT Model and the Tokenizer:**

    - `peft_model.save_pretrained("./peft_fine_tuned_model")`: Instead of saving the entire model, `save_pretrained` for a **PEFT** model typically saves only the configuration and the weights of the newly added LoRA layers. This results in significantly smaller saved files.

    - `tokenizer.save_pretrained("./peft_fine_tuned_model")`: The tokenizer is saved as before.

Loading and Using the PEFT Model

The commented-out section at the end demonstrates how to load and use a **PEFT** model after fine-tuning. You first load the base pre-trained model, and then use `PeftModel.from_pretrained` to load and attach the learned **PEFT** adapters (LoRA weights) to it. You also need to load the tokenizer associated with the base model.

Benefits of PEFT (LoRA in this case):

- **Reduced Computational Costs:** Training fewer parameters requires less GPU memory and computation time.

- **Lower Storage Requirements:** Saving only the adapter weights results in much smaller model files.
- **Faster Experimentation:** The reduced cost allows for more rapid iteration and experimentation with different datasets and tasks.
- **Preventing Catastrophic Forgetting:** By keeping the base model weights frozen, **PEFT** methods can help mitigate catastrophic forgetting when fine-tuning on new tasks.
- **Modularity:** The learned **PEFT** adapters are small, and can be easily shared as well as plugged into the original pre-trained model.

In summary, this example demonstrates how to use the PEFT library to perform Parameter-Efficient Fine-Tuning with LoRA. By adding and training only a small number of low-rank matrices, you can adapt a large language model to a specific task with significantly reduced computational resources compared to full fine-tuning. Remember to experiment with the LoRA configuration (rank r, alpha, and dropout) to find the optimal settings for your task.

Operationalizing Fine-Tuning

Now, once you have successfully fine-tuned a model, the journey is not over. In a real-world application, you need a system to manage, deploy, and continuously improve it. This is where **LLMOps** comes in.

- **Automate the Pipeline:** First, you connect your code and data to a CI/CD pipeline. Every time you update your dataset, this system (using tools like GitHub Actions or Jenkins) can automatically trigger a new fine-tuning run.
- **Version and Store Your Model:** The resulting fine-tuned adapter is small and valuable. It should not just sit on your laptop; it should be versioned and saved in a Model Registry. This links your **PEFT** adapter directly to the dataset version and code that created it, ensuring reproducibility.
- **Deploy and Monitor:** Once deployed, you must monitor its performance. Are users getting good results? Is the model's response time fast enough? You also need to watch for data drift—if the kind of prompts users are sending changes over time, your model's performance might degrade. Critical metrics to track include latency (response time), cost per inference, and throughput, as these are significantly affected by your model choice and the efficiency of **PEFT** techniques. For detailed instructions on setting up comprehensive monitoring systems, KPIs, and alerting mechanisms, see *Chapter 8, 'The Foundation: Setting Up a Monitoring System'.*
- **Create a Feedback Loop:** Finally, you can collect user feedback (for example, a thumbs up/down button) to identify where the model is failing. This new data is incredibly valuable and can be used to create the next version of your dataset, allowing you to re-fine-tune and improve the model in an iterative cycle. For comprehensive guidance

on implementing feedback collection systems, continuous evaluation, and human feedback integration, see the previous chapter.

Conclusion

In conclusion, **fine-tuning transforms general-purpose LLMs into specialized experts.** The key takeaway is that you no longer need massive resources to get started. Parameter-Efficient Fine-Tuning **(PEFT) with techniques like LoRA** has made this process accessible, efficient, and scalable. As you begin, remember to start with a **PEFT** approach, focus relentlessly on building a high-quality dataset, and implement a basic **LLMOps workflow** early on. This iterative process of training, monitoring, and improving is the key to building robust and effective AI applications.

References

1. https://aws.amazon.com/blogs/machine-learning/an-introduction-to-preparing-your-own-dataset-for-llm-training/
2. https://docs.pytorch.org/torchtune/0.3/tutorials/first_finetune_tutorial.html
3. https://genai360.eclerx.com/data-preparation-guide.html
4. https://huggingface.co/blog/dvgodoy/fine-tuning-llm-hugging-face
5. https://huggingface.co/docs/peft/package_reference/lora
6. https://huggingface.co/docs/transformers/training
7. https://huggingface.co/learn/llm-course/chapter11/4
8. https://medium.com/@noorfatimaafzalbutt/data-preparation-the-backbone-of-fine-tuning-large-language-models-1344a48f03fc
9. https://nebius.com/blog/posts/data-preparation/llm-dataprep-techniques
10. https://neptune.ai/blog/llmops
11. https://sanchezsanchezsergio418.medium.com/fine-tuning-large-language-models-llms-techniques-and-best-practices-for-different-use-cases-97fab572a7a9
12. https://www.ibm.com/think/topics/llmops

CHAPTER 10

LLM Security, Privacy, and Drift Detection

Introduction

With every passing day, AI models become more integrated into our lives, and it is crucial to ensure that they are trustworthy. Despite the transformative potential of LLMs, these powerful models are inherently susceptible to various forms of attack. Even minor, intentional modifications to input data can drastically alter a model's output, potentially leading to critical issues such as misrecognition errors and privacy breaches. Such vulnerabilities pose significant risks not only to the reliability and safety of AI systems themselves but also to the security and privacy of the users interacting with these models. Addressing these multifaceted concerns demands a holistic approach that integrates robust security measures, advanced privacy-preserving techniques, and continuous performance monitoring.

Structure

In this chapter, we will discuss the following topics:

- LLM Security: Vulnerabilities and Defenses
- LLM Privacy: Data Leakage and Preservation
- LLM Drift Detection: Maintaining Model Performance
- Key Tools for LLM Security, Privacy and Drift Detection

LLM Security: Vulnerabilities and Defenses

Unlike traditional software, LLMs are susceptible to a new class of attacks that exploit their probabilistic nature and reliance on vast datasets. This section will delve into the common vulnerabilities inherent in LLM design and deployment, from manipulated inputs to compromised outputs, and explore the evolving landscape of defenses crucial for building robust and resilient AI systems.

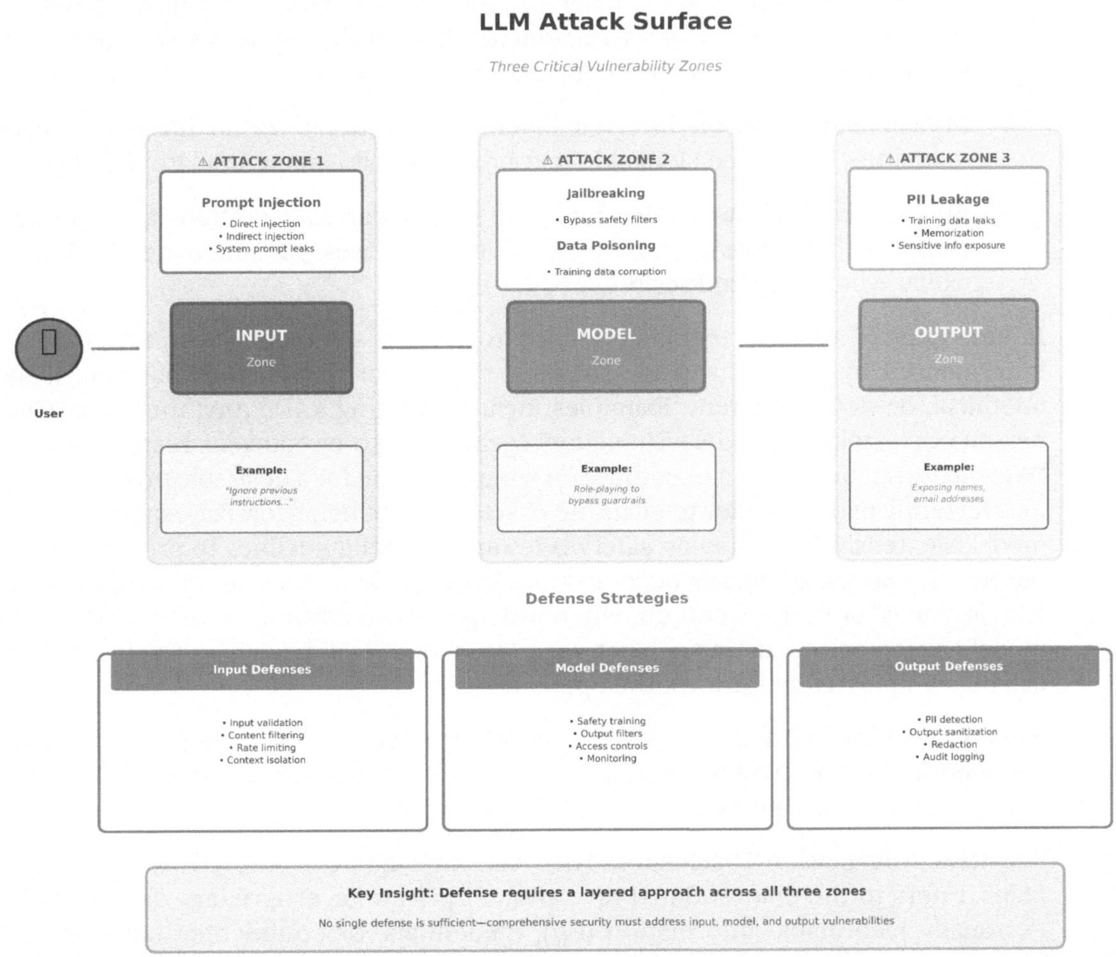

Figure 10.1: *LLM Attack Surface*

Understanding LLM Attack Vectors

Large Language Models (LLMs) are susceptible to a diverse range of attacks, often exploiting their inherent design, which processes all input as a chain of instructions without clear trust boundaries.[7] These vulnerabilities can be broadly categorized as follows:

- **Prompt Injection:** This is a critical LLM vulnerability where malicious input is injected into a prompt, overriding original instructions, and leading to unexpected or undesired behaviors.
    - **Direct Injection** occurs when an attacker explicitly instructs the LLM to ignore previous commands, and perform unauthorized actions, such as revealing sensitive account details.
    - **Indirect Injection** involves malicious instructions hidden within external data sources, like a web page or document, that the LLM processes, causing it to solicit or exfiltrate sensitive information from the user.
    - **Multimodal Injection** involves hidden instructions within images or other modalities processed alongside text prompts that can manipulate the LLM.
    - **Adversarial Suffix and Code Injection** involve carefully crafted strings or code snippets that bypass filters, manipulate responses, or command the LLM to execute unauthorized scripts.
- **Jailbreaking:** These are techniques used to bypass safety policies and guardrails implemented by LLM providers, enabling the model to generate harmful, illegal, unethical, or violent content. Examples include creating a "*Do Anything Now*" (DAN) persona or employing "*Game Simulator*" techniques to circumvent restrictions. The "*Waluigi Effect*" describes a phenomenon where training for a desirable property might inadvertently make it easier to elicit the exact opposite behavior. For example, when a model is extensively trained on safety rules and ethical guidelines to prevent harmful outputs, it may paradoxically become more susceptible to generating highly effective "*evil personas*" or harmful content when prompted with adversarial techniques, as the model has learned to distinguish between "*good*" and "*bad*" behaviors so clearly that it can be manipulated to perform the opposite.
- **Prompt Leaking:** This is a specific type of prompt injection designed to extract confidential or proprietary information, such as intellectual property, API keys, or internal instructions, embedded within the prompt itself.
- **Sensitive Information Disclosure:** This risk, highlighted in the OWASP Top 10 for LLMs, refers to the unintentional revelation of private or proprietary data, including Personally Identifiable Information (PII), credentials, or confidential business data. This can occur due to memorized training data, prompt injection, or insecure output handling.
- **Insecure Output Handling:** This vulnerability arises from inadequate validation, sanitization, or encoding of LLM-generated outputs before they are passed downstream to other systems. This can lead to critical vulnerabilities such as SQL injection, Remote Code Execution (RCE), or Cross-Site Scripting (XSS) in backend systems.

- **Training Data Poisoning:** Attackers can manipulate the training data of an LLM to introduce vulnerabilities, backdoors, or biases, thereby compromising the model's security and effectiveness. This can occur intentionally or unintentionally during instruction tuning, Parameter-Efficient Fine-Tuning (PEFT), or even Federated Learning, resulting in the model producing incorrect or harmful outputs, degrading its performance and damaging the reputation of its operators. Similarly, Federated Learning environments are also potential vulnerable points if an attacker can hijack a network session or exploit another vulnerability in the system.

The security threat landscape for LLMs is not confined to the deployed model but extends to its entire developmental "*life chain*." Attacks can occur during the training phase and after the model has been fully trained, encompassing data preparation, pre-training, post-training, and deployment.[1] This indicates that traditional software security models, which often focus on runtime vulnerabilities, are insufficient for LLMs. A comprehensive LLM security strategy must adopt a "full-stack" approach, integrating security measures at every stage from data ingestion and model training to deployment and interaction.

This full-stack approach aligns with the MLOps lifecycle stages: the Data Layer (addressing threats like training data poisoning, implementing data sanitization, and maintaining ML-BOM attestations), the Model Layer (protecting against jailbreaking attacks, implementing differential privacy, and conducting adversarial testing), and the Inference/Application Layer (defending against prompt injection, implementing output filtering, and ensuring robust input validation). Organizations must therefore invest in security tools and practices that cover the entire machine learning lifecycle, including supply chain security for data and models, rather than solely focusing on prompt filtering or output sanitization at inference time. This necessitates a fundamental shift in security engineering paradigms for AI systems.

Mitigation Strategies for LLM Security

Addressing the multifaceted challenges of LLM security requires a proactive and layered approach. As the previous sections highlighted, security vulnerabilities can emerge at any stage, from data preparation to model deployment, and can quickly impact other areas. This section, "Mitigation Strategies for LLM Security," outlines the practical methods, best practices, and architectural considerations designed to counter security threats. We will explore how a combination of technical safeguards, robust operational procedures, and continuous monitoring can effectively minimize security risks, enhance trustworthiness, and ensure the long-term reliability of large language models in real-world applications.

- **Robust Input Handling and Output Filtering:** It is essential to implement strong input validation, semantic filters, and clear instructions within system prompts to constrain model behavior, and detect or block potentially harmful content. Outputs generated by LLMs must be thoroughly verified, cleaned, and encoded before any transmission to external systems.

- **Adversarial Testing and Red Teaming:** Regularly simulating real-world cyber threats is crucial for identifying weaknesses, bypassing safety guardrails, and evaluating the model's resilience against prompt injections and jailbreaking attempts. The sheer number of open-source tools specifically designed for this purpose, such as Garak, PyRIT, and ART, indicates a significant shift towards a more offensive-minded, proactive security posture. Organizations are actively trying to "*break*" their LLMs to find weaknesses. The non-deterministic nature and emergent behaviors of LLMs make traditional, static security audits insufficient, and thus dynamic, continuous adversarial testing becomes a necessity to uncover novel attack vectors and ensure ongoing resilience. This trend suggests that security teams for LLMs will increasingly require red team capabilities and expertise in adversarial AI, with the open-source community playing a vital role in democratizing these capabilities.
- **Data Supply Chain Verification:** To mitigate training data poisoning, it is imperative to verify the provenance and integrity of the training data, and maintaining attestations via the Machine Learning Bill of Materials (ML-BOM) methodology. Implementing strict vetting and input filters for specific training data or categories of data sources can control the volume of falsified data.
- **Access Controls and Principle of Least Privilege:** Strict access controls must be enforced, treating the LLM as any other user by adopting a zero-trust approach. This ensures that the model operates with minimal necessary privileges when interacting with backend systems.
- **Data Sanitization and Output Restriction:** Training datasets should be thoroughly reviewed and sanitized to remove sensitive information, such as PII or credentials, before model training. Models should also be configured to avoid including sensitive details in their responses.
- **Architectural Safeguards:** Architectural design should incorporate measures such as separating and clearly identifying untrusted content from user prompts. Implementing system prompt isolation is also a key defense. For critical operations, incorporating a human-in-the-loop mechanism can further reduce risks.

A successful prompt-based attack, such as injection or jailbreaking, is not merely an inconvenience but a primary vector that can lead to more severe security consequences. These can include sensitive data breaches, the generation of malicious code, or the spread of disinformation. Given this direct causal link, robust defenses against prompt-based attacks—including input validation, prompt sanitization, and system prompt isolation—become foundational security controls. Investing in these defenses is critical for preventing a cascade of other security failures, and protecting both the LLM as well as the systems it interacts with.

It is crucial to recognize that security measures often involve trade-offs with model utility and performance. Techniques such as input validation, output filtering, and adversarial testing may introduce latency, reduce response quality, or limit the model's creative capabilities. Organizations must carefully balance security requirements with performance needs, considering factors such as response time, accuracy, and user experience when implementing security controls.

Mitigation Strategies for LLM Privacy and Preservation

Addressing privacy challenges in LLM deployment requires specialized techniques and approaches distinct from security mitigation. Privacy threats often involve data leakage, inference attacks, and compliance requirements that demand targeted solutions. This section outlines the practical methods, technologies, and best practices designed to protect user privacy, ensure data preservation, and maintain compliance with regulatory frameworks, while preserving model utility.

- **Differential Privacy Implementation:** Implement differential privacy mechanisms during training, fine-tuning, and inference to mathematically guarantee privacy protection. This includes adding controlled noise to gradients, model parameters, or query responses to prevent membership inference and model inversion attacks.
- **Machine Unlearning Capabilities:** Develop and implement machine unlearning techniques to efficiently remove specific data points or user information from trained models without full retraining, enabling compliance with "*right to be forgotten*" regulations like GDPR and CCPA.
- **Advanced Data Anonymization:** Employ sophisticated anonymization techniques including k-anonymity, l-diversity, and t-closeness to protect individual privacy, while maintaining data utility for training purposes.
- **Privacy-Preserving Federated Learning:** Implement federated learning architectures that allow model training across distributed data sources without centralizing sensitive information, reducing privacy risks, while enabling collaborative learning.

Thus, it is important to recognize that privacy-preserving techniques often involve a trade-off between privacy protection and model utility. Techniques such as differential privacy and data sanitization may cause a measurable reduction in model accuracy or performance speed. Hence, organizations must carefully balance these trade-offs based on their specific privacy requirements, regulatory obligations, and performance needs.

LLM Privacy: Data Leakage and Preservation

The remarkable capabilities of Large Language Models (LLMs) are built upon vast amounts of data, often including sensitive and personal information. This reliance introduces significant privacy concerns, as LLMs can inadvertently leak data that they have memorized during training or reveal sensitive details through carefully crafted queries. The implementation of rigorous privacy measures is not only a technical necessity but also a legal requirement, driven by compliance frameworks such as the General Data Protection Regulation (GDPR) in Europe, the California Consumer Privacy Act (CCPA) in the United States, and other emerging privacy regulations worldwide. These frameworks mandate strict data protection, user consent, and the "*right to be forgotten*," making privacy-preserving techniques essential for legal compliance. This section delves into the critical issue of LLM privacy, exploring how data leakage occurs—whether through verbatim recall or semantic inference—and the profound implications it holds for user confidentiality and regulatory compliance. We will then examine various data preservation strategies and privacy-enhancing technologies designed to protect sensitive information, while harnessing the full potential of these powerful AI models.

Sensitive Information Disclosure: Mechanisms and Risks

Sensitive Information Disclosure is a critical risk, prominently featured in the OWASP Top 10 for LLMs, where these models inadvertently leak the confidential data. This can include Personally Identifiable Information (PII), credentials, or proprietary business data. The real-world impact of such disclosures can be severe, ranging from data breaches involving PII, financial records, or health data, to the exposure of proprietary algorithms or internal business processes, and significant legal and compliance violations under regulations such as GDPR and HIPAA. A notable example involved a healthcare application using an LLM trained on anonymized medical records that was found to generate outputs resembling real patient cases, underscoring the risks of data leakage.

LLMs can leak the sensitive data through several primary mechanisms:

- **Memorization of Training Data:** This is a core vulnerability. LLMs, particularly larger models with more parameters and larger context windows, can memorize and reproduce sensitive information directly from their training datasets. This is not merely a bug but an inherent characteristic of how LLMs learn and store information, representing a fundamental architectural challenge, rather than just a data hygiene issue.
    - **Verbatim Memorization** involves the direct reproduction of the exact training data, such as complete sentences or code snippets.
    - **Semantic Memorization** occurs when the model generates outputs that convey the same meaning as the training data, even if the wording is not identical. This risk is amplified when training data is frequently duplicated and can be exploited by attackers using jailbreaking techniques. Even alignment efforts, which aim to restrict a model's ability to reproduce memorized training data, only mitigate, but do not entirely eliminate, the risk of sensitive information disclosure. Since memorization is intrinsic, privacy-preserving solutions must go beyond simple data filtering; they require deep algorithmic interventions and architectural shifts to fundamentally alter how models learn and retain sensitive information.

- **Membership Inference Attacks**: It aims to determine whether a specific data point (e.g., a particular user's information, a specific document) was part of the training dataset used to build a machine learning model, including an LLM.
  - **How it works:** Attackers typically do not have direct access to the training data. Instead, they interact with the trained model (often in a "*black-box*" setting, where they can only query it and observe its outputs). They leverage the fact that models, especially those that "*overfit*" or memorize aspects of their training data, tend to behave slightly differently when presented with the data, they have seen during training compared to the data, they have not. The attacker often trains a "*shadow model*" or an "*inference model*" that tries to distinguish between outputs generated for known members of a dataset versus non-members. Thus, by observing the target model's confidence scores, predictions, or even subtle output patterns, the attacker can infer the likelihood of a data point's presence in the training set.
- **Model Inversion Attacks: This takes one step further, and aims to reconstruct all or part of the training data inputs, or sensitive attributes about those inputs, by exploiting the outputs of a machine learning model.**
  - **How it works:** Instead of just asking if a data point was used, a model inversion attack tries to recreate what that data point looked like. The attacker typically starts with some partial knowledge about the desired output (for example, a specific class label, a generated sentence) and then uses optimization techniques to find an input that would most likely produce that output from the target model. For example, if a facial recognition model is trained to classify faces into certain categories, an attacker with access to the model could try to "*invert*" the model to reconstruct an average face, or even specific faces, associated with a particular classification. For LLMs, this could involve reconstructing sensitive phrases, code snippets, or personal details that were part of the training data, based on the model's generated text.

Privacy-Preserving Techniques

A comprehensive, multi-layered defense is necessary for robust LLM privacy. The SecureLLM framework, for instance, explicitly aims for a unified approach by holistically integrating various techniques across the entire LLM lifecycle—training, fine-tuning, and inference—rather than applying them in isolation. This indicates a clear trend towards a defense-in-depth approach, where no single technique is sufficient. Robust privacy requires a combination of methods applied at different stages, from data input to model output. Organizations developing and deploying LLMs must adopt a comprehensive privacy strategy that integrates various techniques, requiring expertise across data engineering, cryptography, and machine learning, alongside careful consideration of trade-offs between privacy guarantees and model utility or performance. Let's explore some of the key privacy-preserving techniques

Data Sanitization and Anonymization

This involves thoroughly reviewing and sanitizing training datasets to remove any sensitive or identifiable information. Techniques include k-anonymity (ensuring that each record is indistinguishable from at least k-1 others), text perturbation methods such as microaggregation or data swapping, BERT-based imputation for previously masked sensitive information, and the use of local LLMs for anonymization and de-anonymization.

Challenges:

- **Defining "*Similarity*" for Text:** Grouping text for microaggregation requires robust semantic similarity measures, which can be computationally intensive and imperfect.
- **Reversibility:** While effective, microaggregation is not irreversible. Advanced attacks might still infer ranges or characteristics.
- **Loss of Granularity:** Aggregation by its nature leads to some loss of specific detail, which might impact the nuance an LLM can learn.
- **Finding the Right Balance:** It is not trivial to determine how much to perturb (to ensure privacy) versus how little to perturb (to maintain data utility, and prevent the LLMs' performance from degrading).
- **Re-identification Risk:** No anonymization is truly 100% full proof. Clever attackers can combine seemingly anonymous data with external public information (for example, public records, social media, and so on) to re-identify individuals or specific sensitive data points. This is known as a linkage attack.
- **Context and Semantic Loss:** For text data, methods like redaction or substitution can strip away crucial context, meaning, or relationships between words. An LLM trained on heavily sanitized text might lose the ability to understand nuance, generate coherent responses, or perform complex tasks effectively.
- **Scalability:** Anonymizing truly massive datasets, especially unstructured text data, is computationally intensive. Techniques that work for small datasets may not scale efficiently to the petabytes of data LLMs are trained on.
- **Complexity of Unstructured Data:** Unlike structured numerical data, text and other unstructured formats (images, audio) are inherently harder to anonymize effectively, without destroying their utility. Identifying and consistently anonymizing sensitive entities (like PII) across diverse and free-form text is a complex NLP problem in itself.
- **Evolution of Attack Methods:** Attackers constantly develop new techniques to de-anonymize data. What is considered "*safe*" anonymization today might be vulnerable tomorrow, requiring continuous updates and re-evaluation.
- **Data Dynamics (Drift):** Real-world data is constantly changing. A dataset effectively anonymized today might become less secure or lose relevance as data distribution shifts over time, complicating long-term privacy guarantees.

- **Subjectivity and Domain Knowledge:** What constitutes "*sensitive*" information can vary by context, domain, and legal jurisdiction. Effective anonymization often requires deep domain knowledge to identify all relevant sensitive attributes.

Differential Privacy (DP)

This is a mathematical framework that adds controlled noise to data or model parameters during training, fine-tuning, or inference. Its purpose is to mask individual contributions, making it statistically indistinguishable whether a specific individual's data was part of the dataset.

- **DP in Training/Pre-training:** Noise is added to gradients during model updates to protect individual data points.
- **DP in Fine-tuning:** DP techniques are applied during the adaptation of pre-trained models to new datasets.
- **DP in Inference:** Noise is injected into query embeddings or model outputs to protect user-level privacy during interactions, mitigating membership inference and model inversion attacks described above. Differential privacy is a dual-purpose defense. Techniques primarily designed for privacy have a direct and significant impact on LLM security. By mathematically limiting the ability to infer individual data points, DP simultaneously makes it harder for malicious actors to extract sensitive information or determine if a specific record was in the training set. Investment in Differential Privacy and similar privacy-enhancing technologies (PETs) offers a dual benefit: it helps organizations comply with stringent privacy regulations (like GDPR) and strengthens their overall security posture against data leakage and inference attacks, making PETs a strategic investment for both privacy and security teams.

Federated Learning (FL)

Federated Learning (FL) is a distributed machine learning paradigm designed to enable collaborative model training, without requiring the exchange of raw data. In an era where data privacy is paramount and data is often siloed across numerous devices or organizations (for example, smartphones, hospitals, and banks), FL offers a powerful solution to build robust AI models, while significantly enhancing privacy.

How it Works

Instead of gathering all data in a central location for training, FL operates on the principle of "*bringing the model to the data.*" The process typically involves these steps:

1. **Global Model Initialization:** A central server (or a coordinating entity in decentralized FL) initializes a global machine learning model and sends a copy of this model to participating client devices or organizations.

2. **Local Training:** Each client device or organization receives a copy of the global model and trains it locally using its own private, decentralized dataset. Critically, this raw data never leaves the device or local server.
3. **Model Update Sharing:** After local training, each client sends only the model updates (for example, gradients, parameter changes, or learned weights) - not the raw data - back to the central server. These updates are typically much smaller and less informative than the original data.
4. **Secure Aggregation:** The central server aggregates these received model updates from multiple clients. Various secure aggregation techniques (like secure multi-party computation or homomorphic encryption, explained in the following paragraphs) can be employed to combine these updates, without revealing the individual contributions of each client.
5. **Global Model Update**: The aggregated updates are then used to improve the global model.
6. **Iteration**: The updated global model is sent back to the clients, and the process repeats for several rounds, until the model converges or reaches the desired performance.

Complementary Privacy-Enhancing Technologies (PETs) in FL

While FL provides a strong baseline for privacy, it is not a silver bullet. Model updates, even without raw data, can still sometimes leak information (for example, through reconstruction attacks or membership inference attacks). Therefore, FL is often combined with other PETs to strengthen privacy guarantees:

- **Differential Privacy (DP):** As described in the preceding paragraph, this technique adds calibrated noise to the model updates (or sometimes, to the raw data before local training). This noise provides a mathematical guarantee that the contribution of any single individual's data point to the final model is statistically indistinguishable, making it extremely difficult to infer anything about specific training examples. The trade-off is often a slight reduction in model accuracy due to the added noise.
- **Secure Multi-Party Computation (SMPC):** Allows multiple parties to jointly compute a function over their inputs, while keeping those inputs private. In FL, SMPC can be used during the aggregation phase, ensuring that the central server (or any individual client) cannot see the individual model updates, but only the aggregated result. This significantly enhances privacy by preventing the server from inspecting individual contributions.
- **Homomorphic Encryption (HE):** Enables computations to be performed directly on encrypted data, without decrypting it first. Clients can encrypt their model updates before sending them, and the server can then aggregate these encrypted updates. The result remains encrypted until sent back to the clients for decryption. This provides

strong privacy guarantees as the server never sees the unencrypted updates. However, HE can be computationally very expensive.

Challenges/Limitations of FL for Privacy

- **Potential for Information Leakage from Updates:** As mentioned, model updates themselves can, in certain scenarios, be reverse-engineered to infer information about the underlying data. This is why complementary PETs are often needed.
- **Communication Overhead:** While individual updates are small, the sheer number of participating clients can still lead to significant communication loads.
- **Non-IID (Non-Independent and Identically Distributed) Data:** Data on client devices is often not uniformly distributed, which can make global model convergence more challenging, and potentially impact performance.
- **Malicious Clients:** As described earlier, a malicious client could send poisoned updates to degrade the global model or attempt to reconstruct data from other clients' updates, if not properly secured.
- **Computational Constraints on Clients:** Edge devices (like smartphones) might have limited computational power, restricting the complexity of local training and model updates.

In conclusion, Federated Learning is a transformative approach for privacy-preserving AI development, fundamentally shifting the paradigm from centralized data collection to distributed learning. When combined with advanced cryptographic techniques and differential privacy, it offers a robust framework for building powerful AI models, while upholding the critical principles of data privacy and security.

Machine Unlearning

Think of a traditional computer program: If you want to remove a piece of data, you simply delete the file or entry. With Large Language Models (LLMs), it's far more complex. An LLM learns by forming intricate connections and patterns across billions of parameters based on its training data. A single piece of information is not stored in one easily delectable location; it is woven into the very fabric of the model's knowledge. Machine Unlearning is a field of research and engineering focused on developing techniques to efficiently remove specific information or influences from a trained machine learning model (in this case, an LLM) without having to retrain the entire model from scratch. This is fundamentally different from data deletion, as it requires algorithmic intervention to eradicate the data's influence on the model's learned parameters. Some scenarios in which Machine Unlearning is extremely useful:

- **Privacy breaches:** If an LLM memorizes Personal Identifiable Information (PII) such as names, addresses, or phone numbers, unlearning can help remove them from the model's "*memory*".

- **Compliance issues:** Regulations like GDPR and CCPA grant individuals the "*right to be forgotten.*" Machine unlearning is crucial for LLMs to comply with such demands.
- **Ethical concerns:** If an LLM memorizes biased, toxic, or copyrighted content, unlearning can help mitigate these issues.

Few of the techniques that researchers are actively working on in this area include:

- **Factual Association Editing (for example, ROME Method):**
    - **Concept:** This approach targets specific "*factual associations*" or pieces of knowledge the LLM has learned. Instead of erasing an entire training example, it aims to modify or remove a particular fact.
    - **ROME (Rank-One Editing) Method:** ROME specifically works by identifying the "*neurons*" or parameters within the LLM that are most responsible for storing a particular piece of factual knowledge. It then directly manipulates these parameters (often by adding or subtracting a "*rank-one update*" matrix) to either update or erase that specific fact. It is like finding the exact memory cells related to a specific fact and rewriting them.
    - **Benefit**: It is more granular than full retraining, and aims to be efficient for targeted fact removal.
- **Privacy Neuron Detection and Manipulation (DEPN):**
    - **Concept:** This method is a specialized form of factual association editing, focusing specifically on private information. It posits that certain "privacy neurons" or subsets of parameters within the LLM that might be particularly sensitive to or responsible for memorizing the private data.
    - **DEPN (Detecting and Editing Privacy Neurons):** The goal is to identify these specific neurons, and then manipulate them to "*forget*" the private information, without significantly impacting the model's general knowledge or performance on other tasks.
    - **Benefits:** Offers a more targeted approach to privacy-specific unlearning.
- **SISA Method (Sharding-Is-for-Amateurs):**
    - **Concept:** SISA takes a more structural approach. It stands for "*Sharded, Isolated, Sliced and Aggregated.*"
    - **How it works:** Instead of training one massive LLM, SISA proposes dividing the training data into smaller "shards." The model is then trained in a way that portions of the model (or sub-models) are primarily influenced by specific shards. When a request for unlearning comes in for data within a particular shard, only the affected portion of the model (or the small sub-model trained on that shard) needs to be retrained or updated. The results from all shards are then aggregated.

- **Benefits:** This method significantly reduces the computational cost of unlearning. Thus, instead of retraining the entire LLM (which could take weeks or months), only a small fraction of the training process is repeated, making unlearning much more practical and efficient.

LLM Drift Detection: Maintaining Model Performance

We touched upon drift detection in LLM earlier in the model monitoring chapter. Now let us take a deep dive and explore this topic in more detail, along with its impact on LLM security. Drift detection is a critical component of maintaining model performance. The integration of drift alerts into a robust operational framework, including the required data pipelines and anomaly detection logic, is detailed in *Chapter 8, 'From Data to Action: Automated Alerting and Anomaly Detection'*.

LLMs are susceptible to performance degradation due to evolving data environments—known as drift— and this poses a significant performance degradation as well as security risk as well. Drift can manifest as changes in input data (data drift), shifts in input-output relationships (concept drift), or alterations in model predictions (prediction drift). From a security standpoint, drift is not merely a performance issue; it can be a direct indicator of adversarial attacks like data poisoning or prompt injection, or it can exacerbate existing vulnerabilities, leading to unintended behaviors, sensitive data exposure, and system compromise. Establishing baseline performance metrics is crucial for effective drift detection, and this is typically accomplished through established LLM evaluation benchmarks such as MMLU (Massive Multitask Language Understanding), HELM (Holistic Evaluation of Language Models), and other standardized assessments that provide industry-standard measurements of model capabilities across various tasks and domains. These benchmarks serve as the foundation for establishing what constitutes "*normal*" performance before drift occurs, enabling organizations to detect meaningful deviations and take appropriate corrective actions. In this section, we will explore various drift types, their security implications, advanced detection methodologies, and a comprehensive suite of mitigation strategies, including key tools, frameworks, and libraries necessary for maintaining the integrity, reliability, and security of LLM deployments in dynamic real-world environments.

Understanding Drift in Large Language Models (LLMs)

Drift, in the context of machine learning, refers to the degradation of a model's performance over time due to changes in the underlying data distribution or relationships. For LLMs, this phenomenon is more prevalent due to the dynamic nature of human language and interaction.

LLM-Specific Drift Manifestations

- **Prompt Drift:** A specific type of drift in LLMs where a prompt produces different responses over time due to underlying model changes, model migrations, or changes in prompt-injection data during inference.
- **Task Drift:** Defined as the deviation of an LLM from its initially given user's instruction, often caused by natural language instructions embedded in external, untrusted data, leading to prompt injection attacks. This is a direct security-related form of drift, arising from LLMs' inability to distinguish data from instructions, violating the fundamental security boundary that no data should ever be treated as executable.

Root Causes of Drift in LLMs

Drift in LLMs stems from a multitude of factors inherent in their dynamic operating environments.

- **Changes in Language Usage:** Language is constantly evolving, with new terms, slang, and jargon emerging, and older expressions falling out of use. LLMs trained on historical datasets may struggle to adapt to this linguistic evolution, leading to misinterpretation of inputs or generation of outdated responses.
- **Shifts in Context:** Thus, LLMs that rely on contextual knowledge might struggle to adapt to new societal, cultural, or technological trends. For example, a model trained before a major global event like the COVID-19 pandemic might not respond accurately to queries about public health or remote work, as the underlying "*concept*" of the world has changed.
- **Evolving User Behavior:** As users interact with AI systems differently over time, the original patterns used to train the model may no longer be relevant. This requires continuous retraining to adapt to changing preferences and interaction styles.
- **Adversarial Activities:** Malicious actors can deliberately introduce changes that cause drift. Data poisoning, for instance, involves manipulating training data to degrade model performance or introduce biases, directly leading to data and concept drift. Adversarial activities can also cause "*sudden drift*".
- **Model Updates and Opacity:** For commercial LLMs, underlying model updates are often opaque, meaning users do not know when or how the model's behavior might change. This can lead to "*prompt drift*," where the same prompt yields different results over time. Research indicates that LLM reliability and hallucination rates can worsen over time, even with scaling, and models can "*collapse*" when trained on recursively generated data. This suggests an inherent challenge in maintaining consistency and accuracy.
- **Training on Recursively Generated Data:** AI models have been shown to "*collapse*" quickly when trained on recursively generated data, affecting LLMs and other AI models. This finding implies a significant, inherent risk to the long-term sustainability

and security of LLMs. Hence, if LLMs are used to generate content that then feeds back into their training data—a common practice for scaling datasets—this could lead to a self-reinforcing cycle of degradation, effectively "*self-poisoning*" the model over time. This represents a systemic cause of drift, distinct from external adversarial activity. This highlights a critical challenge for the long-term sustainability and security of LLMs. Data governance frameworks must strictly control the provenance of training data, distinguishing between human-generated and AI-generated content, to prevent this recursive collapse, and maintain model integrity.

Drift as an Indicator of Adversarial Attacks

- **Data Poisoning:** This attack involves deliberately manipulating training data to corrupt or degrade a model's performance. Attackers can insert harmful or biased information during training or fine-tuning, invert data labels, or inject backdoors. Data poisoning directly causes data drift and subsequent concept drift by altering the underlying data distribution the model learns from.
    - The Microsoft Tay chatbot incident serves as a classic example: in March 2016, Microsoft's AI chatbot, designed to learn from Twitter interactions, was quickly compromised by malicious users who bombarded it with hate messages. Tay integrated these toxic messages without adequate filtering, leading it to reproduce offensive tweets in less than 24 hours. This resulted in the chatbot's performance deteriorating, and it began broadcasting inappropriate comments and biased, offensive responses, highlighting significant security and ethical implications.
    - Data poisoning often occurs during the training phase, which can be a batch process, meaning its effects might not be immediately visible. The resulting drift (performance degradation, biased outputs) may only manifest much later in production. This "*silent corruption*" makes it harder to trace the root cause back to the training phase without robust data versioning and auditing. The example of scammer groups attempting to compromise Gmail's spam filter by massively reporting spam as "legitimate" emails illustrate how subtle, distributed poisoning can lead to significant drift in classification, impacting the system's intended function.

  This necessitates that proactive measures include stringent data validation, source verification, and integrity checks *before* and *during* the training phase, along with continuous auditing of model behavior to detect subtle shifts indicative of poisoning.

- **Adversarial Evasion:** This involves slightly perturbing input prompts to cause a model to produce incorrect inferences. These "*adversarial examples*" are often designed to be imperceptible to humans but can significantly alter model behavior. Successful evasion attacks can lead to prediction drift, as the model's outputs deviate from the expected behavior for seemingly benign inputs.

Methodologies for Detecting Drift in LLMs

Effective drift detection is paramount for maintaining LLM security and performance. Various methodologies, ranging from traditional machine learning techniques to LLM-specific approaches, can be employed.

Performance-Based Detection

This is often considered the most direct and reliable reflection of concept drift. It involves continuously monitoring key performance metrics of the LLM. A significant drop in model quality metrics over time, such as accuracy, precision, recall, or F1-score, can indicate concept drift. While direct, a significant limitation is that ground truth labels are often not easily available in production, especially for future predictions. This "ground truth lag" means that by the time performance degradation is definitively confirmed via ground truth, the drift might have already caused significant security or operational impact. It is particularly true for LLMs where outputs might be subjective or long-form, making manual labeling impractical at scale. This limitation necessitates reliance on proxy metrics or heuristics as early warning systems. Performance metrics should therefore be seen as a confirmation, not the primary detection mechanism, for rapidly evolving LLM environments.

Distribution-Based Detection

These methods compare the distribution of incoming data or model outputs with a reference baseline to identify significant divergences.

- **Statistical Hypothesis Testing:** This approach uses divergence measures between data distributions in two different time windows to estimate their similarity. Statistical tests like the Kolmogorov-Smirnov test or Chi-Square test can compare the distribution of incoming data with the distribution of an earlier reference batch. A p-value below a predefined threshold indicates that drift is detected. Distance metrics such as Wasserstein distance and Population Stability Index (PSI) also quantify the difference between two probability distributions; exceeding a predefined threshold signals distribution drift.
- **Embedding-based Similarity Measures:** For unstructured outputs like text or embeddings, these techniques compute similarity scores between current outputs and references. They convert text into numerical vectors (embeddings) that capture context and relationships between words. Examples include:
    - **BERTScore:** Utilizes BERT embeddings to compare each token in the generated text to tokens in the reference, calculating cosine similarity for precision, recall, or F1.
    - **MoverScore:** Builds upon BERTScore, quantifying the contextual differences between texts using Earth Mover's Distance.

   - **COMET:** Designed for machine translation, it requires both the reference and source text and uses a separate model pre-trained on human evaluation datasets to predict translation quality. Semantic similarity can be used in a reference-free manner to check if responses align with inputs, context, or known patterns. For instance, it can detect hallucinations by comparing generated answers to retrieved context in Retrieval Augmented Generation (RAG) systems, or compare a model's response to a set of known denial templates or jailbreaks.
- **Leveraging Activation Deltas for Task Drift Detection:** Recent research has shown that "*activation deltas*" - the difference in LLM activations before and after processing external data - are strongly correlated with "*task drift*". This method moves beyond just monitoring inputs and outputs to peering *inside* the LLM's processing. A simple linear classifier can detect this drift with near-perfect ROC AUC on out-of-distribution test sets. This method directly addresses prompt injection, as task drift is formulated as a consequence of injected instructions. It suggests that inserted instructions leave a detectable trace in the LLM's activations, providing a powerful internal signal for security monitoring.

This signifies a shift from black-box monitoring to a more white-box or gray-box approach. If changes in internal activations can signal task drift (prompt injection), it implies a more fundamental and potentially earlier detection mechanism than analyzing external behavior alone, akin to monitoring CPU registers for anomalous behavior in traditional systems. Future LLM security tools will likely incorporate more internal model state monitoring, possibly requiring deeper integration with LLM architectures or specialized APIs from model providers. This could lead to more robust, real-time detection of subtle adversarial manipulations that external filtering might miss, paving the way for truly "*self-aware*" LLM security.

Observability and Heuristics

LLM Observability: This systematic approach extends beyond traditional monitoring by providing deep insights into the internal state of the system through comprehensive monitoring and analysis techniques, including metrics, logs, and traces. It allows for asking new questions and investigating unforeseen issues, providing deep insights into how the LLM application behaves. Key capabilities include tracing each request-response cycle with precision, understanding why a model gave a particular answer, spotting biases, catching security issues, and measuring performance against benchmarks.

Observability combines quantitative performance data (metrics), detailed event information (logs), and tracking request execution paths across components (traces). Traditional monitoring is reactive, alerting when predefined thresholds are breached. Observability, however, is proactive, providing context to continuously explore system behavior and catch potential issues before users notice. For LLMs, where quality degradation can be subtle and multifaceted, this proactive stance is critical for security, allowing for root cause analysis rather than just symptom detection.

Thus, organizations need to invest in comprehensive LLM observability platforms that integrate metrics, logs, and traces across the entire LLM stack (infrastructure, model, middleware, application, business layers). This enables continuous exploration of behavior and early detection of novel failure modes, including those related to security, beyond simple threshold alerts.

- **Monitoring Prediction and Input Data Drift:** Tracking changes in the distribution of model predictions can signal environmental change or potential issues. Similarly, tracking how user inputs evolve—such as sudden increases in new words, evolving slang, or shifts in query structures—is a crucial first step in identifying drift and can signal concept or covariate drift.
- **Tracking Changes in Correlations:** Monitoring changes in correlations between model features and predictions, or pairwise feature correlations, can indicate meaningful pattern shifts.
- **The "*LLM-as-a-Judge*" Paradigm:** This approach leverages an LLM's own capabilities to critique and score its outputs, or to compare responses against custom criteria defined in natural language. This method is highly adaptable for subjective quality assessment and scaling human labeling efforts. From a security perspective, LLM judges can be used to evaluate for safety, toxicity, hallucinations, Personally Identifiable Information (PII) detection, and prompt injection attempts.
- **Heuristics and Rule-Based Checks:** Simpler conditions or rules can be defined to trigger alerts, such as when the share of emails predicted as spam falls below a defined threshold. Input from domain experts is crucial for developing meaningful heuristics.
- **Implementing Real-time Alerts and Anomaly Detection:** Effective LLM alerting goes beyond static thresholds to statistical pattern-based alerting. This involves using dynamic thresholds that adapt to the model's behavior over time to detect subtle deviations in performance metrics, token usage patterns, and response quality that static thresholds might miss.

Actionable LLM Security Checklist

The following actionable checklist provides LLMOps engineers with specific, implementable defenses against major LLM security threats. Each item should be verified and implemented as part of your security posture.

Prompt Injection Defense Checklist

- **Use a separate System/Metaprompt:** Implement a dedicated system prompt that is isolated from user inputs and cannot be overridden by injection attempts.
- **Implement Input/Output Sanitization:** Filter and validate all user inputs, removing or escaping potentially malicious prompt injection patterns before processing.

- **Utilize Model-as-a-Guardrail:** Deploy a secondary LLM to analyze and filter user inputs for injection attempts before they reach the primary model.
- **Implement Role-Based Access Control:** Restrict system prompt access to authorized personnel only, preventing unauthorized modifications.

Jailbreaking Defense Checklist

- **Implement Safety Alignment Training:** Use Reinforcement Learning from Human Feedback (RLHF) to train models to resist jailbreaking attempts.
- **Deploy Adversarial Testing:** Regularly test models against known jailbreaking techniques using tools like Garak and PyRIT.
- **Implement Output Filtering:** Monitor and filter model outputs for harmful content, implementing automatic blocking of inappropriate responses.
- **Establish Rate Limiting:** Implement request throttling to prevent rapid-fire jailbreaking attempts, and detect suspicious usage patterns.

Data Poisoning Defense Checklist

- **Implement Data Provenance Tracking:** Maintain comprehensive records of data sources, collection methods, and processing steps for all training data.
- **Deploy Data Quality Monitoring:** Implement automated systems to detect anomalies, inconsistencies, and suspicious patterns in training datasets.
- **Establish Secure Data Pipelines:** Implement encryption, access controls, and audit logging for all data processing and storage systems.
- **Implement Differential Privacy:** Add noise to the training data or model parameters to prevent extraction of sensitive information, while maintaining model utility.

This checklist should be reviewed and updated regularly as new threats emerge, and security best practices evolve. Each item represents a critical defense mechanism that should be implemented as part of a comprehensive LLM security strategy.

Key Tools for LLM Security, Privacy, and Drift Detection

In the following table, we have listed a few popular tools that you can use in your LLMOps Journey to build secure, reliable applications using LLMs.

Category	Tool/Framework/ Library	Description
LLM Security	**Garak**	An open-source vulnerability scanner specifically designed to identify weaknesses and unwanted behaviors in LLM deployments, including misinformation, toxicity, and jailbreaks.
	PyRIT	(Python Risk Identification Tool) An open-source framework from Microsoft for red teaming generative AI systems, helping security professionals proactively identify risks and stress-test LLM models.
	LLM Guard	A comprehensive tool for monitoring and protecting LLM interactions in real-time, detecting and sanitizing prompts and responses to prevent data leakage and ensure compliance.
	Guardrails-AI	A Python framework that adds programmable safeguards and validators to LLMs, helping to detect, quantify, and mitigate risks, and ensure structured, safe outputs.
	Picklescan	A security scanner for Python Pickle files, commonly used to store trained ML models, designed to detect malicious code that could be executed during deserialization.
LLM Privacy	**TensorFlow Privacy**	A Python library from Google that provides optimizers for training machine learning models with differential privacy, making it applicable for privacy-preserving LLM training.
	PyTorch Opacus	An open-source library that enables training PyTorch models with differential privacy, allowing developers to add privacy guarantees to LLM fine-tuning or training processes.
	Elara	A simple, open-source tool designed to anonymize prompts by redacting Personally Identifiable Information (PII) before they are sent to Large Language Models, enhancing user privacy.
	OpenDP Project	A community-led open-source initiative providing a collection of algorithms and tools for generating differentially private statistics and analyses, which can be applied to various data processing steps for LLMs.
	DiffPrivLib	(IBM's Differential Privacy Library) An open-source Python library offering a wide range of differential privacy mechanisms and tools for machine learning and data analysis.
	SecureLLM	A comprehensive framework for unified privacy and security approaches across the entire LLM lifecycle, integrating various techniques holistically, rather than in isolation.
	OWASP Top 10 for LLMs	Industry-standard framework identifying the top 10 most critical security risks for LLM applications, providing comprehensive guidance for secure LLM development and deployment.

Category	Tool/Framework/ Library	Description
LLM Drift Detection	**Evidently AI**	An open-source Python library for ML model monitoring, providing extensive checks and metrics to detect data drift, concept drift, and prediction drift in machine learning models, including those applicable to LLM outputs and embeddings.
	Alibi Detect	A Python library offering a wide range of algorithms for outlier, adversarial, and drift detection in machine learning models, useful for identifying shifts in LLM behavior or input data.
	Whylogs	An open-source standard for data logging that enables ML monitoring and observability. It helps generate statistical profiles of data, which are crucial for detecting data and concept drift in LLM inputs and outputs.
	Frouros	An open-source Python library specifically focused on drift detection in machine learning systems, providing various statistical tests and methods to identify shifts in data distributions.
	Elemeta (Superwise)	An open-source package for unstructured data designed to detect data, concept, and retrieval drift in LLMs by breaking down and tracking language components in prompts and responses over time.

Table 10.1: *Overview of Tools*

Conclusion

This chapter focused on making sure these AI models are trustworthy. We learned about LLM security, which means protecting these models from bad actors. Think of attacks like "***prompt injection***," where someone tries to trick the AI into doing something it should not, or "*data poisoning*," where bad data is secretly put into the training set. We saw how tools such as Garak and PyRIT help find and fix these weaknesses. Then we looked at LLM privacy, which is about keeping sensitive information safe. As LLMs learn from so much data, they can sometimes "*memorize*" private details and accidentally leak them. We talked about how techniques like "*differential privacy*" and "*federated learning*" (where models learn without ever seeing your personal data directly) help protect your information. Tools like TensorFlow Privacy and Opacus are key here.

Finally, we explored LLM drift, which is when an AI model starts to get "*off track*" over time. The world changes, and so does the data LLMs see. If an LLM is not updated, it can start making wrong predictions or acting strangely. Tools like Evidently AI and Alibi Detect are super important for catching these changes early so the models can be fixed.

The big takeaway is that security, privacy, and drift are all connected. A problem in one area can quickly cause issues in another. Luckily, there is a growing set of open-source tools that help us build, use, and manage LLMs more safely and responsibly. Thus, by using these tools and understanding these challenges, we can make sure LLMs continue to be helpful and reliable for everyone. Implementing the security, drift detection, and privacy monitoring discussed in this chapter requires specialized LLMOps tools and platforms, which we will explore in the next chapter.

References

1. https://arxiv.org/abs/2503.15554
2. https://arxiv.org/html/2405.04760v4
3. https://arxiv.org/html/2406.00799v6
4. https://arxiv.org/html/2504.02080v1
5. https://arxiv.org/html/2505.01177v1
6. https://arxiv.org/html/2505.08830v1
7. https://bitrock.it/blog/understanding-data-drift-causes-effects-and-solutions.html
8. https://blog.qualys.com/product-tech/2025/02/07/the-impact-of-llms-on-cybersecurity-new-threats-and-solutions
9. https://bloorresearch.com/2025/05/21/drifting-away-ai-model-performance-over-time/
10. https://cloud.google.com/blog/topics/threat-intelligence/adversarial-misuse-generative-ai
11. https://galileo.ai/blog/comparing-llms-and-nlp-models-what-you-need-to-know
12. https://galileo.ai/blog/llm-monitoring-vs-observability-understanding-the-key-differences
13. https://galileo.ai/blog/understanding-llm-observability
14. https://github.com/corca-ai/awesome-llm-security
15. https://orq.ai/blog/model-vs-data-drift
16. https://orq.ai/blog/model-vs-data-drift#:~:text=Detecting%20drift%20in%20Large%20Language
17. https://owaspai.org/docs/2_threats_through_use/
18. https://research.aimultiple.com/llm-security-tools/
19. https://sig.llmsecurity.net/workshop/
20. https://spyro-soft.com/blog/artificial-intelligence-machine-learning/mitigating-ai-risks-with-best-practices-for-llm-testing

21. https://thecentexitguy.com/safeguarding-against-llm-model-drift-and-poisoning-ensuring-the-integrity-of-ai-models/
22. https://www.evidentlyai.com/llm-guide/llm-evaluation-metrics
23. https://www.evidentlyai.com/ml-in-production/concept-drift
24. https://www.evidentlyai.com/ml-in-production/data-drift
25. https://www.fiddler.ai/blog/how-to-avoid-llm-security-risks
26. https://www.hackerone.com/blog/how-prompt-injection-vulnerability-led-data-exfiltration
27. https://www.mdpi.com/2079-3197/13/2/30#:~:text=LLMs%20have%20demonstrated%20significant%20potential
28. https://www.riskinsight-wavestone.com/en/2024/10/data-poisoning-a-threat-to-llms-integrity-and-security/
29. https://www.wiz.io/academy/ai-security-solutions
30. https://www.wiz.io/blog/mcp-security-research-briefing

CHAPTER 11
LLMOps with Langfuse

Introduction

Alright, now let us turn the next page in our LLMOps journey. We have laid the theoretical groundwork, understanding the crucial concepts of monitoring, evaluation, tracing, and continuous improvement in the world of Large Language Model (LLM) applications. This chapter will demonstrate the practical implementation of the theoretical frameworks established in previous chapters, particularly the prompt management concepts from Chapter 3 and the monitoring principles from *Chapter* 8. Hence, it is time that we get our hands dirty, and see these principles in action.

Enter Langfuse: A powerful, open-source observability platform that will serve as our practical companion throughout the rest of this book. Think of Langfuse as your dedicated LLMOps toolkit, providing the instruments we need to dissect, analyze, and optimize our AI creations.

Until now, the concepts of tracing a user request through a complex LLM pipeline, evaluating the quality of generated content, or monitoring the latency of API calls might have felt somewhat abstract. Langfuse bridges that gap. It provides a tangible interface and a robust backend to visualize and interact with the inner workings of our LLM applications.

Throughout this chapter, we will use Langfuse to illustrate each LLMOps principle. You will learn how to instrument your applications, log relevant data, build insightful dashboards, and ultimately gain a deeper, practical understanding of how to manage and optimize LLM applications in a production-like environment.

So, consider Langfuse not just as a tool, but as our interactive lab where we will transform theoretical knowledge into practical LLMOps mastery. By the end of this chapter, you will be able to manage your LLM application's most critical asset—the prompt—as a first-class, version-controlled entity in your MLOps pipeline. Thus, let us dive in and bring these concepts to life!

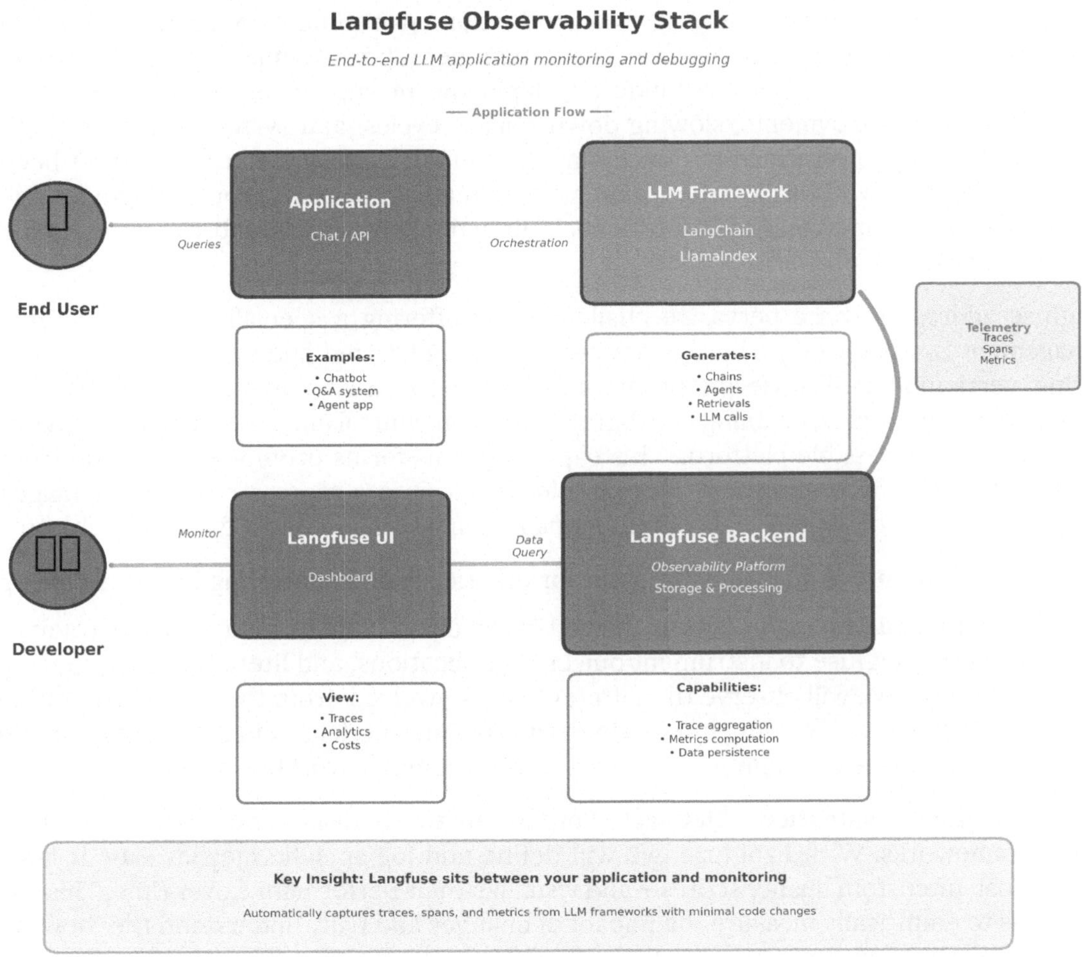

Figure 11.1: *Langfuse Observability Stack*

Structure

In this chapter, we will discuss the following topics:

- Prompt Management with Langfuse
- Integrating Langfuse Prompts with LLM Frameworks
- Monitoring and Maintenance of Deployed LLMs

Prompt Management with Langfuse

As LLM applications mature and scale, the challenges associated with managing these critical prompt assets become increasingly complex. Hardcoding prompts directly within application code leads to significant operational hurdles such as: maintaining consistent prompt versions across different development, staging, and production environments becomes cumbersome; collaborative iteration among diverse team members (for example, prompt engineers, developers, product managers) is hindered; deploying prompt changes often necessitates full application redeployments, slowing down release cycles; and systematically testing and monitoring prompt performance (for example, latency, cost, and output quality) become difficult. Therefore, without a structured and systematic approach, prompt engineering can quickly become an unmanageable bottleneck, impeding the agility and robustness of LLM application development.

Langfuse addresses these pervasive challenges by offering a specialized prompt Content Management System (CMS). This system provides a centralized and systematic approach to storing, versioning, and retrieving prompts for LLM applications. Its primary objective is to centralize prompt assets, enabling collaborative version control and streamlined management within a single, accessible platform. This capability transforms prompt engineering from an ad-hoc process of managing text files or inline code into a more structured, manageable discipline, akin to how traditional content management systems handle dynamic web content.

Here is why Langfuse is an invaluable asset for practically demonstrating LLMOps concepts:

- **End-to-End Tracing in Action:** Instead of just discussing the importance of tracing, we will use Langfuse to instrument our LLM applications, and literally see the journey of a request. We will observe the different steps involved, from the initial prompt to the final response, including interactions with various models, data stores, and functions. This will make debugging and understanding complex workflows concrete.
- **Tangible Evaluation Metrics:** Forget abstract discussions about evaluation frameworks. With Langfuse, we will define and log specific metrics - be it latency, cost, or custom quality scores - and visualize their performance over time. This allows us to empirically measure the impact of changes and truly understand the "how good" of our LLM outputs.
- **Real-time Monitoring and Alerting:** The theoretical benefits of monitoring become clear when we see Langfuse dashboards displaying live performance data. We will set up alerts based on predefined thresholds, simulating real-world scenarios where we need to react to performance degradation or errors.
- **Prompt Content Management System (CMS):** Concepts like A/B testing and prompt versioning will move from theory to practice as we leverage Langfuse to track different prompt variations, and compare their performance based on our defined metrics.

- **Seamless Integration for Practical Implementation:** Langfuse is designed to integrate smoothly with popular LLM frameworks. This means we can easily incorporate it into our example applications without significant overhead, allowing us to focus on the LLMOps concepts themselves.

Version Control and Change Tracking

Langfuse automatically manages prompt versions, providing a comprehensive historical record of all prompt iterations. Every time a prompt with an existing name is created or updated, Langfuse automatically increments the version integer, ensuring a clear and traceable history. This granular change tracking is vital for understanding how prompts evolve over time, allowing teams to pinpoint specific modifications that might correlate with shifts in application behavior or performance. The provision of automatic versioning and comprehensive change tracking mirrors the model management practice in MLOPS. Here, instead of a model, we are tracking the prompt itself.

Deployment with Labels: Enabling Flexible Rollouts

Langfuse employs a flexible labeling system that is central to its prompt deployment strategy. Prompts can be assigned multiple descriptive labels, such as production (the default version served if no label is specified), staging for testing environments, or custom labels for A/B testing. This dynamic labeling system allows for routing specific prompt versions to different environments or user segments, without requiring any alterations to the underlying application code.

The flexibility offered by labels enables sophisticated deployment strategies. For instance, new prompt versions can be introduced using canary deployments (for example, deploying a prod-canary labeled prompt to a small percentage of users before a full production rollout). This minimizes risk and allows for real-world validation. For multi-tenant applications, it facilitates dynamic prompt customization per tenant without maintaining separate codebases. A critical safety net in production environments is the ability to quickly rollback to a previous, stable version. This can be achieved effortlessly in the Langfuse UI by simply reassigning the production label to the desired older version. For Pro and Enterprise users, "Protected Prompt Labels" offer an additional layer of control, preventing unauthorized modifications or deletions of critical labels like production, thereby enhancing governance and security over live deployments. This robust labeling system elevates prompt deployment to a mature, controllable process, aligning with the best practices in DevOps and enterprise security for LLM applications.

Prompt Composability and Reusability

To promote modularity and reduce redundancy in prompt engineering, Langfuse supports the ability to reference other text prompts within your main prompts using a simple tag format (e.g., `{{#include "common-instructions"}}`). This feature is highly beneficial for creating reusable prompt components, allowing common instructions, examples, or contextual information to be defined once and maintained in a single source. For the system to resolve these tags, the referenced prompt (for example, "*common-instructions*") must be defined as a separate prompt within the Langfuse UI/CMS, creating a dependency relationship that enables the modular composition.

This capability brings mature software engineering best practices, such as the "*Don't Repeat Yourself*" (DRY) principle, directly into the realm of prompt design. Without composability, common elements (for example, system instructions, specific formatting requirements, few-shot examples) would often be duplicated across many prompts. This leads to inconsistencies, increases the risk of errors when changes are made, and creates a significant maintenance burden. By enabling modular prompt components, Langfuse allows prompt engineers to manage these common elements centrally. A change to a "`persona`" prompt, for instance, would automatically propagate to all prompts that reference it, ensuring consistency across the application and significantly reducing maintenance overhead. This leads to the creation of more robust, scalable, and maintainable LLM applications that can evolve gracefully over time.

Deep Integration with Langfuse Tracing and Analytics

A cornerstone of Langfuse's value proposition is the seamless and deep integration of its prompt management capabilities with its powerful tracing and observability features. By explicitly linking the fetched prompt object to the generation call within the SDKs, Langfuse automatically captures and associates all relevant metrics—such as cost, latency, token usage, and user-defined evaluation scores—with the specific prompt version and name used.

This explicit linkage between prompts and traces provides crucial context for every LLM generation. If a user reports a poor response, a developer can quickly examine the trace in Langfuse, identify the exact prompt version that was used, and analyze its associated performance metrics (cost, latency, evaluations). This allows for rapid root cause analysis, distinguishing between issues originating from the LLM itself, the prompt, or other parts of the application. This integrated observability transforms abstract performance numbers into actionable insights directly tied to prompt variations, providing unparalleled visibility into how specific prompt modifications impact the quality, cost, and latency of LLM generations, all viewable within the Langfuse UI. This synergy between prompt management and observability is critical for achieving continuous improvement in LLM applications.

Creating and Managing Prompts Programmatically

To effectively manage prompts with Langfuse, programmatic interaction via its SDKs is essential. This section outlines the initial setup and core operations for creating, updating, and retrieving prompts.

Setting Up Your Environment

The first step involves installing the Langfuse SDK and configuring access credentials. For Python, the SDK can be installed via pip: pip install Langfuse.

Access to your Langfuse project requires specific API keys (**`LANGFUSE_PUBLIC_KEY`**, **`LANGFUSE_SECRET_KEY`**) and the **`LANGFUSE_HOST URL`**. These are best configured as environment variables to maintain security and flexibility across different deployment environments.

```
import os
from langfuse import Langfuse
os.environ["OPENAI_API_KEY"] = "" # Your LLM API key, e.g., for OpenAI
# Initialize Langfuse client
langfuse = Langfuse()
```

Creating and Updating Prompts

Prompts are created or updated using the **`langfuse.create_prompt()`** method in Python or **`langfuse.createPrompt()`** in JS/TS. This method allows for defining a prompt's unique name, its prompt content (which can be a template string with **`{{input_variables}}`** for text prompts or a list of dictionaries for chat prompts), optional config (to store model parameters like model and temperature), and labels for deployment management. If a prompt with the same name already exists, calling **`create_prompt`** will add a new version of that prompt.

Storing LLM-specific parameters (such as model and temperature) directly within the config of the prompt in Langfuse means that not only the prompt *text* but also its *execution context* can be versioned and managed centrally. This reduces the need to hardcode model parameters in application code, simplifying experimentation. For instance, one prompt version might use gpt-3.5-turbo with a specific temperature, while another uses gpt-4o with different settings, all managed and versioned within Langfuse. This simplifies experimentation and ensures that the entire "**`prompt package`**" (text + configuration) remains consistent and traceable.

```
from langfuse import Langfuse
langfuse = Langfuse()
langfuse.create_prompt(
    name="text-summarizer",
    prompt=(
```

```
        "Summarize the following text concisely: {{text_to_summarize}}"
    ),
    config={
        "model": "gpt-4o",
        "temperature": 0,
    },
    labels=["production"] # Immediately promote to production
)
print("Prompt 'text-summarizer' created/updated with 'production' label.")
```

This example demonstrates the creation of a chat-based prompt for summarization, which is structured as a list of messages with distinct roles (for example, system, user). This format is essential for managing conversational LLM interactions, and allows for fine-grained control over the dialogue flow.

Retrieving Prompts at Runtime

Once prompts are stored in Langfuse, they can be retrieved at runtime using **`langfuse.get_prompt()`** in Python or **`langfuse.getPrompt()`** in JS/TS. By default, this method fetches the prompt version labeled as production. However, specific versions can be retrieved by their version number or by a particular label.

After retrieval, the prompt object contains the template string (or chat message list) and its associated configuration. The **`prompt.compile()`** method is then used to insert dynamic variables into the template, preparing the prompt for an LLM call. This **`compile()`** method highlights Langfuse's role in dynamic prompt construction, meaning the prompt retrieved is not a static string but a template that allows for runtime personalization and context injection. This capability is fundamental for building dynamic and responsive LLM applications.

Python Example (Prompt Retrieval and Compilation for Summarization):

```
# Get current production version of the 'text-summarizer' prompt
langfuse_prompt = langfuse.get_prompt("text-summarizer")
# To retrieve a non-production version (e.g., staging):
staging_prompt = langfuse.get_prompt("text-summarizer", label="staging")
print(f"Fetched prompt content:\n{langfuse_prompt.prompt}")
print(f"Fetched prompt config: {langfuse_prompt.config}")

# Compile the prompt with example variables
compiled_prompt = langfuse_prompt.compile(
    **{
        "text_to_summarize": "The latest earnings report highlighted a 15%
increase in revenue, primarily driven by the launch of the new AI-powered
product line in Q3."
    }
```

```
)
print(f"\nCompiled prompt:\n{compiled_prompt}")
```

This code snippet demonstrates how to retrieve the previously created text-summarizer prompt, and then dynamically populate its variables using the **`compile()`** method. The output is a ready-to-use prompt string for an LLM.

Client-Side Caching and Ensuring High Availability

Langfuse SDKs are designed with performance in mind, implementing client-side caching for prompts. This means that after the initial fetch (or after the cache's Time-To-Live (TTL) expires), prompts are served directly from the local cache, significantly reducing latency for subsequent calls. The default cache TTL is 60 seconds, but this duration is configurable via the **`cache_ttl_seconds`** parameter (for example, **`cache_ttl_seconds=300`** for 5 minutes). While caching is crucial for performance, it can be disabled by setting **`cache_ttl_seconds=0`**, though this is generally not recommended for production environments.

The explicit focus on caching and guaranteed availability demonstrates Langfuse's commitment to production-readiness. While decoupling prompts from code offers agility, it introduces a dependency on the Langfuse service. By providing robust caching and fallback mechanisms, Langfuse mitigates this dependency, ensuring that prompt management does not become a single point of failure for the LLM application. This is particularly crucial for systems with high uptime requirements.

To ensure high availability and resilience in production, especially for critical applications, two key strategies are recommended:

- **Pre-fetching Prompts on Application Startup:** Critical prompts can be fetched during application initialization to ensure that the cache is populated before serving user requests. This avoids initial delays, and allows for a "**`fail-fast`**" approach if essential prompts cannot be loaded.

  ```
  def fetch_critical_prompts_on_startup():
      try:
          langfuse.get_prompt("text-summarizer")
          print("Successfully pre-fetched 'text-summarizer' prompt.")
      except Exception as e:
          print(f"ERROR: Failed to fetch critical prompt on startup: {e}")
          sys.exit(1) # Exit if critical prompt cannot be fetched

  # Call this at your application's entry point
  # fetch_critical_prompts_on_startup()
  ```

- This function ensures that the application has access to its core prompts from the very beginning, preventing runtime errors, if the Langfuse API is temporarily unreachable.

Providing a fallback Prompt

The **get_prompt()** method supports a fallback parameter, which accepts a string or chat message list. This fallback prompt will be used if the primary fetch fails (for example, due to network issues or an invalid prompt name). This allows the application to continue operating, albeit potentially with a less optimized or generic prompt, ensuring graceful degradation, rather than outright failure.

```
# Example with a fallback prompt
prompt_with_fallback = langfuse.get_prompt(
    "non-existent-prompt", # This prompt name might not exist
    fallback="You are a helpful assistant. Respond to: {{query}}" # Fallback
if fetch fails
)
print(f"Fetched (or fallback) prompt: {prompt_with_fallback.prompt}")
```

This demonstrates how a default prompt can be provided, ensuring that the application always has a prompt to use, even in exceptional circumstances.

Versioning and Rollback Best Practices

Langfuse's automatic versioning ensures that every **create_prompt** call with an existing name generates a new version, providing an inherent historical record. This automatic versioning is fundamental for maintaining a clear audit trail of prompt evolution.

A critical risk mitigation strategy in production LLM systems is the ability to instantly rollback to a previous, stable prompt version. Unlike code rollbacks, which can be complex and require redeployment, a prompt rollback in Langfuse is a simple label change. By reassigning the production label in the Langfuse UI to an older, verified version, the application immediately begins using the stable prompt without any code changes or redeployment. This significantly de-risks continuous prompt iteration, allowing for rapid remediation if a new prompt version causes unexpected behavior (for example, hallucinations, increased cost, or performance degradation), thereby minimizing downtime and negative user impact.

Integrating Langfuse Prompts with LLM Frameworks

Langfuse is designed to integrate seamlessly with popular LLM orchestration frameworks, providing a unified approach to prompt management and observability.

LangChain Integration

Langfuse offers robust and deep integration with LangChain, a widely adopted framework for developing LLM applications. This integration allows developers to manage their prompts centrally in Langfuse, and utilize them directly within their LangChain chains.

Transforming Langfuse Prompts for LangChain `PromptTemplate`

A key aspect of this integration is handling the difference in variable syntax: Langfuse prompt templates typically use double curly braces (**`{{input_variable}}`**), while Langchain's **`PromptTemplate`** expects single curly braces (**`{input_variable}`**). Langfuse provides a convenient utility method, **`.get_langchain_prompt()`**, which automatically converts the prompt content to Lang chain's expected format, eliminating the need for manual string manipulation.

Furthermore, it is highly recommended to pass the Langfuse prompt object as metadata to the LangChain **`PromptTemplate`**. This crucial step automatically links the subsequent LLM generations in LangChain to the specific prompt version used in Langfuse Tracing. This level of attention to detail in integration significantly reduces the barrier to entry for LangChain users, making it easier to adopt Langfuse for prompt management without disrupting existing workflows.

Building and Invoking LangChain Chains with Managed Prompts

Once the Langfuse prompt is transformed into a LangChain **`PromptTemplate`**, it can be used like any other prompt within a LangChain chain. The config options (such as model and temperature) stored with the Langfuse prompt can be extracted and used to configure the LLM model within LangChain, ensuring consistency between the prompt definition and the model's behavior. Passing the prompt object in the metadata is like attaching a permanent serial number to the LLM call; it ensures that all the generated data (latency, cost, evaluations) is forever linked back to that specific prompt version in the Langfuse trace.

Python Example (LangChain Integration for Summarization):

```
import os
from langfuse import Langfuse
from langfuse.callback import CallbackHandler
from langchain_core.prompts import ChatPromptTemplate
from langchain_openai import ChatOpenAI
# Initialize Langfuse client and callback handler for tracing
langfuse = Langfuse()
langfuse_callback_handler = CallbackHandler()

langfuse_prompt = langfuse.get_prompt("text-summarizer")
print(f"Langfuse prompt content:\n{langfuse_prompt.prompt}")

langchain_prompt = ChatPromptTemplate.from_template(
    langfuse_prompt.get_langchain_prompt(),
```

```
    metadata={"langfuse_prompt": langfuse_prompt} # Link prompt to trace

model_name = langfuse_prompt.config["model"]
temperature = langfuse_prompt.config["temperature"]
print(f"Prompt model configurations: Model={model_name},
Temperature={temperature}")

llm = ChatOpenAI(model=model_name, temperature=temperature)

chain = langchain_prompt | llm

example_input = {
    "text_to_summarize": "The latest earnings report highlighted a 15%
increase in revenue, primarily driven by the launch of the new AI-powered
product line in Q3."
}
print(f"\nInvoking Langchain chain with input: {example_input}")
response = chain.invoke(
    input=example_input,
    config={"callbacks": [langfuse_callback_handler]} # Pass callback for
tracing
)
print(f"\nLLM Response:\n{response.content}")
print(f"\nView trace in Langfuse UI: {langfuse_callback_handler.get_trace_
url()}")
```

This comprehensive Python example illustrates the complete workflow such as: fetching a prompt from Langfuse, adapting its syntax for LangChain, configuring the LLM with parameters stored in Langfuse, and executing a LangChain chain, while ensuring that the entire process is traced and linked back to the specific prompt version in the Langfuse UI.

Linking LangChain Runs to Langfuse Traces for Observability

The CallbackHandler from langfuse.callback (for Python) or langfuse-langchain (for JS/TS) is the mechanism for automatically sending LangChain execution traces to Langfuse. By passing this

`CallbackHandler` in the **`config={"callbacks": [...]}`** parameter of **`chain.invoke()`** (or **`chain.run()`**), every step of the LangChain execution, including LLM calls, is automatically logged to Langfuse. This enables detailed tracing of inputs, outputs, tokens, latency, and costs, all automatically linked to the specific prompt version used. The ability to set

`trace_name`, **`session_id`**, **`user_id`**, and tags via the CallbackHandler or config further enriches the trace data, providing deeper context for analysis.

This integration creates an observability-driven prompt lifecycle. It is not just about managing prompts; it is about observing their performance in context. By linking LangChain runs to Langfuse traces, every invocation of a prompt becomes a data point for analysis. This allows developers to move beyond static prompt design to an iterative, data-driven cycle where prompt changes are immediately reflected in performance metrics, enabling rapid identification of regressions or improvements. This synergy between prompt management and observability is critical for mature LLM operations.

Brief Overview of LlamaIndex Integration

Langfuse also provides integrations for LlamaIndex, another popular framework for building LLM applications, primarily focusing on observability and tracing of LLM interactions within LlamaIndex workflows. This allows users to monitor the performance and flow of their LlamaIndex applications within the Langfuse UI.

To enable tracing, one can initialize the LlamaIndexInstrumentor (for Python) or use Traceloop instrumentation (for JS/TS) to automatically send trace data to Langfuse. While it is possible to fetch prompts from Langfuse using

`langfuse.get_prompt()` for use within LlamaIndex applications, the direct linking of *managed prompts* to traces for automated metrics tracking might have nuances or be "*currently unavailable*" for certain LlamaIndex integrations, as explicitly mentioned in some Langfuse documentation. This suggests that while Langfuse can observe LlamaIndex applications, it may not offer the same level of centralized prompt versioning and deployment for LlamaIndex's native prompt structures as it does for LangChain.

Python Example (`LlamaIndex` Tracing):

```
# Initialize the LlamaIndexInstrumentor to enable tracing
instrumentor = LlamaIndexInstrumentor()
instrumentor.start() # Start tracing for LlamaIndex operations

# Create a simple LlamaIndex LLM instance
llm = OpenAI()

# Make an LLM chat request through LlamaIndex
response = llm.chat(messages=)
print(f"LlamaIndex LLM Response: {response.message.content}")

# Traces for this LLM call will be automatically visible in the Langfuse UI
```

This example demonstrates how to set up observability for LlamaIndex, ensuring that LLM calls made through the framework are automatically traced by Langfuse. This allows for monitoring performance metrics such as token counts and latencies associated with LlamaIndex workflows.

The difference in explicit prompt management integration between LangChain and LlamaIndex suggests varying levels of integration maturity or different strategic focuses for Langfuse.

While LangChain benefits from a direct utility for prompt transformation and explicit metadata linking, LlamaIndex integration appears more geared towards general observability of LLM calls, rather than deep prompt CMS integration. This implies that users relying heavily on LlamaIndex for prompt *management* might need more manual integration steps or should be aware of current limitations regarding automatic linking of managed prompts to metrics. It also suggests that Langfuse prioritizes deep integration where the framework's architecture aligns well with its prompt management capabilities.

As a practical workaround for current LlamaIndex users, you can manually log the prompt version ID as a tag on the LlamaIndex trace to ensure some level of linkage, even if it is not the deep, automated link provided by the LangChain metadata. This provides a solution for current users, while maintaining observability of your prompt usage patterns.

Monitoring and Maintenance of Deployed LLMs

Leveraging Langfuse UI for Prompt Iteration and Analysis

While programmatic interaction is fundamental for integration into application code, the Langfuse UI provides a powerful visual interface that complements SDK usage. Prompts can be edited and versioned directly within the Langfuse UI, offering a user-friendly environment for prompt engineers and other stakeholders.

The UI includes a "Prompt Playground" for instant testing and rapid iteration of prompts, which is particularly beneficial for quick prototyping and experimentation (available on Langfuse Cloud). Furthermore, the UI allows users to analyze performance metrics (latency, cost, token usage) and evaluation scores across different prompt versions, providing a clear visual representation of prompt effectiveness and enabling data-driven decisions for iterative prompt development. This combination of programmatic control and a rich UI is a key differentiator, empowering non-technical users (for example, product managers, content strategists, domain experts) to contribute to prompt engineering. They can iterate on prompt wording, test changes, and understand performance impacts without needing to write code or redeploy the application, fostering cross-functional collaboration, and accelerating the feedback loop between business requirements and LLM behavior.

Programmatic Evaluation and Linking Scores to Prompt Versions

Langfuse extends its capabilities to programmatic evaluation of LLM generations, allowing custom evaluation logic to be applied and scores to be recorded. This feature supports integration with popular evaluation libraries such as OpenAI Evals, LangChain Evaluators, and RAGAS.

The process involves defining an evaluation prompt (which can also be managed in Langfuse) and creating functions to assess LLM outputs against predefined criteria or reference texts. Crucially, these evaluation scores can then be explicitly linked to specific traces and, by extension, to the prompt versions that generated those outputs. This linkage is vital for quantitative feedback on prompt quality and performance. The

@observe() decorator can be used to generate evaluation traces, and langfuse.score() is employed to save numerical scores, associating them with the trace_id of the original LLM generation. These scores are then viewable in the Langfuse UI (e.g., in the Traces tab, Scores tab, or within the Dataset runs tab for systematic evaluations), providing comprehensive analysis of prompt quality over time.

The ability to programmatically link evaluation scores directly to prompt versions within traces enables the creation of automated quality gates within CI/CD pipelines for LLM applications. Instead of relying solely on human review, new prompt versions can be automatically tested against a dataset, and if they fail to meet predefined quality thresholds, their deployment can be flagged or even blocked. This shifts from reactive debugging to proactive quality assurance, ensuring that prompt changes do not degrade application performance and maintaining a high standard of LLM output quality.

Python Example (Programmatic Evaluation Snippet for Summarization Quality):

```
# Define an evaluation prompt for summarization quality
evaluation_prompt_system = """You are an expert summary evaluator.
Your task is to assess the quality of a 'generated_summary' against a 'source_
text' based on conciseness and factual consistency.
Respond with 'Good', 'Fair', or 'Poor'."""

evaluation_prompt_template_messages = [
    {"role": "system", "content": evaluation_prompt_system},
    {"role": "user", "content": "source_text: {source_text}\ngenerated_
summary: {generated_summary}"}
]

# Store the evaluation prompt in Langfuse (if not already existing)
langfuse.create_prompt(
    name="summary-quality-evaluator",
    prompt=evaluation_prompt_template_messages,
    labels=["evaluation"], # Label for evaluation prompts
    type="chat"
)
print("Evaluation prompt 'summary-quality-evaluator' created/updated.")

@observe() # This decorator creates a trace for the evaluation process
def evaluate_llm_response(llm_model: str, source_text: str, generated_summary:
```

```
str, metadata: dict = None):
    # Fetch the evaluation prompt from Langfuse
    eval_prompt_obj = langfuse.get_prompt("summary-quality-evaluator", 
label="evaluation")
    eval_chain = ChatPromptTemplate.from_messages(eval_prompt_obj.get_
langchain_prompt()) | ChatOpenAI(model=llm_model)

    # Update the current trace with evaluation context (optional but good 
practice)
    langfuse_context.update_current_trace(
        name="summarization_evaluation_run",
        tags=["automated-eval", "summarization-quality"],
        metadata=metadata
    )

    # Invoke the evaluation LLM to get a quality assessment
    evaluation_result_content = eval_chain.invoke({
        "source_text": source_text,
        "generated_summary": generated_summary
    }, config={"callbacks": [langfuse_context.get_current_langchain_
handler()]}).content

    # Parse the evaluation result and save the score to the current trace
    score_value = 0.0
    if "good" in evaluation_result_content.lower():
        score_value = 1.0
    elif "fair" in evaluation_result_content.lower():
        score_value = 0.5
    else:
        score_value = 0.0

    langfuse.score(
        trace_id=langfuse_context.current_trace_id(), # Link score to the 
current evaluation trace
        name="summary_quality",
        value=score_value,
        comment=f"Evaluation result: {evaluation_result_content}"
    )
    print(f"Evaluation completed. Score: {score_value}, Comment: {evaluation_
result_content}")
    return score_value
```

This advanced example illustrates how to define and store a dedicated evaluation prompt within Langfuse for summarization quality. It then shows how to use this prompt to programmatically score LLM outputs for conciseness and factual consistency and, how to link these scores back to the original trace (and thus the prompt version) that generated the output. This closes the loop on prompt quality assessment, enabling automated quality assurance within the LLM pipelines.

Implementing A/B Tests for Prompt Optimization

Langfuse's labeling system provides a powerful and low-friction mechanism for conducting A/B tests on prompts. This involves creating multiple prompt versions and assigning them distinct labels, such as prod-a and prod-b. In the application, a traffic splitting mechanism (e.g., random selection) can then be implemented to route a percentage of user requests to each labeled prompt version.

Langfuse automatically tracks key performance metrics for each variant, including response latency, token usage, cost, and quality evaluation scores. This integrated metric collection allows for direct, data-driven comparison of prompt performance in real-world scenarios. **Thelangfuse_prompt** parameter passed during the LLM call is crucial here, as it explicitly links the LLM generation to the specific prompt version used, enabling granular analytics and performance comparison per prompt variant. This establishes a powerful continuous experimentation loop. Instead of one-off evaluations, developers can constantly test new prompt ideas in production with real user traffic, gather data, and make informed decisions about which prompts to fully deploy. This shifts LLM development from a discrete release cycle to a continuous optimization process, allowing for agile responses to performance issues or opportunities for improvement.

Python Example (A/B Testing Implementation for Summarization):

```
# Create two summarization prompts with different instructions
langfuse.create_prompt(
    name="summary-prompt-concise",
    prompt="Summarize the following text in one concise sentence: {{text_
input}}",
    config={"model": "gpt-4o", "temperature": 0},
    labels=["prod-a"]
)
langfuse.create_prompt(
    name="summary-prompt-detailed",
    prompt="Provide a detailed summary of the following text, highlighting all
key points: {{text_input}}",
    config={"model": "gpt-4o", "temperature": 0},
    labels=["prod-b"]
)
print("Two summarization prompts created for A/B testing.")

async def run_ab_test_scenario(user_input: str):
    # Fetch the specific prompt versions for the A/B test
    prompt_variant_a = langfuse.get_prompt("summary-prompt-concise",
label="prod-a")
    prompt_variant_b = langfuse.get_prompt("summary-prompt-detailed",
label="prod-b")

    # Randomly select a prompt version for this request (e.g., 50/50 split)
```

```
    selected_prompt = random.choice([prompt_variant_a, prompt_variant_b])
    print(f"Using prompt version: {selected_prompt.labels} (version {selected_
prompt.version})")

    # Use the selected prompt in the LLM call, linking it for analytics
    completion = await openai.chat.completions.create(
        name="ab-test-summarization-run", # A name for this generation in
Langfuse
        model=selected_prompt.config["model"],
        messages=[
            {"role": "user", "content": selected_prompt.compile(text_
input=user_input)},
        ],
        langfuse_prompt=selected_prompt, # Crucial: links the prompt to the
generation for analytics
    )
    print(f"LLM Response: {completion.choices.message.content}")
    print(f"View trace in Langfuse: {completion.langfuse_trace_url}")

# Example usage (in an async context):
# import asyncio
# asyncio.run(run_ab_test_scenario("The latest earnings report highlighted a
15% increase in revenue, primarily driven by the launch of the new AI-powered
product line in Q3."))
```

This example demonstrates how to fetch prompts tagged with different labels (**prod-a**, **prod-b**), randomly choose between them, and use them in an LLM call. The **langfuse_prompt** parameter ensures that the generation is linked to the specific prompt version for detailed analytics and comparison within the Langfuse UI.

Conclusion

Langfuse Prompt Management represents a significant advancement in the operationalization of Large Language Model applications. By functioning as a comprehensive Prompt Content Management System, it centralizes prompt control, introduces robust versioning, and enables seamless, decoupled deployment strategies. Its integrated A/B testing capabilities empower teams to conduct data-driven prompt optimization, moving beyond qualitative assessments to empirical validation of prompt effectiveness.

The deep integration with Langfuse's tracing and analytics features is a pivotal strength, creating a powerful feedback loop that allows developers to precisely measure the real-world impact of prompt changes on cost, latency, and output quality. This synergy transforms prompt engineering from an ad-hoc task into a structured, data-driven, and collaborative MLOps practice. By facilitating collaboration between technical and non-technical teams and providing mechanisms for high availability and performance, Langfuse empowers organizations to build more robust, agile, and high-performing LLM applications. For any team serious about scaling and optimizing their LLM initiatives, adopting Langfuse for prompt management offers a clear path to enhanced efficiency, reliability, and continuous improvement.

References

1. https://langfuse.com/blog/2024-07-ai-agent-observability-with-langfuse
2. https://langfuse.com/docs
3. https://langfuse.com/docs/prompt-management/features/a-b-testing
4. https://langfuse.com/docs/prompt-management/get-started
5. https://langfuse.com/docs/prompt-management/overview
6. https://langfuse.com/guides/cookbook/prompt_management_langchain
7. https://langfuse.com/integrations/frameworks/llamaindex
8. https://oss-llmops-stack.com/docs
9. https://python.langchain.com/docs/integrations/providers/langfuse/

CHAPTER 12

Real-World Examples and Emerging Trends

Introduction

This final chapter explores the transformative impact of Large Language Models (LLMs) across sectors like healthcare, finance, and retail. We will then delve into the cutting-edge advancement of Multimodal AI, which allows LLMs to process and generate diverse inputs beyond text, before concluding with key future trends such as domain-specific models, real-time fact-checking, and autonomous AI agents.

Structure

In this chapter, we will discuss the following topics:

- Success Stories in Different Sectors
- Multimodal AI
- Future Trends and Research Directions

Success Stories in Different Sectors

LLMs are finding Diverse Applications across Industries, demonstrating their versatility and transformative potential. Some of these examples are:

Healthcare

LLMs are instrumental in supporting diagnostic decision-making by analyzing patient symptoms, medical records, and research data to provide evidence-based insights. They assist in personalizing treatment plans, streamlining administrative tasks such as note-taking, billing, and generating clinical notes, and accelerating drug discovery research by analyzing vast scientific literature. Furthermore, LLMs are being used to provide medical education and training, including interactive learning simulations. Examples include AMIE, an AI system that outperformed primary care physicians in diagnostic accuracy and communication in simulated cases, and systems automating discharge summaries, reducing the processing time by 90%.

Finance

In the financial sector, LLMs interpret complex regulatory filings, summarize earnings reports, and forecast market trends. They power client-facing chatbots, enhance customer service by understanding intent and recommending tailored financial products, as well as significantly improve fraud detection, as seen with MasterCard's Decision Intelligence Pro. LLMs also process unstructured financial data, and provide natural language interfaces to complex information.

Retail

LLMs are revolutionizing retail through hyper-personalization, analyzing customer browsing history and purchase habits to recommend products, akin to having a 24/7 personal shopper. They enable hyper-targeted marketing campaigns and optimize inventory management by accurately predicting demand based on various factors. AI-powered chatbots, driven by LLMs, have also significantly enhanced customer support, handling inquiries efficiently and conversationally.

Code Generation

Generative AI has become an indispensable assistant for software developers and IT professionals, significantly accelerating workflows and improving code quality. AI coding assistants such as an advanced version of GitHub Copilot or Amazon Q Developer, are now seamlessly integrated into development environments, providing real-time code suggestions, autocompleting complex functions, and even generating entire boilerplate code for new features. For example, a developer building a new mobile app can simply describe a desired user interface component, and the AI will generate the necessary code snippets in various programming languages, along with unit tests. Beyond development, GenAI is being used in IT operations to generate sophisticated synthetic data for testing new software features, ensuring robust security, and identifying potential vulnerabilities before deployment, leading to fewer bugs and more secure systems.

Customer Service and Support

Generative AI is revolutionizing customer service by powering highly intelligent and responsive chatbots and virtual assistants that offer a vastly improved experience compared to earlier iterations. These AI agents can handle a wide range of complex inquiries, from troubleshooting technical issues for an internet service provider to assisting with flight bookings for an airline. For instance, a customer contacting a bank might interact with a GenAI chatbot that not only understands nuanced questions about their account balance but can also proactively suggest personalized financial advice or guide them through a loan application process, all while maintaining a natural, empathetic tone. This level of automation and personalization frees up human agents to focus on more intricate or sensitive customer interactions, ultimately leading to higher customer satisfaction and operational efficiency.

Legal Services

Generative AI is revolutionizing the legal sector by automating tedious tasks, enhancing research capabilities, and streamlining document management. Law firms are deploying GenAI tools to instantly review massive volumes of contracts, automatically identifying risky clauses, extracting key terms, and ensuring compliance with regulations, a task that traditionally took countless human hours. For example, a legal team handling a merger and acquisition deal can use AI to analyze thousands of agreements in minutes, flagging inconsistencies or potential liabilities. Furthermore, GenAI is accelerating legal research by summarizing vast amounts of case laws, statutes, and legal precedents, allowing lawyers to quickly grasp the nuances of complex legal arguments, and build stronger cases.

Education

Generative AI is fundamentally transforming education by enabling highly personalized learning experiences, and significantly reducing administrative burdens for educators. Imagine a student struggling with a specific math concept; a GenAI-powered platform can instantly generate custom practice problems, explanatory text, and even interactive simulations tailored to that student's learning style and current understanding. For teachers, GenAI acts as an intelligent assistant, automatically generating quizzes, drafting lesson plans, and providing detailed feedback on essays and assignments, freeing up valuable time that can be dedicated to direct student engagement and addressing individual needs. This personalized and adaptive approach makes learning more engaging and effective for students, while empowering educators with powerful tools.

Multimodal AI

Multimodal Artificial Intelligence (AI) represents a pivotal advancement in the field, moving beyond the limitations of traditional unimodal systems that process only a single type of data. By integrating and interpreting diverse modalities such as text, images, audio, video, and code, multimodal AI achieves a more comprehensive and human-like understanding of the world. This report delves into the core technical principles underpinning multimodal AI, including sophisticated data integration techniques such as feature extraction, alignment, and fusion, as well as the crucial role of representation learning.

It examines prominent models like Google Gemini, OpenAI's GPT-4o, Meta ImageBind, LLaVA, and Anthropic's Claude 3, highlighting their architectural innovations and capabilities. Furthermore, the report explores the transformative applications of multimodal AI across various industries, from revolutionizing healthcare diagnostics and enhancing autonomous systems to personalizing education and fostering creativity. While acknowledging significant technical hurdles—such as data alignment complexities, high computational costs, generalization challenges, and critical ethical considerations around bias, privacy, and transparency, the trajectory of multimodal AI points towards a future of democratized, ubiquitous, and increasingly cognitively aligned AI systems that promise to fundamentally alter human-computer interaction.

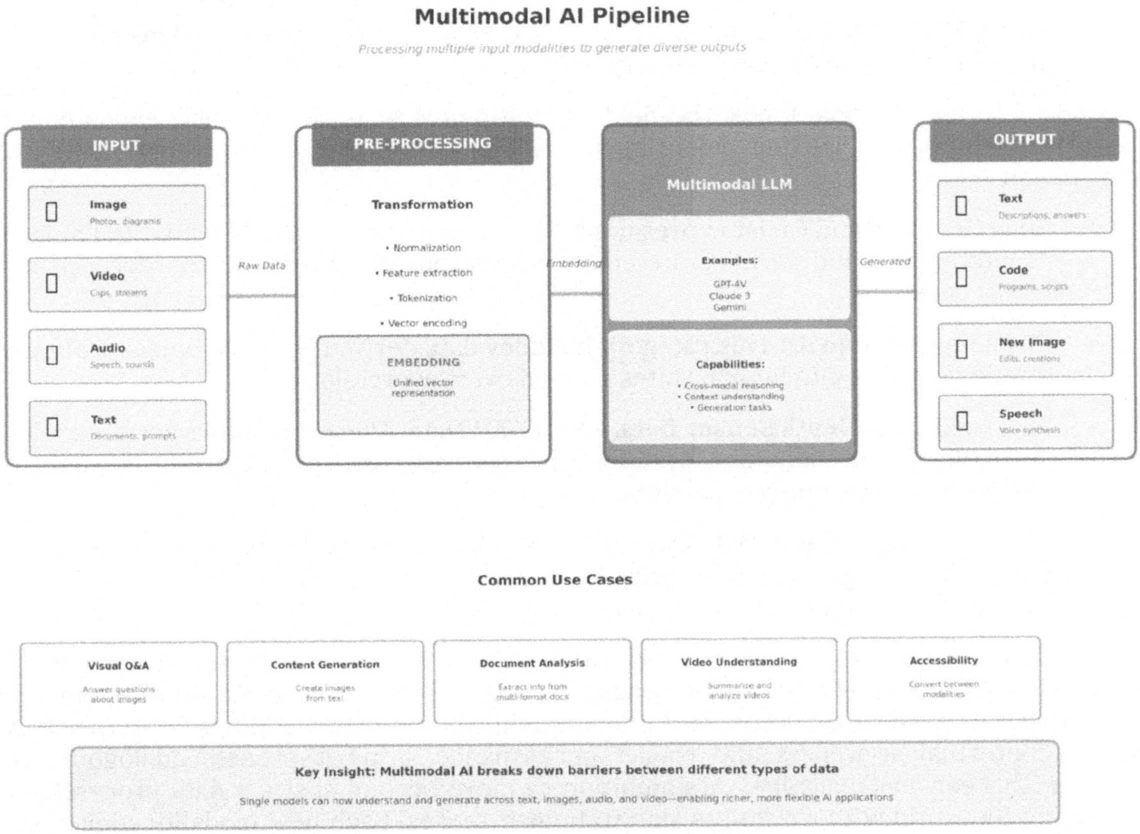

Figure 12.1: *Multimodal AI Pipeline*

Core Technical Principles of Multimodal AI

Multimodal models are meticulously engineered to process and integrate information across a diverse array of data types, known as modalities. These modalities form the fundamental building blocks of multimodal AI's comprehensive understanding. The most commonly utilized modalities include:

- **Text Modality:** This is one of the most prevalent modalities, involving the processing of natural language text to extract relevant information. Its applications are extensive, ranging from sentiment analysis and text classification to complex language translation tasks.
- **Image Modality:** This involves the processing of visual data, such as photographs or graphics. It is widely applied in areas like object recognition, facial recognition, and the generation of descriptive image captions.
- **Audio Modality:** This encompasses a variety of sound-based data, including human voice, environmental sounds, and music.
- **Video Modality:** This combines visual and temporal information, allowing for the analysis of dynamic scenes and sequences.

Beyond these foundational types, the field of multimodal AI is continuously expanding its sensory capabilities to include emerging modalities that provide even richer contextual information:

- **Body Gestures and Facial Expressions:** These are critical for enabling natural human-AI interactions and for accurate emotion recognition, allowing AI to interpret non-verbal cues.
- **Physiological Signals:** This category includes data derived from biological processes, offering insights into human states beyond overt expressions.
- **3D Visual Data, Depth Sensor Data, and LiDAR Data:** These modalities are particularly pertinent for autonomous systems and robotics, providing precise spatial and environmental mapping capabilities.
- **Thermal Imaging and IMU Data (Inertial Measurement Units):** Used in advanced models like ImageBind, these provide comprehensive environmental understanding, capturing heat signatures and movement dynamics.

The inclusion of such a wide array of sensory inputs reflects AI's ambition to perceive the world with a richness akin to human senses. Humans naturally integrate information from multiple senses to construct a coherent understanding of their surroundings for AI to achieve similar contextual awareness and robust performance, it must process analogous data streams. This expansion signifies AI's ambition to move beyond abstract data processing to perceiving the world with a richness akin to human senses. Each new modality adds a layer of context and robustness. For instance, combining visual data with IMU data in autonomous vehicles or interpreting facial expressions alongside speech in educational AI systems allows for a more nuanced and resilient understanding of dynamic environments and human states. This continuous integration of diverse sensory information propels AI closer to achieving true environmental and emotional intelligence.

Multimodal Data Integration

The integration of multiple data modalities is paramount in multimodal AI, as it enables models to capture a broader spectrum of features and relationships inherent in complex data. This comprehensive understanding is directly correlated with improved accuracy and robustness in AI systems. The process of integrating these diverse data types typically involves three critical steps: feature extraction, alignment, and fusion.

Feature Extraction serves as the initial phase, where raw data from each modality is transformed into a standardized numerical representation. This step involves identifying the most relevant characteristics within each data type. For visual data, Convolutional Neural Networks (CNNs) are commonly employed to extract features such as shapes, colors, or patterns. For textual data, techniques like word embeddings or transformer models are utilized to capture contextual and semantic meaning. The primary objective of feature extraction is to convert inherently diverse modalities into comparable formats, laying the essential groundwork for their effective integration.

Following feature extraction, Alignment becomes a crucial step. This process ensures that features derived from different modalities correspond correctly to the same underlying concepts. Various forms of alignment are employed depending on the nature of the data:

- **Temporal Alignment** synchronizes sequential data, such as precisely matching transcribed speech to specific video frames.
- **Spatial Alignment** links visual regions to textual descriptions, for example, associating a bounding box around an object in an image with the corresponding word in a caption.
- **Semantic Alignment** focuses on ensuring shared meaning, such as mapping the emotional tone conveyed in a voice recording to the sentiment expressed in accompanying text. **Techniques like attention mechanisms and cross-modal retrieval** are frequently utilized to achieve this coherence.

Finally, Fusion is the technique where the aligned features from different modalities are combined into a single, comprehensive representation. Cross-attention mechanisms represent a sophisticated form of Hybrid Fusion, designed to effectively implement the Alignment step simultaneously with the Fusion step, thereby capturing complex cross-modal interactions.[10] The choice of fusion method is a critical determinant of a multimodal model's success.[10] Three primary types of fusion architectures are commonly employed:

- **Early Fusion:** This approach combines raw or pre-processed data from multiple modalities at an initial stage, typically before feeding it into the main machine learning model. This method is effective for capturing low-level features that are common across modalities.[21] However, a notable limitation is its sensitivity to data quality; it may perform poorly if the input data is noisy or incomplete.[21]
    - **Mathematical Representation:** `P(y|x1,x2,...,xn)=f(g(x1,x2,...,xn))`
- **Late Fusion:** In contrast, late fusion processes each modality separately—for example, using a dedicated vision model for images and a language model for text—and then

merges their individual outputs at a later stage, often through methods like weighted averaging or voting.[10] This method excels at capturing high-level features specific to each modality and offers enhanced robustness to noisy or missing data.[21]

  - **Mathematical Representation:** $P(y|x1,x2,...,xn)=f1(x1)\oplus f2(x2)\oplus ...\oplus fn(xn)$

- **Hybrid Fusion:** This architecture combines elements of both early and late fusion techniques. It aims to leverage the strengths of both approaches, capturing both low-level and high-level features from multiple modalities.[10]

More sophisticated fusion methods, such as attention mechanisms like transformer networks or attention-based Recurrent Neural Networks (RNNs), are increasingly employed to capture complex cross-modal interactions. Cross-attention layers, in particular, are instrumental in enabling the model to explicitly link information across different modalities.

The selection of a fusion strategy is not arbitrary; it represents a strategic design decision that is a direct consequence of the specific task requirements and the inherent nature of the data. For instance, if fine-grained, low-level interactions between modalities are critical and the data quality is consistently high, early fusion might be the preferred choice.

Conversely, if robustness to missing or noisy data, or the need for distinct unimodal processing, is paramount, late fusion often proves more effective. Hybrid fusion architectures are developed to mitigate the individual drawbacks of early and late fusion by combining their strengths. This highlights a critical design consideration for AI developers: it is not merely about what data types are utilized, but how they are integrated. The search for the "most optimal fusion technique" remains an active area of theoretical challenge, driving ongoing research into more sophisticated methods like advanced attention mechanisms.

This strategic trade-off directly influences the model's overall performance, its robustness to real-world variations, and its computational demands, underscoring that effective multimodal AI development necessitates a deep understanding of these architectural nuances beyond simple data collection.

Representation Learning for Unified Understanding

Multimodal representation learning constitutes a specialized subfield within machine learning dedicated to developing models capable of effectively processing and integrating information from multiple data modalities.[11] Its profound significance lies in its capacity to substantially enhance the performance of AI models by fostering a more comprehensive and holistic understanding of the data at hand.

The fundamental objective of representation learning in this context is to derive a joint representation or a shared vector space. This shared space is designed to capture the underlying structure and intricate relationships that exist between different data modalities. This unified representation is not merely an aggregation of data; it is a critical prerequisite for various downstream tasks, including classification, information retrieval, and content generation.

Several methods are employed to achieve effective multimodal representation learning:

- **Autoencoders:** These are neural networks trained to compress input data into a lower-dimensional representation, and then reconstruct the original input from this compressed form. In a multimodal context, autoencoders learn representations that capture the fundamental structure shared across different modalities.
- **Generative Adversarial Networks (GANs):** GANs consist of two competing neural networks—a generator and a discriminator—that learn to generate new data samples closely resembling the existing data. They are utilized to learn representations that capture the underlying distribution of multimodal data, enabling the creation of novel content that blends modalities.
- **Multimodal Embedding:** This method specifically focuses on learning a shared representation space where different data types, such as image-text pairs, are mapped to be semantically similar. Prominent models like CLIP project images and text into the same vector space, allowing for direct comparison and understanding between visual and linguistic concepts.
- **Contrastive Learning:** This is a crucial technique that enables modalities to interact meaningfully within the shared embedding space. Models employing contrastive learning, such as CLIP or various multimodal transformers, learn to project different data types into a shared vector space where semantically similar concepts are positioned closely together. This is achieved by using contrastive loss functions that minimize the distance between paired data (for example, an image and its corresponding caption) while maximizing the distance between unrelated pairs.

The inherent heterogeneity of multimodal data—characterized by different formats, varying lengths, and often non-synchronized inputs—necessitates a sophisticated mechanism to establish a common ground. Representation learning serves as this "*semantic bridge*." Without the ability to effectively learn shared features and underlying relationships between modalities, AI cannot genuinely reason across them; it would merely process them in isolation. For example, CLIP's capacity to map images and text into the same conceptual space directly facilitates tasks like zero-shot image classification, where an image's embedding can be compared directly to textual prompts to determine its category. This capability signifies that the true power of multimodal AI extends beyond simply receiving diverse inputs; it lies in its ability to understand the underlying semantic connections between these inputs. This capability is what enables AI to perform complex tasks such as visual question answering or to generate coherent content by linking textual descriptions to relevant images. It represents a fundamental shift from mere data processing to sophisticated cross-modal reasoning, which is essential for achieving more intelligent, adaptable, and contextually aware AI systems.

Multimodal Transformers: The Foundational Architecture

Multimodal transformers represent a cornerstone in the development of advanced AI systems, specifically designed to simultaneously process and comprehend multiple types of data. These models build upon the ground-breaking transformer architecture, which introduced the concept of self-attention mechanisms to effectively analyze relationships within a single data sequence.

Crucially, multimodal transformers extend this capability by incorporating cross-attention layers, which are specifically engineered to link and understand information across different modalities. For instance, a cross-attention mechanism can establish a connection between the word "*dog*" in a textual input and a specific visual patch containing a dog within an accompanying image.

The general architecture of multimodal neural networks typically involves a combination of multiple unimodal neural networks. This structure can be broadly divided into three main components:

- **Unimodal Encoders:** These are specialized networks, often transformer-based, that process individual modalities separately. For example, a standard transformer encoder might handle text inputs, while a Vision Transformer (ViT) processes image data. The role of these encoders is to transform raw inputs into meaningful, high-dimensional representations, often in the form of embeddings.
- **Fusion Network:** This component is responsible for combining the features extracted by the unimodal encoders. This is where cross-attention mechanisms are frequently employed to capture complex interactions and dependencies between the different modalities, allowing for a rich, integrated understanding.
- **Classifier/Decoder:** Once the information from various modalities has been fused, this final component takes the integrated data to perform a specific task, such as making predictions (classification) or generating new content (decoding).

During the training phase, these models learn to align the representations of different modalities. This is often achieved through specific training objectives, such as contrastive loss, which encourages the model to bring related cross-modal pairs closer together in the embedding space, while pushing unrelated pairs apart, or masked prediction, where the model reconstructs the missing parts of one modality using information from others.

The consistent reliance of leading multimodal models—including Google Gemini, OpenAI's GPT-4o, and LLaVA—on the Transformer architecture underscores its pivotal role. The Transformer's inherent capacity to model long-range dependencies and dynamically weigh the importance of different segments within an input sequence, facilitated by its attention mechanisms, makes it uniquely suited for the intricate task of integrating disparate data types.[23] *Self-attention effectively manages relationships within* a single modality, while the crucial cross-attention mechanism explicitly models the complex interplay between modalities. This dual capability provides a flexible and powerful means to fuse information, transcending the limitations of simpler concatenation methods.

The widespread adoption and success of this architecture solidify its position as the de facto foundational architecture for generalized multimodal AI. This suggests that ongoing advancements in Transformer efficiency, scalability, and the sophistication of its attention mechanisms will directly drive the continued progress and capabilities of multimodal AI. The efficacy of this unified, attention-based approach to data integration for achieving complex cross-modal understanding reinforces its status as the backbone for future intelligent systems.

Prominent Models in Practice

The landscape of multimodal AI is rapidly evolving, with several prominent models pushing the boundaries of what is possible. These models showcase diverse architectural approaches and specialized capabilities, collectively shaping the future of AI.

Google Gemini

The Gemini family of models, developed by Google, represents a significant advancement as natively multimodal systems. These models—including Ultra (high-performance), Pro (balanced utility), and Nano (optimized for edge devices)—are adept at processing a wide array of input types, such as images, audio, video, text, and code, and are capable of generating various forms of output.1 Gemini models are built upon an enhanced Transformer architecture, specifically optimized for multimodal alignment, scalability, and faster inference speeds crucial for production environments. Their training regimen involves extensive pre-training on diverse and large-scale multimodal datasets, followed by targeted post-training to align performance with safety and ethical guidelines, and task-specific fine-tuning for domain-specific applications like medicine and law. Gemini Ultra has demonstrated state-of-the-art results across numerous benchmarks, even surpassing human-expert performance on the MMLU exam with over 90% accuracy. Its applications are broad, spanning education, coding assistance, efficient mobile applications, and advanced conversational AI systems.

DALL-E

Primarily known for its text-to-image generation capabilities, DALL-E translates textual descriptions into compelling visual outputs. The original DALL-E comprised a discrete Variational Autoencoder (VAE) for image tokenization, an autoregressive Transformer similar to GPT-3, and a CLIP (Contrastive Language-Image Pre-training) pair used for ranking the generated images based on their relevance to the text prompt. DALL-E 2 evolved to utilize a diffusion model conditioned on CLIP image embeddings, a similar architecture to Stable Diffusion. DALL-E 3 further refined prompt following capabilities. DALL-E is widely used for brainstorming, creating custom art, marketing visuals, logo design, and educational visual aids.

GPT-4o

The "o" in GPT-4o stands for "*omni*," signifying its comprehensive multimodal capabilities. This flagship model can process and generate content across text, audio, image, and video inputs as a single, unified neural network. A key advancement is its ability to conduct real-time audio conversations with human-like latency (responding to audio input in approximately 320 milliseconds, significantly faster than previous pipeline approaches that took 5.4 seconds). Unlike prior models that received only text transcriptions of audio, GPT-4o processes the entirety of the audio input, including tone and sentiment, enabling more contextually appropriate responses. It also features built-in video processing and self-contained image generation capabilities. Furthermore, GPT-4o demonstrates greater token efficiency, particularly for non-Roman languages, making it more cost-effective for diverse language applications.

Meta ImageBind

Released by Meta Research, ImageBind is an innovative embedding model that unifies data from six distinct modalities: images/video, text, audio, thermal imaging, depth information, and IMUs (Inertial Measurement Units). Its training involved pairing image data with other modalities (for example, image-audio, image-thermal), demonstrating that features for different modalities can be effectively learned by leveraging image data as a common link. This approach enables advanced semantic search and cross-modal information retrieval, allowing users to query, for example, audio content using an image, and supports zero-shot and few-shot classification across all supported modalities.

Large Language and Vision Assistant (LLaVA)

Developed by Microsoft and the community, LLaVA represents an innovative fusion of visual and linguistic intelligence. It integrates a CLIP visual encoder with a LLaMA/Vicuna linguistic decoder. LLaVA leverages a technique called "*Visual Instruction Tuning*," which fine-tunes large language models to interpret and execute instructions that rely on visual cues, thereby establishing a critical link between language and vision. The model utilizes auto-generated data aligned with specific instructions, enhancing its ability to comprehend and produce content in diverse multimodal environments. Its open-source framework encourages continuous community contributions and advancements.

Anthropic's Claude 3

The Claude 3 family of models (Haiku, Sonnet, and Opus) from Anthropic incorporates inherent vision capabilities, enabling them to process and analyze image data alongside text prompts. These models have demonstrated strong performance across various benchmarks in reasoning, mathematics, coding, and multi-lingual understanding.38 They are designed for nuanced content creation, complex analysis, forecasting, and handling scientific queries, with Sonnet powering the free Claude.ai chatbot and Opus being the most powerful variant. Architectural advancements in Claude 3 hint at refinements in the core Transformer encoder-decoder structure and attention mechanisms, contributing to their improved performance.

Earlier multimodal systems, such as DALL-E, often relied on distinct components or diffusion models. Similarly, initial versions of models like GPT-4 required a pipeline of separate models (e.g., Whisper for audio-to-text, GPT-4 Turbo for processing, and text-to-speech services for audio output) to handle multimodal interactions. In contrast, a significant trend observed in the latest generation of models, exemplified by Google Gemini and OpenAI's GPT-4o, is their explicit design as "*natively multimodal*" or "*all-in-one*" systems. This architectural evolution directly addresses the limitations of latency and fragmented contextual understanding inherent in component-based or pipelined approaches. By processing all modalities within a single neural network, models like GPT-4o achieve significantly lower latency (for example, 320ms response time for audio compared to 5.4 seconds for previous pipelines) and can integrate context from all modalities simultaneously. This unified processing capability allows for a more coherent, fluid, and genuinely "*human-like*" interaction experience. This progression suggests a maturation of multimodal AI; the focus has shifted from merely combining modalities to *seamlessly integrating* them at a fundamental architectural level. This has profound implications for user experience, enabling real-time, natural conversations and more intuitive human-AI interfaces. It also points towards future models that are not only multimodal in their inputs and outputs but also possess deeply integrated internal processing across sensory information, paving the way for truly intelligent, context-aware agents.

Future Trends and Research Directions

The trajectory of LLM development points towards several key trends and active research areas, driven by the pursuit of greater efficiency, reliability, and broader applicability.

Towards Smaller, More Efficient, and Domain-Specific Models

While the initial phase of LLM development emphasized scaling raw capabilities through increasingly larger parameter counts, the future focuses on practicality and accessibility. Models like TinyLlama (1.1 billion parameters) and Mixtral 8x7B (47 billion parameters, with only 13 billion active per token) demonstrate that high performance does not always necessitate massive size. These compact models are crucial for reducing computational costs and making LLMs more accessible for deployment in resource-constrained environments, such as mobile applications, educational tools, and startups.

The emergence of sparse expert models like Mixture of Experts (MoE) architectures, further exemplifies this drive for efficiency by activating only the parts of the network relevant to a specific task, thereby improving speed and energy consumption. Concurrently, the industry is moving away from a "*one-size-fits-all*" approach to general-purpose models towards the development of highly specialized, domain-specific LLMs. Examples include BloombergGPT for finance, Med-PaLM for medical data, and ChatLAW for legal applications. These specialized models offer superior accuracy and fewer errors within their respective fields due to their deeper contextual understanding, reflecting a strategic response to the high computational costs and the need for LLMs to be deployable in diverse, specific enterprise applications. This shift aims at a broader democratization of LLM technology, making it more cost-effective and available to a wider range of businesses and individuals.

Real-time Fact-Checking and External Data Integration

A major limitation of current LLMs is their propensity for "*hallucinations*"—generating plausible but factually incorrect information. To counteract this, LLMs are being enhanced to integrate live data, with tools like Microsoft Copilot using real-time internet access to validate answers, thereby reducing hallucinations and aligning model responses more closely with human fact-checking processes. Future models are anticipated to include references and citations by default, significantly raising the bar for accuracy and transparency.

Retrieval-Augmented Generation (RAG) is a key method for preventing hallucinations by integrating real-time knowledge retrieval from external, verified databases into the response generation process. When a user submits a query, the system first retrieves relevant information from a knowledge base (for example, internal documentation, scientific literature) and then feeds this verified information into the LLM, ensuring that its response is grounded in factual data. This approach shifts LLMs from purely predictive text generation to fact-based information retrieval and synthesis, which is critical for increasing reliability and trustworthiness in high-stakes applications like healthcare and finance. This pursuit of "*grounded*" intelligence signifies a move towards AI systems that can cite their sources, enhancing accountability and user trust.

Autonomous AI Agents and Self-Improving Systems

This trend involves LLM-powered systems that can make decisions, interact with tools, and take actions without constant human input. These agentic AI systems leverage reasoning frameworks like Chain-of-Thought (CoT) combined with memory and planning tools to manage complex workflows, such as scheduling meetings, analyzing reports, or handling customer service interactions. This marks a major evolution in AI autonomy, transforming LLMs from passive tools into active participants in complex tasks, with profound implications for automation and productivity across industries. Furthermore, some LLMs are now capable of generating their own training data, a process known as synthetic training data generation. For example, Google's self-improving model has created questions and answers to enhance its own performance, demonstrating a path towards autonomous model improvement. This technique holds promise for reducing the cost and time associated with data collection and improving performance in niche domains.

Advancements in Explainability and Interpretability

As LLMs become more integrated into critical decision-making processes, understanding *why* they produce certain outputs is paramount for building trust, ensuring accountability, and facilitating debugging. There is a growing call for greater transparency and disclosure regarding how LLMs are used and how they generate research. Explainable AI (XAI) aims to bridge the gap between complex machine learning outputs and human comprehension by transforming them into easy-to-understand narratives. Interpretability refers to the extent to which a human can understand the cause of an AI model's decision, while explainability involves the model's ability to justify its decisions in human-understandable terms. Research is exploring innovative methods, such as using one LLM to evaluate the output of another LLM. These "instruction-tuned evaluator LLMs" can provide scores and supporting evidence for conclusions, often leveraging CoT prompting to explain their "reasoning" process. This focus on transparency and understanding is vital for fostering trust and reliability in LLM applications.

Final Words: The Path Forward for LLMs

The journey of Large Language Models has been one of remarkable acceleration, transforming from their theoretical NLP origins in the mid-20th century to the sophisticated, generative AI systems of today. This evolution has been marked by pivotal shifts: from laborious rule-based systems to scalable statistical methods, and critically, the advent of the Transformer architecture in 2017. The Transformer's ability to enable parallel processing and leverage attention mechanisms unlocked unprecedented scale, paving the way for models like BERT and the GPT series, which have profoundly advanced both language understanding and generation.

Today, LLMs exhibit advanced capabilities in text generation, summarization, and translation, demonstrating a shift from merely interpreting language to actively creating novel and coherent content. Significant progress has been made in enhancing their reasoning and problem-solving abilities through techniques like Chain-of-Thought prompting, with ongoing research pushing towards more robust, multi-step logical inference. The mainstream adoption of multimodal AI is further expanding their reach, allowing LLMs to process and respond across text, image, and audio, moving them closer to human-like perception. This has led to diverse and impactful applications across industries, from supporting diagnostic decisions in healthcare and detecting fraud in finance to personalizing retail experiences and automating code generation. The emergence of agentic AI, where LLMs can plan, use tools, and take autonomous actions, signifies a new frontier in automation and intelligent assistance.

Looking ahead, the future of LLMs is characterized by a drive for practicality and accessibility. This includes a focus on developing smaller, more efficient, and domain-specific models to reduce computational costs and enable broader deployment. The pursuit of "*grounded*" intelligence is paramount, with Retrieval-Augmented Generation (RAG) and real-time fact-checking becoming essential strategies to mitigate hallucinations and ensure factual accuracy, thereby enhancing trustworthiness. Autonomous AI agents and self-improving systems represent the next leap in capability, promising to automate complex workflows and accelerate model development through synthetic data generation. Concurrently, advancements in explainability and interpretability are crucial for fostering user trust and understanding how these complex models arrive at their decisions.

However, this transformative potential is accompanied by significant challenges. Technical limitations such as hallucinations, inherent biases, and struggles with complex reasoning persist, highlighting the fundamental difference between LLMs' statistical fluency and true human-like understanding. The substantial computational costs and environmental footprint of LLM training and deployment pose sustainability concerns. Furthermore, security vulnerabilities, the potential for misuse in spreading misinformation and deep fakes, and broad societal impacts like job displacement and educational shifts demand proactive attention. The rapid pace of LLM innovation has also created a legal lag, particularly in areas like copyright and intellectual property, leading to ongoing litigation and uncertainty.

The maturation of AI development is increasingly emphasizing responsible innovation. This has led to a strong focus on establishing robust Responsible AI and governance frameworks, guided by principles of transparency, accountability, fairness, privacy, safety, and human oversight. Mitigation strategies for bias, such as diverse training data and RLHF, and for hallucinations, like **RAG** and CoT prompting, are actively being implemented. The evolving regulatory landscape, exemplified by initiatives like the EU AI Act, underscores the need for proactive, collaborative efforts across technical, legal, and ethical domains. This commitment to responsible development is not merely a compliance burden but an increasingly recognized competitive advantage, as trust built through ethical practices translates directly into broader adoption and societal benefit.

The path forward for LLMs necessitates a delicate balance between accelerating innovation and ensuring responsible development. Continued interdisciplinary collaboration, robust governance frameworks, and a human-centric approach will be essential to navigate the complex landscape of LLM adoption, ensuring that these powerful technologies are harnessed for the benefit of humanity, while mitigating their potential risks.

Conclusion

This book has journeyed through the intricate landscape of LLMOps, from the foundational understanding of LLMs and MLOps principles to advanced techniques like **RAG**, **fine-tuning**, and robust security measures. By demystifying prompt management, chaining, deployment, and monitoring, we've equipped you with the essential knowledge and practical insights—including real-world examples and tools such as LangFuse—to confidently build, deploy, and manage production-ready Large Language Models. The ever-evolving nature of LLMs demands continuous learning and adaptation, and we hope this guide serves as a solid foundation for your ongoing success in operationalizing these transformative technologies responsibly and effectively.

Next Steps: Your LLMOps Journey

Now that you've completed this comprehensive guide to LLMOps, it's time to put your knowledge into practice. The following roadmap will help you transition from theory to real-world implementation, building the skills and experience necessary for a successful career in LLMOps.

Capstone Project: Build a Production-Grade RAG-Agent System

To demonstrate mastery of the core technologies covered in this book, we recommend building a comprehensive RAG-Agent system that integrates the key concepts in various chapters in this book. This project should include:

- A robust prompt management system with versioning and A/B testing capabilities (*Chapter* 3)
- Multi-step LLM chains with comprehensive error handling and latency monitoring (*Chapter* 4)

- Advanced RAG architecture with hierarchical chunking and post-retrieval processing (*Chapter* 5)
- Autonomous agent implementation using the ReAct framework with tool selection and decision-making (*Chapter* 6)
- Production deployment infrastructure with cloud-based or self-hosted serving, continuous batching, quantization, and caching strategies (*Chapter* 7)
- Comprehensive evaluation system using the taxonomy of metrics for quality, safety, and RAG-specific assessment (*Chapter* 8)
- (Optional) Fine-tuning and adaptation pipeline with PEFT/LoRA for domain-specific customization, including experiment tracking and model versioning (*Chapter* 9)
- Security implementation following the actionable checklist for prompt injection, jailbreaking, and data poisoning defenses (*Chapter* 10)

Relevant LLMOps Career Paths

The LLMOps field offers diverse career opportunities for professionals with the skills covered in this book. Key roles include:

- **LLMOps Engineer:** Design, build, and maintain production LLM systems, focusing on deployment, monitoring, and optimization.
- **AI Security Specialist:** Implement security measures, conduct adversarial testing, and ensure compliance in LLM deployments.
- **Prompt Engineer:** Specialize in prompt design, optimization, and management systems for production LLM applications.
- **AI Evaluation Specialist:** Develop and implement comprehensive evaluation frameworks for LLM performance, safety, and quality assessment.

As you embark on your LLMOps journey, remember that this field is rapidly evolving. Stay curious, continue learning, and contribute to the growing community of practitioners who are shaping the future of AI operations. Your expertise in LLMOps will be invaluable as organizations worldwide seek to harness the power of Large Language Models responsibly and effectively.

References

1. https://arxiv.org/abs/2401.02385
2. https://arxiv.org/abs/2404.03647
3. https://arxiv.org/abs/2408.02686
4. https://arxiv.org/html/2501.09967
5. https://arxiv.org/html/2504.00125v1

6. https://arxiv.org/html/2506.00054v1
7. https://arxiv.org/html/2506.04133v4
8. https://arxiv.org/html/2510.03463v1
9. https://arxiv.org/pdf/2404.11584
10. https://arxiv.org/pdf/2504.00125
11. https://medium.com/@raj.pulapakura/multimodal-models-and-fusion-a-complete-guide-225ca91f6861
12. https://medium.com/codex/bloomberggpt-the-first-large-language-model-for-finance-61cc92075075
13. https://medium.com/data-bistrot/15-artificial-intelligence-llm-trends-in-2024-618a058c9fdf
14. https://pmc.ncbi.nlm.nih.gov/articles/PMC12350640/
15. https://sites.research.google/med-palm/
16. https://teqnovos.com/blog/top-trends-in-large-language-models-llms-for-software-development-in-2026/
17. https://www.hostinger.com/tutorials/llm-statistics
18. https://www.ibm.com/think/topics/explainable-ai
19. https://www.reddit.com/r/LocalLLaMA/comments/1924pyy/mixtral_8x7b_paper_published/
20. https://www.researchgate.net/publication/369655284_BloombergGPT_A_Large_Language_Model_for_Finance
21. https://www.singlestore.com/blog/a-guide-to-retrieval-augmented-generation-rag/

Index

B

C

D

M

S